MEMOIRS OF A HACK MECHANIC

How Fixing BMWs Helped Make Me Whole

BY ROB SIEGEL

D1570819

BentleyPublishers
.com

MEMOIRS OF A HACK MECHANIC

CONTENTS

The '68 VW Camper.

*Rebuilding the engine to Maire Anne's
VW van in the kitchen.*

Rob's 1973 BMW 3.0CSi on the way to Vintage at the Vineyards in 2010.

Removing the engine from a 1999 VW Passat.

Rob Siegel, BMW CCA member Steve Diamond, and an ultra-rare BMW Z1.

The Siegel family

BENTLEY PUBLISHERS™ | Automotive Reference™

Bentley Publishers, a division of Robert Bentley, Inc.
1734 Massachusetts Avenue
Cambridge, MA 02138 USA
800-423-4595 / 617-547-4170

Information that makes
the difference®

BentleyPublishers™
.com

Read the **Warnings and Cautions** on page 410 of this book before attempting any work on your vehicle.

This book is prepared, published, and distributed by Bentley Publishers, 1734 Massachusetts Avenue, Cambridge, Massachusetts 02138. Bentley Publishers is a trademark of Robert Bentley, Inc. [B]˚ is a registered trademark of Bentley Publishers and Robert Bentley, Inc.

Copies of this book may be purchased from selected booksellers, or directly from the publisher. The publisher encourages comments from the readers of this book. Please contact Bentley Publishers by visiting http://www.BentleyPublishers.com.

Memoirs of a Hack Mechanic: How Fixing Broken BMWs Helped Make Me Whole, by Rob Siegel
© 2013 Rob Siegel.

The opinions expressed in this book are the author's, and do not necessarily reflect the views of the publisher.

Portions of this work appeared previously in *Roundel* magazine and are reprinted here with permission where applicable.

ISBN 978-0-8376-1720-6   **Bentley Stock No. GBRS   Mfg. code: GBRS-01-1304**

Library of Congress Cataloging-in-Publication Data

Siegel, Rob, 1958-
  Memoirs of a hack mechanic : how fixing BMWs helped make me whole / by Rob Siegel.
    pages cm
  Includes bibliographical references and index.
  ISBN 978-0-8376-1720-6 (alk. paper)
  1. Siegel, Rob, 1958- 2. Automobile mechanics--United States--Anecdotes. 3. BMW automobiles--Maintenance and repair--Anecdotes. 4. Engineers--United States--Anecdotes. I. Title.
  TL140.S54A3 2013
  629.28'72092--dc23
  [B]
                    2013005035

Cover design by Andrea Corbin. Front cover photo by M. Bentley. Back cover photos by Rob Siegel (top, middle, and background) and Maire Ann Diamond (bottom).

The paper used in this publication is acid free and meets the requirements of the National Standard for Information Sciences-Permanence of Paper for Printed Library Materials. ∞ Manufactured in the United States of America.

For my wife Maire Anne
and my mother Bernice,
both of whom gave me more
legroom than any husband
or son deserves.

WHAT IT MEANS TO BE A CAR GUY

Other than my degree in math and physics summa cum laude, my boyish good looks, and my astonishing sexual prowess, there's absolutely nothing extraordinary about me.

I'm sorry. I've always wanted to start a book that way. Let me try again. Heh-hhem.

Hi. I'm Rob. I'm a car guy. Now, I'm many other things as well—a husband, a father, an engineer, a musician, a typical American living his blissful postwar baby boomer upwardly mobile stressed-out suburban existence. It's just that, in addition to the obligatory wife, house, and 2.4 children, I have eight cars.

So what does it mean to be a car guy? In my case, it's lusting after, chasing, buying, nurturing, driving, keeping (to the maximum extent that I have money and space), and occasionally selling cars, sometimes making just enough money on one to fool myself into thinking that I've finally figured out how this works so I can buy the next one and really lose my shirt, and doing all this within some reasonable bounds of financial propriety. The objects of my automotive affections are predominantly early '70s BMWs, but any cool car will turn my head pretty hard, and many non-Bavarian beasts have graced my garage.

Nearly three decades ago I started writing a column called "The Hack Mechanic" for *Roundel* (the magazine of the BMW Car Club of America), and, through it, learned that I am far from alone. Granted, eight cars may be a bit extreme, but in fact there are a lot of people—overwhelmingly guys—who do what I do, who are drawn to the same things I am, who love cars and use them as a source of relaxation and a conduit for passion.

Pick a car manufacturer and a model. New or old. Doesn't matter. BMW 2002tii. Porsche 911. Alfa Spider. Toyota Land Cruiser. '63 Rambler. Geo Metro. For any of these, hop online and you can find multiple forums full of people exchanging tips on how to fix them, modify them, or just keep them running without having to pay to take them into the dealer every time they hiccup. The number of cars I own may put me on the right edge of the bell curve, but it is a well-populated bell curve nevertheless. And I don't think you'll read many posts that say, "I freaking *hate* working on cars; I'm just doing this because I don't have the money to pay someone to do it." No, we're all doing it because we find it satisfying. Need to replace a clutch in an M3? Spend ten minutes online and you'll find a detailed "how to" document that someone has written, photographed, annotated, posted, and answered questions on.

And people say men can't communicate.

The fact that a very highly focused interest can result in broad human connection has always fascinated me. Why do any of us choose the things that we do for leisure activities or hobbies? Usually it's some combination of attraction to the activity, the physical objects associated with it, and the people involved. That is, even if you liked cooking, you probably wouldn't cook if you hated food and thought every foodie you'd ever met was a jerk. The cars are interesting, and working on the cars is enormously therapeutic for me, but perhaps their highest value lies in their acting as a conduit for human interaction. My writing, many close friendships, and some old-fashioned honest-to-goodness love all trace back to a shared interest in a boxy little two-door German sedan. That's remarkable.

To be clear, I don't consider myself a "collector." In the car world, that term implies having the purse to buy the best, most original, lowest-mileage cars you can find, storing them in a climate-controlled warehouse, and rarely—if ever—driving them. I'm happy for guys with the resources of the 1%, but who the hell do *you* know with a warehouse? I make a decent living but I don't have that kind of coin.

I perpetually have grease under my fingernails. I don't own an orbital polisher. I'm just a guy trying to indulge his passions without risking the nest egg. As Maire Anne likes to point out, the kids have never gone hungry, we've never missed a mortgage payment, and the tuition checks get sent on time. The chunks of money spent on my cars are generally in the sub-$5K range—not even enough to remodel the bathroom. (Well, except the BMW Z3 M Coupe. And the Porsche 911SC. But we'll get to those.) I typically buy high-mileage cars that need work and are therefore in a price range I can afford. Then I just try to keep them running. I hold onto the ones I find interesting and/ or beautiful, and perhaps let one go when another one catches my eye. And I don't "restore" cars. I prefer "rolling rejuvenations," meaning that the car is still drivable as much of the time as possible (this is the equivalent of living in your house while you're renovating it).

Overall, I'm just someone who knows what he likes, is very thorough and persistent about sniffing out good deals, and can pounce quickly on the right opportunity. In a world where we're buffeted about by forces we can't control, this exercise of choice is, in fact, liberating. All those cars certainly didn't wind up in my driveway by accident.

So, come on in. Step inside both my physical garage and my psyche. Spend a few hours with me looking at life through the lens of cars. Learn why men love cars and why we exhibit such passion about them and dedication to them when in general we often appear to have the emotional intelligence of algae. Meet my family members, both those of sinew and of steel. Marvel at Maire Anne and the kids (of which there are not 2.4 but three; I never found fractional children particularly useful), and understand our family dynamic, which is to give one another the space to do the things we love. Develop an appreciation for why working on cars is a form of therapy, and why the relationships men have with cars are, actually, useful. See inside my head—a quirky yet surprisingly stable, rational place.

But watch where you step. There's junk everywhere in here.

CHAPTER 1

HOW CARS IMPRINT ON YOU LIKE BODYSNATCHERS

Men, the story goes, are emotionally limited, taciturn creatures. We don't like to lie on the analyst's couch. We appreciate the brilliance of J. D. Salinger's *The Catcher in the Rye* precisely because *in the first goddam sentence,* Holden Caulfield spits in the eye of the modern self-indulgent confessional memoir by stating, "I don't feel like going into it, if you want to know the truth." So, while I could win your sympathy by telling you that I was a nice Jewish boy from Long Island whose father died when I was ten and my mother is a saint, we're just not going to go there. I mean it's true, but it's not who I am.

I'm a car guy.

For that, like most things, I blame my mother.

Oh, it's not that she was into cars—far from it. My mom and dad owned sensible cars. I fondly remember the black '65 Ford Fairlane with the red interior and the three-on-the-tree transmission. And I remember the look on my dad's face when my sister and I, seven and six years old, respectively, were out in the driveway of that six-room Long Island ranch on a Saturday morning, washing the brand-new Fairlane with a bucket of soapy water. And steel wool. *Daddy! Look! WE WASHED THE NEW CAR! Doesn't it look PRETTY?* He didn't betray his horror at the spider web of scratches the steel wool made. God, what a nice guy. If that were a test, I'd fail it. Miserably.

But it's as if I was wired from birth to be a car guy. I began noticing cars at a very early age. I remember seeing, when I was about eight years old, the 1963 split rear window Corvette Sting Ray that a neighbor had bought, and thinking it was the most beautiful thing on Earth. Imagine my surprise when I learned years later that I was right ('63 through '67 Corvettes are almost universally admired as timeless pieces of American industrial design).

Of course, it's not only car guys that notice cars. *Everyone* notices cars. How many '50s movies have you seen where your gaze is drawn straight to a Cadillac's tail fins or a Buick's basset hound headlights? The car guy will be able to say, "Oh, the car with the droopy eyes, that's a '54 Buick," but everyone is aware of cars as pieces of form, shape, and color that need to mesh with the rest of the industrial design of the surroundings or else the eye is immediately drawn to them as an anachronism. It'll be interesting to see how movies handle the '80s and '90s, car-wise; so far the one iconic automotive example everyone recognizes from '80s cinema is the red Porsche 944 Jake Ryan drove in *Sixteen Candles*. But what distinguishes the car guys from the pack is that they're the ones who wonder if it's a straight 944, an S2, or a turbo.

I have a theory about how we develop these automotive obsessions: Some of us are indelibly imprinted by the first car that really kicks us in the ass. We are then doomed to follow this car, or copies of it, for the rest of our lives like geese who have mistakenly imprinted on a glider. This accounts for the self-perpetuating system that generates seasonal swarms of adolescents with swollen adenoids who imprint on gas-guzzling tire-squealing muscle cars driven by Fonzie look-alikes. They're trapped, unable to break the cycle. Ask the kids hanging around the parking lot at the Store 24. "What's your story, son?" You'll probably hear, "Well, this really cool kid Tommy on my block had a '71 Nova …"

In my case, the imprinting was so severe that it was initially misdiagnosed as a glandular condition. The CDC is now actively investigating the possibility that susceptibility is passed through contact with leather seats. However, what I imprinted on was not a split-windowed Corvette (that would've been a very expensive mother), but a 1970 BMW 2002 that was owned by Nick, a Hampshire College student who roomed with us in the early 1970s in Amherst, Massachusetts, where we moved after my dad passed away. The car—and note that "2002" is the model, not the year—was one of those boxy little German sedans, red with a license plate that said *GEIST* (German for "spirit"). When I was 13, Nick would drive me along the back roads, alternately impressing me with what this decidedly non-Corvette-looking little car could do, and scaring the bejesus out of me. This adolescent exposure to the BMW 2002 infected me with something from which I have yet to recover—car guy-itis.

So why do I blame my mother? Well, before the Car Thing, there was the Bicycle Thing. I rode bikes, built bikes, rebuilt bikes, tore them down to the frame, repainted them, changed the components, and started again. The summer before college I was planning on cycling cross-country. It seemed like a natural culmination of six years of steady interest, and the timing seemed like a window of opportunity large enough to, well, drive a bicycle through. I couldn't find anyone to go with me, so I resolved to go alone. This frightened my mother no end (I, now, as a parent, understand this, but at the time it seemed silly), so she tried the Big Bribe—"If you don't go, I'll buy you a car." It took a couple of weeks for the magnitude of the offer to fully permeate my consciousness, but it worked. I caved.

Damn you, mother. It all could've been so different. I could've stayed a bike guy, saved tens of thousands of dollars, and attracted earthy-crunchy women into my 50s.

For the record, as "the son growing up without a father," my mother was probably too easy on me. The Big Bribe was just one example. My sister, in fact, was furious that I, the problem child, got the cool car, while she, the responsible dutiful daughter, did not. I only learned recently, nearly four decades later, that she's still pissed at me about it.

But I really don't feel like going into it, if you want to know the truth.

CHAPTER 2

THE BRITISH PIECE OF CRAP
(OR, THIS IS YOUR BRAIN ON ADOLESCENCE)

With the Big Bribe from my mother (the 30 pieces of silver for which I sold out my dream of bicycling cross-country), I bought, not a Ford Fairlane, not a BMW 2002, and certainly not a split-windowed Sting Ray (although that would've been one of the shrewdest investments *ever* had I bought one and kept it pristine by not actually driving it), but … a Triumph. A Triumph GT6+, which looks like a little Jaguar XKE. Actually, Nick owned an XKE before he had that BMW 2002, so perhaps it imprinted on me in my sleep, one of those bodysnatcher things. Or perhaps I instinctively understood that the cute little Triumph was a better girl magnet than the boxy Teutonic BMW. Girls, of course, were very important to me. At any rate, starting the summer before college, I owned a very cute, very small, very fast, very troublesome British car.

Of course, "very troublesome British car" is the ultimate automotive redundancy. It is impossible to overstate what a piece of crap this car was. Sure, those British cars of the '60s and early '70s—Triumphs, MGs, Jags—had a lot of panache, but … if you learn only one automotive-related joke, it must be this: Why do the British drink warm beer? Because they have Lucas refrigerators. Why is this funny? Because Lucas Electrical supplied the notoriously unreliable electrical components and wiring in most 1960s–1970s British cars. Sometimes, when I drove my Triumph at night, the headlights would stop working. Sometimes, when I drove it in the rain, the windshield wipers would short out and I'd have to limp the car along in the breakdown lane until I came to an overpass where I'd wait for them to dry out. You can imagine what fun it was at night in the rain. This behavior—ubiquitous in British cars of the era (you'll hear enthusiasts quip that "they *all* did that," and incredibly, they all really did)—coupled with the timing of the release of the first *Star Wars* movie in 1977, gave Lucas a new moniker: The Prince of Darkness. The next time someone complains about warm beer, mumble something about a Lucas refrigerator. Go ahead. Some car guy will high-five you.

(Okay, maybe a few more: "Lucas—inventor of the first intermittent wiper"; "Lucas electrical components—the original antitheft devices"; "Lucas vacuum cleaners—the only Lucas product that didn't suck." And my favorite—"Lucas denies having invented darkness, but they still claim 'sudden, *unexpected* darkness.'" The car guy world is rich with humor and pathos.)

(The other must-know car joke, by the way, is that Karmann—yes, of Karmann Ghia fame—invented rust, then licensed the process to the Italians. We'll circle back to this one later in the book when we have sufficient context. Don't worry; like *Monty Python and the Holy Grail*, *Young Frankenstein,* and the Reagan Revolution, it'll be funnier the second time around.)

Now, it's said that adolescents make poor decisions because their frontal lobes aren't fully formed. The mere fact that I *bought* the Triumph is textbook evidence of that. Once cars are added to the mix, it's a wonder any car guy survives his own adolescence because we do things that are so profoundly stupid. The truly frightening thing is that the adolescent brain is so adept at bending sensory input to fit its short-term desires that the poor decisions make sense at the time.

During the time I had the Triumph, I commuted frequently between Lexington, Massachusetts, where I had gone to high school and Amherst, Massachusetts, where I attended college. It was about a hundred miles, the bulk of it on Route 2. The eastern section of Route 2 is a divided highway, but when you get to the western part of the state, it becomes a two-way road.

Now, I used to drive the Triumph fast—5,000 rpm in fourth gear was 87 mph, and the car seemed quite happy there. One night I made it from Porter Square in Cambridge to the center of Amherst in an hour and 15 minutes. To extend the *Star Wars* analogy, this was my equivalent of Han Solo bragging that the *Millennium Falcon* made the Kessel Run in less than twelve parsecs (except that an hour and 15 minutes is a valid time measurement, whereas a parsec is actually not a time but a distance—the distance light can travel in a year; this error caused many otherwise loyal *Star Wars* fans to geek out). Running the calculation now, there are 50 miles of highway on Route 2 between the Concord rotary to Route 202, so I might have averaged over 90 on that section; the rest is smaller roads. I don't see how it was possible, but I swear that's what my watch said. If the Triumph had a dashboard clock I could blame the time discrepancy on Lucas electricals, revealing that not only was he the Prince of Darkness, but a Time Lord as well.

One night, when I was 18, I was in the Triumph heading west on Route 2 toward Amherst when the fog started to roll in. I slowed down, but I was on the section of road that was a divided highway, and I found that by riding on the dotted line between the two westbound lanes and staying there, I could compensate for the reduced visibility and keep driving at a pretty good clip, perhaps slowing down from 80 mph to 75.

Then I came to the end of the divided section and was on the undivided two-lane portion where there is the potential for cars to be coming in the opposite direction. I slowed down, but then I realized that the dividing line, whether double or dotted, reflected brightly beneath my headlamps. The fog was thicker now, but by plunking the nose of the car down on the dividing line, it seemed that I could still keep driving at about 70. When approaching cars came at me, I could see their headlamps diffusely light up the fog, and I had ample time to move from the center back into my lane. No problem.

Scared yet?

As I approached the turnoff from Route 2 to Route 202, the fog became much thicker, and I nearly missed the exit. Unlike Route 2, Route 202 is just a small, unlit, windy road, but my adolescent logic was firmly in place. There are sections where 202 is just blacktop with no painted dividing line, but I noticed that there *was* a painted strip on the right side demarking the shoulder. Okay, I thought, I can use that strip to navigate. So I continued driving far faster than was reasonable on this narrow, windy, unlit road, through the fog, judging my position on the road relative to the painted line on my right.

The amazing thing isn't that I wasn't hurt or killed, or that I didn't crash the car, though all of those things are in fact remarkable. The amazing thing is that I ran off the road and onto the shoulder *not once, not twice, BUT THREE TIMES* before my frontal lobe accepted that information, processed and analyzed it, and issued the directive to my right foot that said *I guess you'd better slow down.*

I recently told this story to my family. Even though the event occurred in 1976, my mother visibly shuddered when she heard it.

Of course, just because I rode bikes before I got into cars doesn't mean I was any less stupid. I rode everywhere, at all hours of the day and night. One evening a bunch of us were out carousing. It got late. I got tired. I lived on a street at the top of a good-sized hill and I was not looking forward to the ride home. One guy who was with us had just graduated from bicycle to motorcycle. He had a bright idea.

"If you're tired," he said, "I could tow you."

"Um, how would that work?"

"Well, I have these bungee cords I usually use to strap stuff onto the rack on the back of the motorcycle. We can take the bungees, string them together, and hook them to your handlebars."

"Sounds good to me!"

We took perhaps six bungees, each about four feet long, hooked them end-to-end, and connected one end to the rack on his motorcycle, and the other end to the stem on my handlebars, figuring, you see, that the stem was better than the handlebars because the stem is located in the middle whereas if you hooked the bungee to the handlebars it might twist them and cause the bike to pull to one side which would make the whole thing, you know, dangerous, and we didn't want that.

Yeah. I know.

So that's what we did. Then my friend started up the motorcycle and took off. My bike took off after him, with me on it. He accelerated up the hill on Mass Ave. Then the bungee cords started to do what bungee cords do—stretch. So the bike and I drifted farther behind him. And then—and I honestly did not see this coming—as we crested the hill, the potential energy in the stretched bungees did its thing. It turned from potential to kinetic energy, propelling me and my bicycle forward like a slingshot, catching us up to the motorcycle, which must've been doing about 50 mph. I unhooked the bungee from my handlebar stem, thanked my friend for the, uh, tow, slowed down, and took a right turn onto my street like it was the most natural thing in the world.

At the time, I think that my most serious reflection on this profoundly idiotic maneuver amounted to "well that was a little hairy."

Now, of course, with the benefit of my five decades of accumulated wisdom, I think, boy, that was stupid—had we filmed it, maybe we could've won something.

As much as I try to impart a sense of rationality and consequence to my own three sons, I still remember what it was like to have no fear, to slingshot up a hill on a bicycle, to rocket forward through fog, to drive all night through sheer force of will, to be intoxicated by action and worry about consequences later. It was glorious. We measure maturity by how much we can leave behind and still smile. Part of me hopes that my boys don't get the wrong message from hearing about my hour and fifteen minute run from Cambridge to Amherst all those years ago, but part of me wants to fire up my M Coupe and see if I can do it in an hour and ten.

But I digress.

Although the Triumph was quite fast, the thing that accelerated most was its decrepitude. But things that break must be fixed, and I was drawn in. After all, as a college student, you can't afford to take a car—much less a *furrin* car—in to the dealer whenever it hiccups, can you? For years I had taken bicycles apart. The car was just another mechanical system; it really wasn't that different. So when the engine started running hot and I could see antifreeze streaming out the center of the water pump, I caught a ride into town, bought a new water pump, and replaced it. When I heard the sickly rhythmic sound of metal slapping against metal, it wasn't hard to figure out that a universal joint had ripped out, and I replaced it. When the clutch stopped working, I yanked out the transmission and found that the tube the throw-out bearing runs on had disintegrated and the seesaw-like fork that slides said bearing on said tube had a hole in it the size of my thumb, so I grumbled loudly and replaced them. When a rear axle literally cracked in half, I said *what the hell?* (actually that's not what I said) and replaced it, even though it meant having to use a crowbar to push the leaf spring down and reattach it to the top of the differential by holding it in place *with my forehead*.

Now, any car will require maintenance, and any old car will require major refurbishment, but in 1976, my 1973 Triumph *was only three years old*. I've always suspected that British cars suffered this level of basic metal fatigue because the Brits had used up all their steel in World

War II and were left to build cars out of recycled crap I mean scrap.

I eventually learned that, in addition to simply being British, there was a reason why the GT6's drivetrain acted as if it had osteoporosis. The car was derived from the anemic little four-cylinder Spitfire, but had a six-cylinder engine stuffed into it, so everything rearward of the engine was subject to torque (twisting) greater than it was designed for. It's no wonder axle shafts and universal joints were pulverized into cornflakes.

So it broke. I fixed it. It broke. I fixed it. Finally I grew tired of this little game. It broke. I sold it. Panache notwithstanding, the Triumph was a miserable piece of garbage. I never bought another British car (proving that men, in fact, *can* learn, contrary to direct experimental evidence by Dutch scientists).

In the interim, however, in spite of the trouble it caused me, I discovered that *I actually enjoyed working on the car.* This was more than mere economic necessity—I *liked* diagnosing and repairing it. This was, it turned out, a watershed event—the start of a lifelong relationship with mechanical repair as both a source of relaxation and a way of getting into cars I couldn't otherwise afford.

During the time I owned the Triumph, two friends had 2002s (well, a 2002 and a 1600, respectively). The three of us formed a triad of terror on the streets of Amherst. The fact that their 2002s could carry four people, out-handled the Triumph, and broke far less frequently and in far less spectacular ways was not lost on me, and it became increasingly clear that I'd bought the wrong car. However, I could still lose them in second gear on a straight section of road, and with the Triumph's mini-Jaguar looks, let's not forget that all-important girl magnet factor. And, incredibly, despite the Triumph's actively homicidal handling characteristics, it was the only one of the three cars that hadn't been wrecked by the end of my sophomore year.

Maire Anne reminds me that I sold the Triumph the day after our first date. This is true. We met in Earthfoods, a student-run natural food restaurant at UMass Amherst that served positively vile pizza and a lentil loaf better suited to insulation than ingestion (I suppose it's remarkable that the presence of earthy-crunchy women was enough for me to regularly patronize a venue that served undercooked whole wheat pizza topped with raw carrots, but really there's nothing remarkable about it at all). I picked Maire Anne up at her apartment about ten miles north of Amherst. As she tells the story, cute guy, cute car, this'll be great, no more waiting for the PVTA bus. Next day I sold it. Oh well, Maire Anne says, at least the guy is still cute (see why I married her?).

Actually a far better test of long-term compatibility would've consisted of my keeping the Triumph and seeing if Maire Anne stayed with me while the car serially stranded us and I blew food and rent money on repairs. My getting rid of the Triumph when I did—while it was still capable of both attracting girls and moving under its own power—was, I now realize, an early indication of my basic rationality and fundamental sanity. You could infer that my not wrecking the Triumph was an example of this, but really it was more a function of blind dumb luck. (By the way, the one time I actually *did* lie on the couch, the analyst told me that I was a basically stable, rational person with an almost unerring self-correction mechanism that led me away from potentially dangerous situations before I was likely to get myself into serious trouble. I wanted to smack the bastard. Don't *ever* tell a man he doesn't have a dark side.)

The Triumph had well-served my mother's intended purpose of bribing me not to cycle cross-country alone, but it had overstayed its welcome. It was miserably unreliable; you could hear it rust; it was passively hazardous on dry pavement and actively hazardous if you looked at the asphalt with so much as a moist thought. I had nowhere to garage it, and I was a penniless college student. It had to go. It went. But since its last act was taking me on my first date with she who would become my wife, I owe the car a big debt of gratitude. Maire Anne and the GT6+ are wistfully intertwined in my mind by this single encounter. The car that went, the girl who stayed. I'd quote Neil Young's song "Long May You Run," but the odds that the car lasted the remainder of the '70s, much less survived to this day, are vanishingly small.

Interestingly enough, I have a recurring dream in which I stumble across the Triumph, which I've stashed away in a cave somewhere and forgotten about. This is perfect. If anything reveals the schism between the sexes, it is this. Freud said dreams are the royal road to the unconscious. Women have horrific nightmares in which they've misplaced babies (Maire Anne had a doozie in which she heard our child's small voice calling from within a large house that was being devoured by the sea). Men, in contrast, have simple longing dreams about old cars and old girlfriends. It's a good thing we can move refrigerators, miter saw moldings, and sweat-solder copper pipe or we'd have no redeeming social value whatsoever.

But there's something else going on here as well. The relationships that men have with cars can be surrogates for relationships with women. This can cut both ways. Those who serially swap cars like Kleenex are likely exhibiting some degree of displacement behavior, but that isn't necessarily a bad thing; if you're going to get tired of something, get tired of a car. But the other extreme is holding into your baby way past the point of reason.

Dreams of old cars and old girlfriends. Some say men can't commit. In fact, sometimes we don't know how to let go.

I appear to have wandered in and lain down on the couch, so why don't I just settle in for the session?

CHAPTER 3

SO WHY *DO* MEN LOVE CARS ANYWAY ?

They're pretty. The cooler ones have sumptuous curves. And when you hit the gas, they push you back in your seat. The nicer the car, the faster this happens. Pretty simple. Neither men nor cars are really all that complicated. What else do you need to know?

Okay, let me turn the cute dial down a bit.

I'm reminded of the last line in the wonderful film *Almost Famous*, where the kid finally gets his interview with the big rock star and asks him what he loves about music. What do men love about cars? Well, to begin with, *everything*.

Let's talk about speed. To a man, the whole spectrum of sensations surrounding speed is pretty special. Not every car is fast (hell, I lust after a '63 Rambler Classic, and that's a little old lady car), but, well, let's just say it—there is an orgasmic burst accompanying the mashing of the throttle in a fast car. In all senses of the word, and in all senses of the body, speed is a rush. Awareness heightens, the hair stands up on the back of your neck, everything rushes toward you as the car thrusts forward, pistons pumping, engine howling, revving higher, faster, higher, faster, and you shift gears *WWAAAAAAAA waaaaaaaaaaaa* and take it to another level, Christ this thing is fast oh my god oh my god *OH MY GOD* …

Excuse me for a minute.

Now, not every guy is a car nut, but most car nuts are guys. For the record, while I am certain there are women who are into cars, I don't know any of you personally. Perhaps you would be as possessed and passionate as I am, and consequently I would be as reasonable as Maire Anne. Or perhaps we would each spend all of the other's money, then kill each other. It would be interesting to be your husband. In our next life, it's a date. We'll have hyper-gearhead children who will fix this broken world.

Phil Donahue once famously remarked that men are so emotionally constipated they have to drink beer *just to talk with each other*. There's a lot of truth to that. You can ask a guy why he likes a particular car and he'll talk cubic inches and horsepower and tire sizes and 0 to 60 times, but dig down and the answer is probably *well, I just really like it*. You can ask him the same question about his spouse and he'll probably give a similar answer: Why do you love her? *I don't know; I just do*. There may be some design aesthetic (obviously we're back to cars here) he finds particularly appealing (and aside from the universal acclaim of early Corvettes and Jaguars, and almost any Italian exotic, this is highly subjective). Or you may find some imprinting-related story like mine. But he genuinely may not know what is driving his passion. At least we know that women exude pheromones. Maybe, years from now, researchers will identify the peculiar mix of benzene, glue, leather, and burnt electrical insulation given off by British cars and be able to cure the poor bastards who are genetically predisposed to have the receptor sites for this pheromone, thus eliminating a sizable chunk of misery from the human condition.

Reams have been written about the whole *Men Are from Mars, Women Are from Venus* thing, but I'm not sure how much of that applies to cars. In the classical right brain / left brain paradigm, men have been characterized as more dominant in the upper left, or rational (*ha!*) and lower left, or organized (*ha! ha!*) quadrants, with women as more dominant in the upper right, or big-picture (probably) and lower right, or empathetic (definitely) quadrants. Obviously, it's difficult to pull anything concrete out of the intersection of psych-*lite*, pop culture, and *Top Gear* to give a definitive answer to why, if shown a '63 Corvette, most men drool and most women say, "That's nice," but I'll try.

Here's what I think. I believe that men, by and large, lack the nesting behaviors exhibited by many women. Have you ever seen the episode of the British show *Coupling* where Steve rants about cushions? If not, Google it for a good laugh. Maire Anne and I are enormously compatible, and I *still* don't understand the concept of "throw pillows." However, I think that men are very direct, immediate, intimate creatures, and cars are very direct, immediate, intimate objects. Compare a car to a living room. Why does your typical guy have far more interest in a car than the furnishings of his own living room?

You sit in both. You touch both, but you touch the car far more *because you have to control the car*. Think about it. What is there to control in a living room? Just the remote for the big-ass TV. Yeah. Well. So you see my point. Why do many men prefer cars with standard transmissions? One more thing to control. Why do men prefer to be the one driving? Yup. We've also just answered the question of why so many men seem to like playing golf; it's *all* about control.

"A-*ha*!" you say. "So men *are* control freaks!" Yes, but not in the way you think. We all like to have the illusion of control over our own lives. Sure, some men like to grab the remote control, just as some women like to clip coupons, shop, and put little pillows on chairs. These are clearly forms of control as well. With men, though, it's more tactile; we like to feel that we can control the things we lay our hands on. Hunting fits this theory as well. Sure, men talk about hunting in terms of the camaraderie, going into the woods with their buddies and so forth, but if they didn't have weapons to control—deciding the fate of some living creature, whether or not to blow its head off—where would the appeal be? You think men are going to sit around in all that nature, *talking about relationships and feelings?* Just try that, if you want to see someone shoot something.

I realize that this issue of "control" is a prickly one, but bear with me while I try to navigate the ship between the rock and the whirlpool. Certainly there are abusive men who try to manipulate and control women. Such men are scum, and should be neutered. Then again, there are women who regard men as projects (you know, "If I could smooth off his rough edges, get him to lose his football buddies on Sunday, he might be a keeper"), and if that's not an attempt at exercising control, I don't know what is. Any productive human relationship requires us to relinquish control so we can interact as the subtle complex unpredictable beings that we all are, but wildly unpredictable responses are difficult to deal with. Perhaps because of this, the desire to control gets transferred onto the inanimate realm. What do people say when their house is a mess? "The house is getting out of control." What is their response? *To try to control it.* There is comfort in the predictability of inanimate objects.

Look. Men are total sensation junkies. We spend a good portion of our life chasing sensation, be it with women, skydiving, rock climbing, drinking, drug use, or fast cars. I'm not saying that women aren't enamored of sensation; I'm just saying that men are. As men get older, the realistic limits on our bodies and the desire to remain faithful to our spouses may keep us in line, but the craving for sensation often continues. When I was in my teens I worked for a 40-something guy who had an impossibly low unbelievably angular red Lotus Europa. I overheard two 40-something friends of his talking, and one of them said, "A car like that, *you can get sex out of.*" I thought, yeah, girls like guys with cool cars, I get it. But I didn't get it. Not for years. They weren't talking about using the car to pick up girls. *They were talking about the sensation.*

I'll try to word this very carefully. It is bound to be misunderstood, but here goes. As most couples age, passions cool. Sex becomes less frequent. I'll bet you a dollar that this is not the man's preference. Some women may supplant sexual passion with nesting behavior, but most men don't. We don't care what color the sofa is. There's no sensation, no passion in the sofa (unless you make love on it). But a car—particularly a beautiful fast car—now *there's* something to be passionate about. A man can wring a lot of sensation out of a car. Add in the temptation, the lust, the chasing, and the consummation, and you've got the sensational framework of an affair without the actual sexual interaction. To a man, a cool car provides a whole range of sensations on demand. It's a very uncomplicated relationship. Friends with benefits. And the car never asks you to come shopping at Ikea. In some ways, it *is* like that notorious 1998 *SNL* sketch "Mercury Mistress," except that they got the car completely wrong. It should've been a curvaceous Italian exotic. Who the hell would want to make love to a Grand Marquis?

For the record, I don't hunt, I don't care about sports, and I think that golf is among the silliest, most wasteful of human activities. Nonetheless, I am very much a man, and a cool car, like a pretty woman, will turn my head pretty hard. With cars, though, it's socially acceptable to stare. More, it's socially acceptable to *own*. It may not be socially acceptable to stand on the accelerator and leave shrieking smoking acrid plumes of tire smoke in your wake, but man, once in a while, it feels really good when you do it.

I like to own cars that I drive, park, walk away from, then turn around and look back at and say, "*Damn* that's a cool car." At the time of this writing, among the eight cars I own are a 1973 BMW 3.0CSi, a 1973 BMW 2002, a 1999 BMW Z3 M Coupe, and a 1982 Porsche 911SC (more about all of them later), and I literally do the turn-and-look thing with all of them, every single time I park them. Really. Even a '63 Mercury Comet with those jet-age Deco taillights will have the same effect on me. I wish I did that with our living room, but I don't. And I *like* our living room.

I'd be less than candid if I said that I don't care how my cars look. Of *course* I care how they look. But I bought them and I drive them not because I want anyone to look at me—I don't care about that—but *because I like to look at the cars.* Only my 1973 BMW 3.0CSi is a zingy color (red); the others are pretty understated. Are the cars an extension of myself? Sure, absolutely, but not quite in the car-as-avatar sense you probably think. All those stereotypes of Corvette guys with chest rugs and gold chains and *hey, baby*? Maybe, maybe not. Maybe the guy just always wanted a Corvette and could care less what you think. If so, good for him.

Guys are damned if they do and damned if they don't with these highly visible cars. There was a gorgeous red Porsche parked at the gym I used to go to. And not an inexpensive older one like my 1982 911SC—a high-dollar late-model (997) car. I was curious who owned it. I expected it to be someone, you know, hunky. Finally after several weeks I saw the owner get in it and drive it off. The guy was, well, on the small and meek-looking side. *Oh, so he's compensating* goes the conventional wisdom. Fuck that. Maybe he works his ass off and always wanted a Porsche. I hope he loves it, drives it hard, nails it on entrance ramps, and makes it scream. I hope it's good for both of them.

Temptation. Lust. Passion. It's not accidental that these same words are used to refer to the dynamic men have with both women and cars. The caricature of this is the man who is "middle-aged crazy." What does the caricature do? Hook up with a young woman, or buy a sports car. Or both. I have no data and have conducted no survey, but I'd imagine that long-term relationships in which the woman has enabled rather than blocked her man's automotive urges—that is, helped to channel the excess lust, temptation and passion from the sexual arena into the automotive one—are probably more likely to be faithful. Women, if that reads as "let him buy the Porsche he'll be less likely to start chasing tail," it's more complicated than that, but yeah pretty much. And don't think you'll receive less of his passion if he directs some at the car. Trust me, men have *plenty* of passion. Guys, if that reads as "don't even *think* about straying and you'll be more likely to get the Porsche," yes that's it exactly. I have been rock-solid faithful to Maire Anne since Carter was in office (a whole president before we were married), and I own enough cars that I have to count them. Correlation? You be the judge.

One thing I haven't figured out in this cars-as-women thing is: if men love cars, and if cars are women, and if some men love trucks, and if trucks are manly, then … how exactly does that work?

Why do men love cars? Certainly they don't love us back. But they do offer us a complete, rich, heady mix of visual, auditory, tactile, and olfactory sensations. They catch our eye. We respond. We select them. There's a dance. They seduce us. We make them ours. They move beneath us. They are responsive. They are predictable. They can be fixed when they are broken. We can control them, or at least we can try. They jump and twitch when we nail them. Once a man has experienced this sensation, he wants to do it again. And again. And again. There's no mystery here. And if, in addition to all this, the car is visually gorgeous and literally screams and claws when it's driven hard …

Or do I have to draw you a diagram?

CHAPTER 4

BUGS, BOMBS, CARS, AND GUITARS
DAMN IT, HOW COOL DO YOUR PARENTS HAVE TO BE?

My mother, easily the wisest person I've ever met, once said to me, "If your children show interest in anything, treat it like a flower, because if you don't, you'll kill it with neglect or worse." It was easily the best piece of advice I've ever gotten from anyone, anywhere, about anything. Maire Anne and I have raised our boys, Ethan, Kyle, and Aaron, with my mother's *don't kill the flower* mechanism front and center. All three have found their passions (Ethan film; Kyle theater technology; Aaron photography) and have evolved into wonderful interesting human beings.

And as you give, hopefully you shall receive.

What was the theme song from that old TV show? "It's about time, it's about space." I love playing with cars. It is my flower. It appears to be something that is essential to my continuing emotional well-being. My family gets that and gives me the physical, temporal, emotional, and financial space to do it.

Let me lay this out for you. When I'm in the midst of a major repair, I will retreat to the garage every evening for weeks plus consecutive weekends. And if, in the middle of the repair, I catch a whiff of some car that's advertised, I will drop everything on a moment's notice, run out, withdraw several thousand dollars in cash from the bank, drive a hundred miles, and come home with another hobbled car that I'll then work on for months, starting the cycle all over again. Maire Anne won't say *another car? What are you, nuts?* She won't say *we're due at my mother's at 3:00.* She won't put her hands on her hips and shrilly declare *I want to buy new furniture you'll have to sell one of those things if I can't buy new furniture.* She sees that buying and working on cars gives me pleasure. She trusts that I am responsible, and that, for the most part, I know what I am doing. I would say that, for this, I love her, but it's the other way around—in our world, this is how people who love and respect each other behave.

Maire Anne has her flower as well, and unlike my automotive hobby, hers is also her livelihood. Her interest in animals led to a degree in zoology, which then led to her becoming the co-owner of a business called Bugworks. She and her business partner bring insects and arthropods into classrooms to teach kids about respecting the natural world (professionally, she is "the bug lady"). So in our house, in addition to my garage, we have "the bug room," which hosts terraria that contain tarantulas, scorpions, praying mantises, giant African millipedes, lubbers (grasshoppers of biblical proportion), Madagascar hissing cockroaches, meal worms, the beetles they metamorphose into, and a vinegaroon, which sounds like a cookie but I assure you is not. In return for the bliss I receive working in the garage, I leave Maire Anne alone when she is upstairs feeding the tarantulas.

Recently, Maire Anne called me at work, quite excited. "One of my scorpions had *babies!*" she said. "*I'm a grandmother!*" I rushed home with the camera to find ten snow-white baby scorpions, each the size of a thumbnail, on the mother's back, with an eleventh emerging from beneath her. Maire Anne explained that, unlike the majority of arachnids, scorpions are *viviparous,* meaning they give live birth.

It definitely rang my weird-shit-o-meter.

One could say, "Oh your wife brings *bugs* home so she can't really complain when you bring *cars* home," but that misses the point. It's not like we keep score, where one new project car equals two tarantulas and a millipede (though I should try that; the baby scorpions alone should justify at least that '63 Rambler Classic). Maire Anne has no more squeamishness about coming into the garage than I do journeying into the bug room; in fact, she probably has the same overall reaction, which can be summed up as: what is that *smell?* In my space it's the curious combination of brake fluid and rust inhibitor; in hers, high humidity and dead crickets. I did give her a hard time when, one night, while working at the computer, I felt something on my ankle and found a cockroach the size of a Swiss Army knife crawling up my leg. (Response: "Honey, one of your cockroaches got out. *Again.*") But then again, she still doesn't know about the time I used The Good Bread Knife to trim a power steering hose.

At this point, men are probably thinking, "Who *is* this woman and how do I inject her Zen-like emotional state into my wife's body?"

I suspect that many women are thinking two things: "I would *never* let my husband do that. What does *she* get out of it?" (If you have to ask, you don't get it, but how about love, respect, fidelity, and your *own* space?) The second thing is, "Bugs? *Really?*"

Now, you could say, "Well, a woman who handles live tarantulas is the poster girl for nontraditional gender roles, so okay, they're *both* weirdos, no wonder she puts up with him," but, actually, Maire Anne has documented the parameters of her tolerance:

> I don't know what my limit for these cars is, but I'll know it when I see it. Just remember that I have threatened to get dung beetles if you overstep the car line.

> And regarding dung beetles, some insect caretakers have observed that, with respect to dietary preferences, dung beetles can be sustained on something other than poop ("preferred poop" seems more vital to breeding and rearing). Beetle chow can be mixed by adding the following to a blender: half an apple, half a banana, a protein source (a four-inch minnow or about ten earthworms), a quarter cup of wheat germ, a handful of freshly pulled grass grown from bird seed, including the roots and a bit of soil. The resulting mash is rolled into little pellets and stored in the fridge. *DO YOU WANT THIS IN OUR FRIDGE?* Think about *that* when that next ad on Craigslist lights a fire under your creeper.

God I love this woman.

But I must point out that threats of nasty bug-related entities in the refrigerator don't scare me; we have had a dead solpugid (sun spider; go ahead and Google it) in the freezer *for six years*. Why? Beats the hell out of me, but who am I to question passion? It does give me food for thought, though, every time I go in there for a Popsicle.

When both Aaron and Kyle started doing stage crew for their high school theater productions and began spending every waking hour in the theater, initially Maire Anne and I were concerned. I mean, *don't kill the flower* is fine advice, but what about their grades? We quickly realized that, in fact, having them passionate and committed to a constructive activity was a gift. So to any long-suffering spouse of a three-years-to-do-a-frame-off-restoration guy, I can say only this: at least you know where he is. Seriously.

Our kids have always accepted "Dad's working on the car" as just one of many points of interest on the landscape. Professionally, I'm an engineer, working in geophysical applications related to the detection of unexploded bombs on old military training ranges, and sometimes I'm gone for weeks at a time on field surveys. Maire Anne and I were in and out of rock and roll bands together for many years (I'm a guitarist, she's a drummer), and I'm still a quasi-working singer/songwriter. We've often joked with the kids: "Bugs, bombs, cars, and guitars—*damn it, how cool do your parents have to be?*" Familiarity may not breed contempt, but it does foster yawns. The boys' friends may drop jaw when they see the garage full of cars and the terraria with Maire Anne's IOUS (Insects of Unusual Size), but it no longer registers much on the boys' personal radar; it's just part of the furniture.

Now, it is a well-known fact that Dad likes to work on his cars. I am out in the garage many evenings and weekends. Over the years, I've let the kids know that they were welcome in the garage, but I neither begged them to join me, nor hung out a *dad achieving third level of Zen in the garage do not break the trance this means YOU* sign. At dinner, I'd talk about my current automotive project, generally to minimal interest. Now, I am a realist in these matters. In a world of cell phones, instant messaging, and downloaded video, I never constructed wholesale Ward and Beaver fantasies of greasy meaningful father-son bonding over guibos and gaskets. So when the two older boys headed out for the night and the young one queued up in front of the Disney Channel, I shrugged and scooted for the garage. I've solicited their help when I needed a strong back or an extra pair of hands, and I've tried to mandate Ethan's participation when I'm working on his car, but if wrenching is in their genes as it apparently is in mine, it hasn't been expressed yet. Ethan is a big-picture guy. If his car is running, he won't do a thing; if it dies, he'll call me. Kyle, on the other hand, is very much an implementation guy, but he does not yet own a car. When he does, he may be seduced by the sirens of wrenching, as I was. Aaron is still a work in progress. But so am I.

I'll lie, for just a moment, on the couch. Between my father's getting sick, his understandable remoteness, and his dying, he wasn't around much. A few years ago I read *Iron John* by Robert Bly (and anyone who thinks it's a book about men beating drums to get in touch with their inner warrior hasn't read it; I can assure you it is 100 percent drum-free). Mr. Bly's analysis of how, prior to industrialization, sons worked in the fields or in blacksmith shops next to their fathers and absorbed, at the psychic and cellular levels, their "maleness," and how this was lost once men began leaving their families to go to work at factories in cities, is remarkably insightful and quite moving. When I read it, I did in fact begin to think that perhaps I'd missed an opportunity for this kind of bone-level bonding, but I'm not sure what I would've done differently.

I'm sorry, our time is up.

Even if we don't wrench side-by-side, I can't think of a better example to give my kids of how to live than seeing me working toward a goal, doing things that constructively engage my passion and give me pleasure.

A man I know, Jim, has a well-known BMW-specific repair shop. Every few years I'll call him up with a transmission-related question. Last year when I called the shop, his son Teddy answered the phone. I'd never heard Jim talk about his kids, and I was intrigued that Teddy was now clearly part of the family business. As Teddy and I developed a rapport, I told him about my kids having little interest in accompanying me into the garage and asked him what his path was. "Well," he said, "like your kids, my interest was always elsewhere, but my dad always made sure I knew that the door was open. It just took me a long time to walk through it."

Maybe, in this world, the best a father can do is let his kids know the door is open.

CHAPTER 5

WHY ARE SO MANY GUYS INTO WORKING ON THEIR CARS?

You can like buying, driving, and collecting cars and never have the urge to get down, get greasy, get *in there*. But many of us *do* have that urge.

Why?

If you believe what you read in the Sunday magazine sections, you'd think it was all about the real estate. What a load of hooey. Screw that psychobabble about "the man-cave." I see the spreads of some of these spaces with their jukeboxes and retro-'50s chrome Deco stools, where the car is a character in some *American Graffiti* tableau and it looks like someone would get mad if you got oil on something. Feh. I don't know any guy—not one—who looks at those setups and says, "Yeah, that's what I want—another impeccably-decorated space I'm not supposed to mess up." (Although I have to admit that, when I saw an unrestored Texaco Fire Chief gas pump at an antique store, I immediately thought how cool it would look in my garage.)

Real men pull engines and yank gearboxes. My garage is not a place to "hang out." My garage is messy, functional, and glorious, with cars, parts, boxes, jacks, stands, and tools everywhere. There's not a rug, a plasma set, a keg-in-a-fridge, or a Naugahyde Barcalounger anywhere. Hell, there's not even anything to sit on that isn't sharp or greasy. Walt Whitman would love my garage. It is large. It contains multitudes.

But … why would this give pleasure to anyone over the age of twelve? Six reasons.

First, in a world where I'm normally pulled in different directions, when I often think I should be at home when I'm at work and vice versa, my mind and body are deliciously focused when I work on my cars. I'm there for it, totally. I'm not drifting off thinking about some other problem or issue. Not even for a moment. I'm concentrating on one 10mm nut at a time. This is a profound, centering experience, equaled only by locking the bedroom door behind me and she who puts up with me.

Second, I love the laying-on of hands. In my day job, I'm an engineer. I develop proposals, write software, and analyze data—all very analytical and left-brained. So there's something enormously satisfying in catering to the right side of my brain—holding tools, visualizing spatial relationships, dismantling things, and putting them back together. Certainly this is not unique to automotive wrenching; I suspect that people who do carpentry, or woodworking, or plumbing derive satisfaction for similar reasons (Matthew Crawford's fascinating book, *Shop Class as Soulcraft,* talks extensively about this).

Now, there are times when it's not all Zen and green tea. When you snap off a bolt, or draw blood, or are stopped dead in your tracks because you're missing some tool or part, the Hack Mechanic Buddha can sometimes be clearly seen hovering in the corner of the garage, saying *centering experience? I got your centering experience right here, pal,* and laughing his fat ass off at you. When this happens, I usually inhale deeply, take one of my wrenches, feel its shiny cool weight in my hand, and whip it right at his head.

For example, exhaust work has a tendency to bring out my inner axe murderer. Sometimes, when an old, rusty, nasty exhaust just won't come out, I think *okay, you want to mess with ME? You want to tangle with ME?* and I get all Jack Nicholson on its ass and pull out THE SAWZALL. I fire it up—*brrrrAAANGGGG brrrAAANGGGngngng*—and the exhaust trembles and cowers under the car and tries to get away but I go after it and slice it into pieces and rip the bloody thing out of there and we thrash about on my oil-stained floor, transported by animal passion, until I sink back, exhausted, but oddly satisfied, on the cartons of Castrol.

Sorry.

Third, I derive enormous satisfaction from the simple joy of completely solving a problem, experiencing a clear beginning, clear end, and clear success. When I completely squelch one rattle, or resurrect a windshield washer pump, or make anything that wasn't working yesterday work today … that's bliss. How often does this occur in the rest of *your* life? Outside of sex, can anything be more satisfying? Maybe a good Reuben sandwich, if it doesn't kill you.

Fourth, the truth is that men—maligned, antler-flashing, obdurate, loner men, with all the emotional nuance of Chuck Norris—are in fact capable of showing great passion, love, and dedication. Caring for a car is a very intimate and satisfying thing. Yes, I totally just used the word *intimate* in a sentence whose context involves men. The relationship a car guy has with his car is a commitment, albeit without the risk of getting emotionally hurt. He—dare I say it—nurtures the car. He is responsible for it. If he takes that responsibility seriously, he makes the car more whole than it was before. As a result, he personalizes it; he inhabits its space and makes it unique. While I'm sure that some spouses think, "I wish he would direct that intimacy and nurturing toward *me*," it's not an either/or thing.

Although a car is inorganic, working on one is not unlike gardening. Just like you could pay someone else to fix your car, you could hire a landscaper and simply admire the beautiful result, but as any gardener will tell you, *where's the fun in THAT?* The joy is in the process, the smells, the tactile sensation, the way it occupies your brain and body. Both give you something to nurture. Both involve the use of tools and sticking your hands in dirty places. Both keep you off the streets at night. But you can't do zero to sixty in under five seconds in a tomato. And, working on a car, nothing dies that can't be resurrected.

One can even stretch the analogy to parenting. You get enormous pride out of showing off your baby. And, just as there is actively engaged parenting versus shipping the kids off to the best prep schools, there are car owners who merely write the checks, and those who do it all themselves and are there with their car every step of the way.

Fifth, there is the physical component of automotive repair, which ranges from near-yogic contortions to Alekseyev-like brute strength. I don't go in for health club-style group workouts, and as I'm getting older, my outdoor activities like hiking and biking have nosedived, but when I'm yanking an exhaust or installing a transmission, the pretzel twists that my body needs to hold for extended periods of time could be photographed and inserted in yoga guides with Fish, Grasshopper, and Lord of the Dance. There's one in particular that Jim Rowe from Metric Mechanic described perfectly. It's when you lie on your back, put a gearbox on your chest, transfer it to your knees, then, holding the front of it with your feet and the back of it with your hands, align it and press it into place, then hold it there while you finger-tighten one bolt so you can let it go. I call it *Lord of the Transmission.*

Finally, there's the money. The savings in performing your own normal-wear-and-tear repairs is substantial and thus has its own direct rewards in freeing up money to spend on modifications or elective automotive surgeries. I don't know how anyone affords a car, any car, if they have to take it into the service station (or, heaven forbid, the dealer) every time it hiccups. I like to think the best of everyone, but I can't forget the time we took our Previa to the Toyota dealer after having received a recall notice, and the service manager tried to sell us the 60,000-mile maintenance package including replacement of the timing belt, *when the car doesn't have one* (Previas have a timing chain, not a belt; chains do not require routine replacement). Now, I know there are lots of honest mechanics out there, but we all hear stories about dealers' tendencies to perform cash-ectomies. If you don't have a regular independent mechanic you trust and take your car to an unknown wrench who has hung out the obligatory "BMW Honda Toyota" shingle, you run the risk that he's learning on your nickel. A colleague of mine took his six-year-old Nissan Maxima to a convenient nearby shop when the check engine light went on. They charged him for every hour while they got up to speed on his evaporative system issue and presented him with a bill for a thousand bucks. A week later the light went back on. It's no wonder why so many guys just roll up their sleeves and say *damn it I'll just fix it myself.*

The fact that I do fix just about everything myself makes the cost of the occasional paid repair quite conspicuous. Maire Anne was driving my BMW wagon in northern New Hampshire when the alternator died (she was coming home from hiking with four of her friends in the car, so the event, shall we say, did not reflect well upon me, the supposed mechanic husband). Being 150 miles from home, there was little choice but to, as they say, "pay the man." The $500 repair bill from an independent shop struck me as about right for an alternator replacement in a modern car, but Maire Anne was surprised. "Wow …" she said, "this is a little window into how much money you save us."

But—and I cannot stress this enough—we all spend money on many things. For most people, paying someone else to fix the car is the norm. You have to perform extra work (literally) to go outside the norm. When I was young, my entrée into wrenching was certainly motivated by financial need, but now that I am blessed with some amount of disposable income, why would I go to all the knuckle-busting effort to work on a car if I didn't get some kind of satisfaction out of doing it?

One more thought about the money. I can be as guilty as the next guy of spending hours searching for the absolute lowest price with free shipping on some part that's necessary for a required repair (and, thus, saving us money), only to turn around and blow a king's ransom on something that even I'd have to agree is nonessential. But that's not only a car guy thing. We all make choices where to save and when to splurge. I well remember my Auntie Flossie telling us about her most recent travel adventures, while bragging about the 99-cent per pound chicken we were eating, and seeming equally proud of both.

Look. We all have to do *something* with our time. When men stereotypically chase women, play golf, or sit on the sofa and watch sports and drink beer, you're going to give me a hard time *because I work on cars in my garage?*

So, spouses, when your man is out in the driveway or in the garage, tangling with some angular greasy object that looks like it fell from space and then was pulled from a tar pit, he doesn't necessarily want to be left alone, but before you interrupt him, you should know that he is centering himself, focusing on one thing, solving a problem, controlling his world. At least that's what I'm doing. Of course, maybe he doesn't overanalyze everything the way I do and just wants to get that 427 side oiler in there so he can get rubber out of all five gears.

Why do men love cars? I think that a lot of us would be less relaxed, less happy, *less whole* without the garage and the cars, the personal space to tinker, and the epic stories to tell around the fire of the beasts we slew.

TOOLS OF THE TRADE

While you can nearly dismantle a 1970s BMW like a 2002 or a 3.0CS with just 10, 13, 17, and 19mm sockets (plus 11 and 14mm wrenches for the brake lines), the tools you need for sophisticated repairs on a random car vary quite a bit model-to-model. For example, newer cars use odder sizes, and may have Torx (those odd star-shaped) fittings. Nonetheless, like it says in every tool section of every repair manual you've ever read, you need to start with a decent ratchet and socket set.

TOOLS FOR THE DIY-ER VERSUS THE PRO

First let's touch on the issues of quality and cost. Professional-grade American-made tools like Snap-on and Matco have a lifetime guarantee—you break 'em, they'll exchange 'em. Craftsman has a similar guarantee, with an advantage that you can simply go to your local Sears for the exchange. Some folks say Craftsman is junk compared with professional tools; some say even Snap-on and Matco aren't what they used to be. And some worship at the altar of Harbor Freight Tools where cheap Chinese-made stuff is sold. "Made in China" is a double-edged sword. I know this is heresy to say, but while there's no question cheap imported tools have decimated the American tool industry, the influx also has put perfectly usable tools into the hands of a lot of enthusiasts. A weekend-warrior DIY-er simply doesn't need the same level of tool quality as a professional mechanic who uses them day in, day out. Some of my stuff is Craftsman, but most of it is of lesser quality, and even with the volume of work I do, it has held up fine. Of course, you don't want utter junk either. You really don't want that ratchet to let go or that socket to split while you're leaning on it trying to loosen some rusty nut and send your hand into jagged metal. Ideally you'll buy tools that are forged rather than stamped, but this isn't a showstopper. If it looks, feels, and costs dirt-cheap, then it is. Maybe you'll buy it anyway, it'll break, and you'll learn your lesson. You'll develop your own comfort level with the price and quality of tools.

Editor's Note: This memoir is **not** a repair manual. Please read Warnings & Cautions on p. 410.

RATCHET SETS

A basic ratchet set will usually include both ⅜" and ¼" ratchet drive handles and metric and SAE ("English") sockets. The size refers not to the length of the handle but to the square drive chuck. The bigger the chuck, the more torque it'll take. The ¼" is handy for small nuts, but you'll need the ⅜" stuff to take off anything bigger than 13mm. This basic combination set will get you off and running, but for larger, higher-torque nuts, you'll quickly find you need a beefier ½" ratchet set. When you purchase this, be certain to get a good set of 6-point ½" sockets, even if you have to purchase them separately from the set. Unlike the 12-point sockets that are typically part of a set, 6-point sockets have long straight faces to present against the six surfaces of a hexagonal nut. This helps to prevent the socket from slipping off the nut (it's pretty easy to slip and round the corners off a tight nut with a 12-point socket).

You'll need a good variety of both ½" and ⅜" extensions, swivel adapters, and wobble adapters. A swivel adapter is like a universal joint; it'll bend at up to 90 degrees. The problem is you can't deliver any torque through it when it's bent that far back. It'll just rip the adapter. In contrast, a wobble adapter has no moving parts; it's simply a chuck that's curved instead of dead square so it allows the socket to pivot by about 15 degrees. Since the more extensions and wobble adapters you string together, the more they eat up torque by twisting, it's more important to have a multiplicity of extensions and wobbles in the stronger, stiffer ½" size. If you're pulling a transmission, you have to reach virtually inaccessible bell housing bolts at the top of the transmission from behind it, and you'll wind up using every extension, swivel, and wobble adapter you've got, and only one combination will reach the bolt and allow you to put torque on it. But when you find that combination, cajole it into hanging in place, lean on the wrench, and crack that nut, boy, it's one of the best feelings in Hack Mechanic-dom.

At some point, you'll probably find you need a set of deep sockets to reach nuts that are far down on a threaded bolt. You can get these in ¼", ⅜", and ½" drive sizes, but it's the ⅜" deep set I use the most often.

BREAKER BARS

While ratchets and sockets are a must, I find among the most-used tools in my box are the breaker bars. A decent breaker bar (a handle and square drive chuck without a ratchet) is essential for getting off really tight nuts. This is because the ratcheting mechanism in a ratchet handle is actually pretty easy to destroy if a nut is stuck and you put a pipe on the end of the ratchet handle to get extra leverage. The older I get, the more circumspect I am about having my tendon-laden flesh go careening off into the greasy angular automotive unknown if I'm pushing hard on the end of a ratchet handle and the ratchet skips or breaks. The advantage of a breaker bar is it has no ratcheting mechanism to break. Typically you use the breaker bar with a "cheater pipe" for added leverage to "crack" the nut (get it started), then switch to the ratchet handle to speed the thing off. For things like impossibly tight lug nuts, I like having a big-ass breaker bar with a ¾" drive and using a ¾" to ½" adapter. That way, when I need to put a pipe on the end of the bar and stand on it, the bar won't flex. Sometimes, nothing succeeds like massive overkill.

In addition to the big-ass breaker bar, I also have a small ⅜" breaker bar with a swivel head that is incredibly handy in getting sockets onto nuts in tight spaces where a ratchet handle won't fit. I find myself using this simple tool constantly. It easily wins my "if you knew about these and had one, you'd use it all the time too" award. For example, I recently tried to remove the rear calipers on one of the cars, but access to the bolts holding on the caliper was partially occluded by the rear shocks. I couldn't get my impact wrench (see below) or my big-ass breaker bar on there, but the ⅜" bar fit just fine, and by slipping a pipe over the end, I could get the nuts off.

On a BMW, Allen keys are used mainly on the differential and transmission drain plugs and the bolts holding on half-axles, but they show up other places as well. A fold-out set of Allen keys does not offer sufficient leverage to take off anything tight. At some point you'll need to buy a set of ⅜" Allen sockets.

WRENCHES

Ratchets and sockets are employed when you have unimpeded access to a nut or bolt head, but if you don't have access, either because of lack of clearance or because the nut is part of some other fitting, you need a set of old-fashioned wrenches. Combination wrenches, where one end is open (like a crescent) and the other is boxed, are usually the way to go. The open end is needed for brake line and hose fittings where you can't put the wrench fully around the part you want to loosen, and the box end is useful on things like exhaust flanges where you have to loosen a bolt head with a ratchet and socket and need to hold onto the nut at the other end. The combination wrenches with ratcheting mechanisms integrated into the box end are wicked handy, but they should augment rather than replace a traditional set of combination wrenches; you don't want to be putting a lot of torque on that little ratchet.

One of the dirty little secrets of combination wrench use is you sometimes need to put a pipe over the end of the wrench to get more leverage. Usually you have the box end on the nut, leaving the open end available. You need a pretty big pipe to fit completely over both ears of the open end of the wrench, but I have a few different sized pipes that can fit on *one* ear of the open end. This will destroy cheap stamped tools pretty quickly; you need decent forged wrenches to do this.

MISCELLANEOUS HAND TOOLS

A set of small, medium, and large slotted and Phillips screwdrivers is a necessity for any automotive work. Low-quality Phillips screwdrivers loose their bite pretty quickly and then start to damage the slots in the screw head, so you'll appreciate having at least one good-quality medium-sized Phillips.

Two general household tools that kick around the toolbox and rarely get used in an automotive context are pliers and an adjustable wrench. For nuts and bolts, these should generally be avoided as they'll just mung-up the bolt head by rounding off the corners; a correctly sized socket and a ratchet handle is always preferable to an adjustable wrench or pliers. However, a decent-sized set of big-jawed Vise-Grips, a set of needle-nosed Vise-Grips, and a set of needle-nosed pliers are essential.

At some point, you're going to need to beat on something with a hammer. One could write a chapter on different kinds of hammers alone, but the two I wind up using the most are a small sledge with a short (6″) handle, and a rubber mallet.

The evil twin of the Allen key is the Torx. Torx fasteners started showing up as the attachment mechanism for certain BMW trim pieces in the 1980s. A set of Torx screwdrivers is an inexpensive addition to your toolkit; you'll be glad you have them when you need to remove grills and headlights. For less than ten bucks you can buy a ratcheting screwdriver set which has the Torx bits you'll need for small trim, as well as Phillips and standard screwdriver bits. Remember, though, you get what you pay for; the screwdriver bits in these cheap-o combination sets are not going to be as effective, or hold up as well, as a high-quality screwdriver.

More annoying and expensive than the Torx screws are the Torx-head bolts BMW uses on later cars to hold the transmission to the bell housing. If you're going to remove a transmission on anything from an E30 BMW on, you'll need to buy Torx sockets. Be certain to search online for which Torx bolt sizes are part of your car, as that Torx socket set that you've ordered for a weekend clutch job may skip a size you need (ask me how I know).

ELECTRICAL

The moment you ask the question "Why isn't this electrical thing working?" you're going to need a digital voltmeter (DVM), also referred to as a digital multimeter (DMM). Fluke is the, um, BMW of DVMs, but for basic "is the gonkulator getting power" questions, any DVM will do. In addition to the DVM, you'll quickly build up an assortment of cables and connectors that allow you to supply power to components directly from the battery. I don't drive around the block without a pair of 12-gauge 20-foot cables with alligator leads on both ends.

CLOTHING

I used to work in scummy jeans and T-shirts, unwashed for months, and plunge my bare hands onto components covered in the most disgusting scuziod mung imaginable, but these days I am absolutely addicted to Tyvek coveralls and rubber gloves. A Tyvek suit allows me to zip it on, do a quick fifteen minutes in the garage, zip it off, and not risk contaminating the living room sofa with blobs of grease. (Unfortunately, in the summer, they're simply too damned hot, so I switch to the most disgusting pair of shorts and T-shirt in the halls of human experience, and have perpetually greasy knees and elbows.) Similarly, disposable rubber gloves make it so I'm not scrubbing my hands for longer than I spent in the garage. Some folks swear by the nitrile ones, but I still prefer latex. Though they're not as durable as nitrile, they're closer fitting; I find them better in terms of ability to handle small parts. I tried vinyl gloves, and was instantly revulsed; removing them felt like pulling off a used condom.

FLOOR JACKS

If you're going to do even the most basic oil change, brake, exhaust, and suspension work on a car, you need a floor jack and a set of stands. Floor jacks come in a huge variety of sizes and capacities. You can pay $30; you can pay $1,000. If you have to pick one and you're short on money, I'd recommend a 3-ton capacity floor jack. These can be had mail-order for as little as $80. If your car is very low and the jacking point is way underneath, you may need a low-rise long-reach floor jack. It used to be there was one choice in this category—the AC Hydraulics DK13HLQ. A mere 3.1" at the front of the jack, this Dutch-made Rolls Royce of floor jacks used to cost over $600, then as the dollar fell against the euro, soared to $900, then became simply unavailable, so if you needed a low-rise long-reach jack, you were SOL. Fortunately, this is one area where the availability of inexpensive Chinese tools has been to the immense benefit of the DIY-er, as there are now similar jacks available from Ranger and Omega in the $200 range. I have three floor jacks: A DK13HLQ (snagged on eBay) which is indispensable for lifting the front of the Z3 M Coupe and the Porsche; a garden-variety 3-ton workhorse floor jack; and an aluminum 1.5-ton unit which is light enough to easily toss in the trunk of a car for road trips, tire changes, checking out potential car purchases, etc.

(Why would I need to use a floor jack at all when, as you'll read below, I, in fact, have a lift in my garage? Several reasons. Sometimes a car is already on the lift. Sometimes I just need to do something quick, like swap a single wheel or inspect the brakes. Even having the lift, the floor jacks still see a lot of use.)

JACK STANDS

The floor jack will raise the car, but you need to support it on jack stands. Stands of 3-ton capacity are sufficient for most passenger cars. Avoid like the plague the old-school three-legged stands where it looks like the three legs are cut from the same piece of thin-gauge metal tubing. If you have these in your garage, recycle them. You want four-legged stands with a toothed center piece and a ratchet bar which allows you to easily raise the center piece but requires you to lift the bar to lower it.

I can't mention jack stands without hammering home this point: *Whenever* I am working beneath a car, I *always* double-jack it. This means I jack it up, put the jack stands in place, lower the car onto the stands, *then leave the floor jack in place.*

A word regarding drive-on ramps: Don't. On paper, they may sound appealing for oil changes, but too many things can go wrong. Firstly, they're made from cheap, thin, stamped sheet metal. Second, the increased width of modern car tires makes it so they don't fit in the indentation at the top of the ramp, which in turn makes it very easy to drive off the end of the ramp. Lastly, many modern cars are so low that ramps don't work anyway—the air dam hits the ramp and pushes it forward as you try to drive up it. Just don't.

POWER TOOLS

In addition to the hand tools, there are a few power tools you'll need. A drill, a reciprocating saw (i.e., a Sawzall) and a Dremel tool with a supply of cutting wheels are essential for doing battle with exhausts and their attending army of rusted fasteners and convincing them to give it up and release their death grip on the soft white underbelly of your car.

TAP AND DIE

At some point during a repair, a nut is going to come off with difficulty, and is going to be nearly impossible to put back on without cross-threading it. A tap and die set is a collection of tools for recutting threads. The taps sort of look like different-sized screws, the dies like screw holes inside quarter-sized discs. If you've, say, unthreaded a nut from an exhaust stud, you find the correctly sized die and twist it up and down the stud to clean the threads. You can do the same with a tap on the nut. Later in the book we'll talk about "stuckness" and how to use a drill and a tap to repair a snapped-off stud.

AIR TOOLS

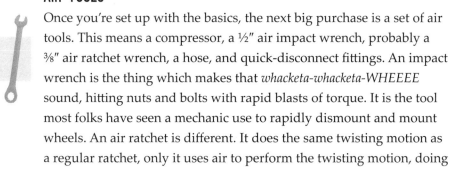

Once you're set up with the basics, the next big purchase is a set of air tools. This means a compressor, a ½" air impact wrench, probably a ⅜" air ratchet wrench, a hose, and quick-disconnect fittings. An impact wrench is the thing which makes that *whacketa-whacketa-WHEEEE* sound, hitting nuts and bolts with rapid blasts of torque. It is the tool most folks have seen a mechanic use to rapidly dismount and mount wheels. An air ratchet is different. It does the same twisting motion as a regular ratchet, only it uses air to perform the twisting motion, doing it in a fraction of the time it takes you to do it manually.

Let me say something that surprises many people. *The utility of air tools is not in removing incredibly tightly stuck nuts. Their utility is in removing normally tight nuts incredibly quickly.* If you have ancient lugs on your wheels, or recalcitrant nuts holding the head pipe to the exhaust manifold, it is not at all unusual for them to sneer at your impact wrench and send it scurrying into the corner to whimper and question its manhood, only to succumb to an old-fashioned breaker bar and a pipe (in the valley of the stuck, leverage is king). This is also true when you've strung together four extensions and two wobble joints to reach an inaccessible transmission nut—the lack of rigidity in that multiple sloppy set of connections eats up torque, and the air impact wrench isn't delivering much of its *whacketa whacketa whacketa* directly to the nut you're trying to remove. The breaker bar and pipe still often win the day against their slicker faster-talking uptown cousin. I'll say it again. *The utility of air tools is in removing normally tight nuts incredibly quickly.*

I bought my air tools in 1987. The compressor is a Craftsman 3hp with a 20-gallon tank. The impact wrench and air ratchet were Taiwanese-made tools (the Chinese tools of their day) from Harbor Freight Tools. The compressor, impact wrench, and air ratchet still work fine. These days you can get everything you need for about $250. The compressor's horsepower governs the peak pressure delivered to the tools, whereas a combination of horsepower and tank size contribute to the cubic feet per minute (CFM) rating. If you're running a small air tool like an air ratchet, it's not running all the time and it doesn't need to deliver either strong or sustained force, so you can use one of those little compressors about the size of a fat bathroom wastebasket. For an impact wrench, however, you'll need a bigger compressor, something in the 2–3 hp and 12–20 gallon range. Even with a properly sized compressor, if you're trying to take off a tight nut, you may have to wait for the compressor to cycle (to fully pump up the tank to peak pressure) to allow the impact wrench to blast it with maximum torque. And, even so, you may still need to resort to the big-ass breaker bar and cheater pipe.

There are times when, working on the car in the morning and evenings, I don't want the *whacketa-whacketa-WHEEEE* of the impact wrench; I want to do the Zen thing, just me and the wrench and the nut. But impact wrenches and air ratchets can really speed things along. Air tools can really save wear and tear on your wrists, too, especially on rusty nuts where, even when you've gotten them loose, you have to keep putting a lot of force on the wrench. When removing the nearly two dozen 10mm bolts holding on a BMW oil pan, the air ratchet is an incredible time saver. When I need to take off half-axle shafts with their six Allen key bolts per side, I clean each bolt hole out with a small pick, insert the Allen socket, tap it lightly into the head of the bolt with a hammer, slip on the impact wrench, squeeze the trigger, and off it comes, no muss, no fuss, no stripped Allen heads. Hack Mechanic heaven. It almost feels like cheating.

An air impact wrench is also incredibly useful for disassembling front struts once you've compressed the spring. Without an impact wrench, you need to hold the top of the strut cartridge still by inserting a small Allen key at the top, then trying to loosen the nut with a big wrench. When doing this, it's very easy to strip the Allen key's hole. But with an impact wrench, you don't have to immobilize the cartridge at all; you just let the impact wrench spin the nut off.

Note that impact wrenches, by their nature, can easily destroy inexpensive sockets. The socket wall cracks, then the nut you were loosening has rounded corners, making it more difficult to remove. At a minimum, you need a set of ½" thick-walled impact sockets. This kind of socket set is, in fact, the only Snap-on tool I own.

Once you have a compressor, you can buy other air tools as the need arises. A tire inflator (a chuck with a trigger and a pressure gauge) is incredibly handy. I have an air chisel which, when used with a pickle fork attachment, makes removing ball joints almost a joy. I don't use it for much else (though one winter I did actually use it to chip major hunks of ice off portions of my driveway). I also have a small air hacksaw, though it doesn't offer much utility that isn't present in the combination of a Sawzall and a Dremel tool.

WORK SURFACE

With all these tools being accessed and all these parts being removed and installed, it's incredibly handy to have some sort of work surface. Until recently I didn't have one; I just left tools and parts on the garage floor during a repair. On the one hand, they were all right there, but sometimes I'd accidentally kick a socket skittering across the floor, or step on a pipe, have it roll under the sole of my shoe, and struggle to retain my balance. I now use an inexpensive roller cart to corral my tools and provide a surface on which to stage parts.

THE LIFT ("ELEVATE ME")

The wet dream of any DIY mechanic is a lift. Ah, to be able to stand up under a car like the pros do, maybe even roll a transmission jack under there … it, uh, jacks me up just thinking about it. (Remember that scene in *Young Frankstein* where Gene Wilder says, "Elevate me," to Teri Garr? Never mind.) I used to drive past closed service stations, see the double-bay roll-up doors, know there were two full-height lifts inside that I *sooooo* could make use of if only I had some legal path to them, and think the automotive gods were mocking me, punishing me for some past automotive sin. Maybe buying the Triumph. Or abandoning my '63 Rambler by the side of the road.

Unlike air tools, lifts are more difficult to justify in a direct return-on-investment sense. But not everything is about return on investment, nor should it be. As we get older, have more disposable income (hopefully), and settle into our hobbies, it is natural to invest in the things that give us pleasure. What is the return on investment on a Weber barbeque grill, or a deck, or the money spent on gardening, or a gourmet kitchen? Spending money on a lift may be the ultimate admission you're working on cars because you like to—because it gives you plea-sure—not simply because you're trying to save money. So what? Tell your significant other I said it was okay.

"Lift" once evoked an image of a single enormous in-ground hy-draulic cylinder, but these days there are many other choices. Far more common are surface-mounted lifts whose arms swing out to support the car's frame and allow complete unimpeded access to the under-side of the car. Four-post lifts can be self-supporting, but two-post lifts need to be bolted to the garage floor; you have to verify the thickness of the concrete and be very certain of the integrity of the installation. So-called "runway lifts" usually have four posts supporting a pair of ramps the car drives onto. Thus they are useful for oil changes, ex-haust, transmission, and alignment work, but not for any repairs that require the wheels to be removed. Several types of post lifts do double-duty as storage devices by lifting a car high enough to allow a second car to be driven beneath. The downsides of a post lift are the cost, and the fact the posts themselves eat up some amount of garage space. At a minimum, it makes it so the space can't easily be reconfigured (once those posts are up, you have to position a car directly between them; there's no putting it fractionally, or crosswise).

If you don't have the fourteen-ish feet of ceiling height needed for a post lift, you might consider a mid-rise scissors lift. Like a floor jack, these lie pretty flat on the ground until you raise them up. They lift the car up about four feet, which is high enough to sit, with your butt on the ground, completely upright beneath the vehicle. Compared with the contortions I used to undergo working beneath a car on jack stands, this is bliss. The downside of a mid-rise is that the body of the lift is in the way—it impedes access to the center part of the underside of the car, though cut-outs in the lift body try to minimize this obstruc-tion. Typically there's a big cut-out at the "front" end of the lift where you'd normally position the front of the car; this allows fairly unim-peded access to the underside of the engine.

A mid-rise lift uses an electrically powered motor to drive fluid into a pair of hydraulic cylinders which, in turn, raise the platform. To keep the profile low, the electric motor and the fluid reservoir are not located on the lift but on a wheeled stand which looks something like a golf bag. Many manufacturers claim their lift is "portable" by using the wheeled stand as a lever to move the lift around. Having tried this, I can tell you, in practice, it's easier to slide it over eight inches at a time with a long crowbar than to use the wheeled stand. But a mid-rise can, in fact, be moved around inside a garage; it is not a permanent installation.

After my garage—with its low nine-foot ceiling—was built, I took the plunge and bought a BendPak MD6XP mid-rise lift for less than 15 hundred bucks delivered. I had recently bought the Porsche 911SC, and the mid-rise was perfect for working on it, as there are very few components in the middle of the underside of a rear-engine car (I'd position the engine over the cut-out on the "front" of the lift).

For working on anything in the front or rear of a BMW, the lift is fabulous, but using it to pull a transmission is challenging, as you can't roll a jack directly beneath the transmission; the body of the lift itself is in the way. There are two separate issues. Firstly, depending on the direction the car is facing, the top of the lift (the horizontal platform) is in the way of the transmission. As I said, one end of the lift platform has a cut-out though which there *is* access to the transmission if the car is facing forward (and this is how you'd pull the transmission if you were strong enough to not need a transmission jack), but for reasons unclear, every mid-rise lift I've ever seen has the cut-out directly above the hydraulic cylinders. Which brings us to the second issue—those hydraulic cylinders are right where you want to place the transmission jack.

I found two solutions to this. One is to position the car backward on the lift so you don't have the advantage of the cut-out but you do have the advantage of not having the hydraulic cylinders in the way. This enables you to lay down a false floor over the leg of the lift (I used two steel wheels, one on each side of the lift's leg, with a heavy piece of sheet aluminum on top) on top of which you can roll a transmission jack. Even with the car facing the wrong way so there's no cut-out beneath the transmission, there's just enough room to pull the tranny (at least there is with a BMW 2002).

The second way to deal with transmission removal on a mid-rise lift is to put the car on the lift facing forward, do everything except actually dropping the transmission (i.e., remove the shields, exhaust, and driveshaft, and unbolt the transmission from the engine but leave one bell housing bolt in place), then take the car off the lift, roll it forward onto the cement floor, and go the last mile the old-fashioned way: Jack up the car, put it on jack stands, and use a conventional floor jack or a transmission jack to drop the tranny. I employed this technique to replace the clutch in my Z3 M Coupe and it worked very well.

As with any relationship, there are some accommodations one has to make in order to live happily with the mid-rise. The first is your car might not clear it; your car doesn't have to be as low as a Viper to have the bottom of the car hit the top of the collapsed lift. The Porsche guys all use—and I copied—a set of ramps made by stacking wooden 2x10s sideways and cutting the ends off at an angle to make a ramp, enabling you to drive and park on top of the lift. Another quirk of the lift is that it takes a certain amount of time to position a car on it. An older, happy-go-lucky car with exposed frame rails such as BMW 2002 or 3.0CS can be positioned quickly and easily on the lift. This strikes me as in keeping with its flexible, roll-with-the-punches, come-out-and-play personality. However, many newer cars are not so accommodating, and have frame rails that are hidden behind plastic under-cladding (or don't have traditional frame rails at all), requiring you to swing the lift's arms out wide and lift the car by the jack pads on the rocker panels. With a wide car, you must center the car on the lift very precisely, which takes time. My E39 wagon was downright persnickety about this; it was so wide, relative to the lift, there was only about a two-inch margin for error on both sides, requiring multiple readjustments of the car on the ramp. It probably took me a good 20 minutes to get it on the lift, aligned, and up in the air.

The mid-rise is not perfect, but what is? It is a pretty good compromise of cost, space, and functionality. Whenever I sit fully upright beneath the car, hanging an exhaust or changing a tie rod, I think, man, I *love* having this thing.

If you're a long-time gearhead looking for an excuse to buy a lift, just do it. It'll cost a tiny fraction of that gourmet kitchen. And I'd wager you'll enjoy it almost as much.

If you're just starting out in the DIY world, don't be intimidated by the litany of tools I've listed. Tool needs will make themselves known in an organic fashion as you wade into a repair. Some of the bigger or weirder stuff can be borrowed from friends or rented from AutoZone. With all my stuff, repairs still get interrupted because I need to run out and procure some tool. Hell, sometimes the thing I need most in the entire world is a milk crate to stand on.

Spouses, if you've come away from reading this thinking, "This is fabulous—I know what to buy him for his birthday," that's great, he will adore you for it, but be careful. Think about the things he buys for you. Does he know *your* tastes? Does he buy you *exactly* what you want, or do you sometimes think, "I wish he'd asked me first; I don't want to return it and hurt his feelings." It's like that. Tools are a very intimate thing. If he's a dyed-in-the-wool American tools guy, getting him a gift certificate to Harbor Freight Tools may not be the best fit. It's difficult to go wrong buying Snap-on stuff, but boy, you'll pay for it. Gift certificates to Amazon or other vendors which carry a whole range of brands offer a lot of flexibility, but little intimacy. I suggest simply being direct, and asking him exactly what he wants. It may spoil the element of surprise, but it will increase your odds of giving him a tool he'll actually use. If he has a car guy buddy with whom he wrenches, you might ask him, "John, what does Fred really want?" You will, however, need to be prepared for a wholly non-tool-related answer.

Why do men love cars? It gives us an opportunity to accessorize.

CHAPTER 7

WHY I DON'T FIX CARS FOR OTHER PEOPLE

(PART I: BAD LUCK WITH FRIENDS' VOLKSWAGENS)

I love to work on cars. I have the knowledge. I have the tools. I have Zen-like experiences in my garage. And I've talked about how the cars are a conduit for human interaction. You might think it would be natural for me to do it professionally, or as a source of additional income, or at least as a favor for friends.

You might think. *But you would be wrong.*

The basic issue is that things go wrong all the time when you're doing mechanical work. If it's my car and I've chosen to do the work, then I'm responsible, but if it's someone else's car, it gets complicated, and you rapidly slide into "no good deed goes unpunished" territory.

Now, there is of course one glaring exception to this: family. I've done any number of repairs for my sister, including once steaming the inspection sticker off my gorgeous 1973 BMW 3.0CSi to put it on her uninspectable piece of crap minivan to keep it on the road for one more season, which resulted in a big permanently discolored patch in the corner of my windshield; it sticks out like a sore thumb to this day. If ever she implies that I don't love her, I'll haul her ass into the garage, point to the obvious clouding in the windshield laminate of my otherwise mint car, and say *oh yeah, well what do you call THAT?*

Then there was the time when I found my sister-in-law Tricia her first car, a Toyota Tercel, and then had to find an identical one with a dead engine so I could transplant the engine from the former into the latter when the former got totaled. Along the way I won the respect of my father-in-law; I did all this in his driveway. Tom was great. I said, "I'm going to have Tricia's wrecked car towed here, then I'll pull the engine, then I'll find a good one with a dead engine and have that one towed here, and that may take a while, then I'll pull some parts off the wreck, then when it's all done I'll have the wreck towed off as junk, so you'll have two cars here for a while, but I think it's doable." To his enormous credit, he believed me (and, I guess, to my credit, I pulled it off). And I'm always working on Ethan's car. But he's my son. That's family. That's different.

This whole "I don't work on other people's cars" thing started when I was at UMass. Friends knew that I had become very adept at keeping the Triumph running. My friend Paul had a Beetle. It needed work on the brakes. It was late November. He was poor. He begged me. Finally I relented and said that I'd do it if he bought the parts. So I put the car up on jack stands in the parking lot of my dorm. I found that, in addition to it needing the expected pads in the front and shoes in the back, one of the rear wheel cylinders was leaking. And, like any New England car, everything was rusty. I explained to Paul that, in order to change the wheel cylinder, we had to unscrew the brake line feeding it, and that with things being rusty, there was a chance that the brake line could snap off. But we were right there, it was three in the afternoon, sun still up, with the car jacked up in the parking lot and everything exposed. What we were supposed to do, stop?

So I tried to unscrew the brake line. And because it was rusty, it snapped right off, pissing sickly smelling brake fluid onto the asphalt. (By the way, I *hate* the smell of brake fluid, which hangs around forever and pervades any automotively purposed enclosure the same way urine pervades subway stops.)

If this happened to me now, I would know how to deal with it. You have to replace the entire length of brake line running all the way to the master cylinder, and, of course, then you run the risk of it snapping off at the other end and having to replace the master cylinder as well. It's quite possible that, by the time you're done, maybe you'd snap off and have to replace every brake line on the car. I understand that now and could deal with it if necessary, though it would completely suck. But in 1977, one snapped line exceeded the limit of what I was able to do as a mechanic.

I was very apologetic. Paul was not pleased, but he understood. But we now had a car up on jack stands in a parking lot, with a snapped brake line, in November, with the sun going down. So I put the thing back together as best as I could, and at some odd hour of the morning, I drove it very carefully to the nearest repair shop. (Note that this is not quite as insane as it perhaps sounds; most cars built after

1968 have a tandem braking system, meaning that even if there's a leak, the car will still have half its braking.)

I had provided my labor free of charge, but Paul was faced with a larger bill than anticipated because of the snapped brake line. Maybe the same thing would've happened to a pro. Maybe not. Who knows? But I had the lingering feeling that I had done something wrong.

So the car was a conduit for human interaction all right—and that interaction was disappointing.

I thought, well, it's easy to avoid this in the future—I won't work on anyone else's car. If asked, I'll just say no.

And I did—for about 15 years.

CHAPTER 8

THE LURE OF OLDER CARS

Why are many car buffs into older cars? Part of it is certainly nostalgia. That imprinting thing runs deep, and many car guys are fanatically devoted to the cars they couldn't afford in their youth and now can.

But nostalgia notwithstanding, there is certainly a lot of appeal in the simplicity of older cars. When you open the hood of a newer car, the engine compartment looks like the top of a Sears Craftsman shop vac, with everything carefully hidden behind molded black plastic cladding. In contrast, on an older car, you see the engine, spark plug wires, distributor, alternator, starter motor, and radiator laid out the way The Great Automotive Creator intended. So wonderfully form-follows-function.

And, with simplicity comes ease of diagnosis. If you turn the key and the engine cranks but doesn't start, the number of things that could be wrong is very small. Old cars have no computers or weird electric doohickeys to fail and interfere with starting and running. Similarly, if the car has no heat, the cable is likely not pulling the heater valve open. There just aren't many other possibilities. It's not going to be some hyper-expensive electronic module jammed way up under the dash. There aren't any. The odds of you getting stumped and having no choice but to tow the old girl to the dealer are exceedingly slim. Plus, when you actually need to get in there and fix it, with simplicity comes ease of repair; unlike on a newer car, there's enough space to stick your hands in and actually reach things like the starter motor and the alternator without having the fingers of E.T.

So what do we mean by "older cars?" A widely quoted but arbitrary standard is that an "antique" car must 25 years old—but this is only relevant in that, in certain states, it affects insurance rates and the ability to get antique plates. What *is* important are the automotive sea changes that occurred in the years 1974 and 1975, effectively dividing the car world into BBAS and ABAS (Before Bumpers and Smog and ... you get it). It's worth taking a moment to understand so that, if nothing else, you can impress your friends by being able to nail the year of a car from a hundred feet away.

Long story short, new federal Department of Transportation (DOT) standards that went into effect for the 1973 model year mandated that front bumpers had to withstand a 5 mph impact. In response, most manufacturers merely pushed the existing chrome bumpers slightly further from the body. However, in 1974 these standards were strengthened to include an impact from any angle with no damage to lighting, requiring car companies to use significantly larger energy-absorbing bumpers and mounts. Because of this, it is trivially easy to tell at a glance if a car is pre- or post-'74. If it has small, lithe, chrome bumpers that are flush against the body and are well integrated with the lines of the car, the car was built prior to 1973 (many pre-'73 American cars even had the taillights integrated into the rear bumper). If it has chrome bumpers that are just slightly pushed out from the body, it is likely a '73. If it has larger bumpers that protrude several inches from the body and do not look integrated with the lines of the car, it is a '74 or later model. For example, 1974 BMWs have bumpers that look like highway dividers. The poster child for bad bumper integration was the MG. The pre-'74 cars are classic, but the post-1974s feature a front bumper abomination that looks like it has trout pout. Talk about your bad plastic surgery.

In 1975, a second, smog-related change occurred. The Environmental Protection Agency (EPA) established rules, and Congress passed laws, resulting in tailpipe emissions requirements that dramatically restricted pollutant levels, requiring most manufacturers to use catalytic converters and burn unleaded gas to meet the new standards. Not surprisingly, it took a while to get all this right and for the emissions systems to be designed-in rather than added-on. In addition to having dramatically reduced levels of performance (the standard engine in the 1975 Corvette, for example, generates a measly 165 horsepower), these post-'75 cars often have short engine lifetimes because they run hot. BMW, for example, eschewed catalytic converters in favor of a similar technology called thermal reactors. These were attached to the exhaust manifold and ran so hot that if you opened up the hood at night, you could see them glowing red. A cracked head was a fairly common result. For all of these reasons, generally speaking, the years 1975 through 1977 comprise the least desirable period for many otherwise collectible cars.

There is a third dividing line created by the dreaded "check engine light" (CEL). Beginning in the 1980s, manufacturers began equipping their cars with an increasing amount of self-diagnostics. One needed only to press a button in a 1980s BMW to verify all of the car's lights were working properly before taking it in for an inspection. However, this On-Board Diagnostic (OBD) capability not only found its way into the emission control system, but emissions soon became its primary concern.

In 1996, the so-called OBD-II self-diagnostic emissions monitoring system was federally mandated on all cars sold in the United States. This included a standardized set of fault codes and a socket into which to plug a device to read them. There are occasional benefits to this. For example, the CEL can warn that the car is running monstrously rich, dumping raw gas into the catalytic converter, before it ruins the cat—an expensive proposition. However, generally speaking, the CEL is a pain in the butt. The light itself provides no information; you have to plug in a code reader. And even then, the diagnosis is usually vague, like "minor evaporative leak." The oft-repeated advice that the CEL is frequently due to something simple and inexpensive, like a loose gas cap, is, in my humble opinion, perilously close to urban myth. Most folks I know have had the opposite experience—paying as much as a thousand bucks simply to make the damn light go out. And, in most states, the light *has* to be out for the car to pass inspection.

While I can't advise you to simply ignore the CEL, there's no question that the CEL is *far* less important than a lit oil pressure light or a temperature gauge in the red, both of which mean *stop the car NOW*. Really, the CEL should be called the RMERIWCWBCOOPTIIL ("relatively minor emissions-related issue whose cost will be completely out of proportion to its importance light"). And there's the whole issue of the CEL impeding modification—if one is considering something like an engine swap, it is far easier in a pre-OBD-II car.

Let me be careful here. I am all in favor of emission controls. I am in no way advocating their removal from older cars. I am simply pointing out that if you lust for a particular model of classic car that was built on both sides of the Bumper and Smog Divide, you'd be wise to do homework and buy one that's either early enough for emission controls to be non-existent or minimal, or late enough for the manufacturer to have gotten them right. But be aware that buying on the early (emissions-free) side has a consequence for those of you with spouses with delicate noses. Early carbureted cars with no emission controls tend to smell of gas. Whenever I fire up my 1973 BMW 2002 in the driveway, Maire Anne, who has an exquisitely sensitive sense of smell, says, "Man, that thing *stinks*!" It took me a while to realize it, but she can smell the unburnt hydrocarbons in the exhaust.

So a car built in 1973 or before has both lithe, well-integrated, aesthetically pleasing chrome bumpers and the simplicity that goes along with minimal emission controls. You can understand the appeal. After that, there's a roughly eight-year window in which you'd really have to present a lawyer's case for why you'd want that particular car rather than an older or a newer one. Except, I guess, if you're into AMC Pacers; those were *only* manufactured 1975 through 1980. Bad timing. Sort of like being born during the plague.

We've established that old cars are cool, have an integrated design aesthetic, and are easy to work on. But it's a great big automotive world filled with nearly limitless choices of enthusiast cars. My particular poison is early '70s BMWs. Why? We may not choose the cars we imprint on, but we can certainly rationalize them. Sure, there is the styling that is quintessential 1970s German industrial design. And yes, they present a pleasing range of visual and tactile sensations. But the main appeal of '70s-era German cars is that they drive and handle very well, even by modern standards, even with their stock skinny 165-series tires. Note that this is not the case for all enthusiast cars. I know a guy who owns a '65 Corvette Sting Ray, one of the icons of swagger and speed, and he says, "Yeah, it's beautiful but it drives like a truck."

I go just as gaga as the next car guy over '50s tail fins and chrome, but I'm certain even the most ardent '55 Chevy owner doesn't kid himself that he loves it because of its handling. And that's fine; not every car is about booting around entrance ramps. I saw a butter-yellow 1950 Chevy pickup truck with bulbous whitewalls that looked like it just drove out of *Who Framed Roger Rabbit* and thought how cool it would look in my garage. And that wouldn't drive *like* a truck; that *was* a truck. But with a '70s BMW, you can easily transform its already excellent handling to go-cart-like with easy bolt-on additions of wider tires, stiffer shocks, and thicker antiroll bars, then simply remove them if you or the next owner is a stickler for originality. Lastly, while these cars drive and handle well even by modern standards, there's no confusing them with their modern counterparts, and in many ways, that's a good thing. A '70s-era BMW has a simplicity and a directness you won't find in a late-model BMW M3. This lets you get your jollies without getting into trouble; you may find yourself going *yeeeeee-HAAA* in the 2002 only to check the speedo and find you're barely exceeding the speed limit.

Now, in defense of newer cars, there's this myth: "These new cars are so computerized you can't work on them anymore."

Bullshit.

No, you can't troubleshoot and field-strip a Motronic unit, but you don't have to. Generally speaking the electronics in newer cars are fairly reliable, unless you own a Jaguar, in which case you have bigger problems than I can help you with. And what you gain in terms of easier cold-weather starts, increased performance, better fuel economy, and lower emissions is worth some loss of I-can-fix-it-by-the-side-of-the-road control in the rather unlikely event that the electronic control unit (ECU) or some crucial sensor does, for some reason, die.

But the more important point is that *not every square inch of a modern car is controlled by a microprocessor*. Brakes, for example, are still brakes. Even on a modern car with antilock brakes, the procedure for replacing brake pads and rotors has changed very little. The same is true of exhausts and suspensions. This triumvirate (brakes, exhaust, suspension) accounts for much of the normal-wear-and-tear repairs on a car. You can save a lot of money by sourcing these parts from somewhere less expensive than the dealer and installing them yourself. This truth is not abrogated simply because the car is "computerized." I recently replaced the clutch in my '99 BMW Z3 M Coupe, and I can assure you that I did not encounter any microprocessors along the way.

And regarding those "computers"—don't be too hard on them. The use of microprocessors in cars became necessary in order to control the engine accurately enough to comply with emission standards while achieving some reasonable balance with power and fuel economy. It took a while to get it right, but once the teething pains were over, the results were better than most enthusiasts expected. All my newer cars start right up even in frigid weather, idle flawlessly, drive away without stumbling, have ample—sometimes spectacular— amounts of horsepower, and get decent gas mileage to boot. In contrast, you're lucky if an old car is able to do even *one* of these things.

Nonetheless, part of the pleasure in owning an older car is *because* of its quirks. I love the fact that the choke sticks in my 1973 BMW 2002, so to start it, I sometimes need to pop off the air cleaner and rotate the choke closed. The car then fires right up. And I know that. It's a special, intimate, secret handshake between you and the car. It's a little bit like Fonzie banging on the hood and going *hey*. It's the automotive equivalent of knowing that, for the toilet on the third floor, you have to jiggle the handle.

So while I can still perform what many would think is a surprising amount of work on my newer cars, there's more love in working on the older ones.

Why do men love (old) cars? Because owning and driving them is like having lunch with an old friend, quirks and all.

CHAPTER 9

THE VOLKSWAGEN BUS, THE IDIOT MANUAL, AND THE GREAT SOUTHERN MIGRATION

In 1980, when Maire Anne had graduated from UMass and moved to Cambridge but I was still living in Amherst, she showed up at my house one day, driving a '72 Volkswagen bus. How cool is this, I thought? I have a hot girlfriend, and she just bought the vehicle synonymous with reefer and sex.

But far more than just being my girlfriend's car, which I became honor-bound to try to keep running, the bus became a talisman into the automotive world by being responsible for my introduction to the best automotive repair guide ever written: *How to Keep Your Volkswagen Alive: A Manual of Step-By-Step Procedures for the Compleat Idiot* by John Muir. Affectionately referred to as "the Idiot Manual," this remarkable volume, first published in 1969 and revised and reprinted annually for many years, is essentially a philosophy lesson disguised as a repair manual. It opens with the admonition to "kindly come to terms with your Ass for it bears you," and then goes on to talk about love and karma and the need to shut up and listen to what the car has to tell you. Yeah, it sounds like Zen hippie hokum, but make no mistake, the book is what it promises to be—a set of step-by-step-procedures. And the procedures are *very* thorough and *very* well written, telling you not only what to do but how to do it (rare in a repair manual). But even more important, John Muir blazed a trail by making it okay to talk about how you feel about your car long before Click and Clack (the "Car Talk" guys on NPR). In addition, the *Zap Comix*-esque hand-drawn illustrations by Peter Aschwanden are so compelling that when my son Kyle first saw the book when he was 20 years old, he grabbed it and said, *"What IS this?* Oh, graphics have really gone downhill since this was published."

Much of the value of the "Idiot Manual" is in its humanity: the remarkable degree of empathy the author has for those who have recently bought both a VW and the book and are trying to use the latter to fix something in the former. For example, Mr. Muir explains that you, as the owner, can do a better job adjusting your valves in your driveway than any mechanic can do in a repair shop because the procedure needs to be done first thing in the morning when the valves are dead cold, before the car has been started and moved. In the valve adjustment procedure itself, he says, "You can do this … take your time. You can build up speed later, but right now you have an eternity." What a great thing to read as you're lying beneath the car trying to do it for the first time. Further, Mr. Muir says, "Doing the valves, timing, and minor maintenance on your own car will not only change your relationship with your transportation but also will change your relationship with yourself." Yes, that's it, exactly. When I first read that, I realized for the first time that I wasn't alone in the way I felt about and dealt with cars.

Even if you don't want to fix anything, the book is quite useful in providing tips for approaching the broader automotive world. Plus, it's funny. In the section called "How to Buy a Volkswagen," Mr. Muir says to:

> stand back and look at it again. Does it stand up with pride? Does it feel good to you? Would you like to be its friend? … Let the data you have obtained soak through from your conscious to your subconscious and grok the car. If it is a bus, crawl around in the back and feel how it is to be back there. Have happy people been back there balling and talking and laughing and living? … Get away from the car … to let your mind and feelings go over the car and the idea of the car. What has its karma been? Can you live with the car? Walk around or find a quiet place, assume the good old Lotus position, and let the car be the thing. At this point, some revelation will come to you and you will either be gently guided away from that scene and can start looking [at other cars] again or you will be attracted toward the car and can continue your inspection. It is important that you neither run the motor nor ride in the car until this

preliminary scene has run its course. It also puts the owner-salespeople up the wall because they have no idea of what you are doing and will be more pliable when the hard dealing time comes.

To this day, when I look at a car, I still follow those instructions. Except for the Lotus position part.

Now, I use the word Zen often enough that failing to at least mention Robert Pirsig's 1974 book *Zen and the Art of Motorcycle Maintenance* would be a conspicuous oversight. *ZMM* intertwines five major topics: a travelogue-style cross-country motorcycle trip the author takes with his son Chris; the author's attempt to rediscover who he was before insanity culminated in personality-altering electric shock therapy; his previous personality's theories on the classical/artistic split and the metaphysics of quality that caused him to go off the deep end; the resolution of his relationship with Chris; and the title topic—his belief that motorcycle maintenance is a microcosm of rationality itself, and therefore, by observing what the machine is doing you can fix it. This last item is easily the smallest of the five topics. In fact, there's but a single instance in which he performs this type of diagnosis (realizing that the high altitude is what is making his bike run hot). So *Zen and the Art of Motorcycle Maintenance*, in fact, contains very little about Zen and the art of motorcycle maintenance.

When I first read *ZMM* in the late 1970s, I was—like many young men overly impressed with their own intelligence—quite taken with Mr. Pirsig's epistemological excursions into the metaphysics of quality. I recently reread the book, and while I was extremely impressed by the skill with which the five topics are interwoven, I now have the perspective of a parent and couldn't help feeling that his parenting style with Chris was so passive-aggressive that … well, there's no confusing him with Bill Cosby.

However, the copy I was reading was the 25th anniversary edition, and when I reached the afterward which began "Chris is dead," I felt a physical blow to my chest. Mr. Pirsig explains, with a terseness that does not hide his pain, that it happened in 1982 and that it was a random act of violence. The fact that I was so viscerally affected by the report of a death that happened three decades ago to someone I did not know, highlights the way in which our humanity connects us. I find this connection to be the most profound of human experiences.

But let's get back to Cambridge. Maire Anne's VW bus had a bumper sticker on the back urging the election of "Sheriff Johnson." For the most part, I'm not big on naming cars, but this was a natural. And the veneer of law'n'order juxtaposed against the happy little curtains Maire Anne had sewed produced just the right touch of irony and chaos.

Like the Triumph, the bus rotted out very quickly. One day Maire Anne jacked it up to change a tire, and the jack went right through the frame rail. Another time, when Maire Anne was driving my mother, sister, and aunt to my UMass graduation in the bus, my aunt opened the sliding door, and the whole thing fell off because the track the door ran on broke away from the rusty body. (Actually, this incident was precipitated by the fact that the bus literally could not make it up a hill whilst laden with so many people, and my headstrong "it's no bother" Aunt Flossie opened the door to get out and walk.) VW busses are now enshrined in the collective consciousness as grainy Technicolor sixties icons, but in 1980 a '72 bus was only eight years old; that's a lot of rust in a short amount of time.

Soon after Maire Anne bought the VW, I got a call completely out of the blue from Nick, the Hampshire College student who had owned that boxy 1970 BMW 2002 in Amherst many years before. He had started a computer company in Cambridge and wanted to know if I would be interested in working for him. So when I graduated from UMass, I went to Cambridge, moved in with Maire Anne, and began working for Nick. Things came full circle when he tossed me the keys to a brushed silver BMW 733i 5-speed that I then used for errand running for the next six months. If I'd swallowed the bait eight years earlier with his 2002, the 733i set the hook.

Also about this time, I was the best man at my friend John's wedding. John's parents were buying him and Elizabeth a new car as a wedding gift. It is traditional for the groom to give the best man a present, and John gave me the 1963 Rambler Classic 660 sedan that he and Elizabeth no longer needed. Well, actually he didn't give it to me. He sold it to me. For a dollar. I still have the bill of sale. The car was powder blue with a powder blue interior. It barely went into reverse. When you parked it, you needed to be very sure that you'd be able to amble forward out of the spot.

But I really liked the car. It had a lot of soul. There's something about these underpowered early- to mid-'60s little-old-lady cars with horizontally opposed headlights that I find irresistible. Maybe it's just that they remind me of my parents' Fairlane (though unlike when my sister and I scratched up the brand-new Fairlane, steel wool might have actually improved the finish of the Rambler). And no dashboard in the world can compare to an early '60s American car, with those beautiful inset chrome gauges and the 180-degree rim-style horn.

Not long after I moved to Cambridge, Maire Anne's job working for a Harvard professor doing research with lizards and snakes moved down to Austin, Texas when her professor was lured away by UT with promises of more money, more research space, and, oh, more money. I on the other hand did *not* have a job lined up, and neither of us knew a soul in Austin. However, in most relationships, there comes a time when the ship sails and you either get on board or you don't, even if you're not sure where it's going. Commitment time. I got on board.

Unfortunately, I couldn't make the same commitment to the Rambler. We were planning on driving Maire Anne's VW bus down to Austin, and we had to figure out what to do with the Rambler. A second car would sure be handy once we were down there, but it seemed wasteful, not to mention lonely and logistically difficult, to drive down in two cars. Plus, we weren't sure the Rambler would make it (although I don't know why we had such faith in the bus). Then, one night, while I was making one last run between Boston and Amherst, the Rambler started losing coolant. I made a strategic decision to try to reach the exit where I knew that there was a service station. I didn't make it. The car overheated. Badly. I wound up abandoning it for the cost of the tow.

I've always regretted treating the car with such disrespect. To this day I still keep an eye out for a 1963 Rambler Classic. I think I need to buy one, take it home, and care for it. It's as if I still have something to atone for.

So, facing an uncertain future in a completely unknown place with no job lined up and no car, I did what any rational guy would do with the small amount of money I had—I bought a really nice car stereo. I already owned a pair of ESS AMT9 audiophile-quality stereo speakers, each about half the size of a washing machine, which I mounted in the back of the VW van. Nick had given me a power amp, so I completed the system with the purchase of a nice cassette deck. Nowadays, high wattage mobile sound systems are a dime a dozen, but in 1981, there was nothing else like this setup anywhere. I showed it to friends, and the uniform response was *you gotta be shittin' me*. Then I mounted a plywood board on top of the speakers in the back of the van and put a mattress over the board so Maire Anne and I had somewhere to "sleep" on the drive down. Hot girlfriend, VW bus with bed and total killer stereo, impending road trip … could my life get any better than this? Thinking back on it, the balance of expectations and reality in my life may never have surpassed this moment. Seriously.

We set out on New Year's Day 1982, in the rusty VW bus with the best sound system on wheels, and a terrarium with 15 lizards. We made it as far as Everett (just north of Boston) to say goodbye to Maire Anne's parents. We asked them for a thermos of coffee, and kind souls that they were, they pretended to make the coffee while we sat down on the sofa and closed our eyes for just a minute (it had been New Year's Eve the previous night, after all). Ah, the wisdom imparted by gray hair: Just let them sleep. I think we woke up 14 hours later. By that time her dad had prepared us a cooler large enough to hide a corpse, packed with enough food to survive the siege of Masada. Anyone who pooh-poohs the whole *food as love* thing hasn't ever had enough of either.

The next day we made it as far as my mother's house in Amherst, where our departure was again delayed, this time by friends, more family, and more food. But the day after, we were honestly, actually, for real, underway.

Now, anyone who has ever owned an air-cooled VW (meaning an old-style Beetle, bus, Karmann Ghia, 411, or squareback) knows that heat in these cars is more of a suggestion than an actual measurable quantity. See, a conventional car has a water-cooled engine, which means that it uses water mixed with antifreeze to carry heat away from the engine, thus cooling it. A side benefit is that once the water has done its job and carried heat away from the engine, that water and the heat it carries can be used to heat up the passenger compartment, so it is sent to what's essentially another radiator up under the dashboard. (This is why, if your car is running hot, it's actually helpful to turn on the heat; it's like giving the car a second radiator. You may have heard this, and it is, in fact, true.)

But one of the unique things about older VWs is that they have an air-cooled engine (actually the oil is cooled as well; it's more accurate to say that they're air- and oil-cooled engines, but everyone just calls them air-cooled). The engine has a bunch of fins and metal shrouding and a fan to move air around. There's no antifreeze and no radiator. It's a very appealing, very simple design.

Except for one problem: The heat sucks. Since there's no water carrying heat away from the engine, there's no hot water to pipe into the passenger compartment. Instead, you have these things called heat exchanger boxes, which, in theory, capture hot air from around the exhaust and send it up to the front in tubes that run beneath the car.

There are two problems with this. The first is that the hot air has to make it from the rear to the front of the car via ducts and tubes, so it has to run the gauntlet of a hundred leaks. The older and rustier the car is, the less well all the ducts and tubes seal, and the lower the odds of actually getting the air up to the passenger compartment while it's still hot enough to make a difference. The second is that, if the hot air *does* make it up there, the heat is always redolent with the scent of exhaust and oil. And if there's a hole in the exhaust that perforates into the heater box, carbon monoxide will be piped directly into the interior, which is downright dangerous.

You also have to understand that the windshield washer in these old VWs is a marvel of German simplicity. There's no motor. It's powered with pressure *from the spare tire*. That's right. You fill the washer reservoir with fluid like any windshield washer, but then you connect a little hose from the top of the reservoir to the valve on the spare tire that's hanging on the front of the bus. You have to love it. Simple. Elemental. And every time you use the windshield washer, you're letting pressure out of the spare tire. So which do you want? A working spare, or a de-iced windshield? You know, it doesn't matter, because in icy cold weather, pretty soon you won't have either.

So that's the car we were driving when we hit an ice storm in Scranton, Pennsylvania: a Volkswagen with no heat and with a windshield washer that has only enough pressure to squirt de-icing fluid for about 15 minutes before the spare tire goes flat. It took us several hours to go several miles. I'd say the interstate was a parking lot, but a skating rink would be a more apt comparison. People in difficult situations develop an interesting camaraderie. Some folks two cars ahead got out of their vehicle, slid up to us, and said, "Hey ... we have some really good home-baked cookies ... you guys wouldn't want to trade some *reefer*, would you?" Maire Anne and I played dumb. "Uh, why would you think we would have any of that?" (I guess that the curtains were more prominent than the Sheriff Johnson sticker.) About an hour later I reconsidered and found myself walking forward two car lengths, trying not to slip on the ice, and inquiring if the offer regarding the cookies was still on the table.

When we were forced to take the next exit, we realized that the interstate was really, actually, officially closed. The car slid sideways down the ice-coated banked curve of the exit ramp. I thought we were going to roll into the ditch, but fortunately the bus stopped sliding.

By the time we got to Scranton (*she'll be rising* ... sorry) Maire Anne and I were bone-chilled, but the 15 lizards in the terrarium were literally frozen. We stopped at the first hotel we saw, which was a formerly grand but run-down old dame, glorious in its decay. The ceilings in the room must've been 15 feet, and the shower had enough water pressure to extinguish Vesuvius. Maire Anne carried in the lizards, with a towel draped over the terrarium in case there was a no-pet rule—and everyone knows that *no pets* means *no frozen lizards* (although this wasn't the kind of place where they cared what you were doing in your room). "Forget it," I said, "they're lizardsicles." But, incredibly, with the warmth and steam from the shower, they revived.

Warm and secure, we smoked reefer and watched Rick James on Saturday Night Live. I'll never forget it. "That girl is really FREAKY.... I'd really like to TASTE HER..." "Who the hell *is* this guy?" we asked each other. "Man, *SNL* really *has* gone downhill."

The rest of the trip to Austin was fairly uneventful. Somewhere in East Texas, the bus died and I had to diagnose the fact that the ignition points had closed up, but that was pretty easy.

To this day, whenever I see a photo of Rick James, I always think of Scranton and those lizards, revived under a high ceiling in a decaying hotel worthy of Miss Havisham.

CHAPTER 10

THE FIRST OF MANY BMW 2002s

So, with the Rambler left for dead in Massachusetts (you can tell I still feel guilty about this, can't you?), Maire Anne, Sheriff Johnson, and I arrived in Austin. Maire Anne settled into her job running a herpetology lab at UT, and I quickly found work; I was a computer programmer, and technology companies were booming.

But I needed a car. I gave in to the automotive obsession that had imprinted me ten years earlier, budgeted a thousand bucks, and looked for my first BMW 2002. I had absolutely no idea the trajectory this simple act would set me on.

Let's get something out of the way right now. If you must delve into the Bimmer/Beemer thing (and really I would rather you didn't), the cars are sometimes called *Bimmers*. (Yes. *Bimmers*. Trust me. This is the name of a BMW-specific magazine. You don't think they'd get it wrong, do you?) The motorcycles are sometimes called *Beemers*. DO NOT CALL A CAR A BEEMER. Just don't. It's wrong. On so many levels. It conjures up the worst 1980s *oh I'm Chad this is my friend Scott from Choate and we're going to take the Beemer to the club and drink some Chardonnay with Muffy.* Don't go there. We just call them BMWs. Really.

I'll try not to let my BMW geek flag fly too high, but a little automotive history will probably be helpful. Although the BMW logo is now synonymous with luxury, performance, and style (and some would say with overly aggressive drivers who have more money than common sense), the company began as an aircraft engine manufacturer. Because of this, the oft-repeated story that the familiar blue-and-white circular logo (or "roundel") originally symbolized a rotating propeller against a blue sky sounds plausible, but the evidence seems to instead point to an incorporation of the blue and white colors of the German state of Bavaria. The postwar years were difficult for BMW, as they were for most German manufacturers, and by the early 1960s they were in dire straits. In 1962 they came out with a line of compact sedans called

Neue Klasse ("New Class") cars that combined an excellent four-cylinder engine and four-wheel independent suspension with a body style that had a boxy yet trim shape and a low hood line that facilitated extremely good visibility. These cars sold well in Germany and helped to return BMW to financial viability. In 1966 BMW debuted a redesigned two-door New Class car, the 1602, that was particularly well proportioned and featured a perky pair of round taillights that made it instantly recognizable. An importer named Max Hoffman sensed its potential for the American market. He convinced BMW to install a larger 2.0-liter engine into the car and sell it in the United States. In this way, in 1968, both the BMW 2002 and the "sports sedan" market segment were born.

Now, up until this point, "sports cars" were, for the most part, either big throaty American muscle cars that handled about as well as an oil tanker, or miserable little British roadsters, or very expensive finicky Italian jobs. Of course there were Porsches, but they were expensive as well. And there was no confusing any of these with family cars. One could argue that Alfa Romeo had sports sedans earlier than 1968, but no matter. The 2002 was the right car at the right time, combining excellent performance and handling, reliability, decent fuel economy, and seating for four, into a particularly trim and well-executed package. Anyone who drove a 2002 was immediately hooked by the whole range of sensations, from the high visibility out an expanse of windows so large that it was referred to as a "greenhouse," to the road feel transmitted through the steering wheel, to the sound and feel of the directional and headlight switches, to that oh-so-snickety gearbox. And because the car was German, it was designed to be driven as fast as it could possibly go—and it felt that way. Eventually other manufacturers—particularly Honda—would copy BMW's tactile feel, but for a while there was nothing else like it on the planet. And in 1968 a 2002 cost about $2,800—a mere $400 more than a Super Beetle.

The press loved the car. In 1968, David E. Davis wrote, in his classic piece for *Car and Driver* "Turn Your Hymnals to 2002," "Down at the club, Piggy Tremalion and Bucko Penoyer and all their twit friends will buy shrieking little 2-seaters with rag tops and skinny wire wheels, unaware that somewhere, someday, some guy in a BMW 2002 is going to blow them off so bad that they'll henceforth leave every stoplight in second gear and never drive on a winding road again as long as they live." Although by modern standards it is highly politically incorrect, my favorite section of Mr. Davis's review is this: "In its unique ability to blend fun-and-games with no-nonsense virtue, this newest BMW also reflects another traditional American article of faith—our unshakable belief that we can find and marry a pretty girl who will expertly cook, scrub floors, change diapers, keep the books, and still be the greatest thing since the San Francisco Earthquake in bed. It's a dream to which we cling eternally, in spite of the fact that nobody can recall it ever having come true. But, as if to erase our doubts, along comes an inexpensive little machine from Bavaria that really can perform the automotive equivalent of all those diverse domestic and erotic responsibilities, and hope springs anew." And you wondered why men love cars.

From 1968 through 1976, about 860,000 2002s were produced, of which about 112,000 came to the United States. Certainly they weren't as ubiquitous as Beetles, but there were enough of them so that, like Beetles, they are enshrined in the collective American consciousness. I love driving my 2002 on the weekends and showing up at some mundane place, like a yard sale, and having nonenthusiasts fawn over it. I particularly enjoyed the 60-year-old woman who said, "Oh, I dated a guy in grad school who had one of these … I *loved* that car!" So when I was 13 and being driven around Amherst in a 2002, I was, as I've been saying, imprinted, but I didn't fully appreciate until years later that I wasn't the only one.

In compliance with the new federal 5-mph standard, bumper changes hit the 2002 in 1974 as they did every other car sold in America. The lithe well-integrated chrome bumpers were replaced with monstrosities that had all the subtlety of bridge abutments. That same year the trademark round taillights were replaced with square ones. You'll sometimes hear the early cars referred to as "roundies," and the later ones as "squaries," which doesn't roll off the tongue in nearly as zingy a fashion. Because the earlier 2002s were lighter, with fewer emission controls, and thus were faster, for many years the rallying cry of the self-appointed BMW faithful was "real BMWs have round taillights."

In the years '72 through '74, BMW imported a fuel-injected version of the car called the 2002tii ("tee-eye-eye"). Eventually, nearly all cars became fuel injected in order to provide a balance of power, economy, and emissions, but in the '60s and early '70s, certain select models were fuel injected to make them *fast*. Because the tii had more horsepower and was substantially quicker than a stock 2002, over the years the tii has become *the* collectible 2002 (well, there is also the rare 2002 turbo, the "touring" [hatchback] and the ultra-rare cabriolet, but these were never commercially imported into the United States). The tii's value is further enhanced by the fact that, through 1974, it burned gas so cleanly that it passed U.S. smog specifications *with no additional emission controls*. When the emissions specs tightened in 1975, BMW stopped importing it rather than try to modify and re-certify it for the U.S. market.

But what I bought in Austin in 1982 with my thousand bucks was neither a tii nor a turbo nor a cabriolet. It was a badly faded, dented, 1971 Colorado (orange) BMW 2002 with a missing front bumper and dents in nearly every body panel, some of which had been partially treated with Bondo (body filler). The orange paint combined with the Bondo and a bit of surface rust to give the car a multicolored hue something like an autumn leaf (well, an autumn leaf that had fallen, been run over several dozen times, and was beginning to rot). Considering the nearly 30 2002s that I came to own over the years, it was a beginning that was, shall we say, inauspicious. Hey, we all have to start somewhere.

In addition to having the common 2002 problem of crunching when shifting into second gear, the car's transmission was incredibly whiny. I checked the transmission fluid level and found that it was dry. *A-HA*, I thought; *THAT'S why it's noisy. Man, I am ALL OVER THIS. Four bucks worth of fluid and I'll have this thing NAILED.* I added fluid and drove the car, and sure enough it quieted right down. Booya! But when I parked it, I found a rapidly spreading puddle of fluid. The transmission's end cover was cracked, which allowed all the fluid to leak out. No biggie, I thought; so I'll replace the cover. I'll have to yank out the tranny, but that's not hard. What I didn't realize was that you can't simply pull the end cover off one of these transmissions; the guts of the transmission are attached to the cover from the inside. By the time you've separated the shaft and gears from the cover, you might as well just jump all the way in and rebuild the damned thing.

So my first repair on a BMW 2002 was rebuilding a transmission, which is like doing brain surgery on your first day of med school. I performed this repair in the carport of our rented Austin duplex. When I found that I needed special tools, I loaded the disassembled transmission into the VW van and parked it outside Terry Sayther's Phoenix Motor Works (PMW—get it?) shop in South Austin. I'd tinker in the van, go inside, ask to borrow one of his special transmission disassembly tools, he'd roll his eyes, etc. I think he only put up with me because he got to sell me a lot of parts.

Now, as I said, BMW 2002 transmissions had this terrible tendency to munch second gear because the synchronizer would wear out (a classic case of "they all do that"), so if there was one saving grace in having to replace the end cover, it was that, while I had the transmission apart, I could also replace the balky second gear synchro.

Once the transmission was put back together and the car was drivable, I had one of those guy-bonds-with-car moments I'll remember my entire life. I took the car for a drive up through the Texas hill country. In addition to the no-longer-crunching transmission, I had just put a new set of Pirelli P3 tires on the car (junk by modern standards, but they were the first set of new matching steel-belted radials the car had seen in many years), and I had installed a sound system with a pair of ADS 200i speakers, which were the cat's ass back in the day. I was, finally—15 years after imprinting on one in Amherst—the owner and driver of a BMW 2002. The car ran great; the stereo sounded superb; the second gear synchro was blissfully quiet. I remember ripping through the hills, working the gears, nailing the car through curves, listening to The Psychedelic Furs singing "The Ghost in You" and thinking … could life be any better than this?

Unfortunately, the bubble popped about a month later when the second gear synchro starting munching again despite my just having replaced it. I later learned that rebuilding transmissions is not mere assembly—there's a lot of precise measuring and shimming of components to tolerance. After that, I never attempted to rebuild another gearbox—I learned to simply swap whole transmissions instead.

But certain things in life are about buy-in. You either do it or you don't. You're in or you're out. I didn't fully understand the concept of buy-in at the time, but I palpably experienced it decades later when, after renting a vacation house on Nantucket for many years, Maire Anne and I put a toe in the water of buying, and quickly realized that there was no possible way we could afford it. After that, every time I went into a hardware store on the island and was in line behind someone who was buying a hinge or a screen for a house they actually owned, I became jealous. It didn't matter how long we had vacationed there. They owned a house. They had buy-in; we didn't.

I had bought my first BMW 2002. It was a piece of crap, but I had buy-in. And it would change my life.

CAR WON'T START

After driving the Colorado 1971 2002 for about six months, I saw an ad for a Malaga (maroon) '73 2002 with air-conditioning—a sought-after option considering that this was, after all, Texas. The ad said it hadn't run in several years. I checked it out and found it parked in the owner's driveway at the top of a steep hill, and, sure enough, it wouldn't start. I tried jumping it with my 2002, but I couldn't get it to turn over.

Let's take a moment and step through a "car won't start" diagnosis. Life is full of shades of gray, but when you turn the key and the car won't start, you're in a hard binary world. You're a zero that really wants to be a one. As Bob Dylan said, "You ain't goin' nowhere."

After many years, I have my family trained not to call me up and simply say, "The car won't start," because they know that such a lack of specificity drives me crazy; it's as useful as saying, "The roof of the house is missing," without providing some context that obviously must exist (for example, "I saw this black funnel cloud," or "I heard this strange whirring noise and looked out the window and there was this spaceship," or even "I looked up and saw that the roof was being gnawed by giant squirrels." Work with me. Give me *something*.).

GAS AND SPARK. AND SPIN.

You've probably heard it said that, for a car to start, it needs gas and spark. That's true, but those come second. Before gas and spark, the engine needs to turn over. Nevertheless, when a car *doesn't* start, it's pretty easy to nutshell it to one of several major possibilities just by using your eyes and ears.

Turn the key to the ignition position but don't try to start the car yet. What happens? What do you see?

USE THOSE DASHBOARD LIGHTS

If *none* of the dashboard lights comes on, there is no electricity coming from the battery, which means that most likely the battery has
been completely drained because someone left the lights or another
electrical accessory on for an extended period of time. If that's not the
case—if it was working a moment ago—I'd wager that a battery cable
has loosened and popped off its battery post or that the connection is
so corroded that is no longer reliably making electrical contact.

USE YOUR EARS

If the dashboard lights *do* come on, turn the key to the start position.
What happens? What do you hear?

If you hear a healthy *RRRrrrRRRrrrRRRrrr*, that's the sound of a
fully-charged battery cranking the starter motor which, in turn, is spinning the engine. In this case, if the car doesn't start, it's not a problem
with the battery or the starter, so jumping it won't help. It's likely a
fuel or ignition problem. And it's actually pretty easy to tell which one.
For extra credit, run down to the auto parts store (in someone else's
car, obviously) and buy a can of "starting fluid." This is like lighter
fluid in aerosol form for cars. You spray it into the air cleaner (better
yet, take the air cleaner off and give it about a three-second blast right
into the carb or throttle body) and then try to start the car. If the engine
roars to life and then dies a few seconds later, it means that the starting
fluid was ignited, so there's nothing wrong with the ignition system,
and thus the problem is in the fuel system. It could be a bad fuel pump
or a clogged fuel filter. If, on the other hand, the car does not even try
to start (you don't hear that "catching" sound), it means there's no
spark at all and some problem likely exists in the ignition system.

If you hear a metallic grinding sound when you turn the key, it
means the starter's gear isn't meshing with the gear around the edge
of the engine's flywheel. This usually means the starter needs to be
replaced.

If, on the other hand, you hear a slower, more sickly *rrrrrr rrrrrr
rrrrrr* sound when you turn the key, odds are overwhelming that the
battery is weak. Similarly, if you turn the key and simply hear a click
and then all the lights on the dash go dim or out, it means that the

battery is so weak that the starter motor can't spin the engine. In both of these cases, the car will probably start if you jump it with another running car by connecting positive-to-positive and negative-to-negative terminals with jumper cables. Be aware, though, that it takes a lot of current to spin the starter motor and start an engine, so the jumper cables must be making good electrical contact at both ends. On cars with old, crudded-up battery terminal connectors, sometimes you need to really dig the jaws of the jumper cable ends into the battery connectors to get a good connection. Sometimes, to truly diagnose the problem, it's necessary to bypass the jumper cables altogether and put a known good battery into the recalcitrant car.

WEAK OR RUN-DOWN BATTERY

Of course there is then the question of why the battery is weak. What caused it to run down? Was it age, or were the lights left on, or was the battery not being properly charged? If it's cold outside and the battery is over four years old, odds are that the battery has simply reached the end of its life. After four years, it's toast. Don't even think; just replace it. Run down to any convenient auto parts store. If they offer several options, buy whichever one best fits your budget. The differences among them are not important; the difference between any one of them and the piece of crap currently in your car *IS* important. It's pretty easy to replace a battery; you can do it yourself. Undo the negative terminal first, then the positive, then the bolt holding it to the battery tray. Yank the offending battery out. Install the new one. There is no more cost-effective medicine for a car than a fresh battery. While you're replacing it, spend the five bucks, buy a terminal cleaning tool, and scrape the crud out of the circular inside of the terminals on the battery cables so they'll make good electrical contact.

However, if the battery is recent, it is possible that it ran down because the alternator is bad and wasn't charging the battery. This is important. The last thing you want to do is jump the car, think all is well, and then have it die again one or five or twenty miles down the road, possibly in a dangerous place. On most cars, you can tell if the alternator isn't charging the battery because the battery light on the dash will stay lit.

There's the possibility that the belt turning the alternator has broken. This also should light the battery light. Modern cars have a single "serpentine belt" turning the alternator, water pump, and power steering pump, so if the belt breaks, you also have overheating and lack of power steering to worry about. Open the hood and visually inspect the belt. If it's missing or jammed up into a tangled mess, there's your problem. But if it's present, you need to test if the alternator is charging the battery.

Back in the day, it was common to test the alternator by simply unhooking one of the battery terminals; if the car kept running, the alternator was working. Conversely, if it died, it indicated that the alternator should be replaced. Maire Anne loves to tell the story of when I bought a ratty but running 1970 BMW 2800CS. I jumped it with her Volvo wagon to get it started, and then I tried to drive it home with her following closely behind. Unfortunately the BMW died right at the intersection of Storrow Drive and Route 28—one of the busiest interchanges in Boston. Rather than try to position her car nose-to-nose to jump the BMW again, I quickly opened her hood, yanked the battery out of the Volvo while it was running, wrapped her battery terminals in rubber gloves so they wouldn't short out against the body, instructed Maire Anne *whatever you do, don't stall,* installed the Volvo's battery in the BMW, started it, and drove off. These days, disconnecting the battery while the car is running is highly frowned upon. In the first place, it's really hard on the alternator's diodes, and secondly, without the battery in the system to act like a big capacitor, the alternator can generate voltage spikes that can harm the computer on a modern car. (Both the Volvo and the BMW, by the way, made it home, but this event was the origin of Maire Anne's aphorism "Behind every Hack Mechanic is a woman in a dependable car.")

You can, however, check the battery with a voltmeter. With the engine off, there should be about 12 volts across the battery, but with the engine running, there should be about 14 volts. If there's only 12 volts with the engine running, the alternator is not charging the battery, and the car will die again. This was the test I did after my BMW station wagon died while Maire Anne and her four friends were on the way home from hiking in New Hampshire. I bought a new battery, drove up there, installed it, started the car, measured the voltage, saw 12 volts, concluded that the alternator was bad, and left the car at a repair shop.

BAD STARTER

Lastly, if you turn the key and hear *nothing*, and you've verified the battery is putting out 12 volts (remember, this is the normal voltage when the engine is off), it can mean one of three things. The first is that the ignition interlock—the system of contact switches and relays intended to prevent you from starting a modern car in gear and requiring you to put an automatic in park and step on the brake, or step on the brake and the clutch in a standard—has malfunctioned. The second possibility is that the starter is actually dead. This can sometimes be verified by reaching down and feeling the starter with your hand. If, after repeated attempts to start it, the starter is hot to the touch, you've found the problem. The last possibility is that the ignition switch itself—either the cylinder you insert the key into or the wiring connecting to it—has gone bad. To tell which one of these it is, it is usually necessary to put a voltmeter on the leads going to the starter.

POP-STARTING A CAR

Now, if the battery is so weak it won't spin the starter but it has at least enough juice to fire the spark plugs, there's a cute trick you can do with an older manual-transmission car called pop-starting. You turn the key to the ignition position where the dashboard lights go on. You put the car in neutral. Then you either roll down a hill or get a few friends to push the car to about 5 mph. Then you step on the clutch pedal, put the car into first or second gear, and quickly let out the clutch pedal, which engages the clutch. This connects the wheels to the engine, which forces the engine to turn. The immediate effect is that the car slows down, since all of a sudden it has the drag of the engine on it (if people are still pushing, at this point they crash into the trunk and swear a blue streak at you). But then, hopefully, the car sputters and starts just as if you'd turned the key, but with the car in gear. Pop starting can be used if the starter motor is bad, or if the battery is too run down to crank over the starter motor but has enough juice to fire the spark plugs. Once the car is running, the alternator takes over, and you should be fine as long as you don't shut it off. I did this once for my son Ethan and he thought I was a god (hey, as a parent, you take these deifying moments when you can get them).

DRIVING WITHOUT A CLUTCH

While we're on the subject of cute tricks to do with clutches on old cars, the mechanical *yang* to pop-starting's *yin* is driving without a clutch at all. Older VWs and Porsches have a cable clutch, and you need to know how to do this because, when the cable breaks, you're stranded. The hydraulic clutches on modern cars fail slowly, but they *can* fail. To drive without a clutch, first make sure there's nothing directly in front of you (this won't work if you're parallel parked), take a deep breath, put the car in first gear, and turn the key. If the car is old enough that it doesn't have an ignition interlock, when you turn the key, it will rhythmically lurch forward like it does when you accidentally try to start it without your foot on the clutch. The difference is that, now, you *want* it to lurch. Rather than going *whoops!* and shutting it off, continue to feed gas. In a few seconds the car will transition from lurching to running. When you need to shift, let off the gas and pull the lever back to neutral, then lean (don't jam) the lever into the next gear and gently rev the accelerator. At some point the speeds of the gears inside the transmission will match and the shift lever will slide into gear. Obviously this is a stop-gap; it is difficult and dangerous to navigate through traffic in this fashion. But one day it may help you get yourself, the car, and the family out of harm's way, or maybe even home and into your driveway. In fact, I know all this because I was driving Maire Anne's bus through the center of the University of Texas campus when its clutch cable broke. Between honking, running one red light, and careful shifting, I *did* make it home, where I changed the cable.

So, back to Texas and the '73 2002 I was looking at buying. I took the battery out of my '71 Colorado 2002 and put it directly into the Malaga '73 2002. About every fifth attempt, the starter motor would try to turn the engine, but it sounded labored. When I reached down with my hand, the starter motor was very hot.

I told the owner my suspicion that the starter was bad. Since the car was at the top of his driveway, I explained that all we needed to do was to roll the car down the driveway and pop-start it. He was leery. The car was currently safe in his driveway. He wasn't thrilled

about tossing it out of the nest, so to speak. But I convinced him. So we pushed it out of the driveway. I let it roll about halfway down the hill, then tried to pop-start it.

It didn't work.

Now there was a dead car at the bottom of the hill. The owner was *not* pleased. I think I bought the car partially to diffuse the implied threat of violence. But, as part of this process, I'd also inadvertently decreased the resale value of the car—that is, it was now a bona-fide dead car that wouldn't even fire up when pop-started. Had I gotten it running, it would've been more difficult for me to drive a hard bargain. Hey, it was just the way it worked out. There have been other times I've resurrected supposedly dead cars only to have the owner go hard-line on the price.

This points to an important dynamic in these sorts of purchases: risk versus reward. If a car is dead, you can't drive it, so you can't do a thorough evaluation of what it needs. If you pick it up for a hundred bucks, take it home, and get it running with little more than a fresh battery and a tune-up, and there aren't other any major issues that need to be sorted out for the car to be reliable, then you're on the Cheshire-cat-grin side of the risk/reward curve. If, on the other hand, you've paid nearly what it'd be worth if it were running and it turns out it needs an engine, you've let lust get the better of you.

I had the '73 2002 towed home, tuned it up, changed the oil, adjusted the choke on the carburetor, and got it to start on those every-fifth-times that the starter motor would engage, so I was quite happy. I figured the starter would give me plenty of warning before failing altogether, so I drove it this way for several months, taking care to park it, whenever possible, on a hill so I could pop-start it if necessary. Obviously this was foolish false economy on my part, but I hated to pitch the part before its time had truly come. One evening, in downtown Austin, I was somewhere flat, and the starter motor gave up the ghost completely. I called for a tow. It took a bit of explaining to the tow truck driver that I wanted to be towed, not home, not to a service station, but just four blocks away to where there was a hill so I could pop-start it. He did it, but he gave me this look that I had already seen more than once while in Austin. The look said: *damn Yankees.*

CHAPTER 12

NOTES FROM TEXAS
HEN'S TEETH AND
REDNECK WIND CHIMES

Maire Anne relied on Sheriff Johnson as daily transportation, but its rust belt history was making it increasingly unsafe. While she was back up in Boston visiting family over the holidays, I found a rust-free '68 VW camper that came complete with the pop-top, sink, stove, fold-out bed, and a blown engine, for 500 bucks. I bought it and surprised her with it when she came home to Austin. I pulled the good engine out of the Sheriff, rebuilt it in the kitchen of our apartment, and installed it in the camper. The fact that she supported—indeed, photographed—my rebuilding her engine in our kitchen was an early indication of good things to come. Not that I expected anything else. I mean, to a woman who spends her professional days handling lizards and snakes, what's an engine in the kitchen?

Very shortly after I bought the '73 2002, Maire Anne and I were planning to drive from Austin to Colorado (the state, not the color) to go backpacking in the Weminuche Wilderness, near Durango. We had the choice of taking her VW camper with its newly rebuilt engine, or the 2002. Although the BMW 2002 was obviously faster, we opted for the "proven" camper. About 100 miles out the camper started running very hot. We dejectedly limped it home and tried to decide whether to fix it, rent a car, postpone our vacation, or take the BMW. The responsible mechanic in me was adamant against driving an "unproven" car to Colorado. Maire Anne gently pressed me: "What's wrong with it?" "Well, it burns oil. There's no spare tire. A million little things." So we bought a case of Castrol and a can of Fix-a-Flat, stuffed the car to the gills with camping equipment and coolers, and made it to Santa Fe the first day and Durango the next. *That*, in a nutshell, is what's so good about 2002s.

What Maire Anne didn't know was that one of the items I'd packed was my grandmother's engagement ring. I planned to ask her to marry

me on top of the Continental Divide—a two-day hike in. Near the
end of the second day, when we were about an hour's hike from the
Divide, I transferred the ring from my backpack into my pocket to
have it at the ready.

Then, as we were approaching tree line, the weather turned bad.
Sheets of rain began pelting us. Maire Anne balked at going over the
Divide in such bad weather. "It'll be slippery. It'll be dangerous. We
won't be able to see anything," she said. "Besides, we can pitch the
tent right here below tree line for the night, eat some food, play some
Scrabble … I'll make it worth your while," giving me her best, rain-
soaked come-hither glance. All rational, reasonable, even downright
seductive statements from the member of the couple without the
engagement ring in her pocket. I was pretty adamant about wanting to
continue, but didn't quite know how to push the point without spill-
ing the beans. As any man will tell you, when you successfully pump
up your courage to ask a woman to marry you, it's not something that
readily deflates. Seek immediate medical treatment for a marriage
proposal lasting more than four hours.

I actually sat in the tent and played Scrabble. In the rain. With the
engagement ring in my pocket.

The following morning, when we were on top of the Continental
Divide, I asked Maire Anne to marry me. I don't recall if there was
anything in her part of the verbal contract about living with a car guy.
She jokes that she said yes because I was the one carrying the food.

When we completed the ten-day hike, we emerged about 40 miles
from where we'd parked the 2002. We hitchhiked and got picked up
by a retired minister and his wife, the kind of people who reaffirm
your basic faith in humanity. Maire Anne noted that as soon as we got
in the car they rolled the windows down (after ten days, we must've
stunk). They took us back to their trailer and let us use their shower.
Then they drove us to where we'd left the 2002, which was a good 30
miles out of their way. Where do you find people like that? All around
you, if you look.

Upon returning to Austin, I rewarded the '73 2002 by beginning
to sort out its mechanical issues. As I said, a big part of the appeal of
the '73 2002 over the '71 was that the '73 had air-conditioning. I got the
a/c working (which made Maire Anne very happy) and drove the car

for the next year. At that point I had the '71 2002 repainted, and sold it. This turned out to be the template for what would happen over the next 30 years—I'd find an interesting car in need of work which made it affordable, buy it, drive it for a while, then sell it when a nicer car came along, or when the siren's song of newer technology started to sing in a price range I could afford.

I love working on air-conditioning. There are few things more satisfying than starting with a hot car and ending with a cold one, and there is *substantial* money to be saved by working on air-conditioning yourself (see Chapter 46: "Getting a Cool Car Cool"). But the '73 2002 was my first foray into this field, and I had a lot to learn. Of course, Texas is hot, and thus there are many sources for both a/c parts and repairs. Even so, air-conditioned 2002s did not exactly grow on trees. At one point I walked into a parts shop and presented the car's defective expansion valve. The proprietor growled a "Whuzzat frum?" "Old BMW," I told him. He grumbled a bit as he examined the part. "Man," he said. "*Them things are rarer than hen's teeth.*" Hen's teeth? I paused. I did a brain scan like Arnold Schwarzenegger in *The Terminator*, scanning for Most Appropriate Response. Okay, hen's don't have teeth. I get it. Most Appropriate Response: "Uh, so, do you know who else might have one?" Ding ding ding ding right answer. "Yeah, this German stuff's purty specific; best talk to Terry Sayther." Small victories can be surprisingly sweet.

Tom, a colleague of mine from work, helped me rejuvenate the a/c in the '73 2002. Tom loved to portray himself as a gruff pickup-truck-driving red-meat-eating Real Texan. But about a centimeter beneath that surface was the sweetest guy you'd ever want to meet. I drove out to his house in the hill country. This was old-school shade tree mechanic work—literally working under the shade of a tree in his yard. While we were taking a break, Tom invited me in for lemonade (no beer while we were working; his rule not mine), and in his living room was this absolutely beautiful glass menagerie—the prettiest hand-blown glass animals you'd ever seen this side of a Tennessee Williams production. Some redneck.

When we came back outside, we walked past his pickup truck, and I noticed that in the bed was a layer of beer cans two-deep. Now, at this time, there was no open container law in Texas; in fact there were drive-through "beer barns." I noticed the beer cans and made some wisecrack about how I guessed he didn't always drink lemonade.

"You know," Tom said, shrugging off the fact that I'd just seen his glass menagerie, putting his thumbs in his belt, and putting back on his best Redneck, "when you get enough of these back there, and you get up to speed on the highway, they start whipping around and around really fast in a circle. You know what we call that 'round here?"

"Uh, no."

"Redneck wind chimes."

For the remainder of my stay in Austin, 2002s seemed to just start coming at me. Maire Anne used to say that they followed me home like lost puppies (hey! now they're *imprinting on me!*). There was the one I bought for three hundred bucks because an overzealous Brake Check employee ran it over an embankment. There was the one that was abandoned behind the apartment building across the street. I looked inside, found a registration, tracked down the name, and discovered that the guy to whom it was registered had sold it, but the guy who'd bought it from him apparently never registered it, had gotten a bunch of parking tickets, and then skipped town, and the city was chasing after the seller to pay the fines. He was thrilled to transfer title to me literally for nothing and have it officially off his back. Unfortunately, four months later, the buyer who never completed his paperwork returned from Argentina and, title in my name or no, was none too pleased to see that I had "stolen" his car. I paid him a hundred bucks, essentially, so he wouldn't beat me up.

Then there was the one I bought as a running parts car (incredible how convenient it is to store BMW 2002 parts in a running BMW 2002-shaped container) until, one day, I parked outside a store and went inside only to hear some jerk leaning on his horn. When I went out to investigate, I found that "the jerk" was my car—a short circuit had burned the insulation off the horn wire and touched it to ground, which is why it was spontaneously blaring. It turned out that the entire wiring harness leading up to the steering column had burned, at which point the car fulfilled its destiny and became an actual parts car.

And there was the 2000CS. This was an elegant European-issue two-door coupe with a wood dashboard and badass-looking Euro headlights. Unfortunately the guy I bought it from turned out not to have actual title to the car. He said it had been abandoned on his property in exchange for back rent. I wanted it. I paid him, and I had it towed home, as it had any number of issues that made it undrivable. The seller said he'd straighten out the paperwork. I was in no rush, as I had to order parts from Germany in any case. This was years before the internet was even a gleam in Al Gore's eye. But, five months later, when I had the car running, the guy still hadn't lifted a finger to get title and have it transferred to me. I finally had a hearing with the county tax assessor, who, with me in his office, called the seller up and put him on speakerphone. The seller said that I was impatient and out of control, that I'd threatened him, and that if I'd just calm down he'd get the paperwork done. After he hung up, the tax assessor paused, thought for a moment, then drawled, "Well obviously he's a lying scum … by the power of my office, I hereby grant you title." It was one of those moments when you're glad for a bureaucrat who wields absolute power over his little domain.

My "car thing," as friends and family came to call it, was all so much fun that I basically never stopped doing it. The volume of activity and the number of cars have cyclically surged and abated, but much of my leisure time is still spent chasing, buying, and fixing cars.

Why do men love cars? Just look at the places they've taken me. I mean where else would I ever have learned about hen's teeth and redneck wind chimes?

CHAPTER 13

NORTHWARD HO, ALEX, AND BERTHA

In the spring of 1984, Maire Anne and I were engaged and living in Austin, and planning the wedding for the summer in Boston. That seemed natural—both of our families lived there. The question was what to do after that. We talked and thought about it very carefully, and decided that if we returned to Austin after the wedding, we'd likely buy a house there, put down roots, have kids, and before you know it we'd be dug in. Since raising kids around our families was a big priority for both of us, we made the difficult decision to do a preemptive move. We both gave our notice at work, forged ahead with the wedding plans, and wondered what the hell we were doing.

I sold the '73 2002 and bought a rust-free '74 with big bumpers. Though I love the round taillights and svelte small chrome bumpers found on '73 and older 2002s, I figured that a big-bumpered BMW made far more sense to use in the, ah, bumper car game of parking on the streets in Boston. I christened the car "Bertha," because with those bridge abutment bumpers, she was anything but dainty. Her paint was faded (actually her paint looked like it had been mixed with cement), but dent- and rust-wise her body was damn near perfect. And, like the '73 2002, Bertha had air-conditioning.

When we moved up to Boston, my friend Mike and I towed Bertha on a dolly behind the miserable decrepit U-Haul truck we'd rented (is it even *legal* to rent a truck in Texas without air-conditioning?). Maire Anne and her sister, Tricia, drove the Volkswagen camper. So, convoying across East Texas in August, the only car that had air-conditioning—the 2002—was the empty one being towed. What was wrong with this picture?

The other relevant event here involved the cats. We had three. Two were relatively even-tempered, but Phoebe, our Siamese, never liked going in the car. She would massively stress out and do that creepy vocalization thing that Siamese do that makes you think they're

possessed and about to rip your face off. Our vet, a lovely gentle
man, prescribed some kitty tranquilizers for the trip. We gave them to
Phoebe as we were loading the last items in the truck.

Bad idea.

"Tranquil" was about as foreign to Phoebe as consensus is to
American politics. First she stumbled about the apartment with this *oh
God what is happening to me dude my paws are like HUGE* look in her blue
Siamese eyes. Then it all really kicked in. It was as if she had knocked
back two Quaaludes and chased them with three cans of Red Bull. She
acted like a drunken kitty in the throes of a bad acid trip. So Maire
Anne and Tricia had this stressed-out, psychotic, vocalizing Siamese
cat in the camper as they headed across East Texas in hundred-degree
heat. Phoebe was panicked when she was in her cage so they took
her out and put her on a leash with a chest harness, like the other two
more even-tempered kitties.

This was fine until she jumped out the window.

Poor Phoebe, looking so stressed and bewildered, flapping in the
breeze until they could stop the car and pull her back in.

In any case, we finally arrived back in Boston and temporarily
moved into a house in Brighton that my mother and sister had recently
bought. It was a decaying old fifteen-room Victorian that they were
beating into submission and turning into a three-family home. My
mother lived on the first floor; my sister and her family lived on the
second. The apartment on the third floor had just become habitable.
They'd been planning to find a tenant when Maire Anne and I showed
up and moved in until we could figure out what to do. We lived there
for eight years. I still have easily 3,000 pounds of 2002 parts in my
mother's basement and under her porch. Needless to say, Mom is one-
quarter enabler, three-quarters saint.

Maire Anne and I got married in August 1984. I have some wonderful photographs of us driving Bertha, the car covered in shaving cream
with cans attached to her massive bumper, away from the reception.

We blew most of our remaining money on a brief honeymoon, and
then returned to my mother's house and both began looking for work.
I soon found the job I still have—developing technology to detect
unexploded shells on old military training ranges. Maire Anne began
writing science abstracts.

My mother's house (though I lived there for eight years, I will always think of it as "my mother's house") had a two-car garage, and I quickly took that space over to accommodate my "car thing." My mother and sister were remarkably tolerant of my excesses; between keeping Bertha off the streets and working on whatever my other project car was at the time, I usually occupied both bays.

One day I had a brain fart while backing Bertha out of the garage. Her driver's door was slightly ajar. The door caught on the garage opening and bent back, preventing it from closing and thus ruining it. So much for Bertha's perfect Texas body.

I needed to procure a replacement door. It's hard to imagine, but before the internet, there were mail order sources for parts. You learned about these sources in archaic literary forms called magazines (which were sort of like thin, flexible tablet computers permanently set to a single web address), and ordered the parts via an ancient device called a telephone or even—gasp—a letter. Maire Anne and I were planning to use the car for a road trip the following week, so there wasn't much time. I removed the bent door and ordered a new one.

The new door arrived in a big box, with a big ominous hole punched in the side. Uh-oh. I opened the box and found that the door had been dented in transit. This was a problem. I called the vendor, who agreed to send me another door, but it wouldn't arrive in time for me to install it for our trip.

Then I remembered—there was a shop across Commonwealth Ave from my mother's house called McCray's BMW that repaired cars and sold parts. I hopped in Bertha and drove her across the street. And into McCray's. Without a driver's door.

"Can I help you?" asked a young man working there. He was cheery and engaging, with "I can see that perhaps you need a door" written across his face.

"Yes," I said, "I want to borrow a door."

His expression changed from cheer to amusement mixed with mild incredulity.

"You want to … *borrow a door?*"

Monty Python had nothing on this sketch.

I explained what had happened, that I'd damaged my door, that I'd ordered a new door, that it had arrived dented, that I'd sent it back, but that a new one wouldn't arrive in the necessary time frame; hence my entirely rational request. (There have been many times in my life when it all seems so logical to me, yet I know I must sound like Ignatius J. Reilly.)

The young man's name was Alex. To this day, when asked how we met, Alex says, "Rob showed up in my shop and asked if he could *borrow a door*." Incidentally, no, he did *not* have a door I could borrow—something I try to remind Alex of when he tells the story lest he portray himself as more helpful than he actually was.

Even though he could not help me with my immediate door-related needs, Alex and I became fast friends. We often hung out, talked cars, and helped each other out on automotive projects—from installing transmissions and engines to stripping whole parts cars.

At one point, Alex bought, for very short money, a nearly new BMW 533i that had taken a brief swim in Boston Harbor (in insurance-speak, this is called a "flood car"). He'd hoped to get it running, but the electrical gremlins were too pervasive. The truism "a car just needs gas and spark to run" applies far more directly to primitive carburetor-equipped beasties than cars with computers that have been immersed in salt water. After giving it his best shot, Alex realized that he (like the car) was in over his head, and reluctantly sold it for parts.

Regarding Bertha's door, I wound up hammering out and temporarily reinstalling the original door so Maire Anne and I could travel. When we got back, the new door had arrived. I sprayed it with a coat of primer and installed it, thinking that sometime soon I would have Bertha repainted.

When Alex and his fiancée Heidi got married in 1988, our band played at their wedding. Heidi asked us to play a song she had written about how they'd met. It was to the tune of the old Sinatra standard "Strangers in the Night." I still remember singing "Scoobie doobie doo … he had an old 2002 … and it was *blue*." It was very sweet.

For their honeymoon, they were planning on doing "the grand circle" road trip—a six-week swing through the big Western national parks. Two days before they were supposed to leave, however, Alex was still working on his car (a BMW 2002, though not the blue one of "Scoobie doobie doo" fame), and things weren't looking good. I said, "You know, Bertha is running really well, and has working air-conditioning, a sunroof, and really comfortable Recaro seats. Do you want to take her? It'll be my wedding present." Alex was, well, a guy. We don't ask directions, and we don't easily admit that we're in over our head. "No, I'll get my car working," he replied. Heidi gently implored him to take me up on my offer. She had to work on *him* a little, but the next day he relented. So Alex and Heidi and Bertha literally drove off into the sunset.

It was five years after Alex and I had met.

Bertha's driver's door was still in primer.

CHAPTER 14

DAS COUPE (MY 1973 BMW 3.0CSi)

They say there's no accounting for taste, but they're wrong. The two-door BMW coupes built from 1968 through 1976 (the 2800CS and 3.0CS/CSi/CSL, body code "E9") are among the most beautiful driving machines ever to grace the blacktop. Their lithe lines, wood dashboard, huge glass expanse, and silky-smooth six-cylinder engine have stolen the heart of many BMW fanatics and non-BMW-philes alike. Although the 2002 is the car that established BMW's reputation in this country, the 3.0CS is the model that is most frequently listed as the most gorgeous BMW in the buff magazines. A major factor is that the lines of the car include elegant slender pillars holding up the roof in the front and back. These are the so-called "A-" and "C- pillars." A true coupe like the 3.0CS has no "B-pillar" between the front door and rear side window, so when you roll the front and rear windows down, there's this immense unbroken space from front to rear. Of course, the lack of a B-pillar means the front and rear windows have nothing to seal against but each other, so even when E9s were new, the wind noise was high and they leaked in the rain, but when you're this gorgeous, you can get away with murder.

If you really want to get BMW-geeky, the C-pillar on a 3.0CS has a beautiful example of a "Hofmeister kink," a design element originally introduced on the 1961 BMW 1500 (and widely copied throughout the industry) where the base of the C-pillar juts forward before rejoining the rear quarter panel. The total design, combining the "kink," the sweeping unbroken window space of a true coupe, and a surfeit of glass, continues to be stunning 40 years later. This timelessness and looks-just-right sense is all the more remarkable for the following reason. One can safely argue that iconic car designs—Jaguar XKE, Porsche 911, Corvette Sting Ray, etc.—tend to come out of the box as sheer perfection, and the "freshening" they received at later points did nothing but screw them up. With this in mind, consider that the 3.0CS

was not a clean-sheet-of-paper design; the car's graceful body did
not, in fact, spring full-grown from the head of Zeus. It evolved incrementally from the previous four-cylinder model—the BMW 2000CS,
whose body is nearly identical from the doors back, but whose shorter
nose exhibits long slits of glass-covered headlights, making the front
of the car look like a cross between a praying mantis and an electric
razor. The fact that, in lengthening the 2000CS's nose to accommodate
the new six-cylinder engine, they got the design of the car so right is
utterly amazing. It's like adding a dormer onto a split-level house and
expecting the result to look as elegant and integrated as something
penned by Frank Lloyd Wright.

The 3.0CS isn't beach-body curvaceous like a high-dollar Italian
exotic—it's more like the elegant 40-something woman you just can't
take your eyes off. I first saw a 3.0CS in the flesh while living in Austin,
and was immediately, utterly, and completely smitten. Screw 2002s, I
thought, I want me one of *these*.

Unfortunately, the coupes' Karmann-built bodies are extremely
rust-prone (remember that joke about Karmann inventing rust, then
licensing the process to the Italians?), and thus like other European
rust buckets such as the Jaguar XKE and Porsche 911, coupes tend
to fall into three categories: perfect, near perfect, and basket cases.
In 1986, I did not have the disposable income to procure a perfect or
near-perfect one. And unlike the more plentiful 2002s, you rarely find
coupes in body-good-but-needs-mechanical-work condition. Plus, I
had moved back to Boston where they lay down enough road salt to
dissolve bridge decks, so finding a rust-free affordable coupe seemed a
pipe dream.

And then I saw the ad: "1973 3.0CSi hit front partially repaired no
rust many new parts $5200." I repeatedly called the number in the ad
(this was 1986; most folks didn't even have answering machines) and
finally got in touch with the owner's mother, who informed me that
the car was in her driveway and hadn't run in over a year. She warned
me that it had been in an accident and was currently in a million pieces. Like some automotive version of Clint Eastwood, I assured her this
was okay: "That's all right, ma'am; I'm a mechanic." The two essential
ingredients were there—the dead, abandoned restoration project, and
the parent breathing down the owner's neck to "get that hunk of junk

out of my driveway" (always helpful when negotiating a purchase). So, with tools in trunk, checkbook in hand, and lump in throat, I drove off to have a look at the coupe of my dreams.

When I arrived, I found the car in the driveway under a tarp. Like a nervous bridegroom, I slowly untied the grommets and slid the tarp off. My sense of expectation gave way to disappointment as I found, true to Mom's promise, one seriously ugly coupe. The car had been hit in the front, and the damage to the nose and fenders had been attended to ("repaired" is too delicate a word for this abomination) with Bondo, fiberglass, aluminum, pop rivets, duct tape, Brillo pads, and almost everything else you can think of. The right fender was the worst. A major dent had been dealt with by taking a jigsaw to it, slicing the offending area in half, banging it out, *overlapping* the seams, *riveting* them together, and—egad!—*filling* the area with Bondo. In addition to the nose damage, the right door and rear quarter panel had been sideswiped and the silver paint was badly cracked. The bumper, grilles, and headlights were gone, the front windshield was smashed, the rear windshield was missing, and the interior was a jumble of removed panels and hanging wires. "How much does my son want for this, uh, car?" the owner's mother asked me. She nearly gasped when I told her his asking price. "My god!" she said. "If I had my say, you could haul it off for 50 bucks."

This was promising.

After the initial horror, I gathered my wits and looked carefully at the rest of the body. Amazingly enough, the car *was* remarkably rust-free. The interior, although partially removed, appeared to be complete, with the wood dash, trim, and velour in pretty good shape. All four of the electric window motors were there. Damn, though, no a/c or sunroof. After several tries I was able to coax the big six-cylinder engine out of its slumber, but it wheezed and stumbled ominously, belching clouds of oil smoke out both the valve cover and the exhaust (and you know a car hasn't run in a while when you start it and frighten a family of mice living beneath the windshield wiper motor). A compression check revealed only 80 psi in five cylinders, and 0 in one. *Oh, well*, I thought, *needs body AND engine work*.

I tried to recall what the ad had said to make sure I hadn't missed anything. "1973 BMW 3.0CSi." Check. "Hit front." Big check.

"Partially repaired." I supposed. "No rust." Well, maybe. "Many new parts." Generally when people say this, they mean that the car has new brakes, shocks, and exhaust (any old car had better have "many new parts" or it isn't likely to run at all), but this one turned out to be different. When I asked Mom about it, she led me into the basement where I found, to my stunned surprise, factory-logo'd boxes of parts including a huge one that held a brand spanking new rear windshield (no front one, though). There were new grilles, a new front bumper, new rubber seals, new side marker lenses, new visors, new molding, new electric window switches, and new trunk emblems. All in the original plastic bags with the part numbers still attached. It turned out that the owner worked at a BMW dealership and, before he lost interest, he had ordered many of the parts he needed to at least cosmetically restore the car. Why he'd shelled out for all these pricey parts and wasn't willing to repair the body correctly is a mystery rivaling the purpose of Stonehenge and why anyone ever bought a Renault.

Clearly the term "project car" did not do justice to this one. The apparent lack of rust and all those new parts made it appealing, but I made up my mind not to get involved. The thing needed massive amounts of work. On cars that sit for a year or more, the rings rust themselves to the cylinder walls, the exhaust rots out from the inside, the brake seals dissolve into the brake fluid, and the clutch sticks to the flywheel. Since you can't drive a dead car, you can't hear a rumbling rear end or a whining gearbox, so you really don't know what else it needs. And coupe body parts are ridiculously expensive. I'd bought, repaired, and sold many older BMWs, but I wanted a coupe for *me*, and when undertaking a project of this type, the adage is to "start with the car you want to finish with," and this one had no a/c or sunroof. All true. A litany of good reasons to let it pass.

But it's amazing how the mind works. You start off thinking "no way," temper that with a dose of "but I've never seen one this cheap," and wind up at "I wonder how low the guy will go." The owner's mother assured me that while she could not give away her son's car, she'd let him know that his asking price was not grounded in reality. About a month later, for $1700, the affordable dream coupe was mine. Once again, as with my first 2002, I had buy-in.

I was tempted to test my mechanic's pride and see if I could get it running well enough to drive the 25 miles home, but reason prevailed and I shelled out the money for a flatbed tow. As I stood in my driveway beaming at my purchase, Maire Anne came down and had a look. Her words were supportive, but her eyes said, "I don't know about this one." I'd been talking excitedly about the coupe ever since I first saw it, and now here it was: a silver car with one smashed and one missing windshield and enough orange Bondo to make Tammy Faye Bakker appear natural. Any rational being would have labeled it an eyesore. A neighbor stared in disbelief. "Is that thing supposed to be *worth* something?" he asked. Boy was *he* in for a surprise.

Having bought a rust-free 3.0CSi for $1,700, I thought I could surely restore it, slowly, a bit at a time, when I had the money, doing all of the mechanical work myself and shopping around for bodywork and paint, for under ten grand. Boy was *I* in for a surprise.

CHAPTER 15

RESTORATION AND WHY IT MAKES NO FREAKING SENSE

Before I go into the details of the coupe project, some terminology might be in order. The exact meanings of many of the buzzwords used in automotive restoration are very subjective. *Absolutely positively no rust anywhere ever cross my heart and hope to die* is pretty unequivocal, but little else is guaranteed. It's been said that when an ad says *no rust,* that means *rust,* and there's some truth to that. Above, I describe the coupe as *rust-free,* but really that means *not enough rust to lose any sleep over* (when I bought it, the only rust holes were on the edge of the trunk lid).

The phrase *no rot* implies that there may be some surface rust or paint bubbling, but no blatantly obvious holes in the outer body. *No structural rust* is supposed to mean that the frame, shock towers, and suspension attachment points are solid, but I have found that cars so described often have holes in the floorboard large enough to stick my head through. *Original condition* describes a car that hasn't had any restoration work done, but *original and ready for restoration* seems to guarantee a total rust bucket.

Restored is the least precise of all, as it can mean that the paint is recent and nothing is broken, or that everything is brand spanking new right down to the undercarriage and the engine compartment decals. When a car has had fanatic-level work like replacement of the firewall insulation or wiring harness, or removal, sandblasting, and repainting of the subframes, sometimes the terms *ground-up restoration* or *better than new* are used. If a car has been stripped, de-rusted, and correctly repainted, but the underside has not been redone, sometimes the phrase *outer body restoration* is used. It is hard to draw an absolute line between a car that is restored and one that just looks and runs okay; I'll use the term somewhat loosely to refer to any systematic body and mechanical rejuvenation.

RESTORATION PARADIGMS

There are three basic ways to restore a car: do it by yourself with the car on the road, do it by yourself with the car *off* the road, or pay someone else to do it. All three have their appeal. If you can afford it, professional car-off-the-road restoration is the way to go. Just give someone your car for a year, and half your annual salary. But then you can only say, "I'm having a car restored," not "I'm restoring a car." If you decide to do some or all of it yourself, having the car on the road makes the project quite a bit easier. It facilitates taking the car out for professional work if you find there's something that you can't do, it gives you the pleasure of actually driving your car during the process, and it offers you the option of selling a running car if you find you've bitten off more than you can chew (rather than a dead hulk and a garage full of parts). It is impossible, however, for such a "rolling resurrection" to be as thorough as a full ground-up restoration during which you spend two years of nights and weekends taking the thing apart, peeling back wiring harnesses, putting it on the rotisserie, painting the subframes, zinc-plating individual nuts and washers, and putting it all back together.

THE COST-BENEFIT ANALYSIS YOU NEVER DO, BUT YOU SHOULD

But whether you're doing restoration or *RESTORATION*, it's hellishly expensive, and if you view it coldly, it doesn't make much sense even if you have a classic candidate and the money to bring it back. If you wind up selling the car once it is restored, you will *never* get back the money you put in, so rather than buying a restorable heap, you're *always* better off buying a car that someone else has restored, even if that means spending four times as much on the car.

Of course, if you don't *have* the money, the "it's better to spend four times as much" argument is specious. If you don't own a home or have a stock portfolio to borrow against, the only money you can borrow is through an unsecured personal loan at nosebleed rates, and these generally are capped at a few thousand dollars—a fraction of what you'll need to either restore a neglected car or buy a restored one.

Now, when I bought the 3.0CSi in 1986, I simply ignored all this. I was young, I was short on money and long on lust, and the only way I could figure out how to get my hands on the coupe I so craved was to buy the only affordable rust-free one that I found, condition be damned, and, well, I'd figure out the rest later. So, yes, I did what everyone tells you not to do. With nearly 25 years of hindsight, I can now lecture people on why this was foolish, how you should *always* spend more and buy a restored car, etc. But the mind filters information in wonderful ways; when I try telling this to younger BMW enthusiasts, what they *hear* is "You bought that beautiful red coupe when you were 28 years old? *Man!*"

So here's the tip no one tells you: Yes, you're always better off buying a restored car, but if you can't, by purchasing a car that needs work and spreading that work out over a period of years, *you become your own credit agency*. You give yourself the money no one else will give you. You turn impossible into possible, no into yes. Of course, if the car is rusty, it still makes no sense; it still has to be the right car. I didn't fully appreciate at the time how lucky I was that, while mine had been hit, it was nearly rust-free.

WHY IS PAINTING A CAR SO DAMNED EXPENSIVE?

So let's talk about paint and bodywork. Maybe you, like me, bought something you probably shouldn't have. Or maybe you or your spouse are scratching the itch and thinking of buying an enthusiast car. Some of the classics you see are so pretty they just, you know, *pop*, but people want so much money for them. And then you see other cars, maybe not so shiny, for a quarter the cost. Can't you just buy a cheaper one and paint it?

Sure, and you can buy an inflatable structure that slides over your slab-ranch house and makes it look just like a McMansion, so that, from the street, no one will be able to tell the difference.

Was there sufficient sarcasm there or am I being too subtle?

Over the years, many folks have seen the ads from chains like Maaco advertising $250 paint specials, and so when they hear about it costing thousands of dollars to paint a car, they don't understand why. I'm not a paint and body guy, but let me try to explain.

PREPARATION, PREPARATION, AND PREPARATION

When you see a car that is to die for, with a finish that reflects the whole world and looks as if you could fall into it, what you're seeing is, in fact, the sum of four related things: 1) the body panels beneath the paint lying extremely flat, 2) the paint itself lying extremely flat, 3) the paint having a shine on it, and 4) the combined effect of the paint and all of the other outer body components (especially the chrome) on the car.

I once took a car to Earl Scheib, whose slogan was that he'd "paint any car any color for $99." Do you know what? *They literally didn't even wash the car. They painted over dirt.* They masked the trim, bumpers, windows, and lights, and simply sprayed the car and gave it back to me. That's what you got from Earl and his dentures for 99 bucks.

Did the car look better than before it was painted? From 50 feet, absolutely, but from close up, the finish was very uneven, because they didn't properly prepare the car. Painting requires preparation. Preparation takes time. Time costs money. The more preparation involved, the better the paint job, but the more it costs. Perhaps nowhere else is the adage "time is money" so directly applicable.

If a car's finish is so bad that it needs to be repainted, it is likely that the body panels aren't smooth. If you just spray paint on an uneven surface, it will look like makeup applied over obvious acne. It's just like painting the outside of your house—you need to scrape the flaking old paint off the shingles before you can lay down a new coat. First, at minimum, the car's surface needs to be lightly sanded to remove any bumps and help the new paint adhere. Second, if the old paint is cracked, it will have to be sanded off or else the cracks will show up through the new paint. Third, there will likely be the usual distribution of small dents and door dings. If you don't fix these beforehand, when the old dull paint is replaced with new shiny paint, your eye will immediately be drawn to the imperfections because of the different way that they reflect light. So prepping a car usually involves roughing-up or sanding off much of the old paint, hammering out minor surface imperfections, and leveling them with small amounts of body filler. Earl didn't even do this much.

PAINTING MISSION-CREEP:
PLAN ON REPLACING TRIM AND RUBBER

Now, if you're going to this much effort, it is silly to leave the trim on the car (and by trim I mean anything that bolts onto a painted surface—bumpers, molding, mirrors, door handles, emblems, headlights, taillights, windshield washer nozzles … anything). You can try to sand around the trim pieces, but it is very easy to damage them with the sander. So the trim pieces really should come off to enable unimpeded access to all body panels.

And, if the car is 30 years old, odds are that rubber seals at the front and rear windshields are hard as rocks. If you're going to the effort of painting the car correctly, you should at least consider pulling the glass out, painting under it, and replacing the seals with new rubber. And, if the windshields are badly pitted (and in any 30-year-old car with original glass, they are *always* badly pitted), there's never a better time to replace the glass as well.

So we've slid easily from "just paint it" to "just sand it and paint it" to "pull off all of the trim, sand it, level the body panels, paint it, and reassemble it" to "and while you're in the neighborhood, replace the front and rear windshields and rubber seals." Note that all of the above takes place before anyone has even sprayed a lick of paint, or has said anything about rust. Time is money. The clock is ticking. The register is going *cha-ching*.

ANYONE CAN PAINT. CAN'T THEY?

Next there is the physical act of painting. Waving a spray gun back and forth at a fixed distance from the car isn't exactly rocket science. However, you need a dry place to do it, with good lighting and temperature control, because unless the temperature and humidity are precisely controlled and the paint is mixed just right and the spray gun is adjusted correctly, paint tends to clump and exhibit what's called "orange peel," meaning that when you look at it closely, it resembles the surface of an orange. Actually, all just-sprayed paint has some degree of orange peel; it's a question of how much. Even new cars have it if you look up close, but it's usually not enough to interfere with the shine. However, a much greater degree of roughness is typical in an inexpensive aftermarket paint job.

When a car has a reflect-the-sky shine, it is because the paint is lying flat enough to act like a mirror. Bumpy mirrors don't work very well. I can assure you that even if you wax the living daylights out of an orange, it is not going to be a good mirror. So the presence of orange peel is a big roadblock in the way of a deep shine. The tried-and-true way to get paint to lie flat is to wet-sand it. That's right—actually sand the paint while keeping the surface wet with water. When you see a car with an oh-my-god mirror finish, odds are that the car has had multiple coats of paint wet-sanded between coats. It is, needless to say, a time-intensive and thus expensive process.

AND THEN THERE IS THE PAINT ITSELF

Lacquer used to be the choice for pampered classics driven only on sunny Sundays, but the industry has moved to enamel paints that are essentially liquid plastic, which can expand and contract as the metal flexes and swells with vibration and extremes in temperature. Acrylic enamel is the less expensive option. Urethane enamels are more expensive, and are generally two-stage paints—so-called base coat / clear coat systems—where the pigment (the color) is in the base coat, followed by a clear coat that preserves the color by blocking the sun's ultraviolet rays. For that reflection-so-deep-you-can-fall-into-the-paint result, typically both the base coat and the clear coat are wet-sanded.

Next, the outer layer of paint—whether it's a straight color or a clear coat—is buffed and wax is applied. If the paint is lying perfectly flat, this is the final step that gives it luster and produces that "fall into it" quality.

Finally, there are the other outer body pieces. If you're repainting an older car, odds are that every component on the outside of the car, including the bumpers, molding, mirrors, grilles, headlights and tail-lights, the glass, and the rubber seals, are in the same condition as the paint, meaning … they're old and dull. When you suddenly change the paint from old and dull to new and shiny, every nonshiny outer body component sticks out like a sore thumb. This dynamic is particularly strong on older cars precisely because so much of the trim is chrome. Put another way, once you've removed all that trim, just throw it in the garbage because now that you've dropped two grand on painting the car, you're not going to want to reattach any of it. Hello, slippery slope.

WHY I LOVE CARS WITH PATINA

One other thing to keep in mind is this: The finishes used on older cars were usually single-stage paints with no clear coat, making them extremely vulnerable to sun fading. Sometimes it is possible to bring back the shine on an old single-stage paint job by compounding and polishing the original paint. Personally, I *love* the slightly irregular patina you get from polished original single-stage paint. One of the best approaches to maintaining sanity and a positive bank account balance is to buy neither a restored car nor a car needing restoration but instead one in this in-between condition, because less-than-perfect outer body chrome looks just right against less-than-perfect paint with a nice patina on it. The whole thing is balanced. This is also something to keep in mind if you have an older car and want to get it shinier without sliding into the bottomless pit of full outer body restoration. Although the term "rat rod" referred originally to low-budget hot rods, it is now sometimes applied to B- and C-condition unrestored cars that are driven proudly, blemishes and all.

OH, AND RUST. YEAH. THAT.

Note that nothing I've said above even touches on the issue of rust. There's a whole spectrum of rust, from the nearly trivial (surface rust in the spare tire well) to the structural (rust-through on the frame or in the "shock tower" areas where the suspension is attached to the car). I don't do bodywork, but I think I can safely say that no one has ever taken a car in for restoration and been told, "You know, that rust isn't nearly as bad as we thought."

Even if a car has only surface rust with no rust-through, there are difficult choices looming for you and your budget. If there's flaking paint and surface rust on an outer body panel, obviously you sand it and paint it, natch. But what about flaking paint and surface rust on the back of the lip at the bottom of the doors? On the underside of the trunk lid? On the top surfaces of the frame rails in the engine compartment? On the floorboards? If you don't address these, and if the car isn't kept dry, what is surface rust today will be rot next year. In simply trying to paint even a 99 percent rust-free car, it's easy to stray across the line from painting to restoration. Suddenly it's not the firm fixed price the body shop quoted you—it's time and materials. It costs whatever it costs.

Now, I'm not saying that it *never* makes sense to paint a car. I'm just explaining why you're not going to buy a $3,000 car, give it a $500 paint job, and make it look like a $15,000 car. If the goal is a shiny, rust-free car, you should buy a shiny, rust-free car. If you try to start with a car that is neither rust-free nor shiny and make it both, it can easily break both your bank account and your heart.

DO WHAT I SAY, NOT WHAT I DID

So I, of course, ignored everything I've just said and tried to figure out how to fix this (admittedly rust-free) heap of a 3.0CSi. There was no way I could afford to have all of the outer body restoration done at once, so I broke it into phases. In the first phase, I scrimped and saved my money, searched for the best price I could find on a nose and fenders ($1,400 at the time), and bought them. Then I saved more money. Then I paid someone to pull the old nose and fenders, install the new nose and fenders, paint them with black primer and undercoat them, and install a windshield ($2,300). After taking this nearly $4,000 whack, I drove the car that way—half silver, half black primer—for two years while I saved even more money for even more work.

In the second phase, I had the car painted. I found a body shop in the Boston area that advertised in the local BMW Club magazine. When I drove up there, I found Giovanni, the shop owner, painting his own 3.0CS—always a good sign when the proprietor shares your passion. I left the car with him, and over the next few weeks, he completely stripped my car down to bare metal, repaired the sideswipe damage, leveled the body panels, primed the car, and sprayed seven coats of base and seven coats of clear. The body panels were all wet-sanded to remove orange peel and give the paint that deep look. Because I was changing the color of the car from silver to Signal Red (a deep rich Mercedes color), the interior, engine compartment, and trunk were also painted. Giovanni was quite creative, and he painted the engine compartment by masking the engine and painting around it instead of pulling it out. The cost for all this was four grand, and that was back in 1986 (I had another quote for ten grand). In an attempt to hold the cost down, I pulled all the trim off the car before I brought it to him, delivered the car, and pulled the interior out in a bay in his shop. I supplied him with new windshield seals, as both the front and rear windshields had to come out to paint the car. The fresh black rubber seals made a subtle yet startling difference against the fresh red paint.

In addition to removing the trim yourself to hold down cost, you may be tempted to reattach it yourself, but be careful. It is *very* easy to scratch the paint putting on trim, particularly while installing bumpers. If the shop nicks the paint, the onus is on them to make it right, but if you take delivery of the car and *you* put a decent gouge into the paint, you have no one to blame but yourself. I compromised and had Giovanni put the bumpers on, leaving the beltline trim to me.

This third phase—trim installation—was the slippery slope. As I mentioned, when I bought the car, it came with some brand-new trim pieces, but what this meant was that as I started reattaching any remaining original chrome trim pieces—all of which were dull, pitted, and scratched—I realized how completely out of place they looked against the new paint. I eventually relented and replaced all the trim.

THE PAY-OFF

But when it was reassembled, the car was absolutely drop-dead freaking gorgeous, and the deep Signal Red paint and new rubber made the chrome just pop. It must be noted that this was the late 1980s. BMWs were still synonymous with yuppies. And I looked less like Michael J. Fox and far more like Jerry Garcia (well, a 140-pound version of Jerry Garcia).

So I considered it the ultimate compliment when I was stopped at a red light in Boston and a guy in the adjacent vehicle took a long stare at the car, and said, "Hey, *nice car.*"

I said, "Thanks."

Then he asked, "*How does a guy like you own a car like that?*"

I smiled. "Drugs," I said, and drove off.

CHAPTER 16

COUPE SPARE PARTS

I added up the costs for the purchase of the 3.0CSi, the body panels and their installation, the paint, and all the trim. It came to about 15 grand, which was about what the car was worth, so in the "you'll never get it back" paradigm, I did very well.

The car's navy velour interior never looked right against the red paint, but changing the interior was prohibitively expensive. Then the impossible happened. I saw an ad for a purportedly rust-free 3.0CS for $4,800. Yeah, right, I thought. But you never know unless you look, and when I checked it out, I found that the car had come over from Saudi Arabia, *was* in fact completely rust-free, and had a beautiful tan leather interior. In addition, it had working air-conditioning, and was considerably tighter and had far fewer clunks and rattles than mine. Why the guy was asking less than half what it was worth I'll never know. I bought it on the spot.

The Saudi car's white paint had blotches of sap from sitting beneath a tree. I did something I never would've done with my freshly painted red coupe—I took it through a car wash. Coupes, as you now know, have no B-pillar, so the seal around the side windows typically lets in a lot of wind noise and some amount of water, but, I thought, it's just one car wash, I'll get the sap off and be done with it. I sat in the driver's seat as the car was pulled through the wash. The high-pressure water started to spray. A trickle through the side seals rapidly turned into a deluge. I realized I'd made a huge mistake. In about 10 seconds I was drenched. *Then came the soap.* I watched helplessly as massive amounts of suds penetrated my car like something out of a Woody Allen movie. I tried to block the gap in the seals on the driver's side with my forearm, but the soap monster was coming in the passenger side too. I relented and just sat in the driver's seat, drenched and soapy, laughing my ass off, thinking, well, the interior *could* use a good shampooing.

I seriously considered keeping the Saudi coupe and selling my freshly painted red one (the siren's song of air-conditioning sings pretty loudly), but in the end I swapped interiors, putting the gorgeous tan leather seats, door panels, and a new tan rug into my red car and the navy pieces into the Saudi car, and sold the Saudi car for a tidy profit. Despite having nearly 50 BMWs pass through my hands over 30 years, nothing remotely resembling this near-windfall ever happened to me again.

Shortly after my coupe was painted red, I got geeky and sprung for a vanity plate that said WARP9, the significance of which is two-fold. Firstly, this was the fastest the *Enterprise* was ever ordered to go on the original *Star Trek*. Second, BMW's platform code for the 3.0CS is "E9." One day I was driving to work and got bagged. It wasn't a flagrant violation—something like 43 in a 35 zone—but my wisdom in having painted this car arrest-my-ass-red and driving with a license plate that might as well say ISPEED seemed questionable. The officer took my license and registration and went back to his car. When he returned, he asked, "What does the WARP9 stand for, son?"

I felt like a total idiot geek having to actually say the following words to a police officer: "It's the fastest they ever ordered the *Enterprise* to go on *Star Trek*. Sir."

"Well," he smiled, "try to fly your spaceship a little lower to the ground. I only wrote you up for a warning."

The coupe was gorgeous, but the engine, though functional, wore its age and miles on its sleeve in the form of mechanical noise, low power, and oil consumption. Then in 1991 I stumbled across an engine from a 533i offered for such a low price that there had to be a catch. The seller said, "Yeah, it came out of a flood car that had less than 10,000 miles on it. Story was some idiot drove it into Boston Harbor." My mind went through a series of hyperlinks. 533i … flood car … Boston harbor … searching … searching …"You didn't buy this from a guy named *Alex*, did you?" Yes, incredibly, this guy had wound up with the engine from Alex's ill-fated 533i (see Chapter 13: "Northward Ho, Alex, and Bertha"). I bought it and tore it down. I didn't see any salt damage, but I replaced the rings, bearings, and seals while I was in there. The fact that Alex's engine landed in Das Coupe is one of those circle-of-life things that you can't plan on.

The red 3.0CSi has been the sun around which other things revolve in my automotive universe. In addition to the updated engine in 1991, I installed a 5-speed transmission. In 1998 I retrofitted air-conditioning into her. This dramatically increased my enjoyment of the car by making it more comfortable to drive in hot weather. In 2004 I outfitted her with L-Jetronic fuel injection which made her start right up and idle smoothly even after not having run in months. I guess if you were cynical, you'd call her "the black hole around which other things try to revolve but get sucked in." But I've had the car so long and done so much to it that it feels like part of me, and I part of it.

In truth, people have cars restored because they *want* to have cars restored. Often they look before they leap, and sometimes they're like the frog in the pot of water not knowing to jump out when the temperature is gradually being turned up, but people do it because it gives them the chance to personalize a car, to make it an expression of who they are.

Fundamentally, a restoration is all about choice and control. You may not feel like you had a choice when the car imprinted on you when you were 13, but you certainly exercised a huge degree of choice when you ponied up real money as an adult and brought home its sister. I mean, I *like* '63 Rambler Classics, but in a resource-limited world, I would never spend time and money restoring one over a '70s-era BMW. For many people, once they've anted up and bought in, it doesn't matter if you tell them that restoration makes no freaking sense—they're on a glide path to disposing of their disposable income. If you're up for it, it can be incredibly satisfying to delve into a restoration and have control over whether that restoration is factory-correct down to the zinc plating on the washers, or a wild customization, or somewhere between. All those color choices. All those component options. The car that pops out at the end of the process is the sum-total of all those choices. It sure as hell didn't wind up in your driveway by chance. That baby's *yours*. Hell, it's more than yours. It's you. Why do you *think* you love it so much?

Okay, I'm circling the couch, so why don't I just lie down on it for a moment.

If you want a window into who I am and what I value, look at my 3.0CSi. It has a vanity plate that combines fast-car-bravado with geeky humor. Its gorgeous styling, flashy red paint, and well-maintained leather interior make it a head-turner, plain and simple. Most importantly to me, it runs great. Open up the trunk, though, and you'll see things that would make a purist gag, including questionable adaptations, missing panels, and turn signals connected with speaker wire. Because I don't care about that stuff. There are not enough hours in the day or days in a lifetime to worry about things like that. That's who I am.

I'm sorry, our time is up.

Why do men love cars? Because looking at a car you've spent years with is a bit like looking back at your life. You might quibble over this piece or that, or laugh at how you spent so much time obsessing over details that seem trivial now. But hopefully you have no major regrets, and enjoyed most of it along the way.

CHAPTER 17

YALE

Sometime in June 1987, the phone rang.

"Hello, is this Rob Siegel?"

"Yes."

"This is Yale Rachlin. I'm the new editor of *Roundel* [the magazine of the BMW Car Club of America]. I like your stuff. How'd you like to write for me?"

It's cliché, but it was the phone call that changed my life.

Prior to that, I'd written two or three unsolicited articles for *Roundel*. The magazine ran them. I was happy. Mr. Rachlin ("please call me Yale") explained that he had just taken over the editor's position and was interested in having a staff meeting in Boston. *Roundel*, he explained, was not like other magazines in that there wasn't a full-time centrally located staff. Instead, club members working in locations around the country provided content. So to kick off his editorship, he wanted to assemble existing and future writers and have a face-to-face.

The meeting was remarkable. If I was a small fish in a small pond, I didn't realize it then. All of a sudden I was peer-to-peer with *Roundel* people I idolized. There were a few other new writers as green and awestruck as I was. And there were folks whose names I recognized and I haven't seen since.

I'd be lying if I said I remembered sweeping visionary statements about the direction of the magazine. I don't. Maybe there were. I don't know. What I remember is that there was just something about this guy I really liked. Earthy confidence. Verve and aplomb without bravado. A bit shorter and quite a bit older than I imagined over the phone. The patrician demeanor peppered with a sailor's tongue. That magnificent Semitic schnozz.

We hit it off immediately. I soon found out that Yale's house was on my way to work, and was invited over. "You mean the magazine is done … here? In your basement? What's that smell?" "Oh, it's the hot glue machine that we use to paste up the type." I asked to see the closet where the stone knives and bearskins were kept.

In the pre-internet days, handing in an article meant physically submitting a floppy, so I took to dropping them off. It became an excuse to hang out. Over the next 15 years we talked about anything and everything, from cars to kids to wives to work. We naturally found in each other eager, interesting companions. Regular lunches at a local Chinese restaurant would extend long after the fortune cookies were put on the table. Phone calls would run on and on, eventually ended with Yale's trademark flat baritone, "See ya later." It was easy, relaxed; he was so damned interesting, and neither of us ever seemed to tire of anything the other had to say.

Writing a monthly column was not like sending in unsolicited articles. With the latter, you hone and burnish every word and send it in when it's good and ready; with the former, there's a deadline. You can't write your life's masterpiece every month. The first three months were okay, but by the fourth I thought I had run out of ideas. I called Yale in a lather.

"Boss, I got nothing," I said.

"You do own cars, don't you?" he deadpanned.

"Uh, yeah."

"Did you *do* anything with any of them?"

"Uh, yeah."

"Well, write about that."

It was a turning point; I stopped writing about what I *fixed* and started writing about what I *did*. This is how my *Roundel* column, "The Hack Mechanic," was born.

Yale came to BMWs and track events relatively late in life, but he loved track driving and was very good at it. As with many of us, his 1974 2002tii became the repository of his passion and a good deal of disposable income. When age caught up with the car and it started leaving oily puddles on the ground, he had a new engine, transmission, and suspension installed.

Shortly after the car came back from the shop, I was over at Yale's house for lunch and asked how his newly modified baby drove. "Check it out for yourself," he said, tossing me the keys. I nestled into the Recaro seat and twisted the ignition, but the car wouldn't start. I got out of the car, went back into the house, and barely got out a "Hey, Yale, how do you start the …" when I heard a stomach-sickening crash. I ran into the garage to find that I'd left the car out of gear with the handbrake off and the driver's door ajar, and the minor tilt of the garage floor had sucked the car out and—shades of Bertha!—caught the tii's door against the garage wall, bending it on the hinges like one of those awful "agony of defeat" moments in the Olympic videos. Good thing, too—had the door not impinged on the wall, the car would've kept rolling until it hit the stone wall at the bottom of the driveway.

Obviously I was mortified. Yale, on the other hand, was unfazed. He told me that the car had an antitheft device—the high beam stalk needed to be pulled toward you while starting. "Go drive it," he said. Certainly he loved the car, but this just wasn't a big deal to him. In fact, we recreated the incident, and he photographed me with my best *Home Alone* expression for an article titled "Crashing Dad's Car" in the July 1990 *Roundel*. Our relationship did not need cementing, but there it was, cast in concrete.

If I can lie on the couch for a moment … it would be unnecessarily maudlin, and incorrect, to say that Yale was the father I never had. In the first place, I met Yale when I was 28 and was well out of diapers. And in the second place, I had a father. By all accounts, he was a really nice guy, too. But, as I've said, he died when I was 10. So, over the years, without even realizing it, I've found myself attracted to older men, most of whom (unlike my dad) swore like sailors.

I'm sorry, our time is up.

Yale's wife Bette had a bad knee, and as it got worse, she couldn't drive the tii with its four-speed stick, so he had to buy a modern car with an automatic transmission. Reluctantly he sold the tii to, if I recall, BMW CCA club founder Michel Potheau's dentist. During one of our lunches, Yale reported with chagrin that the word on the street was that the tii was rusting and badly neglected. "He lets his *babysitter* drive it," he confided. Wistfully, he added, "I *never* should have sold it." I recounted an experience that I had when I sold a well set-up '74 tii and wished I hadn't. A year later, the owner called me up and gave me first crack at buying it back, but when I checked it out, the car was nowhere near how I remembered it, and I passed without even making an offer.

I reassured Yale that these decisions we make at the time are usually the right ones. I hope that made him feel better.

Shortly before he and Bette moved to Florida in 2003, I took both Yale and my ex-boss (who drove me nuts but who also was something of a mentor) to lunch. Perhaps losing a father so young caused me to make sure that important things do not go unsaid. Yale and I had regular verbal exchanges of affection over the years, but the father/mentor thing had not been explicitly broached. I don't remember exactly what I said at this lunch—it was probably something simple, coupled with a brief thank you for the inspiration, the example, the affection, and the light shining down the road. But what was important for me to say was wholly unexpected for them to hear. It left them speechless and moist-eyed, and left me knowing that I'd never been so right about doing something so simple in my entire life.

The last year that Yale and Bette were still in Newton, they made an appearance at our annual New Year's Eve party, a sit-down dinner with my closest friends. They stayed for appetizers, but began putting on their coats as the dinner bell was rung. "You're not leaving?" I asked. Pretending to whisper in my ear, Yale said loudly enough for everyone in the room to hear, "If we leave now, Bette says we can have sex later." She just rolled her eyes. My friends still talk about it. We achieve our immortality in small ways such as this.

When Yale moved, I helped him clean out his garage, and inherited much bric-a brac, including his old Bell racing helmet with his hand-stenciled "Yale" logo on it. It kicked around my old garage for years. When I tore down the garage, the helmet, scummy with grease and cobwebs, was thrown out, a decision I deeply regret.

I am, without question, my mother's child. My worst, most selfish impulses were tempered by her patience, and my bedrock values come directly from her. But many of my best personal characteristics were reinforced by Yale, through example. Work hard. Tell the truth. Love your wife. Be nice to people. Don't knuckle under to pressure. And have fun. And all of this—the writing, the mentoring, the close friendship, the love—because of a shared interest in a boxy little two-door German sedan.

Yale passed away in 2005. He was my dear friend, and I miss him terribly. I'm a little old to go looking for new father figures, so I guess I'll just have to run with what I've got.

A few years back, a young BMW car club member tracked down Yale's tii and bought it, saying that the car had "historical significance." Initially I thought this was a little nerdy, but when he sent me photos of the restored car and I found out that it still had the infamous antitheft switch on the high beam stalk, I cried.

Man, I wish I still had that helmet.

CHAPTER 18

BROAD HUMAN CONNECTION THROUGH RIDICULOUSLY SPECIFIC SHARED INTEREST
STEVE AND THE Z1

As we've surely established by now, I'm into cars. Mostly German cars. For the most part, BMWs. Actually, BMW 2002s built between 1968 and 1976. And really only the round taillight models built between 1968 and 1973—I'm not as keen on those later ones with the big bumpers and square taillights. And actually it's only the fuel-injected ones—the '72 and '73 2002tiis—that really blow my skirt up.

Damn, that's specific.

But the world is a great big place, and even with this drill-bit-narrow interest, I am hardly alone.

Perhaps it's just basic human nature that makes us willing to open up to people with whom we have a shared interest. Maire Anne and I once went to a cat show and absolutely fell in love with Abyssinian cats. All of the animals there were of show quality, but we got the name of a breeder who we were told sometimes had less expensive pet-quality animals. I called her on the phone. This woman didn't know me from Adam.

"Hello?"

"Hi. You don't know me. My name is Rob Siegel."

Nothing.

"I got your name from someone at the cat show."

"Yes?"

"Uh, I'm interested in a pet-quality Abyssinian, and heard that you sometimes have them to sell."

"*OH*! Well …"

I think she stopped talking 20 minutes later.

But here's the point: The bond shared by people who are drawn to the same thing is very powerful. Whether it's cats or cars or cooking or gardening or something else, the physical objects and what you do with them may be interesting, maybe even beautiful if that's what you're into, but really it's the relationships among interested people that are the important part.

And the relationships are remarkable. I frequent a number of marque-specific web sites, and while some posters can get a little anal (you know, pointing out that, in some photo, the fuel line is running on the wrong side of intake plenum #3, that sort of thing), the degree of support for one's fellow human being can be absolutely astonishing. Someone can write a post like "Help! I just bought my first BMW M3, and I was driving it, and the thing just died," and he'll instantly discover twelve best friends that he didn't know he had. All because of shared interest in a physical object.

I guess people only become assholes once they get to know each other.

This ability to find people through the web who share your interest, and connect with the one person who knows exactly how to solve your problem, never ceases to amaze me. My 3.0CSi was experiencing an odd oscillatory idle, and not a smoothly varying sinusoidal one—more like a sawtooth where it would hold the idle for less than a second, then the idle speed would drop sharply, then resume. The problem would cease as soon as the throttle was cracked open even a little. This car has L-Jetronic injection retrofitted from a later model BMW, so the engine closely resembles that of an early 6 Series like a 633CSi. Thus, rather than post the problem on the 3.0CS-specific web site www.e9coupe.com, I posted to the 6 Series site www.BigCoupe.com. "Brucey," one of the site gurus (in Cambridge, UK), quickly posted back, "When the idle contact is closed, you *do* have the Overrun Fuel Cut-Off (OFCO) above about 1200rpm. As soon as the engine speed gets below about 1000rpm, fuel cuts back in again. Thus if you have too fast an idle, the OFCO kicks in and then it'll oscillate as you have experienced." Light bulb time. I didn't have an idle oscillation problem. *I had an idle speed problem*. I lowered the idle speed and the problem went away. All this from my one-paragraph description, served back from across the pond. Remarkable. Obviously, if "Brucey" and I ever meet, I owe him multiple libations of his choice. Hell, if I had daughters, I'd marry them off to him.

My friendship with Yale was certainly the deepest, most important relationship that resulted from a shared interest in cars, but there have been many others. If I hadn't driven my 2002, in need of a door, into Alex's shop, we might never have met. And that was just the beginning.

A wonderful example of pulling the rope of connection and meeting the person at the other end is the experience I had with Steve Diamond in 1999. Steve lives in Boulder. He knew me from my *Roundel* column. He called me up out of the blue and asked me if I could look at a BMW Z1 for him. Why would anyone think this was even a reasonable request? Two reasons. First, if you can't cold-call a member of a car club to look at a cool car, who you gonna call? Second, this was a *very* cool car.

The Z1 is the predecessor of the BMW Z3 roadster, but unlike the Z3, it has doors that drop down into the sills, and a multilink rear suspension. Only 8,000 Z1s were built, and none were commercially imported by BMW into this country. However, Steve had stumbled across one that was here legally. Apparently the Z1's plastic body panels were sourced from General Electric, and for this reason a seldom-driven Z1 had been on display for many years at the GE pavilion at Epcot Center in Disney World. The display was being retired and the car wound up in the hands of a broker in the Boston area. At least that was the story.

Initially when Steve asked me if I'd check the car out, I was concerned that he wanted me to certify a full mechanic's bill of health, but really all he wanted was to know if the condition of the car jibed with the story—did it *look* like it was a Z1 with only 3,000 km on it that had spent its life under glass? I looked at the car, it *did* check out, and I relayed that information (and the handful of flaws I found) to Steve. And I got to drive a Z1; it was only a two-minute trip around the block, but bragging rights are bragging rights. Steve was grateful. He apparently made an offer, it was apparently rejected, and that was, apparently, that.

Until about three months later. It seems that Steve's offer was the only real one, and the broker said he could have the car for the offered price if he could get him the money in 48 hours. Steve called me back and asked me if I could middleman the sale of the car for him—make sure it is still intact and exchange bank check for title and keys—oh, and if I could also figure out somewhere to store the car for a week or two while he arranged transportation to Boulder, he'd love me more than he already did.

I tried to think ... I had only my decrepit one-car garage (and even if there was room in it for the Z1, I'd be afraid of the car's getting dented by falling rust), but Yale was still in Boston at that point and he had an unused bay in his garage. I roped Yale into being a party to the crime. Steve sent the check and the check got lost in the mail. Steve nearly had a heart attack, but the check showed up, and he began breathing again. The seller arrived at Yale's house with the car, and we passed papers. Yale and I resisted the temptation to drive it, but we shot a video to document the receipt of the car. The situation quickly degenerated into two grown men in a pristine red Z1, watching the doors go up and down into the sills, making *vroom vroom* car noises, that sort of thing. A few days later the largest car carrier in the world showed up and took the Z1 off to Steve in Colorado, where it showed up a few days before his 40th birthday.

Four years later, I was on business in Denver with a weekend off, so I called up Steve. I finally got to meet him and his wife Dee Dee, and we spent a magical hour driving the Z1 through some of the canyons around Boulder.

All because of a phone call about a car.

Last spring I was in San Luis Obispo on business for three weeks. I had my evenings and weekends free. I remembered that there was a long-time BMW 2002-specific repair shop there. End of day one Friday, out of the blue, no phone call no warning, I stopped in and introduced myself to the owner, Rob Torres. That Saturday morning I helped him and a customer assemble an engine, then we went for a long drive up through the mid-coast wine country in two of the nicest 2002tiis I'd ever seen. How special is that? It's the shared interest that makes these wonderful moments possible.

One of the most satisfying cars-as-vector-for-human-connection moments occurred when I answered the following Craigslist ad: "My fiancé owns a BMW 2002. Unfortunately it needs quite a bit of work before it can be out on the road again. We're having our engagement photos taken in Provincetown at the beginning of April—and I'm hoping to find someone with a 2002 who will let us borrow/rent/trade their car for the day. Let's talk!"

I made contact with Lara and learned that Peter's 2002 has been a big part of both of their lives, but was partially disassembled and sitting in a storage container in New Jersey with an uncertain future. She said, "I'm a photographer who shoots a good deal of weddings. When thinking about my clients' engagement shoots, I often suggest having props that reflect who they are, or going to a place that they feel connected to. When thinking about Peter's and my engagement shoot we decided on Provincetown—a place we love. And then I got to thinking about what things (props) we feel reflect us. My mind immediately went to the 2002—and then I got a little sad realizing we couldn't actually have it in our photos. But then I thought about all of the wonderful 2002 owners out there who may allow us to use their car. It won't be exactly the same, of course, but all 2002s have wonderful personalities of their own—and it's the quirkiness of them that we both love."

Lara and Peter came over and met my far-from-mint '73 2002 whose faded Agave paint has a complex patina. We exchanged a word-of-mouth agreement that if it died, they'd pay for a flatbed tow. And that was it. It was that simple. They picked it up, drove it to P-town, had zero problems, and the photographs came out great. It was as if the car orchestrated the whole thing, and all I needed to do was sit back and smile.

Sometimes the enthusiasm and the specificity can get a bit geeky. Once, when I was advertising a car that I was parting out, Maire Anne had the experience of encountering a possible buyer when answering the phone one night while I was out of town. The caller was interested in some very small trim piece inside the trunk. No matter how many times she said, "I'll have Rob call you back," the caller wouldn't let go. "Is the car *there*?" he pressed. "If you go out to the car, put your head inside the trunk, then turn around 180 degrees and lie on your back *with your head sticking up under the shelf* that's beneath the rear window and look into the corner …" When I got home, Maire Anne described this interaction, and said, "You know, I used to think that you were obsessive, but now I see that actually, in the bell curve of this sort of thing, you're pretty well-grounded."

So I'm into cars. Mostly German cars. This funnels down into intense interest in one variation of a model imported to the United States for two years. Damn, that's specific. But more generally, I am a human being. We are all flesh, we walk this world together, we have interests, we grow old, eventually we die. Hopefully, in between, we talk to one another. If the cars provide one of many conduits to facilitate interaction with other human beings, that's not such a bad thing, is it?

CHAPTER 19

DRIVING WICKED FAST

Back at the start of the book, I said, "I used to drive the Triumph fast—5,000 rpm in fourth gear was 87 mph, and the car seemed quite happy there." Later I described how the Hampshire College student who'd given me a ride in that BMW 2002 all those years ago hired me as his errand runner and tossed me the keys to his 1979 BMW 733i 5-speed. This was, at the time, BMW's top-of-the-line model. Its poise and stability at high speed was startling, and made you believe everything you'd ever heard about how BMWs are designed to be driven as fast as they can possibly go. I would take the car up to 100, 110, even 120 for short bursts, showing off to friends how utterly planted it was. Anyone who rode in the 733i was simply astonished. It was as if, at high speeds, every molecule in the car seemed to be vibrating at the same frequency. If the Triumph seemed happy at 87 mph, the BMW must've been experiencing the automotive equivalent of multiple orgasms at 100.

A year later, I was pumped when I finally bought my first BMW 2002, but it was certainly a big step down from Nick's 733i. After all, the 733i was BMW's brand-new tour-de-force with a then-stratospheric $25K price tag, whereas the 2002 was an eight-year-old beat-to-crap thousand-dollar car with two fewer cylinders and about half the horsepower. Still, even in its shitbox condition, the 2002 felt extraordinarily stable at 80 mph, though I never tried to verify its reported 106 mph top speed. The fact that I drove it a bit slower than the Triumph had nothing to do with its capability and everything to do with a modicum of sanity finally beginning to seep into my then-20-something brain.

In truth, speeds like 80 mph, 100 mph, or even 120 mph pale in comparison to those achievable by any number of high-performance road cars that can easily see the high side of 150. A buck-and-a-half was once the exclusive territory of Italian cars with names ending in *i* but no longer. Hell, it's not even expensive new car territory anymore.

You can explore insane speeds in a well-used E39 BMW 540i sport for five grand, though you'd better replace those worn-out front bushings and check the brakes thoroughly if you're going to try to verify its 155 mph spec.

And that's nothing compared to the right edge of the bell curve you can experience if you have oodles of cash. *Top Gear* verified that a Bugatti Veyron not only can actually reach 250 mph but can maintain it with a surprising lack of drama. Of course, at that speed, the tires wear out in 15 minutes. But that's not the problem you'd think, because, as Jeremy Clarkson noted, you run out of gas in 12.

As I ease into my AARP target years, I've become fairly risk-averse. *Old enough to know better* seems to be taking the wheel more and more, letting *young enough to do it anyway* recede in the rear-view mirror like a hitchhiker you've decided not to pick up. Sure, I'll drive 85 when that's the prevailing traffic speed, but I'll use the radar detector only to avoid being the one gazelle in the pack that the lion chooses as prey. When the Z3 M Coupe starts whispering *come on you know you want to* in my ear, I can't help think how many points a reckless endangerment charge would add to my insurance. On one hand, this is, in fact, part of the value of being attracted to older cars—they're simply not as fast, and thus are less likely to get you into triple-digit trouble. But I do somewhat miss the insanity.

Years back, I did have the opportunity to drive at sustained triple-digit speeds, legally, several times. You'll be surprised to learn that none of these experiences were on the famed German *Autobahn*. Yes, the one time I traveled to Germany for work, I found myself driving clear across the country, from Berlin to Dusseldorf, at night, on *der Autobahn*, in a Mercedes. Unfortunately it was a Mercedes cargo van the size of a UPS truck—not the *oh god I can't believe I'm finally getting the chance to put the hammer down in a fast German car on the best highway in the world* experience I'd imagined. Life is often like that.

One of the benefits of being a member of the BMW Car Club of America is that the Club, and other organizations like it, conduct "driving schools." These are one-day events on a racetrack where, using your own car, you learn how to "drive the line" that carries the most speed through a turn. Through a combination of classroom and track time, instructors teach you how to brake in advance of a corner, then turn in smoothly, hit the apex of the turn, and accelerate out. People get addicted to driving schools and will tell you with proselytizing fervor that it's an opportunity to improve your driving skills. I've always taken issue with that. When you're on a two-lane public road, "driving the line" through a curve takes you into oncoming traffic, so the degree to which the mechanics of the *set-up-for-the-turn-then-enter-apex-exit* skill set are transferable to your daily driving is, in my humble opinion, highly debatable.

However, I have no argument with the position that a driving school is an opportunity to test and experience your car's limits in a highly controlled environment gloriously bereft of traffic lights, utility poles, cars coming at you, little old ladies crossing the street, and children chasing balls rolling out of driveways. I wholeheartedly agree that, by experiencing those limits on the track, you're less likely to push a car past its limit on a public road. And there's no shame in admitting that a driving school is *an opportunity to drive fast*; many tracks have a straightaway on which you can hit 120 mph and higher before you must brake hard to execute the turn at the end.

(That having been said, more than once I have experienced the situation where someone test-drives a BMW I'm selling or demonstrates one I'm thinking about buying, takes it out on the highway, and proceeds to wind it up over 100 mph and weave through traffic like the other cars are cones, with the justification "I did the Skip Barber racing school at Lime Rock." Thus, the *do it here and get it out of your system* value of driving schools doesn't apparently work on everyone.)

After years of Yale Rachlin giving me his best *come on all the cool kids are doing it* speech, I relented. After all, the cost for the day was only about $100 (now, more like $250), and all you needed was an approved helmet and for the car to pass a tech inspection. I did several schools at Lime Rock in Connecticut and at the old Bryar track (now New Hampshire Motor Speedway), first in my highly-modified 2002 Bertha, then in my 3.0CSi, and finally in two of my 5 Series sedans.

Most folks who own fast crisp-handling cars regard themselves as good drivers, and I'm no different, so I expected to take to it like, well, like a good driver to a road. However, despite having Yale himself as my instructor (and a more patient, supportive track mentor one could not ask for), I was, to my intense disappointment, anything but the next Stig. I was not smooth. I was not terribly fast. I was not at one with the rhythm of the track. People would ask me, "What's your approach to turn three?" and I'd ask, "Which one is turn three?" I realized that, until I had the entire track committed to memory, it would continue to be an exercise in frustration. Thus I needed to either do driving schools more frequently, or stop altogether. Since one of Siegel's rules is *Conservation of the Number of Expensive Hobbies*, I stopped. While the $100/day track fee wasn't prohibitive, the improvements you wind up wanting to make to the car (bigger brakes, stickier tires, stiffer shocks, beefier antisway bars, then moving on to hotter engines, close-ratio gearboxes, and limited-slip differentials), combined with travel and hotel costs, started to roll into serious coin. I haven't done a school in nearly 15 years.

My next opportunity for legal speed did not even require my own car. It was at a journalist event I used to attend regularly called International Motor Press Association (IMPA) Test Day, held annually at Pocono Raceway in Pennsylvania and attended by manufacturers who sell cars in volume in this country (meaning Ferrari no, BMW yes, Porsche some years yes some no). Manufacturers stage cars at the track for automotive journalists to sample. The keys are simply sitting in the ignitions. You can just hop in any car and drive it a couple of hot laps around the racetrack, though the track is configured to force you to come back through the paddock after the main straight. This is both to keep the speeds down and to accommodate the high demand for some of the hotter cars for which only one lap is allowed. It was such a kid-in-a-candy-store experience that I kept expecting someone to grab me by the ear and yank me out ("Get out of here, kid—you're not a *real* automotive journalist—you only write for *a car club magazine*").

So from the late '80s to mid '90s, I had the chance to drive some of the most desirable production sports cars in the world at IMPA Test Day—Acura NSX, Dodge Viper, Corvette ZR1, Mazda RX8, Toyota Supra, and more. In some of these cars, I briefly saw a white-knuckled 130 mph before needing to stand on the brakes and turn back into the paddock. I learned that the NSX is a car your grandmother could drive fast, and that the Viper has so much torque it is possible to spin it coming *out of* a curve if you mash the throttle at the apex.

But the most surreal triple-digit experience was the time I was flown to Europe on a *Roundel* assignment to cover the European press introduction of the brand-new BMW E36 325i in 1992. Since it was winter in Germany, the event was held at BMW's testing facility in Miramas in the south of France. There, BMW had a small twisty road course, a flat oval, and a banked oval. And, in addition to the new 3 Series, they brought 5 and 7 Series cars for comparison.

On the banked oval, you could simply put your foot to the floor and leave it there. So not only were the primary cues of speed—objects rushing past—missing, as they are on any track, but because the track was banked, there was an utter absence of lateral g-forces. The car did not lean. My eyeballs were not floating to the side of my skull. There were no tires squealing as they approached the limits of grip. And, to top it off, *the speedometer was marked in kilometers per hour*. Now, my '73 3.0CSi's speedo is also in kph, and you learn that 100 kph is 62 mph and estimate accordingly, but when you're inside two tons of steel rocketing around a track, you don't do the conversion in your head; at least I don't. I mentally filed the number (230 kph) away for later. When I got back to my hotel, I worked it out. I'd been driving a Euro-spec 7 Series at 143 mph. Around and around. Like it was nothing. Without white knuckles. Without a helmet. I consider that wicked fast. Did I mention they offered wine and beer with lunch?

With the benefit of age and experience, I think about this now, and considering the number of idiots I see checking their text messages while I drive back and forth to work every day, it was probably one of the safest things I've ever done on a road.

HOW TO MAKE YOUR CAR DEPENDABLE
(WELL, MORE DEPENDABLE)

What are you, nuts? I can't tell you how to make your car dependable. I'm a Hack Mechanic, not a miracle worker. As a car gets older, any part—*any part!*—can and probably will fail catastrophically, causing the car to grind abruptly to a halt, bursting into flame before flinging you through the windshield. No. Wait. Flinging you through the windshield before bursting into flame. I never remember which way that goes.

OK, I exaggerate. Every part of your car is not in imminent danger of breaking. Rear axles don't spontaneously snap. Clutch release forks don't suddenly break in two. What? You recall that both of these things actually happened to my Triumph GT6+? Yeah, but that only shows what outliers old British cars in general, and overpowered British cars with under-engineered drivetrain components in particular, are. Such things are, in fact, highly unlikely to happen on a classic BMW, much less on the 10-year-old Honda your wife is using as a daily driver.

I'm giving you mixed messages for a reason. Somewhere between the image of late-model Japanese cars as ultrareliable and the carica-ture of old cars as spontaneously dissolving, lies the truth. A car has many normal-wear-and-tear parts (brakes, shocks, and exhaust being primary among them), but most of these components are unlikely to fail in a sudden and catastrophic manner. The single most likely thing to cause a car to stop and you to go *oh crap* is a flat tire. It's not acciden-tal that the one spare part your car comes equipped with is a tire. We're so conditioned to this that we call the spare tire simply *a spare,* as if having a spare anything else is unthinkable.

But besides a flat, the things that are most likely to cause a car to die and leave you stranded on the side of the road are pretty mundane and fairly predictable. They're the battery and alternator, cooling sys-tem, belts, fuel supply, ignition-related issues, and ball joints.

Editor's Note: This memoir is **not** a repair manual. Please read Warnings & Cautions on p. 410.

Now don't get me wrong. I'm not saying you should avoid routine maintenance. Far from it. Your car is not *safe* if the brake pads are down to the metal or if the tie rods are so worn it doesn't track straight. And your car will not *last* if you don't change the fluids. But, to make the obvious bad pun, weak brakes are not likely to stop your car. Likewise with bad shocks and a hole in your exhaust. You need to get these things fixed, but if you don't, the car isn't likely to strand you.

At the other end of the spectrum, bad karmic stuff *can* happen. Automatic transmissions can fail with very little warning. (Reliability hint: *Don't drive a car with an automatic transmission.*) Nuts holding flanges on splined shafts can loosen. And, to be sure, there are model-specific shortcomings. On a BMW with the M42 engine like the 318is and 318ti, the plastic coolant neck can snap off the back of the head and the profile gasket can fail, both causing sudden catastrophic coolant loss. And if you drive *any* modern BMW in very cold weather, the crankcase ventilation valve (CVV) may freeze and send oil into the intake manifold, hydro-locking your engine. These last two things are particularly maddening precisely because they can fail with no warning and leave you in the lurch.

And if you're driving a four-decade-old car like a '70s era BMW, whole new layers of potential failure open up. Your clutch master or slave cylinder can fail, making it nearly impossible to shift gears. Rubber bushings attaching the shift platform can dissolve to the point where the back of the platform hits the driveshaft and sounds like a lathe. The differential may give up the ghost with a loud *bang* and a gnashing of teeth, though it'll usually howl loudly for hundreds of miles beforehand.

But the point is this: If you start with the near-universal list of *battery and alternator, cooling, belts, fuel, ignition, ball joints,* add any model-specific shortcomings, then address these most-likely failures prophylactically, you've gone a long way to making a car, if not dependable, at least *more* dependable.

BATTERY AND ALTERNATOR

Early in the book, I discussed the logic tree relating to *car won't start* and advised that the single biggest thing you can do to increase reliability is to replace the battery. If you buy a used car and need to rely on it starting, particularly in cold weather (and who doesn't?), and you don't know the age of the battery, just replace it. Buy a $5 battery cleaning brush and clean the battery posts and the insides of the connectors. If they're corroded past the point of cleaning, replace the battery cables. This does wonders for the reliability with which you turn the key and have the car start in cold weather.

Inextricably related to the battery is the charging system consisting of the alternator and the voltage regulator. Earlier I described how a voltmeter can be employed to verify that the alternator and voltage regulator are charging the battery at the correct voltage. The alternator and regulator are both easy and relatively inexpensive parts to replace prophylactically. If you do so, along with a fresh battery and clean connectors, you will have largely eliminated the possibility of the battery running down and leaving you stranded (unless, of course, you leave the lights on).

COOLING

A car's cooling system can strand you in several ways. It can get overwhelmed gradually (overheating in traffic) or fail catastrophically (sudden total loss of coolant). Newer BMWs with their plastic cooling systems are famous for the latter; to address these in a way that makes the car dependable, you need to do the full "plastic kit" described later in Chapter 39: "What to Buy—Daily Drivers." But on an older car with metal cooling system components, or on any car you plan on driving farther than around the block, you should at an absolute minimum inspect the hoses and water pump. With the engine cold, lay your hands on each and every cooling hose and squeeze it. If a hose is soft and pillowy, with the hose billowing up around the hose clamp, or if it is rock-hard, it should be replaced. In addition, I like to give each hose a good hard tug. If it shreds, good. Better to do so in the driveway than on the Mass Pike. If you need to replace any hose, you must drain the cooling system, and this gives you the opportunity to do it all—replace the radiator, water pump, thermostat, and every hose. But if the hoses seem decent, the radiator isn't leaking, and the thermostat opens up when the car is at operating temperature, and you're trying to save some scratch, at least pull the hoses off and use an old penknife to scrape off the corrosion that forms at the neck of the engine and radiator components the hoses attach to, then reseat all the hoses and retighten all the clamps.

"Inspecting the water pump" means looking, feeling, and listening. *Look* at where the water pump mates to the engine block and where the shaft protrudes from the front of the pump housing for signs of leakage or corrosion. With the engine off, loosen the alternator, remove the fan belt, spin the water pump, and *feel* for smoothness in the bearing. Then feel for play in the bearing by gently rocking one of the fan blades fore and aft. With the engine running, *listen* for rumbling or squealing of the pump bearing (an inexpensive mechanic's stethoscope is great for this). If you don't know how long the pump has been in there, prophylactic replacement is certainly best, but if the water pump passes these tests, it's probably fine, at least for a while. If it fails any of them, factor into your driving that the water pump may give up the ghost at any time. When I buy an older car, I squeeze and tug the cooling hoses and check the water pump in this manner. If they pass, I move on *for now* to see what matters are more pressing. But if I know I need to rely on the car, including not having it overheat in summer traffic, or if I'm planning a thousand-mile drive to an event in the car, or it's a newer BMW with all that plastic, I prophylactically do the entire cooling system. The peace of mind gained is so good it should be classified as a controlled substance.

Before we leave the cooling system, a word on the fan. Although I talk about the fan belt below, note that many modern cars don't have a belt-driven cooling fan; instead, to save space, they have a slender electric fan. If the fan stops turning, your car may run fine while going down the road, but will overheat quickly when stopped. Prophylactic replacement of this electric fan, particularly on a German car, can be pretty pricey, but at a minimum I like to fabricate and travel with a cable with an in-line fuse so I can hard-wire the fan directly to the battery. This won't help if the fan motor itself has died, but it has saved my butt when the problem is in the fan relay or one of the sensors that's supposed to tell it to turn on.

BELTS

Though I give them their own category, belts don't operate in a vacuum; they're there because they use the engine's rotation to turn something else. The *something else* is the alternator and the water pump. Thus, belts are part of the electrical and cooling functions. Older cars typically have one *fan belt* that runs both the alternator and the water pump, with separate belts running the air-conditioning and power steering if they are present. The fan is usually bolted to the water pump pulley, hence the name. In contrast, most newer cars have a single *serpentine belt* that runs everything. In either case, a belt failure will strand you because it causes both the alternator and the water pump to stop turning. Of the two, it is the water pump that is the more critical item; your car can overheat in a minute if the belt breaks. This is why replacing the belt is critical. Like hoses, I'll inspect the belt on a car I've just bought. If it's obviously cracked, I'll replace it immediately. If it's not, I'll leave it there for now and see what else needs to be sorted out.

In addition to the fan belt, many cars have a *timing belt* that spins the valvetrain in the head. Opel actually produced the first overhead cam engine with a timing belt in 1966 (a design that is now ubiquitous), but most Americans were introduced to timing belts during the fuel shocks of the 1970s when they bought Japanese cars. Because it replaces a traditional heavy timing chain, a toothed timing belt makes for a lighter, sewing-machine-quiet engine. However, it is a belt, and thus can break, and thus must be replaced at regular intervals. And because the timing belt is *inside* the engine, it is out of sight and out of mind, and many folks forget about it until it lets go. When that happens, whether it is a minor inconvenience or a big deal depends on whether the engine is an *interference engine* (one where the valves open into the cylinder space also utilized by the pistons). If the car has a *non-interference engine,* when the belt breaks, the car simply and abruptly dies. A tow, a repair bill, some grumbling, and you're on your way. However, on an *interference engine,* when the belt breaks, you are greeted by the sickening expensive sounds of the pistons smashing into the valves. If you're lucky, the belt lets go when you're starting the engine. If you immediately shut it off, all you've done is bend some valves. Expensive, but perhaps not utterly catastrophic. More likely, though, the car is under load with the engine spinning, and the impact breaks valves, cracks piston crowns, bends rods, possibly even blows a hole in the side of the block—in short, lunches your engine, generates a repair bill large enough to make you cry, and ruins your whole damned day.

The M20 engine used in BMW E30 3 Series cars (325e, 325, and 325i) and in the 528e is the only BMW engine to use a timing belt. It is an interference engine, so prophylactic replacement of the timing belt in these cars at 60K intervals is absolutely crucial. This departure from the traditional BMW timing chain raised eyebrows when the M20 came out in the mid-'80s, but with time, it has proven to be an extremely stout and reliable engine *provided the timing belt is changed regularly.* This is *not* a case where you should look at the belt and see if it shows signs of wear. Unless someone shows you a receipt proving the belt was recently done, prophylactic replacement of the belt and the tensioner is the *first* thing you should do on these cars. You cannot afford to be wrong about this.

On early fuel-injected cars with a mechanical fuel injection pump such as the BMW 2002tii, the Porsche 911S and 911E, and the Alfa Spider with SPICA injection, there is one additional belt: a toothed belt that synchronizes and drives the fuel injection pump. Prophylactic replacement of this belt is part of any resurrection or maintenance, as you ain't goin' nowhere if it breaks.

FUEL

Of all the things that can shut you down, fuel is perhaps the scariest. Sure, you may risk a cracked head by driving an overheating car to the next exit, or experience the sick feeling in your gut when a timing belt breaks, but if there's an overwhelming smell of gas, you need to stop *now* or risk getting burned alive. I've seen fire consume a car, and it is astonishing how quickly it goes from a little bit of smoke to a full-on conflagration. Fuel problems can be loosely categorized as *too much* or *not enough.* If you smell fuel, it's clearly *too much,* and is usually due to a torn or leaking fuel line. Fuel is not like antifreeze, oil, or power steering fluid; *never* drive a car that's "just leaking a little fuel." Stop, now, and fix it, *now.* When I'm checking out a car I've just bought, I'll feel and tug the fuel hoses under the hood and where they attach to the gas tank. Like the coolant hoses, if they're neither rock-hard nor soft and pillowy and bulging over the hose clamps, and if they don't tear or leak when I pull them, I'll move on for now, but if I need to rely on the car or drive it long distances, I just replace them all. Fuel hose is cheap, and changing all of it in the car is perhaps an hour's work and a little bit of gas running down your arm. Really, it's silly not to do it. In addition, mechanically fuel-injected cars like the 2002tii have high-pressure fuel lines connecting the fuel injectors to the injection pump. On a tii, these lines are plastic and can become brittle with age and break. Folks either replace them prophylactically or carry spares.

In the *too little* category are the fuel pump and fuel filters. If a car feels like it's running out of gas, it probably is, so if there's gas in the tank but the car is acting like there isn't, there's probably a fuel delivery issue. Fuel filters clog up with age as they do their job keeping contaminants out of the engine. One of the failure modes of a clogged fuel filter is a car that starts and runs, then after a few minutes, loses power when you try to rev it up. What often happens is the contaminants accumulate against the filter's screen. When the car is shut off, some of the crud falls off the screen, enabling the flow of fuel again, only for the process to repeat itself. I prophylactically replace the fuel filters in any car I buy. The tomato-paste-can-shaped fuel filters are easy to spot and change (except in modern BMWs where they're hidden beneath the car under plastic cladding). In addition, some fuel-injected cars also have a small screen where the fuel line goes into the injection pump; it took me a while to find this in my first 2002tii.

Fuel pumps can and do die. On carbureted BMW 2002s, the mechanical fuel pump is a known normal-wear-and-tear item. With time, the diaphragm gets weaker and pumps less fuel. A known roadside repair is to remove the nylon block separating the fuel pump from the head, and shave it against the asphalt as if the road was a belt sander to remove some material, effectively making the fuel pump rod longer and pumping more fuel. I've rescued several 2002 owners, including myself, with this trick. A spare mechanical fuel pump is part of any 2002 owner's road kit.

Modern fuel-injected cars have a high-pressure electric fuel pump located beneath the car or in the gas tank. These also can, unfortunately, die. The OEM versions of BMW fuel pumps for old fuel-injected cars like the 2002tii and 3.0 CSi are either ungodly expensive or no longer available. I hate to throw away an OEM electric fuel pump before its time, so I keep a reasonably priced aftermarket fuel pump in the trunk. I do not prophylactically replace electric fuel pumps in my newer BMWs, but doing so is not out of the question, as the fuel pump in my 200K E36 325i failed. Fortunately it happened right in my driveway.

On old fuel-injected cars like the 2002tii, the fuel pump comes on immediately when you turn the key, but this raises the specter of it continuing to pump gas in the event of an accident, so newer cars employ a variety of interlocks connected to a fuel pump relay. Unfortunately this adds to the number of things that can cause the fuel pump not to run and the car to die. When I buy a new daily driver, I learn where the fuel pump fuse and relay are, and find, download, and print the appropriate information on how to test and bypass the fuel pump relay, and put the printout in the glovebox. That way, if the car acts like the fuel pump has died, I can quickly determine if it is the pump or the fuse or the relay. I've gotten home more than once by bypassing the relay, even wiring a fuel pump directly to the battery. If you learn from reading the message boards that the relay in your car is a known trouble spot, buy a spare and put it in the glovebox.

IGNITION

Over the past 35 years, ignition systems in cars have gone through four basic generations, with each becoming more and more reliable. The oldest ones have a conventional distributor with spark plug wires coming out of it and with breaker points inside. These first-generation conventional distributors have two mechanical systems at play—the points have to physically open and close to cause the coil to fire and generate the spark, and the distributor has to spin around, advance the spark by an amount related to engine speed (this is the ignition timing) and distribute that spark to the plugs by having the rotor touch each of the contacts inside the cap. Points are *the* replaceable normal-wear-and-tear item in the ignition system in an older car. Every backyard mechanic can tell you a story about a car that died because the points closed up, and having to yank them out on the side of the road, file the surface with a Swiss Army knife, and set the gap with a matchbook. Yes, you *can* do this, but do you *want* to, on the Tappan Zee Bridge at rush hour? Timing, on the other hand, is usually not a reliability issue. The weights and springs inside the distributor may, with age, gum up and stick and lose the ability to advance the ignition timing with higher engine speed. This may make it run a bit hotter, but it is unlikely to cause your car to go from running to dead. You can get around the inherent unreliability of points by upgrading to the second generation of ignition systems that use a points-less electronic ignition. Many BMW 2002 owners run an aftermarket Pertronix electronic ignition module. They're very reliable, though it's wise to keep a set of points and condenser in the trunk in case they go bad. For a knock-around-town older car, points are fine, but for something you need to rely on, the electronic ignition modules do remove this inherent weak point.

FYI, the third-generation (Motronics 1 through 1.3 in Bosch BMW-speak) still has a "distributor," but it no longer controls ignition timing. Its function is *only* to distribute the spark from the coil to the cylinders; spark advance is handled by an electronic control unit (ECU) that looks advance up in a table as a function of engine rpm and load and compensates for it electronically, not with spinning weights and springs. The fourth generation does away with the distributor and plug wires entirely, instead using "stick coils" directly affixed to every spark plug. If a coil goes bad, you lose spark to only that cylinder, not to all of them. Although these systems are, in general, quite reliable, there are a myriad of sensors that affect how the car runs. This is not my area of expertise, but I'm told that, of these, the one that can cause the car to die is the crankshaft positioning sensor, so if you're looking to increase reliability and prophylactically replace one sensor, that would be it.

BALL JOINTS

A car's ball joints connect the front suspension to the steering. The struts in the suspension may wear out but are highly unlikely to cause the car to stop. Likewise with the steering; the myriad of bushings and tie rods may clunk and cause the car to wander, but they're unlikely to strand you. But the ball joints are on the front lines of all that pounding from potholes. The struts prevent the pounding from coupling into the body of the car, but the ball joints take it all. If a ball joint fails catastrophically, you will almost certainly first lose control of the car, then the wheel and the strut will likely fold under, as there's nothing keeping the wheel in line with the rolling direction of the car. Google "ball joint failure" and look at the images. Then look at the years and

models of cars. It's scary. I never used to worry about this until I saw a BMW 2002 with a ball joint that failed at about 40 mph. It nearly to-taled the front end of the car (fortunately the driver was not injured). I can't say that I always replace ball joints prophylactically, but I change them if they show any signs of play, if they look like they've never been replaced (on a 2002 the original ball joints are riveted in place, so if you see rivets, they've been there 40 years), or if I'm performing other substantial front end work and just want to do it all and be done with it.

Repeat after me. Battery and alternator. Cooling system. Belts. Fuel. Ignition. Ball joints. I recently attended The Vintage in Winston-Salem, an event to which nearly three hundred vintage BMWs collec-tively drove tens of thousands of miles. The failures I heard of? Two seized water pumps, a failed set of ignition points where the nylon block riding on the cam lobes broke, one bad alternator, and one blown head gasket, changed in the parking lot by Paul Wegweiser and Ben Thongai in one hour and 56 minutes, a stuff-of-legend repair that will set the standard for generations. I can assure you that this event has triggered many long and substantive discussions as to whether the head gasket should be prophylactically replaced on an old car.

Anything still *could* happen. The ignition switch inside the steer-ing column could fail, preventing you from starting the car. Mice could eat your wires. I once had a woodruff key (the little half moon metal piece that forms a slotted fit) on the front of the crankshaft fail. The symptom was the alternator light coming on and the temperature climbing. I looked at the engine. The fan wasn't turning but the fan belt was in place. What the …? I looked closer. The *crankshaft pulley* wasn't turning. When the woodruff key failed, the pulley was no lon-ger fixed to the front of the crankshaft. Worse, the failure ruined the crankshaft's key slot. I had to pull the engine and replace the crank. Not a good day, that.

But these are far less likely than my top six. Address this list, and the lightness achieved by your peace of mind will probably gain you a few extra miles per gallon.

CHAPTER 21

THE MADNESS OF BUYING A BUDGET ROADSTER

In 1990, the impending birth of our second child, Kyle, brought on a wave of iconoclastic jam-the-thumb-in-the-eye-of-responsibility impulses. I started looking at roadsters. The Mazda Miata had just been introduced, re-igniting pop culture interest in the roadster. But these were new and expensive. I needed old and cheap.

Understand that when I say "roadster," I mean "zippy little two-seater convertible with a stick." Though there certainly are American roadsters (the Corvette of course being the king), most American drop-tops aren't roadsters but roofless sedans. While there's nothing wrong with that (and in fact a '63 Comet convertible with its jet-age taillights is on my lust list), I didn't want a cruiser to tool around in—I craved a little screamer I could stomp on and wind out. The beauty of the roadster is its purity of purpose, its consummate impracticality. It's the piccolo in the orchestra, the tweezers on the Swiss Army knife, the Buzzcocks who play nothing but 200-beat-per-minute power punk but do it perfectly.

To those of us who got our drivers licenses in the '60s and '70s, "roadster" meant "European roaster," which meant, basically, "crap." You had your choice of British crap (Triumph, MG, Austin-Healey, Jaguar, and some oddball marques like Jensen-Healey, Sunbeam, and TVR) or Italian crap (Fiat), but you were in serious denial if you didn't understand that these were failure-prone rattletraps that would rust visibly if you increased the moisture content by sneezing in the car. Hell, a good sneeze could short something out and cause an electrical fire.

Yeah, I know—this is a cheap laugh line directed at cars that nowadays are beloved classics with hard-core enthusiast followings. However, particularly with British cars, I am to be excused for my insolence. Firstly, recall that I owned a Triumph GT6+ which, when just three years old, was rusting so badly its rear subframe mount broke loose, changing its handling characteristics from merely passively hazardous to actively homicidal, and subjected me to electrical maladies that validated every Lucas joke ever told. So, yeah, I have the street cred to dispense the diss.

Second, just as I started my search for a budget roadster, I had an experience that pointed up the dated nature of beloved British marques. In 1990, journalists at IMPA Test Day were all abuzz when Mazda brought the recently introduced Miata. Coincidentally, a company called British Motor Heritage, which sold a variety of British Leyland restoration parts including entire body shells and replacement panels for MGs and Triumphs that they fabricated using the original press dies and assembly jigs, brought an MG that they'd built using their panels and parts—essentially a 1990-issued 1973 MGB. It was no surprise that everyone loved the Miata, and that, in acceleration, handling, braking, ride quality, comfort, indeed in every category except the ineffable qualities of breeding and heritage, it kicked the MG's ass nine ways from Sunday. That was to be expected. No, the surprise was that *every* car out there, even the recent little suckling Hyundais, pretty well kicked the MG's ass.

(A newly remodeled Alfa Spider was there at IMPA Test Day too, but I don't think I drove it. It didn't generate a lot of attention. It was more of a curiosity, an anachronism, like the aged actress on a late-night talk show who you're almost embarrassed to watch because her facelift is so obvious, or a once audacious rock star who hadn't had the good sense to die young. Oh, is this thing still around?)

While the red MGB was gorgeous, a legitimate object of automotive desire (there's nothing like sitting in a Brit behind a row of Smiths gauges), progress is a bitch. You have to love an old car—*any* old car— to own it, and British cars are particular problem children. Nowadays, these are beloved classics, but in 1990 they were just interesting 15- to 20-year-old horrifically rust-prone cars with a litany of known mechanical and electrical deficiencies, and even if you wanted one, it was challenging to find one that wasn't a Fred Flintstone mobile.

In addition to these rust problems, you have to remember that the EPA and DOT standards enacted in the mid-'70s (the big bumpers that came in in 1974 and the catalytic converters and use of unleaded gas that started in 1975) wreaked havoc with *all* cars. These requirements for performance and appearance changes basically destroyed British and most Italian roadsters in the American market; the Brits and Fiat didn't survive long enough here to see light at the end of the tunnel. As I said earlier, a good rule of thumb is to buy before 1974 or after about 1982, but by that time, MG, Triumph, Austin-Healey, and Fiat were gone from our shores. Jaguar survived, if you call what happened to Jaguar survival.

There were, of course, German cars. VW Beetles and Karmann Ghias were both available as ragtops with sticks, but these weren't what I was looking for. (This broaches the delicate subject of the dividing line between legitimate automotive objects of desire versus cute cars no self-respecting car guy would want to be seen in.) Mercedes 230, 250, and 280SL roadsters are timeless and classy, and can be found with a rare 4-speed stick (there's even an ultra-rare 5-speed), but they were never cheap. Later 8-cylinder Mercedes SLs like the 380 and 450 can be found cheaply now, but they're all automatics, and were still very pricey back in 1990.

During my budget roadster search, Porsche 356s were not on my radar. Personally, I've never found the lines of a 356 to be particularly lust-producing. Compared to the flawless shape of the 911, the 356 is like watching Woody Allen's *Love and Death* when you've already seen the far-superior *Annie Hall*. If memory serves me correctly, 356s were pretty affordable in 1990. File that under "if I knew then what I know now."

Porsche 911s and 914s were available with a Targa top that gave you an open motoring experience nearly equal to that of a convertible, but you could never get into a 911 that still had even half its sheet metal for a few grand, either in 1990 or now. 914s were (and to some extent still are) cheap, and definitely have their appeal, but their bodies were Karmann-built. Remember your mandatory automotive joke *Karmann invented rust, then licensed the process to the Italians?* It's not just for laughs; it's to keep you out of trouble.

But (speaking of Italians) although Fiat vanished from America in 1981, Alfa survived through 1994. And understandably so. Although Alfas had the same rust issues as any other ungalvanized car, the Alfa Spider was simply too cool to go gently into that good night. It was a low, narrow, snappy Pininfarina-designed two-seater that looked like nothing else on the road, oozed Italian panache, and emitted an absolutely addictive double overhead cam timing chain raspy howl when you nailed it. The phrase "ahead of its time" is hyperbolic, but unless you wanted to pay big bucks for something with a prancing horse on its hood, there was little else you could buy in 1969 that had an aluminum double overhead cam engine, fuel injection, a 5-speed gearbox, and four-wheel disc brakes.

Spiders went through four body styles, three engine sizes, and three intake systems. The Series 1 cars built '66 through '69 featured a unique teardrop-shaped tail whose contours were similar to its nose; these are colloquially referred to as "boat-tailed" or "round-tailed" Spiders. The first of these Series 1 cars were commonly called Duettos but officially named "Spider 1600s" (not to be confused with the Guilia Spider 1600 — the predecessor and a completely different body style). In 1967 the engine size was increased and the car was designated a 1750 Spider Veloce. Regardless of the name, you know a Series 1 car instantly when you see it. That silhouette — where both the rounded nose and the rounded tail slope down — looks like nothing else (well, it *does* look like something; the Italian nickname for the car is "Osso di Sepia" — cuttlefish bone). In an absolutely perfect product placement before product placement was coined as a term, Dustin Hoffman wound out a Duetto within an inch of its life in the 1967 movie *The Graduate*. It made every guy want to own a car he could wring out like that, *waaaaaaaaaaa WAAAHHHHHH*, to drive with such passion, such brio, such urgency, as if his whole life depended on it. And if he needed to use it to rescue Katharine Ross from a future with the wrong guy, so much the better.

In 1969 Alfa ditched the carburetors on Spiders destined for the American market and outfitted them with a SPICA mechanical fuel injection system adapted from a diesel truck engine. Not unlike the Kugelfischer system in a BMW 2002tii, the SPICA system provided such precise metering of fuel that, at least for a while, Alfa got away with very few additional emission controls on the car. Also not unlike the tii, some percentage of owners became impatient with the SPICA fuel injection and ripped it out and replaced it with carbs. Folks who own these cars now would doubtless like to find the original owners responsible for that ill-fated decision, beat the crap out of them, and re-install the SPICA components, as the value of cars whose fuel injection is intact is now considerably higher.

The Series 2 Spider appeared in 1970 and had a twelve-year run. The redesign lopped off the unique rounded tail, incorporating instead a "Kamm tail" common in automotive aerodynamics (just look at the back end of a Prius). The 5-mph bumpers came in in '74, cats in '75, predictably resulting in a performance drop and drivability issues. Alfa stuck with the SPICA system until 1982, when they replaced it with the same electronic Bosch L-Jetronic fuel injection system being success-fully used on many other European cars.

The Series 3 Spider debuted in 1983—a year after the L-Jet conver-sion—and featured better-integrated bumpers but also boy-racer accou-trements such as an air dam under the chin and a pert little upturned trunk spoiler commonly called a "duck tail." A Quadrifoglio version added side skirts, a removable hard top, and phone-dial wheels.

Much was made of Pininfarina's redesigned Series 4 cars pro-duced 1990 through 1993 that jettisoned the jagged, boy-racer spoil-ers of the Series 3, keyed the bumpers to the body color, and gave the car a smoother, more uniform look. This was the car that was at IMPA Test Day in 1990. I think that, to non-Alfisti, the Series 1 looks like the period-correct rolling sculpture that it is, the Series 2 and 3 look like two slightly different versions of the same car, and the Series 4 looks like the nose of something you're supposed to recog-nize as a Spider grafted onto the body of a different car, like the sort of heritage-based design that resulted in the 2002 Ford Thunderbird. With any of these classics that had long production runs during which they kept tweaking the body, be it the Datsun 240Z, the Porsche 911, or the Spider, it's difficult to credibly argue that they didn't nail the bullseye with the first arrow. As Robert Frost said—midsummer is to spring as one to ten.

In total, Spiders were produced for an incredible 28 years. A long production run tends to carry with it the advantage of a ready supply of parts. This is less of an issue in our modern big web-enabled world, but in 1990, you had to rely on newsletters and ads in *Hemmings Motor News*. The pre-web world was not an easy time to own a short-run or rarely imported car like, say, a Datsun 1600.

Original or restored round-tail Spiders have been big-time collectible for quite some time. Clean S2 cars with the SPICA injection intact have become more difficult to find. None of the Spiders had a galvanized body, but the Series 3 and 4 cars seemed to have the benefit of better steel, drainage, and undercoating. They are certainly not immune to rust, but they don't go away as quickly as the S1 and S2 cars.

In 1990, the S3 cars represented the vertex on the parabola—too new to be collectible, but old enough to be affordable. So, I took the plunge and bought an '84 Spider Veloce with 42,000 miles. It was new enough to have Bosch L-Jet and electronic ignition and be nearly rust-free. It was, however, a very risky purchase. The car had oil in the radiator and antifreeze in the oil—a clear sign of a blown head gasket. The clutch was slipping so badly that the car had trouble getting up hills. And, at the end of the test drive, the oil pressure light flickered. The owner said, "Oh, is it low on oil *again*?" I was horrified. An oil pressure gauge is *not* an oil level sensor; the fact that he treated it as such was a clear red flag. But it was so cheap I took the risk.

I pulled the head and changed the head gasket. As I waded into the Alfa enthusiast community and read newsletters, I learned this was par for the course with the two-liter engines (everyone say it together—*they all do that)*. Bad head gaskets at 42,000 miles. Incredible. This did not bode well for the idea of a "reliable" Alfa.

But after I replaced the head gasket and the clutch, not a lot else went wrong with it. The Bosch L-Jetronic injection was not as interesting or exciting or exotic as a SPICA system would've been, but it just simply worked. The car's seating position was unique—with the seat positioned so your knee was slightly bent when your foot was on the accelerator, your arms were out straight with your elbows locked. *Very* Italian. And the position of the transmission and shift platform was so far forward that the shift lever wasn't on the transmission tunnel as on nearly every other rear-wheel-drive car; instead, it practically went through the dashboard—it stuck out about where the radio is in the center of the console on most cars. And, like its Duetto progenitor, my S3 made incredibly satisfying boy-racer raspy Italian overhead cam timing chain noises when I wound it out. With the seating position, the shift lever, the timing chain rasp and exhaust note, I could think … hang on, Katharine, I'm coming!

It was a fabulous car. It wasn't close to nastyfast, but it was the real Italian thing. Once, when I shifted it into third, I somehow trapped the radio's power wire between the shift lever and the body of the car, raising a burst of acrid smoke and nearly starting an electrical fire, but, hey, it's Italian—you have to expect *some* drama.

I drove the Alfa for two years, then sold it along with a few other cars when we started house-hunting and I needed to scare up a down payment. (I also put out to pasture a largely rust-free but beat-up 3.0CSi that I was deciding what to do with, and a Vanagon camper that I owned just long enough to take one road trip in with the band and camp out in once with my kids in our driveway.)

The history of the Alfa Spider and the Miata are intertwined in ways more global than my trip to IMPA Test Day. There's little doubt that the Miata's introduction in 1990 sucked a lot of the oxygen out of the room and doomed the Spider. It's incredibly ironic to me that the thrice-facelifted yet authentically Italian S4 Spider was upstaged by the Miata, when the Miata's basic design is itself patterned after a (British!) Lotus Elan, right down to its little mouth below the bumper line. Why buy the Italian roadster with the bad reputation when you can have a Japanese-reliable version of a British roadster? Why go to Italy when you can experience it at the Italian pavilion at Disney World? But, with time and distance, the Alfa Spider has achieved classic status. We'll see if the Miata is elevated to that pantheon, or if it is regarded no differently than a Toyota Corolla.

Eventually I would scratch the roadster itch in several other ways. I drove a BMW E30 four-seat convertible for a while. I had a long-term relationship with an '82 Porsche 911SC with a removable Targa top. And my two-seater BMW Z3 M Coupe, while not a drop-top, offers a similar purity of purpose. But only the Alfa was a true roadster, and only the Alfa made me want to wear a linen shirt and smoke stubby little cigarillos and pretend I was descending the winding road on the Amalfi coast into Positano with a leggy woman in the passenger seat wearing a white dress, the wind blowing it dangerously high up over her knees.

Fast-forward 20 years, and, ironically, if you tell me you have a few grand to blow on a budget roadster and ask me for my advice, I'd say … buy a Miata. That is the responsible advice to give. Unless of course you want something else. My friend Alex has a serious jones for a Datsun 1600 roadster. I know a guy who craves a Jensen-Healey roadster more than any other physical object on this planet. They're called passions because you *know* they don't make a lot of sense and you *don't* want someone to talk you out of them, thank you very much.

There's a well-known joke that Fiat stands for "Fix It Again, Tony." But in the enthusiast community, Alfa stands for "Always Looking For Another." I've occasionally looked for an affordable fixer-upper rust-free Duetto (yeah, right), but have not re-Alfa'd.

Why do men love cars? For the love of god, beg borrow or steal something Italian and *drive* it. *Hard*. Maybe you'll hear the aria. If you don't, that's cool. But you're poorer for not having had the experience, like missing the moose as it lumbers across the stream at dusk, or the hummingbirds that dart just outside your range of perception.

CHAPTER 22

SIEGEL'S SEVEN-CAR RULE

I've long said that a car nut needs three cars. There's mom's family hauler, there's dad's daily driver, there's the convertible for sunny days, there's the massively oversized four-wheel-drive beach / snow attack vehicle that can also tow a trailer, there's the track car with stiff suspension, and there's the pampered classic. And there's whatever the current project car happens to be. Oh, wait—that's seven cars.

For years, this has been a running joke with anyone who knows me. I've become an expert at making the indefensible sound downright rational. After all, I'm not a rich collector like Jay Leno or Jerry Seinfeld—I'm just a guy, with a family and an engineering job, who happens to be into cars. I've even been chatting with car guys at events and had them drag me over and introduce me to their long-suffering spouses and say, "Here's Rob. This is the guy I told you about—*the one who's much worse than I am.*" Well, if I can't be a role model, at least I can be a perfect example of wretched excess and utter lack of self-control.

Obviously most folks don't have seven cars. Some cars, in fact, do a nice job of converting, like a Swiss Army knife, to fill more than one role. For many families, an SUV performs dual roles as family-and-stuff-hauler and poor weather vehicle. And for many enthusiasts, a "sports sedan" is appealing precisely because it is, in theory, both a daily driver and a car with sports-car-like reflexes. BMWs, especially M3s, perform the dual role of daily driver and track car exceptionally well. So that compacts four vehicles into two. And, if you have sufficient space and money to support a third car, often the convertible and the pampered classic and the project car are in fact the same physical entity. That's three into one. So if you have a BMW, an SUV or crossover, and some miserable little British roadster, you're all set, right?

What the hell kind of fun is that? Maybe I don't like Swiss Army knives. Maybe I want a hatchet *and* a sushi knife *and* a jeweler's screwdriver *and* a pair of nail clippers.

If you're a non-car-person, you must first understand the concept of a "daily driver." Simply put, it's the car you drive every day. Non-car-people at this point are perplexed, mumbling something like, "Soooooo ... the 'daily driver'... it's like, uh, *your car*? Duh." No, really, to a car person, a lot of thought goes into choosing the car you drive every day. It's like selecting a religion. And, whenever the phrase "daily driver" is thrown around, it essentially implies that there's another enthusiast car in the wings somewhere, sort of like how "mistress" implies "wife," except that the degrees of passion are reversed.

I think I'd best back out of this particular analogy before more than just sheet metal gets bent.

The idea is that, if you're into cars, you may own a car you absolutely adore. Maybe it's new and you want to keep it that way. Maybe it's old but in great shape. Maybe it's neither but you've had it for many years and it's part of you. Should you drive it every day? Doing so subjects it to the elements, puts a lot of wear and tear on the car, and exposes it to the statistical likelihood of damage. Also, if it's old, or it's a convertible, or it's really small, or it doesn't have air-conditioning, you might not want to or be able to use it to commute to work or ferry the family around on a regular basis.

Old cars may have their charm and style, but they typically don't hold a candle to even the cheapest new car in terms of things like heat and a/c, ventilation, and not having wind noise and water leaks at highway speeds. Not to mention safety. So at some point you buy something new, or at least new-ish, and use that car as a "daily driver," leaving your baby for evening excursions and weekend jaunts. By doing that, you've staked out a nontrivial financial position in the money tied up in both your daily driver and your enthusiast car (that you no longer drive every day), and the insurance for both, and the garage space for at least one. Add your spouse and her wheels, and poof, you're talking about three cars. Not cheap.

With that as background, for many years the magic number for me seemed to be four. I had my daily driver, Maire Anne had the family hauler, there was the 3.0CSi, and there always seemed to be some other project car lurking about.

Now, understand that while I earn a good living as an engineer, we all make choices on how we spend money. Maire Anne and I have *never* owned a new car. For 27 years I had a five-mile commute, meaning I could drive to work in just about anything, and as such, my daily drivers have been interesting high-mileage BMWs that veer across the line into being "project cars" themselves. I could've afforded the monthly payment on one new BMW, but that's something I never even considered; I've always preferred having three or four old ones. I buy a fair number of parts to keep the cars running, but, averaged over time, the cost doesn't come close to a pair of monthly car payments. And the insurance costs on older cars are quite a bit less as well. Our collective goal has been to have at least one car new enough and reliable enough that I don't have to work on it. Until of course I do.

When the body restoration was complete on the 3.0CSi in 1988, I had to keep it out of the elements. The unintended consequence of this was that it usurped Bertha's (my 2002) space in the garage at my mother's house, where we were living at the time. I realized that if I left Bertha exposed through the salty Boston winter it would kill her, so I decided to sell her ("If you love something … let it go"). I had previously loaned Bertha to my friend Alex and his wife Heidi for their honeymoon. Alex loved the car. I gave him right of first refusal, and he snatched her up.

Our first child, Ethan, was born in 1988—which coincides with the dates on many of the receipts I still have for the body restoration on the coupe. I chalk this timing up to a sense of urgency on my part ("If I don't do this *right now*, it'll never get done"), as well as to my rising income as an engineer and Maire Anne's consummate reasonability.

When our second child, Kyle, was born in 1990, we maxed out the space in the third floor apartment at my mother's house. In 1992, as we started thinking about having a third child, we finally began seriously house-hunting. We looked primarily in Newton, which is close to Boston and has great schools. But the houses in Newton are on postage-stamp-sized lots—certainly not a town where you'll buy something with a back 40 on which to build a big garage.

Our Realtor kept repeating the timeworn aphorism, "When you see the right one, you'll know," a concept that is reinforced in print and television ads. You know the ones—impossibly attractive young couple, wife hanging on husband's arm, walk into some ridiculously well-lit front hallway with a thousand square feet of glass looking out onto rolling hills. She tosses him a knowing "this is the one" glance that implicitly promises him 20 years of uninterrupted sex if they buy it. What a bunch of bull. You look at houses in the price range that the mortgage company will qualify you for. That's what you can afford. The *oh my God, look at this kitchen! Look at this yard! This is so much better than everything else we've seen! Let's buy this on the spot!* house is not going to be an outlier in your price range; it is going to be in a higher price range. Expecting something like this to happen is about as likely as finding a running rattle-free rust-free 3.0CS from Saudi Arabia with a tan leather interior and working air-conditioning for $4,800.

Okay, perhaps that's not the best analogy.

The point is that, unless you have an unlimited budget, it's all compromise. Obviously we had minimum requirements for number of bedrooms and some sort of yard. But then there was the "highly desired but not strictly required" list. Maire Anne wanted a decent kitchen and I wanted a decent garage. It all hinged on the word "decent." A good working definition of "decent kitchen" turned out to be "I can prepare meals for my family in here without the physical surroundings making me acutely ill." "Decent garage" became "I don't think hail can get through these holes in the roof." I'm sure that, between the appointments, the open houses, and the drive-bys, we easily looked at a hundred houses. Nothing came even close to ringing the "you'll know it" bell.

Then, one evening as Maire Anne and I were methodically performing a postmortem, she said, "Do you remember that brown house on Mague Place?"

"Not really."

"It had awful wallpaper, not enough light, and it stank of cigarettes."

"Nope."

"Maybe we should have another look at it. It did have three bedrooms, a walk-up attic, and a nice yard that backed onto a park."

"Why did we rule it out?"

"I rejected it because of the kitchen."

"Why? What was wrong with the kitchen?"

"You're kidding me. How could you not remember the kitchen? It's had aqua tiles from floor to ceiling and maroon wainscoting."

"Sorry. Did it have a garage?"

"Let me see … I think it was corrugated metal …"

"OH GOD NOT THAT PLACE YOU CAN'T BE SERIOUS."

The garage was a tiny World War II-era corrugated metal structure. It was rusting. It was leaning to one side. It was a garage only in the broadest sense of the term ("Garage? I suppose … check"). And, yes, the kitchen did have plastic aqua tiles from floor to ceiling. It was like eating in a swimming pool. With maroon wainscoting. And a wrought iron lighting fixture that looked like some high school shop student's version of something that had blown off the Atlas sculpture in Rockefeller Center.

So, with kitchen and garage dreams put equally on hold, we made an offer. Compromise. The nature of politics. The stuff of life. We bought the house. It is where we still live. I love our house. I hope we die in this house. (Well, I don't really *hope* we actually *die in the house*, but you get the idea.)

But the reality of Maire Anne having to live with the kitchen, and me having to live with the garage proved more challenging than we expected.

CHAPTER 23

DISCOVERING CLASSIC CAR INSURANCE

The minute we signed the papers on our first home, we pounced with fervor. The ink wasn't even dry before we ripped out the cigarette-reeking rugs. The seven layers of wallpaper we found on the walls of most of the rooms, however, took several years to steam off one square foot at a time.

I remained in touch with Alex. After all, we were both BMW guys with a penchant for wading into hair-brained projects (and I still had visitation rights to Bertha). Not long after Alex's wedding, he left the BMW parts business to become a general building contractor. Honest, hard working, and incredibly creative, Alex is one of those people blessed with an architect's right brain and a can-do attitude that sees all things as possible. He can walk into a space and say, "Well, we can move this wall over *here*, and put up a new wall over *there*."

But, as evidenced by the "I'll resurrect a flood car" episode, even insanely productive people have limits. After Alex bought his house in Brighton, he decided that the addition the previous owner had built on the house was "wrong" and ripped the addition down. I drove over there on my birthday, in my freshly repainted 3.0CSi, to convince Alex to run away with me for the day and ride roller coasters at Riverside Park. I found him standing in the ruins of what had been half his house, with this overwhelmed *oh god what have I done* look on his face. I'm not sure why I'm so attracted to human imperfection, but it was a moment I never forgot. Soon after, I and some other friends helped him raise the post-and-beam frame for the new addition. I even banged in a few of the pins myself.

When our third son, Aaron, was born in 1993, Ethan and Kyle were sharing a room, but we soon began planning how to maximize the space inside the house. We had Alex turn the walk-up attic into a master bedroom suite for Maire Anne and me. This freed up a bedroom for the boys. Alex also designed and constructed the kitchen addition Maire Anne always wanted. The place became quite comfortable. But the garage was still a disaster.

The cars came and went. Maire Anne occasionally drove my BMW 2002s, but loading a toddler in and out of a child seat in the back of a two-door got really old really quickly. Her VW camper had accompanied us when we moved back to Boston, and she had continued driving it after the kids were born, but New England winters were starting to rust it. And like any VW bus, it had a surplus of karma and a deficit of power, making it harrowing to drive among Boston's aggressive drivers who are always in a hurry. I wish I could've held onto the old girl and kept her out of harm's way. These old VW buses, particularly the campers, have become quite collectible. I have great warm thoughts whenever I see one ("warm," of course, being more descriptive of feelings than actual heat output).

After the camper came six Vanagons (built 1980 through 1991). The successor to the original VW bus, Vanagons are larger, faster, better in just about every way, but perhaps less amenable to "Idiot Manual" writer John Muir's Zen-like approach to care and repair. Both Maire Anne and I really liked Vanagons—they are far larger than any other "minivan" and swallowed band equipment when we had gigs—but they were also fairly high-maintenance vehicles. As the years passed, Maire Anne's cars got newer and somewhat more conventional. We owned a Volvo 245 turbo wagon for a while, which I sold when I learned how expensive the turbo was to replace and how fortunate we were it was still running. For a long stretch we had a Toyota Previa, the last year they were made with a 5-speed transmission (Maire Anne prefers driving a stick, bless her).

Eventually we bought a fairly conventional two-year-old Mazda MPV minivan, which negated everything you've heard about Japanese design and reliability by going through three alternators in three years. On these cars the alternator is mounted so low in the engine compartment you have to pull out either the exhaust manifold or the entire right front axle assembly in order to get at it. This was one of the most miserable repairs I've ever performed, on *any* car—so bad that, when the replacement alternator died, I (gasp) paid someone else to put in the third one. *Inconceivable!*

Also coming and going was a succession of Chevy Suburbans. Maire Anne and I have rented a place on Nantucket every summer for 20 years (for years I told the kids, "I'm spending your college education money," and they thought I was joking). You need a four-wheel-drive vehicle to negotiate the six miles of sand out to the tip of Great Point where I like to go fishing. Plus we needed a truck that big to haul the kids, extended family, bikes, boogie boards, guitars, fishing rods, and later the windsurfer and surfboard. Renting a big SUV was expensive, and it seemed to make little sense for us to own a new one when neither of us wanted an SUV as a daily driver.

So, for many years, I'd buy a cheap Suburban in the spring, attend to its needs, use it for vacation, and then sell it in the fall. I preferred the big, truck-like pre-1992 'Burbs with a bench seat across the front and seat belts for nine people. I especially liked the non-Silverado versions with no carpet (the smell of bluefish is hard to get out of a rug). I could go on vacation with my family of five and my brother-in-law's family of four and have all of us pile in, belt up, and drive out on the sand to go fishing. When I finally found a rust-free 'Burb that was a steal, I held onto it for seven years, but I only registered it during the summer.

If I may digress, I suppose it's understandable that, while gas was cheap, many families thought that SUVs had the right balance of features. We were just never one of those families. I've always thought that, unless you live in a climate where there's so much snow, and on such an unpaved boulder-strewn road that four-wheel drive and high ground clearance are true necessities, the minivan is a better compromise. It's a lighter vehicle, so its fuel economy is better, and the layout with the flat floor makes it much easier to put in a third row of seats. Only the largest SUVs have a third row of seats, and now you're driving 6,000 pounds.

Of course, the size and weight of full-sized SUVs were marketed as a safety factor, in particular toward women, who were manipulated into feeling that they and their children "just weren't safe" unless they were driving a three-ton vehicle. With a wink and a nod, the message was, "You and I both know that in a full-sized SUV you're bigger than anyone else; you'll crush them before they crush you." I strongly object to this perversion of safety. In fact, I'll go further: I think it's unethical to market and sell (and, perhaps, to buy) a vehicle if the intent is for your increased safety to come at the expense of someone else.

And then there is the misconception of how much safety four-wheel drive actually buys you. Many folks living in New England will tell you that, when it's snowy, SUVs are the cars you're most likely to see spun off into the median strip. You know why? Because most people driving pickup trucks do not confuse them with sports cars, whereas many people driving SUVs seem to think these top-heavy vehicles that do not handle particularly well in the dry suddenly trans-form into freaking Lamborghinis when it is slick out.

My daily drivers were a succession of high-mileage BMW 3 and 5 Series cars, which I bought needing work, fixed, and sold when I found I could buy something nicer for incrementally more money. Actually, with both my cars and Maire Anne's, the event that triggered a turnover often involved examining the underside of the car. Over time, more and more cars are being built with galvanized bodies and have under-sides that have been undercoated and covered with plastic panels. This makes the bodies far more immune to rust. However, the exhaust, the brake lines, and the myriad of clamps are all still subject to corrosion. It's not unusual for me to look under one of our cars, see the exhaust in an obviously compromised state, look up the cost of replacing the exhaust, find that it's a dealer-only item (no inexpensive aftermarket substitute available), and decide that it's time for the car to go.

Around the time that the underside of my all-wheel-drive BMW 325iX got scary, I developed a serious hankering for a convertible. This pole reversal (all-wheel-drive winter car to convertible summer car, yang to yin) had a lot of appeal. Because of the de-facto limits imposed by insurance and lack of garage space, I told myself I could buy a convertible if and only if it was my daily driver, and that meant a *real* daily driver—a car I would drive through the winter. So I bought a well-used '89 BMW 325i convertible for very little money. Great little car. I'd recommend it to anyone. It lacked the Italian panache and the timing chain rasp of the Alfa, but it did have a full-size back seat so I could use it to drive the three kids to school in the morning on my way to work. With the top down. We all loved it.

True to my promise to myself, I used the convertible as a daily driver, even through the winter. It was miserable. If you *don't* brush all the snow off a ragtop, the snow freezes, thaws, and leaks right through the roof, but you *can't* scrape the snow off because the scraper will rip the top. Plus, on a frigid New England winter day, the heat loss through the cloth roof was so high that if I turned the defroster on full to keep the windshield free of ice, my feet would freeze, but when I tried to direct a little heat to my toes, in a few minutes the windshield would ice up. There's not really a great answer to either of these problems other than not driving it in the winter (i.e., *what were you thinking using a convertible as a daily driver?*) or buying and installing one of those removable hardtops, which are pretty expensive. Fundamentally, going back to Siegel's Seven-Car Rule and the Swiss Army knife analogy, this was a silly attempt at combining two blades (daily driver and convertible) into one. Because I didn't have the garage space for it over the winter, after a year, I sold the convertible and went back to daily-driving BMW sedans.

And then an enabling event occurred: I discovered classic car insurance policies. Certain specialty insurance companies such as Hagerty understand that owners of classic or enthusiast cars are excellent insurance risks because they baby their babies—they avoid traffic jams, they don't leave the car parked on the downhill side of the Costco lot where all the shopping carts roll, etc. The catch is that you can't use a car insured in this way to commute to work—that is, you can't both insure a car as a classic and continue to use it as a daily driver. There are other restrictions as well (typically there's an annual mileage limit; the car must be garaged; every driving member of the household must be listed as primary driver on another fully insured car), but if you are ready to give up the show-off rides to work and already own another daily driver, the cost advantage is huge. Initially it was difficult to acclimate to not being able to simply hop into my 1973 3.0CSi and drive her to work, but once I accepted this limitation and began insuring the car under a Hagerty collector insurance policy, I was paying only about $135 annually to insure the car for 14 grand. Yes, you read it right. No, it's not a misprint.

The unintended consequence of insuring the 3.0CSi as a classic was that, by saving all that money, *I felt justified in buying another car*. And that leads us, inexorably, to the story of the frog-faced interloper.

CHAPTER 24

THE FROG-FACED INTERLOPER

THE 1982 PORSCHE 911SC FORCES THE GARAGE ISSUE

The Porsche 911 was born in the 1960s, screaming something not everyone understood. It continued screaming it for 25 years. The perfectly proportioned double teardrop shape, flawlessly uncluttered interior, and unique driving experience have seduced many a motorhead. Designer Ferdinand "Butzi" Porsche is often quoted as having said, "Design must be functional, and functionality must be translated into visual aesthetics, without any reliance on gimmicks that have to be explained." But the beautiful thing is, even if you've never heard that quote, you're imbued with its meaning every time you look at a 911. If you need a translation, the car has been screaming *form follows function.* It's been screaming "I am what I am." The 911 is freaking Popeye. It even ate its spinach and sprouted muscles.

It's not accidental that a 911 resembles a speed-smoothed VW Beetle. The Beetle was designed by Butzi Porsche's grandfather (also named Ferdinand Porsche) and shares the same basic design and layout that incorporates a rear-mounted horizontally opposed air- and oil-cooled engine coupled to a transaxle that combines the functions of a transmission and a differential into a single unit. If you've ever driven a Beetle, a Porsche 911 will feel, sound, and smell surprisingly familiar. There's the same light, responsive steering, with power assist not being necessary because there isn't the weight of an engine sitting over the front wheels. There's the unmistakable "packed" sound of an air-cooled engine behind you. There's the notchy shifter. And there's that *smell,* faintly redolent of oil and exhaust. There's even the same pair of levers between the front seats to release the hounds of heat from the heater boxes.

Of course, people don't drive Beetles the way they drive a 911, and that's a good thing. It's been said that the 911 is a flawed design, flawlessly executed. Some sports cars and many race cars are mid-engined to optimize weight distribution and thus improve handling, but a 911 is *rear-engined*, not *mid-engined*. This means the weight of its motor sits *behind* its rear wheels. Imagine dragging an anchor around a corner. What is the anchor going to do? Swing to the outside and try to yank the car around with it. If you keep your foot on the gas while scooting around a corner in a rear-engined car, the rear tires grip the road as they try to propel the car forward. This grip keeps the back of the car planted. But if you chicken out and lift off the throttle, the weight of the car transfers from the rear to the front, making the rear tires lose their grip, and often causing the car to spin off the curve, ass-end first. This is the so-called *trailing throttle oversteer* that is inherent in rear-engined cars. Ralph Nader wrote about it in *Unsafe at Any Speed*, the book that effectively killed the rear-engined Corvair. Over the years, Porsche lightened the engine and outfitted the 911 with fatter tires and bigger sway bars to mitigate the problem, but it has never completely gone away.

Let's talk about the look of the front of a 911. Human beings tend to anthropomorphize things. We see faces in the fronts of cars. Headlights are eyes. Radiator grilles morph into noses or mouths. But with an air-cooled car, there's no radiator in the front, thus no grille or slots to let air through, thus no nose, and thus the car's "face" is not humanoid (unless you count the nose-less members of the "trade federation" in *Star Wars: Episode I*). There's a reason the officially named "Type 1 VW" is referred to by everyone as the "Beetle" or "Bug"; the lack of a grille gave it a non-human quality and resulted in it being nicknamed after an insect, lack of antennae notwithstanding. Similarly, the Porsche 911's nose lacks, well, a *nose*. I've always thought 911s look slightly amphibian. You have to admit, with those headlights protruding up above the low hood line, stuck at the very ends of the fenders rather than inset into a front panel, it looks more than a little frog-like.

(If I may digress, in the "cars have a face" department, the double kidneys in a BMW's grille evoke not only a nose, but actual nostrils. In the '60s and '70s these were a slender design element, but their width has been increasing alarmingly. Why BMW thinks the "nostrils" should be more and more pronounced is beyond me.)

The branches and leaves on the 911 family tree have been written about exhaustively (see Karl Ludvigsen's *Porsche: Excellence Was*

Expected for a comprehensive history), but for the models built from
1965 through 1989 there is both a mechanical and a stylistic continuity
that is unique among car brands. As an enormously simplified starting point for the casual enthusiast, it's helpful to think of these 911s
as breaking into five subtly different groups (and don't go looking for
these "groups" in any other literature; this is just the way I think about
it). The car that debuted in 1965 doesn't just look like the car sold in
1989; in terms of the chassis code, it *is* essentially the same car. There
are folks who've taken early 911s and grafted on big bumpers, fender
flares, wide wheels, and whale tails to make them look like later cars,
and conversely, people who try to backdate later cars to look like early
ones. This is possible because the body panels, doors, glass, engine,
suspension, and brake parts all interchange.

The first group consists of the earliest 911s, built 1965 through
1968 These are unique in their short wheelbase and 2.0-liter engine. In
'69 the second group followed, whose wheelbase was extended by 2¼
inches to make the car less twitchy at high speeds. The engine displacement was increased to 2.2 liters, then to 2.4 in 1973. All of these small-
bumpered pre-'74 911s have become highly collectible (especially the
higher-performance "S" and "E" versions), but because of their ungalvanized bodies, they rust at the mere suggestion of moisture.

The third group consists of the big-bumpered cars built from 1974
through 1977. U.S. federal 5-mph impact standards affected the 911
in 1974, eliminating the slender but ineffective chrome bumpers and
replacing them with functional but uninspired ones. The rear bumper
is reasonably well integrated into the car's hindquarters, but the front
bumper wraps around from headlight to headlight and gives the car's
face a pretty good-sized lip, further accentuating its frog-like characteristics. Far worse than the bumpers, though, was the incorporation of
a 2.7-liter engine whose magnesium case was warp-prone and whose
studs had a propensity for pulling out. To add insult to injury, Porsche
had to deal with U.S. federally mandated emission controls in 1975,
and they adopted the same thermal reactor technology that BMW did,
with equally catastrophic results—the thermal reactors caused the
already-problematic 2.7-liter engines to run hot. A 50K engine lifetime
was not uncommon. For these reasons, the mid-'70s cars are easily the
least desirable 911s. The one bright spot is that, in mid-1975, Porsche

began using galvanized steel throughout the entire body of the 911, which made it much less rust-prone than the earlier cars.

The fourth group, called the 911SC, debuted in 1978. Extending through 1983, the SC is instantly distinguishable from its predecessors by its flared rear fenders and fatter tires, both of which effectively and dramatically imply motion by evoking the image of an animal crouched on its haunches and ready to spring forward. But, coupled with the car's nose-less nose and high headlights, the haunches only accentuate the amphibian family resemblance. Hey, I say this with love. Nothing else on the road looks like a frog preparing to pounce.

In addition to the changes in appearance, the SC had a new aluminum-cased three-liter engine. Initially, many of these engines suffered timing-chain-related failures, but once you retrofitted oil-fed Carrera timing chain tensioners, and installed a "pop valve" in the airbox to prevent it from blowing up if the car backfired, SCs were simple, straightforward, surprisingly bulletproof cars. Because the SC still has a conventional ignition with a coil and distributor, it is sometimes called "the last of the analog 911s," a term that is a bit misleading because the SC does, in fact, have an electronic control unit (ECU) box that's tied into the car's oxygen sensor.

The SCs were followed by the fifth group, built from 1984 to 1989. These are the 3.2-liter cars that say "Carrera" on the back. Carreras utilized Bosch Motronic fuel injection (L-Jetronic injection with an air flow meter and a computer-controlled load map for spark advance and fuel delivery), resulting in a better balance of power, fuel economy, emissions, and overall drivability than K-Jet. The best of the Carreras are often regarded to be those built '87 through '89, which had a new Getrag G50 transmission that was smoother and less notchy-feeling than the old 915 gearbox, and a hydraulically actuated clutch that replaced the "I can't believe this thing still has a cable" clutch.

From 1967 on, there was a "Targa" version of the 911 with a flat removable roof panel coupled with a large curved rear window and a wide flat roll bar. In his entertaining book *The Gold-Plated Porsche*, author Stephan Wilkinson is merciless on the Targa. He begins with the tendency of Targa tops to leak like a sieve (true), moves on to the increased body twist from the lack of a fixed roof (also true), continues with the way the Targa top destroyed the 911's classic shape (a matter of debate), and concludes with the questionable taste, intelligence, and moral attributes of Targa buyers (bite me, Steve). Personally I think Targas are a great compromise—they're so much more open than a sunroof, and give nearly the experience of a full convertible without the hassle of a full-sized fabric top.

The SCs and Carreras were available with an aerodynamics package that included a small chin spoiler and a monstrously large trunk-mounted rear spoiler to help keep both the nose and tail planted at high speed. While there are distinctions between "turbo tails," "tea tray tails" and "Carrera tails," most folks call them all "whale tails," as all of them are truly bodacious appendages that look like the last piece you see of a cetacean's anatomy when it dives.

The big bumpers notwithstanding, the 911 not only survived the mid-model "freshenings" that killed so many other cars (just look at the poor Datsun 240Z)—it thrived. While the girl-in-braces-prettiness of the early chrome-bumpered cars is unmistakable, for most men it's the wide fenders, fat rubber, and big tail of the later cars that produce genuine mature lust. The way the 911 managed the trick of looking the same for over 25 years while simultaneously maturing in this gorgeously seductive manner—like a woman aging from 16 to 41 and becoming even more desirable—is possibly unique in the automotive realm.

There's an odd unintended consequence that comes from not changing a car's body for 25 years: Because the real estate remained finite while the needs placed on it kept growing, there is stuff crammed in every crevice. There's an oil thermostat up under the right rear fender. The a/c dryer is up under the left front fender. There are a myriad of little control modules stuffed wherever they would fit.

If you wish to include "Porsches that like look like a 911 and still have an air-cooled engine but technically are different cars," add the "964" and "993" chassis code cars. The 964s were built from 1989 through 1994. If you're not a Porsche person and you see a 964 drive past, you'd think it's the same car as a Carrera, but about 85 percent of the parts are different. These cars are badged as "Carrera 2" and "Carrera 4" denoting the two-wheel- and all-wheel-drive versions. Engine displacement increased to 3.6 liters, conventional coil springs replaced the rear torsion bars, the car was outfitted with power steering and ABS, and the byzantine system of sliders controlling the heat and a/c was finally jettisoned and replaced with a modern climate control system.

The 993, built between 1993 and 1998, is the last of the air-cooled 911s. The 993's hindquarters are similar to the earlier cars, but the nose is markedly different, with the bumper being an integral part of the nose rather than simply protruding from it, and the headlights being a bit less frog-eyed. The big design difference is the addition of a multi-link rear suspension to help deal with the persistent trailing oversteer problem. As with anything that is the last of something desirable, 993s have held their value incredibly well.

I learned all this because I've always wanted a 911, and in the fall of 2003, with my 3.0CSi safely ensconced as a Hagerty car, I decided to scratch a lifelong itch and go looking for one. While I lusted for a small-bumpered pre-'73, I couldn't afford it and had nowhere to garage it even if I could, as my 3.0CSi was occupying my sole garage space. So I set a ten-grand budget and began looking for a 911SC, preferably a Targa, likely in need of work. I looked at several, but in that price range it seemed there were only beat Euro cars with no air-conditioning.

Then I saw an ad for a 1982 911SC Targa with a whale tail. The color was listed as Rosewood. *Rosewood*? What the hell color is *Rosewood*? I learned it was some sort of metallic brown with a love-it-or-hate-it reputation. A guy up in Swampscott, north of Boston, had the car. Imminent divorce was forcing a sale in the middle of the winter. He said the car was unregistered and uninsured, so it could only be driven very short distances. I drove up to check it out in the middle of a snowstorm. The guy opened the garage door, and I couldn't even see the car—an apartment's worth of furniture sat between it and the door. We stepped over and around the furniture to reach the car.

Though the car was under a cover, any car guy would've immediately recognized it as a 911 with a tail. You have to love a shape so distinctive you can tell what it is *under a cover.* The owner unveiled it, and I fell instantly in love. I should've known. Maire Anne will tell you that I went through my "brown phase" in college. It was all I ever wore. *Rosewood* isn't for everyone, but it had me written all over it.

And the *tail.* I thought tails were ostentatious *look at me*

appendages for boy racers and hedge fund managers. I thought tails
were useful only to slap the face of "Butzi" Porsche's statement about
good design not including gimmicks you need to explain. But combined with the Targa top, and set off against the *Rosewood* paint, I
thought … I *love* this tail! I can't fully explain how I can go ga-ga over
both the pure double-teardrop shape of a 911 coupe *and* one adorned
with the "gimmicks" of *both* a Targa top and a tail, but, hey, sometimes
we have pockets of untapped lust just waiting to erupt if they're drilled
into. Sometimes we surprise ourselves.

   "Self," I said, "you are either going to buy this car, or you are going to shut the fuck up about how you've always wanted a 911."

   I checked it out as best as I could. It had only a few small oil
drops beneath it. It started right up, sounded great, didn't smoke,
and appeared to have only one quarter-sized rust hole, on the right
door. Though the car was very well-priced, there was an unacceptable
amount of risk in buying it without a test drive. But it was snowing,
and the guy didn't want it driven in the snow for fear of cracking up
an uninsured car. And even if it wasn't snowing, a ton of furniture
needed to be moved before the car could reach the garage door.

   So I did something I've never done before or since. I negotiated a
$100 nonrefundable deposit for him to hold the car for two weeks to
allow for me to test-drive it, meaning both for him to remove the furniture impeding its exit, and for the weather to clear so it could be driven.

   Both of these things happened. Maire Anne and I returned a week
later and I drove the SC twice around the block. I took a deep breath,
handed him a check for just under ten grand, slapped a plate on it
(back when I used to do that sort of thing), and started to drive it the
25 miles home.

   So, there I was, illegally driving an unfamiliar 911SC home in the
dead of February, trying to attract as little attention as possible, as if a
Porsche 911 with a whale tail doesn't attract attention. It wasn't snowing, but it was brutally cold. I started monkeying with the sliders and
heater levers whose functions are only understandable if you read the
manual several times and crawl inside the designers' German head-
space. I felt only the most vague suggestion of heat.

   Then I nudged one slider and the car started howling like a stuck
pig. *SCCCCCRRRREEEEEEEEEEEEEEEEEEEEEEEEEeeeeeeeeee*. I was

driving through the Ted Williams Tunnel, which has a low speed limit and video monitoring. The combination of the tile walls of the tunnel and the thin fabric roof of the 911's Targa top magnified the squeal. I thought the car was possessed. It was so loud, and I was so paranoid, that I expected a roadblock at the end. Of course, no such thing happened. The squeal was caused by me moving the slider that switched on the blower motor, which was what was needed to push the air from the heater boxes, but, unfortunately, the blower motor was seizing. It was the first of many small things that needed to be sorted out.

As spring came around, I became more and more comfortable with the 911 and began to push it around entrance ramps. Interestingly, for everything you read about the 911's trailing throttle oversteer issues, that's not the dominant handling characteristic you experience during spirited cornering. It's the centering force. The front struts on a 911 have a lot of caster, which is like rake on a motorcycle. The effect of this is that, the harder and faster you turn into a corner, the more the steering wheel fights you. You wind up gripping the wheel. Hard. Remember, this car has no power-assisted steering. Cornering hard requires real effort. The term "white knuckles" comes from the restriction of blood flow due to hard grip, and that's exactly what's going on. If you're accustomed to BMWs that you can drive hard while holding the steering wheel with two fingers, as you would a pair of tweezers, this is a completely unfamiliar feeling. It becomes instantly addictive. Nothing else feels like this.

When my mother first saw the Porsche, and I explained that, despite its ostentatious looks, it cost me less than a five-year-old Honda Civic, she made one of the trademarked breathtakingly level-headed observations that makes her my mother. "So it's frivolous but not irresponsible." I thought, that's perfect. *Frivolous but not irresponsible.* I should have bumper stickers made and place them on every one of my cool cars costing less than ten grand. It's pithier than "You could be driving me—I cost less than a five-year-old Honda Civic."

To keep its engine temperature in check, a 911 relies on multiple oil coolers, which are essentially little radiators. One of these sits on the top right front of the engine. The seals for this and other oil-related components tend to deteriorate and leak. It's not unusual to park a 911 in the fall, make note of its small oil leaks, start it in the spring, and find that a small leak has turned into a gusher from a seal that has further dried and cracked through disuse. Such was the case after my first year of ownership. This required me to undergo that fundamental 911 initiation, the engine drop.

Having pulled VW bus engines, I wasn't at all intimidated. However, there's a difference. On a VW, the sheet metal for the rear cowl unbolts, so you just need to support the engine and roll it away, or roll the car away from it. In contrast, the rear cowl is integral to the 911's body, so the term *engine drop* is literal; you have to jack the back of the car up high enough that the top of the engine will clear it when the engine is lowered. This turns out to require putting jack stands at a two-foot height under the rear torsion tube covers to get roughly three feet of height under the lowest point of the body at the rear of the car. Every auto repair manual that describes jacking up a car says, "Once it's on jack stands, push the car and be certain it doesn't move." I'm here to tell you, with the back of a car nearly three feet up in the air, if you shove it, it moves. When I had to drop the engine again several years later, by that time I had bought the mid-rise scissors lift and a lift table, the pair of which made it so trivially easy and safe to drop the 911's engine that it almost wasn't fair.

I sorted out many minor things and drove the 911SC as often as I could. It was nearly a daily driver. One thing you rarely read about is that the 911 has two little foldable jump seats in the back, so until my kids sprouted gangly adolescent legs, I could squeeze all three of them in and drive them all to school on my way to work. And with the Targa top off, it felt like a fully open car. It was bliss. Reliability-wise, the car was great. It completely lived up to its reputation as a relatively bullet-proof 911.

At this point, the car count was at five—the eternal 1973 3.0CSi, the frog-faced interloper '82 Porsche 911SC, my supposedly-still-the-daily-driver BMW sedan, Maire Anne's daily driver Mazda minivan, and the off-the-road-eleven-months-of-the-year Suburban. Kind of sneaks up on you, doesn't it? From the Seven-Car Rule standpoint, I suppose you could say that in buying the Porsche I was actually trying to be responsible by combining the daily driver, the convertible, and the track car into one, but of course there was no such logic—I just really wanted it.

And then I learned that, in Massachusetts, when a car is 25 years old, it is technically an antique, which is generally a meaningless term except that in Massachusetts unless a car is an "antique" you can't insure it under a collector car policy. So when, in 2007, the '82 Porsche turned 25, it went onto the Hagerty policy along with the 3.0CSi, and the cost of insuring it dropped from about $900 a year to about $125. This meant that I could no longer daily-drive the 911, but my kids' butts were no longer cute or small, so fitting them in the 911's tiny jump seats was less and less appealing for everyone anyway.

So insurance was no longer the thing limiting the number of cars— it was space. And, indeed, I was already running into space problems with the Porsche. Though its modern galvanized body makes it far more resistant to rust than an older car, and though its removable Targa top is sturdier than a ragtop, having a car like that sit outside is far from ideal. I borrowed garage space from a neighbor the first winter I owned it, but the second winter it sat outside and water got in. One frigid day I went to move it, and found that the brake, clutch, and accelerator pedals were immobilized *because they were encased in a block of ice*. Then I remembered that the car's ECU sits beneath the passenger seat. With sickly anticipation I looked, and was horrified to find that the ECU was also encased in ice. I thought, oh man, if I don't garage this 911, I am going to be responsible for its death.

The Great Garage Quest was on.

CHAPTER 25

THE GARAGE GETS BUILT AND ENABLES ALL MY WORST TENDENCIES

Despite the fact that I functioned with the corrugated one-car garage for nearly 15 years, it really was abominable. It had no electricity; I stretched an extension cord from the basement of the house and worked on the cars with the only illumination coming from a single bare bulb. The concrete floor was so cracked that you couldn't roll a mechanic's creeper across it. The corrugated metal radiated heat like an oven in the summer and was beastly cold and drafty in the winter. It did keep the coupe out of the elements, but if another car needed work over the winter, it often had to get done in the driveway. The Rubicon was crossed one February when I had to replace the exhaust on Maire Anne's minivan; I was lying in the driveway in a stream of melt, my insulated mechanic's suit soaked clean through with ice water. This experience along with with seeing the Porsche ECU-under-glass lead to one of those seminal "okay this officially sucks" moments that finally force change.

Let's talk about this for a minute. Why would anyone lie in ice water to replace an exhaust rather than simply taking the car to a repair shop? Well, when you're quoted 1,500 bucks for an exhaust and find the parts online for 400 … the ice water starts looking pretty good. (See why Maire Anne tolerates me? I'm not quite the untethered wing nut I sometimes appear to be.)

As the kids got older, and as college began rapidly approaching like a brick wall on a racetrack in a car with bad brakes, it was hard to justify spending the money it would take to build a garage. But for that very reason, it also seemed like it was now or never. I rationalized it any number of ways. As I said, neither Maire Anne nor I owned new cars—at one point the odometers on Maire Anne's and my daily drivers had over 300,000 miles between them. Jeez, that cost saving alone was probably about the price of a garage. But, really, it was an emotional issue. Maire Anne had gotten her kitchen. I needed my garage.

Obviously I once more turned to my friend Alex, and in 2003 we began conceptualizing a 2¾-car garage (two cars pulled in straight through a big roll-up door, plus one car in the back that you'd have to position crosswise on wheel dollies for winter storage) with a pitched roof high enough to enable a full-height two-post lift—the holy grail of any seriously DIY-oriented car guy. I thought that we would be able to build a new structure in place of the old garage (which was barely a foot from the property line). After all, who in their right mind would object to our tearing down a rusting, leaning, 60-year-old corrugated metal eyesore and building a nicely designed new one?

Well, my neighbor, that's who. I've had a rocky relationship with the retired gentleman on my right ever since we moved in. He's lived here forever, and apparently at some point I had broken some unwritten law. Maybe several. Let's be clear: Yes, I've owned and repaired many cars, but none was ever up on cinder blocks in the driveway; none was ever stripped for parts on the property; none was ever parked in the yard white-trash-style; I never made noise in the garage late at night; I wasn't running a business; and I never *ever* fixed anyone else's car for money. As that great philosopher Groucho Marx once said, "Why can't everyone just leave everyone else the hell alone?"

Long story short, in the city of Newton, in order to build a structure within four feet of the property line—even if it's replacing an ugly existing structure—you have to apply for a variance and subject yourself to a hearing. Because the hearing requires detailed plans stamped with an architect's seal, I had to pay an architect to draw them. But the plans were irrelevant. My neighbor showed up and complained that I was running a repair shop and the problem would only get worse with a larger structure. The head of this kangaroo court pompously intoned, "No one needs a garage, no one needs a two-car garage, and certainly no one needs one of the size you're proposing. Request denied." (Obviously not a car guy.)

I was crushed.

But, as is often the case, there were unintended consequences. Getting shot down was the best thing that could have happened.

After Maire Anne, Alex, and I licked our wounds, we regrouped and considered our options. There were only two ways to build a structure that was compliant with the four-foot setback rule. One was to plop a garage down in the middle of the backyard, which would've eaten up all our property. Maire Anne is tolerant of my excesses but even she has her limits. And I was unwilling to do this as well. The other was to attach a low garage to the back of the house, with half the garage peeking out from behind the house and half obscured by it (think of a rectangle attached by half its shortest wall to the back of a large square). This meant not having a roll-up door for each car but instead needing to pull the cars in through one single-width door facing the street. We designed another door at a right angle to the street, but to use it you'd have to make a frighteningly sharp turn-in from the driveway, risking impact with my neighbor's fence. So this was a three-car garage, but with some torturous moves required to drive any car in or out except the one directly behind the roll-up door facing the street. And, because the structure had to be low enough not to obscure any of the windows in the house, it meant that the ceiling wouldn't be high enough for a post lift (sniff).

But, like politics, the garage was a study in the calculus of the possible. All we'd need to construct this configuration was a building permit, so we wouldn't have to subject ourselves to the capricious whims of variance approval. As part of the conceptual design process, I had a rare think-outside-the-box moment that literally involved space outside the box of the garage. Since the new garage would be adjacent to the deck off the kitchen, we could build a sliding door to access the underside of the deck and, if necessary, park a car under there. Alex submitted the application for the building permit; approval seemed like a minor formality. There was a brief panic when the City of Newton informed me that the old garage might be a "historic structure" and couldn't be removed. But that abated as soon as a city representative came and, uh, experienced its magnificence firsthand.

Then, in the summer of 2005, I learned that the smallish privately held firm I'd worked for since 1984 was about to be purchased by a ten billion-dollar-a-year corporation. My future was suddenly very uncertain. I can be pretty risk-averse when it comes to big-picture finances, and every instinct told me to put the brakes on the garage project. However, since I write my own proposals to fund my own work, I convinced myself that I was still somewhat in control of my destiny.

Right choice. Damn the torpedoes, the new company, the City of Newton, and anyone else. Full speed ahead. I was on an eight-week field survey for work in Albuquerque when I got the news that the building permit had been approved. The old metal garage was demolished immediately. I think Alex's crew insulted it and it fell over. Alex e-mailed me photos of the smashed hulk on the ground. Though I was grateful that it had kept my 3.0CSi out of the elements for nearly 15, I can't say that I shed a tear.

Once I was back home, the fact that construction was actually underway was like an emotional green light telling me that I could buy more cars. The garage's concrete foundation was barely hard when I started looking at BMW 2002s again. I bought a green '73 2002tii—the first 2002 I'd owned since selling Bertha to Alex nearly 20 years earlier. The owner had recently had it repainted, but wound up in a dispute with the body shop over a pretty visible paint drip that ran down the left rear quarter panel. All the glass and trim were off the car, but he'd pulled it out of the body shop, taken it home, stuffed it in his garage, and then lost interest. I bought it with the proviso that I'd pick it up when my garage was ready to receive four-wheeled tenants.

When the frame, walls, and roof were up, I began pulling cars in. The driveway had been extended but not yet paved so I couldn't play chicken with my neighbor's fence and try to make the abrupt left turn through the side door. Instead, I pulled two cars straight in … and they fit nose-to-tail. Wow, I thought … this isn't a three-car garage; *it's a four-car garage*. I called Alex.

"Were we this smart?" I asked.

He laughed. "No," he said. "Basically, you're lucky. You own small cars. The Porsche and the 2002 are both less than 14 feet long. Try it with the minivan and the Suburban and it'll never work."

It was nearly three years from the initial design of the first failed garage plan until the completed construction of the attached garage, but I now have the impossible—a four-car garage (plus a fifth under the deck) in the City of Newton. Because it's attached to the house and has a low roofline, it's remarkably unobtrusive. And, as I wrote in the tools chapter, although the ceiling height was too low for a post lift, I bought a mid-rise scissors lift, which allows me to sit fully upright, blissed-out and Buddha-like, beneath a car.

I cannot stress sufficiently how much my garage is *not* a man cave. Matching stainless steel cabinets? Ha! Diamond tread flooring? Feh! You want a fridge and a plasma screen? Go to a bar. If my garage isn't totally jammed with cars and parts, with an uncompleted 5-speed conversion over here, and the parts for an air-conditioning rejuvenation over there, then I'm not busy enough, and it's time to buy another car.

Regarding my neighbor … he's now elderly and in ill health. Just as you don't know when you've transgressed an unwritten code, you often don't know when a trivial effort on your part will be important to someone else. Last winter when I was snow-blowing my sidewalk, I continued walking and cleared his. It took me all of 30 seconds. My neighbor opened his door, came out on the porch, and shouted, "Robby!" I thought, "What, he's going to yell at me for blowing his sidewalk?" I shut off the snow blower and waited for him to yell, chew me out, whatever he was going to do. Instead, he said, "I haven't been able to clear snow myself since I've been sick. Thank you so much!" Relations have been much better since then.

And Bertha? Alex still owns her, but she hasn't been driven since the mid-'90s. Someone stole her and damaged her transmission. She was recovered, and sat at Alex's house for a year. He was overwhelmed with work and personal issues, so I absconded with Bertha, did a five-speed conversion, and presented her to him as a surprise. But then she was stolen and recovered again, and this time there was engine damage. Alex had her towed to the house of a neighbor who owed him a favor. She's been sitting in the neighbor's garage ever since. For all that I owe Alex, I keep offering to tow Bertha over to my garage and nurse her back to life. Alex is oddly resistant. I think he's concerned that, if I do, I'll run away with her and he'll never get her back.

And yes, three decades later, Bertha's driver's door—the mechanism by which Alex and I met—is still in primer.

Why do men love cars? Well, that big-ass garage would look pretty empty without them.

CHAPTER 26

WHY I DON'T FIX CARS FOR OTHER PEOPLE
(PART II: MORE BAD LUCK WITH FRIENDS' VOLKSWAGENS)

In the late 1990s, Maire Anne and I were in a band with a guy named Blair who had a 1978 VW bus. Blair knew we'd owned a number of buses and Vanagons and that I did all of my own repair work. So when his bus needed an exhaust, he asked me if I would help him replace it.

I explained that things go wrong when doing any kind of mechanical work. I told him that when doing exhaust work on air-cooled cars in particular, it is very easy to snap the studs holding the exhaust to the head, and then you're screwed. I warned him that if these studs snap, you may need to pull the head and take it to a machine shop to replace the studs, or accept that the exhaust will never seal, will be loud, and may cause the engine to run hot.

But Blair was poor, and over the months, as his bus's exhaust got louder and louder, he begged me. Finally he asked me to just give it my best shot, *swearing* that he understood the risk of snapping a stud. I relented.

I soaked the nuts on the exhaust studs in penetrating oil. But sure enough, with my hand on the wrench, I felt that sickening shearing sensation. When a tight or rusty nut breaks free, you hear an audible *crack* and then there's continued resistance on the wrench as rusty threads turn against rusty threads, but when something begins to turn unaccompanied by the *crack*, you know that in two seconds you'll wish you had never touched it.

I felt terrible. I put things back together as best as I could with the new exhaust parts. It was quieter than it had been, but clearly the exhaust wasn't sealing against the head. Blair was philosophical, but obviously this wasn't the way either of us had wanted it to turn out. I think he just lived with it that way. And, once again, the outcome of doing a favor was this feeling in my gut that I had done something wrong. *Screw this*, I thought, *I am never, EVER doing this again.*

I did some very small automotive favors for a friend of Maire Anne's and mine. I replaced her battery; another time I fixed her seat belt. These were utterly trivial repairs (well, trivial to me, hugely important to her, very satisfying therefore to both parties). But other than that, I don't think I worked on anyone else's car for another 15 years.

CHAPTER 27

A CHAPTER ABOUT ME AND HOW FIXING BROKEN BMWS MAKES ME WHOLE. REALLY.

Needless to say, this is couch. Deep couch. Maybe a bottomless sectional. I hesitate to go here, but I'm not sure how else to explain how cars have helped to save my sanity and make me whole. It goes much deeper than the simple discovery through repetition that I enjoy fixing broken cars.

It's not just that I like cars, though I do. It's not that I'm a pushover for the whole cars-as-women-and-relationship-surrogates thing, though that's powerful stuff. Those things don't help keep me sane. It's something else. It's the joy that comes from working with my hands, combined with the satisfaction of being able to completely solve a problem. I'll settle in on the couch and tell you about the part of myself that *isn't* a car guy. We'll deal with all of it, here, right now, get it all out of the way, I'll get up off the couch, write the check for the co-pay, and never come back here for analysis again.

When I was in the fourth grade, I had to do a "what do you want to be when you grow up" assignment. I still have it. It says, "I want to be a rock and roller or a man of science." I remember selecting those specific words because, in fact, I did not know how to spell either "musician" or "scientist." You'll note that there was nothing in there about being a mechanic. And that's fine. In white Jewish upwardly mobile Long Island circles, "mechanic" wasn't a respectable profession anyway (though I'm sure that, had I expressed a strong interest, my mother would've found a way not to kill that flower).

But, in fact, since I was a teenager, most of the gravity in my universe has been generated by the trinary system of computers, guitars, and cars. Computers have been responsible for most of the income, guitars for most of the creative output, and cars for much of the simple enjoyment and relaxation. Of the three, it's actually the guitars (that is, playing music and writing songs) that reach deepest into my soul. It is necessary to meet and understand *guitar guy* and *computer guy* in order to appreciate why *car guy* is the good-natured fellow that holds this psychological band together.

I started playing the guitar when I was ten. My sister Amy was taking lessons. I'd sit outside her door and listen. At the end of each lesson, I could pick up the guitar and play the piece being taught better than she could. She gave it up. Now I am well aware that there have been moments in my life when I am positively insufferable, and I'd imagine that, for both my mother and my sister, this one ranks fairly high. To this day, my mother has a photograph on her bureau of my sister and me, ten and eleven, with Amy playing the guitar. Fleeting things can be so precious.

But in my defense, although Amy gave up the guitar, I never put it down. Sitting either in my room or on the roof over the garage in the house in South Amherst that my mother moved us into after my dad died, I would play my guitar endlessly. We're talking hours, every day, for years. As a parent, I've never understood the pressure placed on kids to practice their instruments because it's supposed to be good for them. Feh. If it's important to them, they'll practice. It's only called "practice" if you don't want to do it. You couldn't *stop* me from "practicing." All through junior high and high school, always in love with some girl, generally broken-hearted, frequently lonely and depressed … the guitar saved my sanity. I just played and played and played. It was so simple. It was a form of unconditional love. My entire young adulthood, I was the guy with the guitar. I played frequently at coffeehouses, corners, and bars, showcasing an encyclopedic repertoire of anything from Elvis Presley to Elvis Costello.

When I went to college, however, I was not a music major. I really did double-major in math and physics at UMass Amherst and graduate summa cum laude. I worked my tail off. I'm enormously proud of it. I find it funny when people say, "I understand that there's a link between music and math." There is, but it's not what you might think. As someone who has studied both, I can tell you that the mathematics necessary to analyze music is very simple. It's whole steps, half steps, intervals, and overtones. Really, it's arithmetic, not math. You can go further and model vibrating strings and other acoustic entities with differential equations, but doing so does not make you a better musician. Do you want to design and build a better guitar, or do you just want to pour your heart out, playing Neil Young songs, at two in the morning? It depends what the goal is (I say this a lot in my life). At one point, I bought a synthesizer keyboard, thinking, "This is perfect. I understand the math behind constructing the waveforms. I will so totally dominate this instrument." You know what? I never used it. I realized that I play music to *feel something*, not to be a geek during my off-hours. Understanding this distinction has been a major dynamic in my life.

While studying physics I tended to rely too much on mathematical formalism, but I was good at formalism; it's a left-brained activity that was far easier for me than actual physical insight, which is a creative right-brained activity. This was an early example of a pattern I've struggled with my entire life. To this day, if Maire Anne says, "How do you think the living room would look if we moved the couch to the other wall?" I say, "I don't know—let's pick it up and move it and then we'll see."

One of my few creative right-brained moments in college came in the computer lab that the physics department had on the tenth floor of the graduate research tower. In addition to the big ker-chunky Teletype keyboards, the lab also had something new—a Tektronix terminal with a green phosphor screen on which you could display not only text but also graphics. Connected to this terminal was a printer that, at the push of a button, would create a hard copy of the graphics on paper that had a smell somewhat reminiscent of mimeograph fluid (a little slice of heaven to anyone who grew up in the '60s). Since this device enabled faculty and students to, for the first time, display and print x-y graphs, face time on the machine was at a premium.

One night when no one was on the Tektronix terminal, I began playing on it. I wrote a simple program that allowed me to input the radii of two spinning circles and display the resulting flower-like patterns (essentially a digital version of the Hasbro Spirograph toy with its gears and pens). This was cutting-edge computer graphics in 1976, but it clearly had nothing to do with freshman physics. As I was displaying plot after plot on the green screen and banging out hard copy after hard copy, I heard the door to the lab open. I could see the large, physically imposing form of Fred Byron, the department head, reflected in the green monitor. Although I had never had a run-in with Dr. Byron, I was certain he would not take well to a geeky frosh flagrantly and wantonly wasting limited computer resources. I waited for the other shoe to drop. After he had watched me for what seemed like an eternity, it did.

"Excuse me," his baritone voice boomed, dripping with departmental authority.

I turned around. "Yes, sir?"

"Those, uh, patterns you're drawing …"

Gulp.

"They're absolutely fascinating. Can you tell me how you're doing that?"

I believe that I can trace my tendency to trust people, and to assume the best rather than the worst of them unless there is direct evidence to the contrary, to this very moment.

It also illustrates how some of the best, most fulfilling moments in life often come from rocking across that thin line separating creatively driven from obsessive-compulsive.

Although those pretty electronic Spirograph patterns were the jackal laugh of my right brain (and their appeal to Dr. Byron a triumphant example of the connection resulting from a shared interest), they were also the exception that proves the rule. That is, though the results of software development can sometimes be quite creative, the activity itself is, in fact, numbingly rational, detail-oriented, and left-brained. Although I didn't realize it at the time, I had a natural talent for writing computer software, and this would become a very marketable skill.

Over the next decade, music and computers wove themselves together in my life like a yin-yang symbol, one feeding off the other. As I neared graduation, the relative worth of my ability to write software as compared with the market value of my bachelor's degree in math and physics (summa freaking cum laude notwithstanding) became glaringly apparent. The out-of-the-blue phone call I received from Nick, the ex-Hampshire student who'd taken me driving in his BMW 2002 and now had a computer business, was one of those serendipitous events you just can't plan on. I moved in with Maire Anne in Cambridge, worked for Nick, and put together the first of many bands—having left my early acoustic phase and taken a hard right into rock and roll.

When Maire Anne and I moved down to Austin, I quickly got another programming job and started auditioning band members. At some point, Maire Anne got tired of helping me haul equipment at 2 A.M. I taught her how to play drums and she became part of the band.

When we moved from Austin back up to Boston in '84, one of our bandmates moved up with us, keeping the band mostly intact. Once again, finding a programming job was easy. There were a lot of software jobs relating to Reagan's Strategic Defense Initiative ("Star Wars"), but I didn't want to do that. I answered a small ad that talked about magnetostatic modeling for detection of unexploded ordnance (dud bombs left over from military training activities). It's the job I still have. Over the years I've moved from programmer to project manager, but I still write a lot of software.

Maire Anne and I played together in bands on and off for more than 25 years, doing both "cover tunes" (other people's songs) and my own original material. It is an understatement to say that I was not the easiest person to deal with when we began doing my own songs ("perfectionist" doesn't begin to describe my Stalinist tendencies), but it was still a great activity to be able to share as a married couple. We continued doing it even after the kids were born, playing several fund-raisers a year for their public elementary school in Newton. Our days of playing out in clubs are long since over; these days, playing rock and roll music is just an excuse to drink beer and play too loud in the basement with ex-bandmates. Talk about an easy, uncomplicated right-brain activity. There are few things in this world that I get such unabashed enjoyment from.

So, for many years, I really viewed my vocation—computers—as a means to pursuing my avocation—playing music. And, yes, the paycheck from writing software also allowed me to buy cars, but that was a hobby. Anyone who called the music a "hobby" would bear the dagger-like pierce of my blue eyes. Eventually, around the time that our second son, Kyle, was born, I had to admit that I was never going to form the next R.E.M. It was time to give my interesting, well-paying day job the focus that it deserved. Yet the death of a dream is a difficult thing. There were other cover bands for Maire Anne and I, and some of that was fun. But, in terms of putting original rock and roll music as the most important thing in our life, there was a last gig, and when it was over, it was over. For the next few years I was not a particularly happy camper.

Then, in the mid-'90s I returned to the acoustic singer/songwriter world. I write songs rooted in my idyllic yet stressed-out suburban life, about raising moral children in a world where the major religions appear blood-sworn to kill each other, and about—to steal a line from the brilliant British poet Philip Larkin—*the million-petalled flower of being here*.

Fundamentally, other than the health of my family, there is nothing I care about as deeply as songwriting. There is nothing from which I derive such deep satisfaction as calling the shot Babe-Ruth style ("I'm going to write a song about *that*"), then crafting the song, burnishing every stanza, every line, every word until I'm satisfied with it, and playing it for an audience.

But the downside of caring so much about songwriting is that it is real work. Although both music and songwriting are generally thought of as right-brain activities, my own songwriting style is so analytical that, for me, it is without question a left-brain activity. That is, I approach songwriting the way most people would approach putting an addition onto a house. You don't just start knocking down walls to see what happens. You think. You plan. You design conceptually, then in preliminary detail, then in final detail. It is exceedingly rare for me to simply pick up a guitar, start playing, and have a song pop out of the toaster. Thus, I don't just pick up a guitar these days and play the way I used to in my room in Amherst, for the simple joy of it. There's too much expectation associated with it now. I always have a mental queue of songs that need to be written, like an architect who has ideas for houses for potential clients, like airplanes at a congested airport trying to land. When I grab a guitar, I automatically think, "I should be working on that song about the Dodgers leaving Brooklyn." It's like that classic *New Yorker* cartoon showing the 30-ish man and woman at an idyllic picnic setting, sitting on a blanket beneath a tree, basket open, wine being poured, when he says, "I should be working on my grant."

In contrast, being a car guy is much simpler. It's deliciously uncomplicated. It appears to satisfy the right side of my brain without the baggage and the expectations of songwriting. As a guy who tends to overanalyze everything (you can tell, can't you?), it is such a simple pleasure for me to go into the garage and fix something, or to displace job-related stress with the thrill and anticipation that comes from looking at another car. And the metrics for success are so straightforward. I can't make a client award me a geophysical survey contract, or book me as a performer in some coveted venue, but I can replace a water pump. In a world where I can't fix health care, I can diagnose and replace a bad alternator and know the problem is fixed, completely. I can take something that wasn't working yesterday and make it work today. And while one may not have complete control over anything in this life, Jeez Louise I have an awful lot of it in my garage. I can make decisions without seeking approval from anyone. And most of the time they're such gloriously inconsequential decisions—do I buy this part or try to fix the one that's in the car?—with so little real consequence even if I'm wrong.

By occupying my hands, working on a car occupies my mind. Cars give my brain the vacation it needs from itself. *Car guy* plays rhythm and lets *computer guy* and *guitar guy* take all the solos. He lets them sneak out to the bar for a couple of quick ones.

He really does save my sanity and help make me whole.

CHAPTER 28

OF KLINGONS AND KLUGES
FIXING THE PORSCHE'S OIL RETURN LINE

There's a saying. "Do it once, do it right."

I hate it. I've always hated it. It is easy, pompous advice, bereft of empathy and creativity, often intoned from on high by someone with anal-retentive tendencies who is not experiencing *your* problem and does not have to spend *your* money. Certainly "do it once, do it right" applies to building bridges and invasive medical procedures, but for common repairs, it must be tempered with common sense, lest every repair result in a rebuilt engine and a fully detailed undercarriage.

First I must tell you the story of the air-conditioning in my high-mileage '92 Suburban. When I first bought the car, I started to rejuvenate the dead a/c and found that the compressor was seized. A by-the-book compressor replacement involves flushing out every a/c line to clean out any junk that the compressor might have thrown when it seized. I saw no metal shavings in the lines feeding the compressor, but I wanted to "do it right." The 'Burb had rear air, so this meant undoing the line that plumbs the rear evaporator so I could flush it. When I tried to remove the metal line, it snapped off (shades of fixing the brakes on Paul's Beetle 20 years prior). I now had to replace both the rear evaporator and this 20-foot-long metal line. When I tried to remove the broken line from the front of the car, that end snapped off as well. It was classic cascading failure. By the time I was done, I'd replaced most of the major a/c components, and it probably wasn't necessary.

It's a lesson I've never forgotten. Look the beast in the face. If you're not prepared to battle it to the death, back slowly out of the cave. (I'm reminded of the *Star Trek* parable of the brave Klingon warrior who stays outside when a ferocious sandstorm is approaching. He says he is not afraid. The storm comes. He dies. Moral: The wind does not respect a fool.)

Case in point: After sitting over the winter, my '82 Porsche 911SC was leaving small puddles of oil on the garage floor (the *new* garage floor). I cleaned the engine to isolate the leak, and found two sources—one from an oil return tube (these carry oil from the outer regions of the engine back to the engine block), and the other from an oil line. As originally designed, you'd have to partially disassemble the engine to change the oil return tubes, but many years ago someone came up with the clever solution of a collapsible telescoping pair of tubes with an integral oil seal in the middle. You pull out the old tube by cutting it in half, put the new pair in, slide the two halves outward, lock them with a circlip, and voila.

I ordered a full set of these tubes, thinking that obviously I'd "do it right" and replace all four. I put the car up on the lift, and immediately realized access to the tubes is blocked by the exhaust, and like any exhaust, attempting to remove it runs the real risk of snapping the exhaust studs that hold the manifolds to the engine. Fortunately the tube that was leaking was by far the most accessible. I replaced it and left the other three tubes alone. Leak gone for 20 bucks. No snapped exhaust studs. No trips to the machine shop. No two weeks of nights and weekends. Is this "doing it right?" For a car used only on weekends, it is—at least it is in my book.

The other oil leak seemed trivial but was in fact far more pernicious. Porsche 911s are called air-cooled cars, but this is a misnomer; they're really air- and oil-cooled cars. A 911 has a nose-mounted cooler that's essentially an oil radiator. This means that there are oil lines running the length of the car. The leak was coming from one of these oil lines, half metal and half rubber. I easily undid the engine end, but the other end that terminated in an oil thermostat would not budge.

Reading online, I learned that the oil thermostat is aluminum and the 36mm nut on the line is steel, so you have 25 years of corrosion of dissimilar metals to break. Both heat and force are difficult because the thermostat is located way up underneath the right rear fender, and there's very little clearance. I ordered the correct 36mm wrench from Pelican Parts (the premier Porsche enthusiast web site) and heated the nut up as best I could, but only succeeded in bending the jaw of the wrench.

One trick is to drop everything together and lay it all on the floor so you can have the access and clearance necessary to try to disassemble the damned thing. But that doesn't save you; it just gives you enough rope to hang yourself. The oil thermostat has four connections on it, and if removing one of them cracks the thermostat, you have to replace all four. Online were plenty of horror stories, complete with photographs of sheared thermostats and snapped-off oil lines.

The mind hyperlinks. Suburban. Evaporator. *Cascading failure.*

No.

Back slowly out of the cave.

I decided my basic tack would be to try the least invasive path first—to see if I could save the metal line with the frozen end and only replace the rubber end. If I couldn't, then I still had the option of cutting the metal nut off the thermostat. This oil line had two parts—a hard metal section with an integrated 36mm flange nut (the one affixed to the oil thermostat), and a rubber section that ends in a second 36mm flange nut. I thought that if I could find the 36mm fitting, I could simply replace both it and the rubber section.

First I verified this was *not* a high-pressure line; it is a scavenging line, maintaining no more than 100 psi. The next step was seeing if I could successfully cut off the old rubber line where it was crimped onto the metal one. With a Dremel tool and metal-cutting wheel, this was trivial; I just carefully cut around the top of the old crimp-on fitting, then cut longitudinally down it. What was left was a nice clean barbed metal fitting that was practically begging me to put a nice new section of hose on it.

And thus we come to the concept of the *kluge* (pronounced *klooj*)—an improvised engineering solution. A kluge can be something as simple as holding on a license plate with zip ties if the bolts have rattled out, but *kluge* usually carries with it the connotation that it is ugly and half-assed, such as duct-taping a leaky window shut, or using a coat hanger for an antenna.

I have rules (more like guidelines, actually) for what I consider "a good kluge." These are: 1) it saves time and money over the "correct" way; 2) it is safe; and 3) it is easily undone if you have to go back and redo the repair. To deal with my oil line, I came up with a beauty. Once I'd exposed the nice clean barbed metal fitting on the metal end,

I knew I could slide a new section of rubber hose onto it. I bought the correctly sized piece of high-pressure rubber oil line (high pressure for the safety margin), and found the correct 36mm fitting and two wide T-bolt clamps (these are far stronger than traditional worm gear hose clamps). Using these, I clamped the hose to the barbed end of the metal line, and clamped the new 36mm fitting to the hose.

I photographed the entire procedure and put it on the Pelican Parts web site. Some folks gasped at such a, well, such a kluge. Some misunderstood and thought I did this because I was cheap, not because I was concerned about cascading failure. Some warned that there would be no early indication of failure and the likely end result would be twelve quarts of oil on the street and a lunched engine. Some said they'd done the same thing with no ill effects, and agreed this was entirely appropriate for a nontracked car. Some recommended I replace the T-bolt clamps with professional crimp fittings. No one offered a principled explanation why a T-bolt clamp shouldn't be as strong as a crimp.

I refilled the car with oil, checked for leaks and found none, and began enjoying my whale tail Targa in New England's glorious but short spring driving season. I checked the T-bolt clamps annually. Four years later they were still tight as a drum, and the Porsche wasn't leaking a drop of oil.

Saved time and money. Safe. Easily undone. A good kluge.

Do it once, do it right? Don't impose those subjective terms on me unless you're prepared to pay my repair bills. There are times when I'm spoiling for a fight, and will gladly commune with my inner Klingon, enter the cave, battle the beast, and emerge victorious with blood smeared on my cheeks. But discretion can be the better part of valor. A stripped stud does not respect a fool.

CHAPTER 29

WHEN CARS ATTACK

It is said you're not a real musician until you've had an instrument stolen, a real software engineer until you've lost three days of code, or a real mechanic until you've drawn blood. I am, I'm sorry to say, a real musician, a real software engineer, and a real mechanic. As much as I enjoy working on cars, they are inherently dangerous entities to be around. The following examples stand out over and above the usual background level of bloody knuckles. They even eclipse the occasional emergency room visit to remove a metal filing from my eye, and the time I swung at the pickle fork with a hammer, missed, and nearly broke my wrist.

One day, early in the fall semester of my junior year at UMass Amherst, a new professor came into our mechanics class (and this is "mechanics" as in the study of motion and the forces that keep things in stasis) and explained, to our stunned surprise, that Dr. Goldenberg, our professor, had been killed over the weekend when the car he was working under fell on him. I don't know the details. I don't know if the car was on a hill, or supported by a jack with no jack stands. But even not knowing, this is why, to this day, whenever I need to crawl under a car, I *always* double-jack it. That is, I use a floor jack to raise the car, put the jack stands in place under the frame rails, let the car down off the jack until it rests on the jack stands, *then leave the floor jack in place.* You could call this "belt and suspenders," but that really trivializes things. This ain't your pants falling down and embarrassing you. This is a car potentially crushing you.

I said, "Whenever I need to crawl under a car, I *always* double-jack it." This implies I don't double-jack a car if I don't need to crawl under it (*modus tollens* for you logic geeks). There is a dangerous game some mechanics and DIY-ers play where they draw a distinction between sustained work which requires you to actually lie beneath the car, versus short bursts of work which requires the car to be up in the air without you actually under it, and use jack stands for the former but not necessarily the latter. I have, at times, been guilty of this. Until it nearly injured me.

Here's what happened. I was checking out a car that was for sale. I wanted to evaluate the car's front end. The time-honored technique is to jack up the front of the car and grab the front wheel at 3 and 9 o'clock and push-pull it, then do the same at 6 and 12 o'clock. If there's no play in any direction, you're good. If there's play only at 3 and 9 o'clock, the car probably has a bad tie rod or other steering component. If there's play in all directions, it's got a bad wheel bearing.

I'd brought one of those small 1.5-ton floor jacks which comes in its own carrying case about twice the length of a shoebox. This form factor is useful in that the case keeps the jack from rolling around in the trunk, but the width of these jacks is pretty narrow, making them somewhat unstable on anything other than a laser-leveled cement floor.

The car's owner and I rendezvoused in the parking lot of a CVS. The parking lot had a very slight downhill slant and had been freshly repaved. It was about 80 degrees outside. You can probably see where this is going.

I slid the floor jack beneath the front of the car and jacked it up until both front wheels were off the ground. Then I crouched next to the left front wheel and did the 3-and-9, 6-and-12 evaluation. With the nose of the car still in the air, I walked around to the right front wheel, crouched next to it, and began to do the same thing. All of a sudden I heard the owner yell, "Look out! Look out! LOOK OUT!"

The combination of the new asphalt, the warm temperature, the slight downhill pitch, and the jack's narrow width caused the jack to sink slightly into the asphalt and the car to topple sideways off the jack. I never had the wheel off and was never beneath the car, but it still scared the crap out of me.

I now won't ever—ever—do anything on a raised car unless it is double-jacked.

My most bizarre injury was at the hands of a BMW 2002's windshield wiper motor. I had a car whose wipers worked only intermittently. While diagnosing the problem, I turned on the car's ignition, hit the wiper switch, and checked the power at the wiper motor connector with a voltmeter. There was power, but the wipers still weren't turning. I then plugged the connector back into the wiper motor. Still nothing. I wiggled the connection. All of a sudden the wiper motor engaged. It spun the wiper linkage around, and the long part of the linkage pinned my wrist against the sharp edge of the car's firewall. Incredibly, it did not puncture the skin, but it held my wrist so tightly my hand turned white. The power was still on, so it continued to hold it actively pinned.

My first thought was to cut power to the wiper motor by pulling off the connector, but my wrist itself was in the way of the connector; I couldn't access it to pull it off. I couldn't reach inside the car to either turn off the wipers or pull out the ignition key. Fortunately there were a few box-end wrenches lying on the fender. I used one to disconnect the battery. Even with the power cut, it took me several minutes to be able to free my trapped wrist. It didn't feel right for weeks, but there was no permanent damage. I was incredibly fortunate not to have been seriously injured.

There was, of course, the close call I had while driving my winter beater BMW 1600. I heard a rhythmic *chunka-chunka-chunka* coming from the rear of the car, and no sooner had my mind formed the thought *gee, that almost sounds like a loose lug nut* when the car went *BANG*, the left rear wheel fell off, the brake drum skidded on the asphalt, *and the wheel passed me on the left* like something from the aftermath of a Wile E. Coyote Road Runner-killing scheme gone wrong. I watched, with that peculiar mix of horror and fascination that accompanies unfolding accidents, as the renegade wheel rolled down the road at about 20 mph, hit a curb, jumped up in the air, and headed straight for the picture window of a house. It missed it by perhaps a foot and lodged in a rhododendron bush. I sheepishly retrieved it, jacked up the car, threaded it back on the mangled studs, and waited for my pulse rate to return to normal.

In racing, there's what's referred to as *red mist*. This is the adrenaline rush which makes you want to win (or at least to beat some other guy) so badly it clouds your judgment and causes you to take inappropriate risks. I've long noted that, in fixing cars, there is something like a *mechanic's red mist* that has similar numbing effects on the logic centers of the brain.

I was doing some exhaust work and had to cut off a stuck bolt that mated the catalytic converter to the muffler. I was replacing every other exhaust component but re-using the cat, so I had to drill out the part of the bolt that was stuck in the flange. This is tedious work that goes much quicker with a drill press. So I took the cat into work where we have a machine shop. I clamped it in a 40-pound vise which sits on the drill press. The vise itself is not clamped to the drill press; it just sits on the flat surface, allowing you to line up the drill bit as needed.

I got impatient and leaned on the lever arm of the drill press and pressured the bit downward to save time. As it neared the bottom of the hole, the drill bit started to smoke. Rather than back off, the mechanic's red mist made me think "almost there … just a few seconds more …" Then the bit seized in the hole. The rotating torque of the drill caused the catalytic converter and the 40-pound vise to spin around, rotate off the drill press, and fling themselves crashing onto the floor. Six inches from my right foot. Which was wearing a Birkenstock sandal. Stupid! Stupid! Stupid!

I've had many other instances of mechanic's red mist. I've drilled holes in pieces of metal I'm holding against a block of wood with my bare hand, and witnessed my brain form the thought *you know, you really should hold this in place with a clamp not your hand because if that drill bit grabs it's going to swing that metal piece around like a cutting wheel and slice the crap out of your hand* and ignored the thought only to have the drill bit grab two seconds later and swing the piece of metal around and generate a nice emergency-room-worthy gash.

Recently I did something so profoundly stupid I literally laughed through the pain. A gentleman named Pat Allen hand-builds and sells a little diagnostic tool called the Wunderbox that plugs into the diagnostic port of a 1970's-era BMW and gives digital readout of engine rpm, dwell, and voltage. In addition, it lets you turn on the ignition and trip the starter motor from under the hood. This is a tremendous time-saver when tuning an older car where you need to take a dwell (points gap) reading, shut the engine off, adjust the gap, re-start the car, and take another reading. Of course, it also means you can start the car in gear with the flick of a toggle switch, despite the box's literally coming wrapped in a sheet of paper warning not to do so.

I was setting the dwell, starting the engine, stopping it, re-gapping, and repeating, all using the box. When I'd gotten the gap right, I took the car for a drive. Resetting the dwell changes the timing slightly, and it felt a little off. I pulled back into the garage and prepared to adjust the timing. I stood beside the car, hooked the box back up, hit the start switch, and immediately ran over my foot. The mind takes a few seconds to process such unexpected events. *Oh. You left the car in gear. By the way … ouch!* The car didn't actually run *over* my foot; it ran *onto* it and stopped there. And thank heaven it did—had my foot not been there to stop the car, the ignition would have "caught" and propelled the car into the back wall of the garage. I shut off the box but could not reach into the car to take it out of gear until I managed to wriggle my foot out of the shoe.

When this stuff happens, I do try to file it in a place in my brain that I can check back with so it won't happen again. I like to think I'm older and wiser and try to recognize the mist when it rises in me and clear it from my vision. But in truth, it's challenging. OSHA doesn't maintain a presence in my garage. I'm not watching football. I'm out there to get things done. When you're hot and sweaty and bitching and griping at some stuck bolt, or when you're nearly done with a repair and you're so close to success you can smell it, it's pretty tough to keep your wits about you. When I'm tempted to do something questionable, I try to remember what I've said for years as a joke, but it's really not all that funny:

If I died in the garage, Maire Anne would kill me.

CHAPTER 30

THE RHYTHM OF REPAIR

There is a web of dynamics surrounding working on cars that I refer to as "the rhythm of repair." These all have to do with how you fit needed repairs into your life. For most people, the answer is "I don't—I pay someone else to do it." And that's fine. But if you're mechanically inclined and enjoy working on cars, the repairs naturally knock at your door. The question is whether you welcome them like old college buddies with whom you then stay up way too late talking about the old times over too many beers, or treat them like people you never really liked but let in out of politeness and then can't wait for them to leave.

Even if you pay someone else to do them, you *do* need to fit repairs into your life. It's a pain to take a car in for a repair. I doubt anyone looks forward to it any more than a trip to the dentist. At a minimum, you need to drop the car off at a shop and get back home or to work. Then you have to reverse the process when the work is completed. Unless the service station is literally around the corner, this takes a nontrivial amount of time. If it's 30 minutes each way, by the time you've dropped off and picked up the car, that's two hours. I look at that as two hours I could have spent fixing the thing myself. I can get a lot fixed in two hours.

When you've been working on cars for a while, you begin to realize how good a real repair shop has it. Big roll-up doors, high ceilings, every tool you could possibly need or want, *a lift* for heaven's sake … but also ready access to parts. That is, if you take a car into a dealer for a repair, they probably already have the parts it needs, whatever those are. If they don't, they can just park your car, maybe even leave it up on the lift, and get the parts quickly from some regional warehouse. Wouldn't it be sweet if *you* could do that?

Let's take brakes as an example. A few years back I was repairing the brakes on what was then Maire Anne's daily driver, a Mazda minivan. In this instance, the car was exhibiting a specific brake-related symptom—the pedal was pulsating when stepped on at highway speeds. So, symptom ("brake pedal pulsating") translates into rough diagnosis ("the front brake rotors are probably warped") translates into a potential parts list ("I need to buy front brake rotors and pads"). In most cases, these are items you can source much cheaper through the web than from a local dealership. So you do that. You comparison-shop on the web, balancing price and delivery. For ground shipping of parts, a week to ten days is not unusual. And, since most do-it-yourself repair work has to occur on a weekend, either the parts are there Saturday morning or they're not; thus the difference of one day in delivery time can effectively put the repair off a week.

So you choose a vendor. You verify the parts are in stock. Perhaps you trust the "in stock" status listed on the website, but to be absolutely certain, it's best to call them. You order the parts. Hopefully they arrive when you expect. You set aside a Saturday morning, jack the car up, set it securely on stands, pull the wheels off, replace the left rotor and pads, then the right, then take the car down, test drive it, put away all the tools, and pat yourself on the back for having saved yourself some nontrivial coin.

Except when you're wrong. Well, maybe not wrong; if you think the car needs brakes it almost certainly needs brakes. But maybe you find that the right brake caliper is seized. Or that the rubber brake hoses are so swollen they look like they're about to burst. Or, in my case, you find that one brake rotor arrived damaged. You now have the car "down" (meaning disabled, although "up" more accurately describes its vertical coordinate). Things are apart. Parts and tools are lying everywhere. And it needs something you don't have. And it's 4 P.M. on Saturday. And this is your wife's car, which she needs to use first thing Monday morning.

In these situations, it's incredible how quickly one can swing from search-20-web-sites-to-find-the-best-price-mode to *I don't care how far I have to drive and how much I have to pay what do I have to do to get my hands on this damn part RIGHT NOW* mode. I recently experienced this quite viscerally while repairing the air-conditioning on the truck for our impending vacation. I gladly would've driven a hundred miles and paid list price if that's what it took to lay my hands on the part I needed. And this cuts to the heart of the rhythm of repair.

Those of us who are "handy" around the house know this dynamic only too well. How many of us have had a home repair go from *something-I-need-to-do-sometime-in-the-future* to *need-to-get-it-done-before-company-comes-for-Thanksgiving*, and gone to Home Depot three times in one day? Oh, I need this. Crap, forgot that I need this too. Oh, man, I can't believe I need *this*. If it's a nonessential repair, like putting up shelves in the spare room or making the basement more habitable, you can just simply stop at whatever point you want and close a door; just add the item to the "next time I'm at Lowe's" list. But if you're fixing something critical like heat or a burst water pipe, you've already rolled the dice, made that crucial decision not to call the plumber, and bet that you can save a couple of Franklins by doing it yourself. Okay, separate-the-men-from-the-boys time. Will the family have hot water in the morning or not? Fortunately most Home Depots are open till 10 P.M. In contrast, parts counters at auto dealerships are, unfortunately, not.

Much of the issue revolves around whether you're doing a small repair or the Big Job. Normal-wear-and-tear stuff like brakes, shocks, and exhaust, for example, should be small repairs—constrained, prescribed, no surprises, repaired over the weekend, car drivable by Monday. In contrast, the Big Job is something you know in advance will render the car undrivable for weeks, maybe months. Obviously an engine swap is a Big Job. A pro can do a clutch replacement in a day, but for me it's something that will take more than a weekend, so it's a Big Job too. While I get enormous satisfaction out of simple repairs with clear beginnings and endings, I also enjoy the Big Job. My retrofit of air-conditioning into the 3.0CSi in 1998, and fuel injection in 2004, were Big Jobs (huge, actually) that stretched over months. I still take enormous pride in them, and still receive e-mail about them. But knowing which category your repair falls into is crucial for managing time, budget, and expectations.

Then there's the question of "mission creep." I'm a practical guy. Certain repairs go together like beer and pretzels. If you need to replace a clutch, you have to pull the transmission, and to do that, the driveshaft and exhaust have to come out, so if the exhaust is weak and the driveshaft center support bearing is making noises and the shift linkage is sloppy, now is the time to replace them. That's just common sense. The problem comes when the small repair on your daily driver mission-creeps into the Big Job, and you're not prepared for it.

A few years back I bought a 1999 BMW 528iT sport wagon to replace my 318ti hatchback and use as my daily driver. It's a very interesting car with a very rare combination of options : a 5-speed manual transmission plus the sport package featuring hunkered-down suspension and 17-inch wheels. I like it a lot, but it has been, by far, the most troublesome BMW I have ever owned. This is the same car I mentioned earlier that died on Maire Anne and four of her friends up in New Hampshire. Now, I didn't hold this against it; *any* car with 135K miles might eat an alternator (the damned Mazda ate three). But other things have happened that are just unforgivable.

It began last winter while I was driving the wagon on a very cold day. I shut the car off, ran a quick errand, and when I started it back up, it began belching copious clouds of oil smoke. I quickly shut it off and had it towed home. By reading on a BMW repair-related website, I learned that a component called the crankcase ventilation valve (CVV) or oil separator had frozen, dumping oil into the part of the engine that usually sucks air. If I hadn't shut it off as quickly as I had, I would've ruined the engine as surely as if I'd driven through a flood.

 The separator is located deep under the left side of the engine, and if you're going to replace it, you might as well attend to any number of other maintenance-related items at the same time. This car had no repair records, so I used the separator replacement as an opportunity to replace the entire cooling system and the seals for the variable valve timing. This is mission creep of the most practical, responsible form. Dealerships and independents routinely perform these repairs in no more than a day or two (and charge you three grand), but I'd never done it before, so learning about it and planning it was like mapping an assault on Annapurna. *Doing* the repair became like an assault on Annapurna when the weather turns bad.

It quickly became clear that the separator replacement plus the related maintenance was a Big Job and would take long enough for me to officially change the status of the wagon from daily driver to project. I cancelled the registration and insurance. We had just bought a used

Honda Fit for Maire Anne and were thus about to sell the Mazda mini-van, but I decided to keep the Mazda so I'd have something to drive over the winter. I gave the BMW wagon a coveted space inside the garage and began tearing it apart. I approached purchasing parts with the no-rush paradigm appropriate to the Big Job. That is, I could be in my left-brain glory and take my time, figure out what I needed, compare prices from six vendors, maintain the information in a spreadsheet, submit parts orders when they satisfied minimum requirements for free shipping, etc.

Even so, the parts orders seemed to be never-ending as I found that I needed a little more, a little more. Eventually I bit the bullet, slid all the way down the slippery slope, and replaced every normal-wear-and-tear part of the cooling system. That probably cost me $1,200 in parts. But it still wasn't the same as replacing "every part in the cooling system." There are components that basically don't break. Until they do. For example, there's a small electric motor underneath the car that helps to push the coolant around. Like most little German electric motors, it's expensive, but reading online I didn't see it as having a reputation for breaking. So I didn't replace it. So of course that little electric motor died later, but not until everything was put back together.

With life, work, and other projects competing for my time, the Big Job on the wagon took five months. My daily driver had truly become my project car. When it was finally complete, I insured the wagon, transferred the plates from the Mazda, and drove it around the block to test it out. There was an acrid smell and lots of smoke. Oh, it's oil burning off the exhaust; that's expected. Then came a loud bang and the car pulled to one side. It had a flat right front tire. I limped it home, put it up on the lift to change the tire, and found that the flat was caused by the right front spring having broken and the jagged edge having punctured the tire. What the …? This wasn't a case of "they all do that." Nor was it mission creep. It was just bizarre. Very few people break front springs in a BMW. I was beginning to truly loathe the car.

Now, springs really should be replaced in pairs. And to replace them, the front strut assemblies have to come out. So while they're out it makes sense to replace the front struts, which, in my car, were actually bad. While you're in there, the wheel bearings, tie rods, ball joints, and bushings are all weak points on these cars that you might as well attend to. This *was* mission creep, but it made perfect sense, so I did it. But, since I'd just transferred the plates off the Mazda, the Mazda was now off the road, and the wagon—disabled by a broken spring—was legally and philosophically the designated daily driver. All this front-end work was a Big Job, but the repair rhythm had abruptly shifted to "get it running, now." I was very unhappy. But I got it done.

Shortly after I got the front end together, I began having problems with the rear end (the pneumatic self-leveling rear suspension on these wagons is an interesting but troublesome system). At that point I was so fed up I nearly sold the car. (Why do men love cars? Some days, I don't; some days I think *they all suck*.) But I toughed it out and replaced the pneumatic bags, the pressurized tanks and hoses, and the rear bushings. And after completing all three Big Jobs, with thousands of dollars in parts and probably hundreds of hours of my time, the wagon was rock-solid reliable.

Sometimes it seems that the real rhythm of repair is *pay a little more, do a little more, pay a little more, do a little more.*

Once the seemingly endlessly expanding work on the wagon was contained and completed, I thought about the whole question of mission creep. Actually I did pretty well. I fixed what needed fixing on the wagon, plus what made sense while I was in the neighborhood. On the web you can always find someone who's so much worse than you, and sure enough, I found reports of people who started off replacing their rear pneumatic bags and, by the time they were done, had removed the entire rear subframe, sandblasted and repainted it, and replaced every rubber bushing. There but for the grace of an anal retentive personality go I.

Truth be told, I *have*, over the years, tilted a bit in this direction. But just a bit. If I'm working on a car that I'm keeping for the long haul, like my 3.0CSi, and it needs, say, a left outer tie rod, these days I'm likely to order not just the left outer tie rod it needs, but the whole tie rod assembly with both inner and outer tie rod ends *and* the same assembly for the right side of the car *and* the center track rod that connects them *and*, perhaps, both ball joints. I've learned to value and appreciate that, once these parts are installed, I've just done most of the front-end work the car will likely need for the rest of my stewardship. To me, that's a big tilt in the direction of "do it once, do it right." To many guys, that's nothing. I don't, for example, use the replacement of front struts as an opportunity to media blast and power coat the springs and strut assemblies while they're out of the car so they look like new. It just doesn't matter to me. My cars aren't trailer queens. I drive them. But if someone else gets pleasure out of both the process of blasting and painting suspension components and the end product, more power to them.

Sometimes it seems that there are two kinds of enthusiast owners—folks like me who just try to keep their cars running, and folks who will not rest until they and their car have achieved perfection. I simply don't chase perfection in *any* corner of my life (well, okay, I lied; I do in songwriting). The strip-it-down-to-bare-metal restoration thing is all about control. It's a primal, man-versus-machine dynamic. You *will* master this pile of steel, glass, and wire. You *will* get this iron to bend to your iron will by beating it to death with tools, time, and money. You *will* take it all apart, zinc-plate every washer, and put it all back together. There's nothing wrong with that, but the time and money requirements are bottomless. It costs what it costs. It takes however long it takes. You have to be in love with the process, because you're going to be involved with the process longer than most committed relationships. Don't get me wrong—there's beauty in the pursuit, and possibly the attainment, of perfection. The end product can be a stunning juxtaposition of form and function. Personally, I am absolutely in awe of the guys who do the whole rotisserie restoration thing and coat the under and inner surfaces of the car with POR-15. But, man, it's a long row to hoe.

Even folks who get off on removing, zinc plating, and reinstalling every nut and bolt are subject to burnout. People have different strategies: visualizing the end product; working on the car for 30 minutes every night; leaving the car alone for a month and coming back to it. And they still get in over their head. I recently saw, and passed on, a '72 2002tii project where a guy wanted to build himself a show-quality car from the ground up and had cut out the rust and acquired a full assortment of new and used body panels awaiting installation. Now, everything was piled on top of the car in the garage, threatening to crush anyone who disturbed it, and he had to admit that he was never going to get this done and wanted out. In the old-buddies-showing-up-at-your-door analogy, this qualifies as your ex-roommate getting shit-faced, throwing up everywhere, passing out in the spare bedroom, then staying around your house, hung over, for 20 years.

Speaking of long-term projects, Maire Anne once noted that even my running cars are often missing things like door panels, center consoles, and glove boxes. Generally there are good reasons for this: Door panels are off because I'm chasing down some rattle; center consoles are out because I'm repairing something in the air-conditioning. But I have to admit (and, yes, this is the car-guy equivalent of revealing the magician's secret of how to saw a person in half), even to someone like me who gets such enjoyment out of closure, there is something safe and comforting about an unfinished project.

For example, I pulled off the long pieces of rocker panel trim (they run beneath the doors between the front and rear wheels) from my 3.0CSi to check for rust and found some very minor bubbles in the paint. That was well over a decade ago. I never put the trim pieces back on. And now, if I must be completely honest, it occurs to me that— even though this is not the reason I took them off—there is a stabilizing effect in leaving them off. After all, even if I needed money, I couldn't sell the car without photographing it, and I couldn't even think about photographing it until the rocker trim pieces are back on, right? And I can't put them back on until I grind off the surface rust and touch up the spots with primer, and the little screws that held it on are long since lost so I'd have to look those up and order them, etc.

Another observation: When the door panels are off a car, you have to reach inside the door frame and pull something metallic and po-tentially greasy just to get the door to open. This makes the car totally uninviting to Maire Anne. Now, that's not *why* the door panels are off. I encourage Maire Anne to drive my cars. Seriously. Really. I do. (The red 3.0CSi, she once noted, would be a great car to meet an old boyfriend in.) But I can't help it if she has an aversion to grease. Maire Anne also notes that, while she can simply take her keys and start her Honda, driving any of my cars requires that she first listen to me clock off a litany of issues that could be as simple as "the check engine light is on but don't worry about it" but could also include "you might have to put the fuel pump relay back in I think it's in the glove compartment you remember where it goes, right?" or "I just had both half axles out I *think* I remembered to torque both of them back down but if you hear something smacking underneath stop and call me."

So, by the simple mechanism of removing a few parts, I've taken a car that could potentially be both driven by a spouse and sold and—*voila!*—negated either possibility. Not that I would *ever* do that intentionally. It's just an unintended consequence. Spouses, I'm not implying that your car guy would ever do this intentionally. He may not even be aware of it.

To quote my father-in-law, "I'm just sayin'."

I'd like to beat the drum in one additional time signature before leaving "The Rhythm of Repair," and that's the subject of splitting a repair with a shop. Working on your own car isn't an all-or-nothing thing. You may be able to find some middle ground where you do some work yourself but pay someone to do the things you can't, or can but just don't like. For example, you might generally enjoy automotive work but hate dealing with the rust falling in your eyes and stuck bolts inherent in exhaust work. Or perhaps you're fine at removing and installing parts but you just can't figure out what's making that *thunk* in the front end. You should be able to find a repair shop with whom you can work as a partner. If a shop is worth its salt, they should regard your instructions to "look at such-and-such *and then call me*" not as a challenge to their authority but as an opportunity to gain a well-informed customer.

For several years I had this kind of relationship with a local BMW dealer (the now-departed Foreign Motors West in Natick, when Lance Mitchell was their service manager). I'd bring them a car with dead air-conditioning to diagnose, they'd tell me which major component needed replacing, I'd take the car back, make my own decision on using new OEM, aftermarket, or used parts, replace the offending item, and bring the car back to them to be evacuated and recharged. It worked out well for both parties—they made a little money off me, and I still felt like I was coming out ahead of the game because I was selecting and installing parts myself.

Whether you're just doing a Saturday repair to the daily driver, or fighting mission creep that's threatening to turn a small repair into a Big Job, or up to your hips in a full-blown restoration, the overriding issue about the rhythm of repair is that you, the car, your needs, and your expectations should all be in harmony. If you're always working on a daily driver as if it's a project car, you're likely to get frustrated and burn out, and that's not helpful to anyone. Why do it if you're not enjoying it? Being able to measure the repair and do the work on a schedule dictated by *you* is key.

Why do men love cars? Because, when the repair rhythm works out right, when you get your baby back on the road with a new exhaust or suspension or air-conditioning or whatever it is you've done, it brings a sense of personal accomplishment and pride that is elating.

CHAPTER 31

OVERHAUL *THIS* (ACTUALLY, DON'T)

While we're talking about the rhythm of repair, I need to rant for a moment about how totally distorted cable shows like *Overhaulin'* are. If you haven't seen this show, they pick a guy with some old beat-up classic car, use him as "the mark," take away the car using a ruse (for example, pretending it's been stolen), then have a team work furiously on the car for two weeks, stripping it completely bare like throwing a carcass into a tub of dermestid beetles (and Maire Anne thinks I don't listen), sand-blasting, patching rust, painting, then reinstalling and customizing everything. New drivetrain, new interior, new over-the-top sound system, everything. Finally they bring in "the mark" to identify the stolen car, and voila! It's been transformed. Hugs and tears. "Oh, it's so beautiful. I never imagined. Thank you. *Thank you. THANK YOU!*"

Seriously moving shit.

This show bothers me in oh so many ways. First, in project management there's an old saying: "On time, in scope, within budget—pick any two." This means that, typically, you can't do everything you want within the planned time frame for the planned cost. At least one thing has to give, whether it's the scope (doing less than you'd planned), the time frame (taking longer than you'd planned), or the budget (costing more than you'd planned). For real restoration work, this is actually incredibly optimistic—you're fortunate if any *one* of these three things comes out as expected. If you have a lot of money, the scope, budget, and time all increase. If you're on a truly fixed budget, the scope gets reduced and the time frame gets lengthened.

The situation presented on *Overhaulin'*, where the scope pretends to be a full restoration plus customization, the time frame jams all of the work into a two-week period, and the cost to the owner is zero, is more than simply unrealistic and more than just a total warping of the rhythm of repair—it is a complete and utter perversion of *any* kind of a project, all driven by the presence of the camera. (If I might wax quantum philosophical, it's observation of the system interfering with the system.) And, yes, I am aware that the presence of the camera is necessary because *this is just a television show.* But imagine if there was a show that short-circuited the trial-by-jury process and presented a totally warped unrealistic view of adjudication on the basis of the single attribute of an unnaturally compressed time frame. Oh. There is. It's *Judge Judy.* Sorry.

Secondly, I imagine that the warped time frame also distorts the experience of the owner. If you're driving a beat-up rat rod of a Camaro, there are probably reasons why. At minimum, a) you probably like it, and b) you probably don't have the money to restore it. What happens when the *Overhaulin'* fairy suddenly sprinkles the restoration dust? Be careful what you wish for. It's like someone giving you a castle, at which point you realize that you have to maintain it and pay taxes on it. Does the guy have a place to garage the transformed car? A safe place to park it at work? Can he afford to insure it? Is he going to keep using it as his daily driver? If not, can he afford to buy another car? I wonder what happens to these cars—what percentage of owners feel that their subtle connection with the car has been severed, yearn to have their old beat-up friend back, and wind up having to sell the pretty shiny Barbie doll whose soul has been excised.

Many years ago, I had something similar happen with a guitar. In 1972, when I was 13 years old, I bought a new Guild D40 with my bar mitzvah money. Over the years it was a somewhat troublesome instrument, but I had an intimate relationship with it; it was the guitar I logged endless hours playing as a weepy angst-soaked adolescent, and through the years I dragged it all over hell and creation. And that *smell.* When I'd open up the case, I'd smell the mahogany and spruce, and my brain would instantly channel Marcel Proust, do the "remembrance of things past" thing, and transport me back to the second-floor guitar store in Northampton where I'd bought the instrument new in 1972. After 35 years, the guitar's bridge started to pull up, so I sent it back to Guild—again—under the lifetime warranty. When they returned it, I opened up the case to find that they'd re-lacquered the surface of the guitar. Who the hell asked them to do that? It broke the intimate link I had with the instrument. When

I opened up the case, all I smelled was lacquer. For months I tried to play it, to reestablish that intimate relationship, but the bond was broken. I finally sold it.

That's how I'd feel if one of my cars were "overhauled" without my permission.

However, if anyone wants to simply write the checks for a restoration that I direct, let's talk.

My only photo of the infamous 1973 Triumph GT6+. It broke. I fixed it. Over and over. Finally, it broke. I sold it.

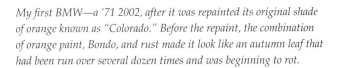

My first BMW—a '71 2002, after it was repainted its original shade of orange known as "Colorado." Before the repaint, the combination of orange paint, Bondo, and rust made it look like an autumn leaf that had been run over several dozen times and was beginning to rot.

The Malaga (maroon) '73 2002 at the trail head in Colorado (the state, not the color. I know. It gets confusing.). Buried within this backpack was my grandmother's engagement ring. Maire Anne and I hiked in single, and hiked out engaged.

I knew Maire Anne was a keeper when she was thrilled that I was rebuilding the engine to her VW van in the kitchen.

Me, pulling the engine out of the '72 VW Bus in preparation for rebuild and installation into the '68 Camper. If memory serves me correctly, I had the engine on its side to remove the pressure release valve. Either that or I was checking its prostate.

The engine from the '72 VW Bus on its way for rebuild and transplant into the '68 Camper.

I don't understand it. The engine should be in here somewhere. Oh, right, I took it out.

I don't recall the VW engine moving from the kitchen to the living room, but it was a small apartment.

My '74 BMW 2002 ("Bertha"), dolled up by my friends with shaving cream and streamers, ready to take us away from our wedding.

Our Siamese cat Phoebe in the '68 VW Camper in which she was forced to transit from Austin to Boston. During the trip, she jumped out the window, and was briefly dangling by her harness.

The '68 VW Camper, me, and Holden (the cat who had the good sense NOT to jump out the window).

My '73 BMW 3.0CSi stripped to bare metal during its outer body restoration.

The just-painted '73 3.0CSi wearing seven coats of Signal Red urethane and seven coats of clear.

When Yale Rachlin let me drive his 2002tii, I accidentally left the car out of gear and the door ajar, and the car rolled backward out of his garage, catching the driver's door on the way out. Rather than chew me out, he grabbed his camera and we recreated the incident for the Roundel *article "Crashing Dad's Car."*

In 1999, BMW CCA member Steve Diamond, whom I'd never met, called me from Boulder and asked me to check out an ultra-rare BMW Z1 for him in Massachusetts. I did, and later helped Steve buy the car. Yale Rachlin stored it in his garage for a week while we waited for it to be shipped. Four years later, Steve, the Z1, and I were finally in the same place at the same time.

The 1989 BMW Z1 that I looked at for Steve Diamond. Note how the doors drop down into the sills. Very cool.

The old garage before demolition. Difficult to believe I worked in this space for 15 years, with electricity supplied via an extension cord from the house and illumination from a single droplight. Even more difficult to believe the City of Newton briefly tried to have it declared a historic landmark.

The old garage after demolition. I think the workers insulted it and it fell over.

The doors weren't even on the new garage when I started buying 2002s again. This '73 2002tii was the first 2002 I'd had in 18 years.

The new garage. Considering its capacity to hold four cars and a fifth beneath the deck, it's remarkably unobtrusive as seen from the back of the house.

A shot of the sliding door in my garage that opens up under the deck. Three of the other cars need to be moved out of the garage to access it, it's a tight fit, and once a car is under there, it's not moving till spring, but I do have the ability to stash a fifth car largely out of the elements. As someone recently noted, "Dude, your garage has a garage."

Nothing is as audacious as a Porsche with a Targa top and a tail. My relationship with the 1982 Porsche 911SC lasted eight years.

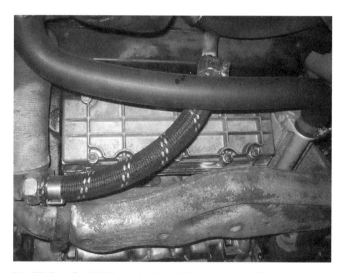

My '82 Porsche 911SC was leaking oil from where a rubber hose was permanently crimped to a hard metal line. Rather than risk stripping nuts or breaking fittings that hadn't been removed in 25 years, I replaced the rubber section with high-pressure oil hose and held it in place with T-bolt clamps. This follwed the rule of a "good kluge"—one that saves money, is safe, and is easily undone.

My middle son Kyle and his prom date posing in front of the 1999 BMW Z3 M Coupe. My older son Ethan was pissed he hadn't thought of it first.

My '73 BMW 3.0CSi on the Blue Ridge Parkway on the way to Vintage at the Vineyards in 2010.

Putting the coupe to bed for the winter. This photo, shot by Yale Rachlin, so beautifully captures the care and intimacy that men are capable of feeling for their car. (Yale Rachlin)

Three BMW coupes in the garage—the '73 3.0CSi I've had for over 25 years, another '73 3.0CS, and a '85 635CSi. The big pile of junk on the left is the detritus of swapping engines in Alex's Passat. You can see the old engine strapped to the lift table.

Pulling the dead sludged-up motor from Alex's Passat. It looks like I'm harnessing the power of Robby the Robot on the movie poster to augment the engine hoist.

Alex and I savoring the moment of triumph after the engine swap in his piece of shit 1999 VW Passat.

*In many ways, this book is my life viewed through the lens of cars, but that lens isn't neces-
sary to view everything. It's the people, not the cars, that are important. My family hasn't
been much for portraits, but Maire Anne really wanted one before Kyle went off to college. I
called our friend Kim Cox and asked her to meet us in the park behind our house. I shouted
to everyone in the house "wear white." Sometimes it's just that easy.*

CHAPTER 32

THE COMING OF THE ASTEROID

Years ago, I mentioned to Alex what I sometimes refer to as the Asteroid Theory of Parenting. It goes like this. Any course corrections you make with your children had better occur very early on because, like redirecting an asteroid, if you're trying to alter its course two days before it's about to smash into the planet and obliterate all of life, it's too late. You should've made small course corrections sooner.

Now, my oldest boy, Ethan, is a classic first child. A headstrong alpha male, he loves to construct a lawyer's argument and stick his toe over any line we draw. When he turned 18, we took the docking clamps off. He had free run of my '96 BMW 318ti for nearly a year. Every time he left the house, I'd say, "Don't do anything stupid." It was a running joke. I'd close e-mails and phone calls the same way—"Don't do anything stupid." Hey, I'm the guy who ran his Triumph off the road in the fog three times and was towed uphill on his bicycle at 50 mph by a motorcycle. With bungee cords. Stupid is bred in my bone.

When, after graduation, Ethan began coming home after 3 A.M. nearly every night, we had a little chat. I know what kids do at these hours, I explained, and they are bad habits that, once engrained, can last a lifetime. I restricted his use of my car to driving to and from his place where he was working; permission for any other use was given on a case-by-case basis. But as he began his final summer at home before college, he announced that he wanted to buy a car.

"Well," said I, his hyper-rational parent. "There are two situations—the first is while you're still at home; the second is when you go off to school. You're 18. I can't legally stop you from buying a car. But with me owning all these cars, there is always at least one you can drive, and it makes absolutely no sense for you to buy another. Plus, if you think you want to buy a car so you can get around my restriction and party all night and drive home, you need to stop and think about what you're proposing. So, can you buy a car while you're at home? No.

"The second issue is once you're at college. The school may not even allow freshman to have cars. Plus, cars are very expensive. For someone your age, it'll be about two grand a year for insurance. Registration, title, taxes, and inspection will run you hundreds. Then there's gas, and repairs, and tickets. I don't think you can afford it. Your mother and I started off college with cars and we both had to sell them because we couldn't afford them."

Now, I said all this, quite pleased with myself, and just brimming with the kind of "wouldn't any kid *just love* to have a father like me" self-satisfaction that can make me absolutely insufferable.

But the adolescent mind is a fascinating thing. Despite what I *said*, I think what he *heard* was "I can't legally stop you," and "your mother and I had cars at college."

A red 1989 Firebird appeared in my driveway. It had no plates. It had no exhaust. Ethan paid $200 for it. He drove it home illegally. He said he was "tired of us rationalizing away his good ideas," he wanted to "make his own mistakes," and was going to "fix it up."

So much for not doing anything stupid.

I cannot begin to describe the ways in which this car pissed me off.

Shortly after Ethan acquired the Firebird, Alex came by the house. "Remember that speech you gave me about parenting being like redirecting an asteroid?" he said. I nodded ruefully. He motioned at the Firebird. "What happened?"

Actually, I take it back. I *can* describe the ways in which this car pissed me off.

Way 1: It was a freaking *Firebird*.

Way 2: He's my son. *How the hell did he imprint on a Firebird?* I had failed him.

Way 3: Years back, when Ethan was learning to drive, I bought an uber-high-mileage 1991 BMW 525i for peanuts. Solid, airbag, ABS, it seemed like a good first car for him in the days before gas averaged three bucks a gallon. "Can I help you work on it?" he asked. "Sure," I said. Never happened. The car had no small number of electrical quirks that took huge amounts of my time with no clear resolution.

Finally, with him having no interest in helping and me preferring to spend my automotive time elsewhere, I sold it.

Way 4: For Ethan to show up with this, this interloper, and to not have consulted me (me!) about buying it, and with the expectation that I would fix it … Perhaps this wasn't his expectation. Kids don't think this stuff through. Maybe it was just *my* expectation, borne on the waters of reality and experience. To keep the car at arm's length felt negligent. To embrace it felt like I'd been conned. And, despite my "no," I had, in fact, been looking for the right car for Ethan.

Eventually, like the *Enterprise* engaging the Borg (resistance is futile), I visually inspected the Firebird. The exhaust needed to be replaced. All the rugs were missing. The floor had plainly visible rust holes large enough to do the Fred Flintstone thing. It was doubtful that it would ever pass Massachusetts state inspection. I recommended that he not register it, get out of it, even donate it to charity. But then I found myself online, looking at exhausts and state inspection laws. Just in case he asked for my help. I ain't Ward and he certainly ain't the Beaver, but I am his dad and that's my job.

If I couldn't redirect the asteroid, at least I could help guide it safely into the ocean.

Ethan never lifted a finger to "fix up" the Firebird. It was still there a week before he started college. After telling him that I was going to do so, and encountering no resistance, I had it towed off, donating it to the local public television station. The Firebird was not spoken about for years. Now we all joke about it. If Ethan seems too full of himself, "Firebird" is best expulsed as part of a mock cough, the way "blow job" was in *Animal House*.

CHAPTER 33

THE Z3 M COUPE AND EVA MENDES'S BUTT

In 2007 I stumbled into The Dream. Most folks recognize the little BMW Z3 roadster built 1996 through 2002, but there is a rare variant called the Z3 Coupe that is the roadster with a hardtop hatchback grafted on. The body style is what is known obscurely in automotive circles as a "shooting brake"—a low, two-door wagon with a squared-off hatchback. The terminology is deliciously British, referring to a sporty personal-sized hunting wagon from which you can grab the rifles and release the hounds. The most recognizable example of a "shooting brake" is the early 1970s Volvo P1800ES sport wagon.

Then, there is a rarer variant within a variant: The BMW M Coupe—also called the Z3 M Coupe—is a Z3 Coupe with M3 goodies (engine, suspension, brakes), plus *massively* wide fender flares and tires. *Nothing* else on the road looks like this car. The rear end is just so … planted. When it was released in 1999, critics complained that it looked like a different car from the front and the back. And there's some truth to that. But over time, because the shape is unique and because the car was only built in fairly small numbers during 1999–2002, it quickly became a cult car. Plus, at the time, it was BMW's fastest car, getting from 0–60 in just 5.3 seconds.

Now, owning the Porsche 911SC, I was not in the market for another slot car. But when a '99 M Coupe showed up on Craigslist, I e-mailed the owner out of curiosity. A few days later he called me. "I think the car is sold," he said. "That is, I've taken a deposit, though the guy has been slow in closing the deal. If it falls through I'll let you know." Oh well. The last thing I needed was another non-daily-driver, and this one was a two-seater priced in the $15K range—not "whimable" money by any means.

But six weeks later the seller called me back, telling me that the buyer couldn't close. He'd returned the guy's deposit, and would be happy to show me the car if I wanted. Oh, man, I wanted. I wanted *baaad.* I drove down to the Massachusetts / Rhode Island border in the dead of winter to see the car. It was gorgeous—silver with a solid black interior. M Coupes are available in a number of really zingy colors with eye-popping two-tone interiors, but the lines of the car are so extreme that I think they look best in understated colors that soften the lines. So I adored the basic silver/black. The owner loved the car but by no means babied it—he used it as a daily driver to commute into the financial district in Boston. It had just under 100K miles and nine Boston winters on it. He was selling it both because it needed work and because he'd found a $199 per month lease deal on a new 3 Series BMW that he just couldn't pass up.

When I drove it, it would not have taken an aficionado to notice the combination of bent wheels, bad shocks and struts, and worn-out rear shock bushings—the car banged audibly and rode just horribly. But when I got on the highway and mashed the accelerator in sec-ond gear, redlined it and shifted into third … none of that mattered. I looked at the speedometer and found that I was doing 90. Oh, *baby*!

Because the car needed work, I was, incredibly, able to keep the lust at arm's length in order to drive a steely-eyed bargain. It was win-ter, the owner needed to sell it, I had a new garage to put it in … the planets were aligned. I bought it, bumping the car count up to seven. I paid more than I've ever paid for any car, yet less than anyone had ever heard of a running M Coupe selling for—about the price of a four-year-old Honda Civic.

I never, *EVER*, have owned anything even remotely this nice. It is the jewel in the crown. It has a back end like Eva Mendes. It is drop-dead gorgeous. It is quirky. It is twitchy. It is stiff. It is a little uncomfortable. It is nastyfast. It snarls and claws when you nail it. I absolutely adore it. Moving or standing still, it is an object of obses-sion. Even my normally laconic son Kyle had me take his prom photos in front of it so he could post them on Facebook (which made Ethan jealous, at least partially because he hadn't thought of it).

Why do men love cars? Because once in a while, one will make you completely understand a 40-year-old offhand comment: "A car like that, *you can get sex out of.*"

SHOCK AND AWE, STRUT YOUR STUFF

Having bought Eva I mean the Z3 M Coupe, the immediate task was to address the fact that it rode horribly. For a BMW with 100K on it, that meant the shocks and struts were probably toast. Fortunately, shocks and struts are well within the envelope of the DIY-er.

Taking the wider view for a moment, the immutable troika of repairs for both the do-it-yourselfer and the non-model-specific repair shop is shocks, brakes, and exhaust. This is not surprising since a) these are major normal-wear-and-tear items on most cars, b) the procedures to replace them vary little from car to car, and c) working on them generally does not require expensive model-specific tools. To many, shocks, brakes and exhaust represent the sweet spot of money-saving DIY repair work (if you own a modern BMW, add cooling system and CVV replacement to this unholy trinity).

So let's talk about suspension work. Even if you don't want to replace your own shocks and struts, at least this will give you some idea what the friendly young man at Midas is talking about when your car is clunking, you bring it in, and he gives you a 1,200-dollar estimate.

SUSPENSION 101

As any kid who has ever ridden a Red Radio Wagon down a hill knows, it has no suspension whatsoever. The wheels are bolted directly to the wagon's body. Hit a bump or pothole and you go flying out of it precisely because the jolt is transferred directly to you. Fortunately, every car is equipped with a suspension to lessen this coupling of pavement to passengers. The suspension consists of a set of springs to hold up the body of the car and allow it to move over bumps, and shock absorbers to dampen the action of those springs so the car doesn't continue to bounce up and down after it hits a bump.

Rear-wheel independent suspension was used on many cars, including BMWs, for decades. In the '80s and '90s, multilink rear suspensions, originally employed on race cars, gravitated onto passenger cars. This design allows the rear wheel to move up and down without changing the angle (called the camber) the wheel makes with the road. Cars with multilink rear suspensions have a wonderful self-correction capability; if you go into a curve a little hot, you correct once with the steering wheel, and the rear end snaps itself into place instead of fishtailing wildly.

FRONT SUSPENSION DESIGN

The front suspension is more complex than the rear because, in addition to hosting attachment points for the springs, the front wheels must also turn so they can steer the car. For this reason, the front suspension of most modern cars utilizes a configuration where the front shock absorber is also the axis around which the steering pivots. This design is called a MacPherson strut. In this design, the front shock absorber is a long replaceable cartridge forming the central structure of the strut. Like the rear shock, this strut cartridge has a piston that goes up and down, the motion of which is damped by either fluid or gas.

Attached to the bottom of the strut housing is the stub axle on which the front wheel and its bearing ride. The coil spring sits in a spring perch at the top of the strut housing. The cartridge's piston passes through the center of the spring and extends through a bushing that looks like a donut with a bearing in the middle and three studs sticking out the top. When the strut is assembled, the spring is compressed, and a nut is threaded onto the end of the cartridge's piston, thereby using the bushing and the nut to hold the compressed spring. The studs sticking out the bushing at the top of the strut assembly are then bolted to the underside of the front fender, and the bottom of the assembly is attached to the ball joint or analogous steering component. The wheel is attached to the stub axle at the base of the strut. In this way, the car is suspended by the spring, the weight is borne by the strut housing, and the bearing in the bushing at the top and the ball joint at the bottom allow the entire strut assembly to rotate when the steering wheel is turned.

(If you want to get geeky, the major alternative front-end design to the MacPherson strut is the double-wishbone suspension, in which the shock absorber is just like the one in the rear and just as easily replaced.)

Struts come in two basic styles. On older cars, the strut has a permanent tubular metal housing about a foot and a half long. The stub axle is an integral part of the housing, permanently affixed at the bottom. This housing lasts the life of the car; it is only replaced if it is damaged by an accident or if catastrophic failure of a wheel bearing ruins the stub axle (ask me how I know). A replaceable strut cartridge slides inside the tubular housing. In contrast, many newer cars employ a design where the replaceable strut cartridge *includes* the housing, and the axle and steering components bolt to it.

Thus, unlike the rear shock, the strut cartridge is tightly integrated; there's no way to drive a car without the strut cartridges installed. Although the strut cartridge is a "shock absorber," the terminology that's usually employed is *rear shocks, front struts.* Most people don't say *strut cartridge, strut housing,* and *strut assembly*; I'm just being overly pedantic for the sake of clarity. When a shop tells you "you need struts," they mean "strut cartridges."

BOUNCING A CAR TO TEST FOR BAD SHOCKS

Although suspension design can vary dramatically car to car, the primary normal-wear-and-tear items are the shocks and struts, and the procedure to replace these doesn't vary much. How do you know they *need* to be replaced? Presumably something feels wrong with the ride—too bouncy or not enough give. The time-honored technique, as old as dirt, temptation, and corruption, is to do the "bounce test"— walk around to each of the four corners and push down sharply on the top of each front fender and rear quarter panel. The car should dip when you push it, then rebound smoothly when you let go. If it continues to bounce, the shock or strut is blown—it has lost its fluid or gas pressure and is no longer absorbing anything. If, on the other hand, you can't push it down, the shock or strut may be seized—not moving at all in its cylinder. The bounce test works well on cars with soft suspensions, but pushing down a modern sports car with very stiff springs is often so difficult that the bounce test is inconclusive. This was the case with my Z3 M Coupe. I did the bounce test and couldn't tell a thing. When I pulled out the front struts, I found one was seized and the other was blown.

REPLACING REAR SHOCKS

Changing rear shock absorbers on most cars is trivial. On a rear suspension, the springs and shocks are usually separate components. (The exception to this is the so-called *coil-over* suspension where the shock absorber goes up and down in the center of the coil.) To change a rear shock, you jack up the back of the car, support it with jack stands, undo the top of the shock absorber (which is usually accessible through the trunk and merely requires using two wrenches to undo two nuts that are tightened against each other), undo the bottom of the shock which is held on by a single bolt, and pull out the old shock. To install the new shock, you may need to put a jack beneath the hanging wheel in order to push the trailing arm up high enough to allow the top and bottom nuts and bolts for the shock to be installed. There are bushings at the tops of the rear shocks. On older cars they're literally just a pair of small rubber donuts that are squeezed between the lock-nuts. On a newer car like the Z3 M Coupe the bushings are in a plate that bolts into the rear shock tower. But it's all easy stuff.

REPLACING FRONT STRUTS

However, changing the front strut cartridges is somewhat involved. Recall that the top of the strut cartridge has a nut threaded onto it that holds a bushing that, in turn, holds the compressed spring. Thus, in order to replace the strut cartridge, the bushing at the top has to be re-moved. To do that, the spring has to be compressed to take the tension off the bushing so the nut and the bushing don't *sproing* themselves off and embed themselves in your face. And to do *that*, the entire strut assembly usually has to be removed from the car.

On certain cars, the geometry may be hospitable to allowing you to leave the strut attached at the bottom, swing the top of the strut out from beneath the fender, get a spring compressor onto the spring, undo the nut, and withdraw the strut cartridge. But unless you've read online and seen pictures of it actually done with your model of car, you risk gouging the paint on your fender. Usually you need to unbolt whatever steering component is attached to the bottom of the strut (a simple ball joint on older cars), unbolt the brake caliper and slide it off the brake rotor, then undo the bushing from the top of the fender, drop the entire strut assembly down, lay it on the floor, and attack it with a spring compressor. The procedure is involved enough that it makes sense to replace any worn related parts (i.e., strut bushings, ball joints) at the same time.

I cannot stress strongly enough that replacing a strut absolutely requires a spring compressor. In the old days you'd read about people compressing springs with hose clamps. I love a good kluge, but this is not the place. If the spring lets go, it can injure or kill you. Don't jury-rig it. A Chinese-made set of spring compressors can be purchased for 15 bucks. AutoZone will loan you a set for free.

There are several types of spring compressors. The most basic is simply a threaded rod with two claws that look like your fingers when you're using them to make quotation signs in the air (think Doctor Evil saying "laser"). You employ a pair of these to compress a spring, one on each side, with the claws at the top and bottom. You tighten them, one at a time, with a ratchet wrench (or better still, air tools). Another type of compressor looks like the hand-cranked jack that comes with many cars, but with an angled plate at the top and the bottom. You insert the angled plates between the coils of the spring and turn the handle to bring the plates together and compress the spring.

When the spring is compressed sufficiently that it is no longer pressing on the underside of the bushing, you remove the bushing by undoing the nut at the top of the strut cartridge. The problem is, when you start to turn this nut, the strut cartridge simply spins around, so the nut doesn't loosen. If you look in the center of the threaded top of the strut cartridge, you'll see a small Allen key hole. You're supposed to put an Allen key (preferably in socket-and-ratchet form) in there and hold it still to prevent the strut cartridge from turning, then use a wrench to loosen the nut. This is problematic for several reasons. If you have an Allen key in the hole, you can't also put a socket over the top to loosen the nut, so you have to use a wrench instead, and depending on the car, the center of the strut bushing is sometimes recessed and it is not always easy to get a wrench in there. But even if you can, if the struts have been in the car for a long time, this nut may not want to come off easily, and it's very easy to strip that little Allen hole trying to hold the thing still. Removing this nut is one of the single best applications for air tools. With an impact wrench, you don't need to hold the top of the strut still; the rapid successive impacts will simply spin the nut off.

When taking off the bushing, pay careful attention to the sequence of spacers and washers and tie them together in the correct order with a zip tie. Inspect the bushing to make sure it's okay. If it's cracked, procure a replacement. Once it's off, you can slide the spring, with the compressor still attached, off its perch. If your car has the newer style of strut with an integral housing, you can transfer the still-compressed spring onto the perch of the new strut, transfer the bushing, tighten the nut, release the compressor, and install the new strut assembly back into the car. If it's the older style of strut where the cartridge slides inside the strut housing, you need to undo the collar nut holding the cartridge in place. This nut may be hexagonal or may have a notch on both sides to receive a special wrench used to remove it. Earlier I said strut and shock replacement didn't require special tools, and I meant it. Removing the notched nut usually isn't a big deal; a big pair of pliers, a Vise-Grip, a plumber's pipe wrench, or a hammer beating a screwdriver into the slots is usually more than enough to spin the collar nut off.

SPRINGS

Unlike shocks and struts, springs are not really normal-wear-and-tear items (yes, some cars such as the E46 BMW 3 Series have a reputation for breaking rear springs, and yes, you can be simply unlucky and break one, as I did on my 528iT). And on very old, very beat-on, very high-mileage cars, the springs may sag. But, for the most part, springs last the life of the car and don't wear out like shocks and struts do.

You may, however, wish to change springs to lower a car for performance or appearance reasons. On a BMW, the most popular aftermarket shocks and struts are Bilsteins. The Bilstein Heavy Duty (HD) is usually employed with the stock springs to firm up the ride, but the Bilstein Sport (SP) is designed to work with lowered springs. Thus, when shocks are being replaced for performance reasons, it's not uncommon to do springs at the same time. Obviously, since the front springs have to be removed to get at the struts, this works out nicely.

But the same is true for the rear as well: If you need to change the rear springs, unbolting the shock is a necessary first step, as the shock itself prevents the rear trailing arm from dropping down low enough to allow the spring to extend to its full length and be taken out. Depending on the car, you may need to unbolt the rear half-axle to let the trailing arm drop all the way down.

Speaking of replacing rear springs, I'd like to revisit the spring compressor issue. Recently, the tide of inexpensive Chinese tools brought another kind of compressor to our fair shores—a small hydraulic unit that, when you pump the lever, it squeezes a pair of angled plates together which compress the spring. Part of the appeal is that, because the hand-pumped cylinder sits on the floor, the portion that actually compresses the spring is fairly compact and can be slid between the spring coils as your hand could if your hand had great strength and could simply reach in, squeeze the spring, and pluck it out. This sings the siren song of being able to compress the spring without having to remove the front strut (or, on the rear of the car, without having to undo the half-shafts).

I was planning on doing some work lowering my 3.0CSi by cutting a coil off the springs and trying different-sized rubber spring perches, so the idea of being able to pop the spring in and out quickly had a lot of appeal. I spent the $125 and purchased one of these units (search for "hand pump spring compressor" to find it online). I was mystified when the unit wouldn't fully compress the spring. The 8" distance between the jaws in the fully extended position was plenty, but no matter how hard I pumped, I couldn't get the jaws closer than 4 ½", for a total travel of only 3 ½". I tried playing with the valves to bleed it but couldn't improve it. Finally I noticed that, on the assembly diagram (there was no manual), it said "stroke 100mm." Doing the math, 100mm is about 3.9". I looked closer on the assembly diagram, and in the middle of the piece pulling the plates together was a small spring. I figured the spring was there to automatically spread the jaws back apart when you release the hydraulic pressure, and wondered if it was what was impeding the compression (beyond a certain distance, the coils of this internal spring were probably stacking up and binding). In other words, the little spring inside was preventing me from compressing the big spring outside. I wondered … could you just take out this internal spring?

Reading online, I found a post on a Subaru-related forum from an enterprising young man who had the same idea. He'd bought one of these units, undid the screw-in plug at the bottom, pulled out the seal, pulled out the spring in the middle, and put it back together. He reported success, so I did the same thing. Initially it worked perfectly, allowing me to quickly pluck the rear springs back out of my 3.0CSi, shorten them, and put them back in, but after several uses it began leaking like a sieve. I don't know if I damaged the seal pulling it in and out, or if pulling the plates that much closer together places too much internal stress on the seals, or if this is simply all you can expect of inexpensive Chinese-built crap.

BUSHINGS

Having said shocks and struts are the big normal-wear-and-tear parts of the suspension, that doesn't mean other suspension components don't need periodic replacement as well. They do. Whenever you hear the term "bushing," it means "piece of rubber between two pieces of metal." Anywhere in the front or rear suspension where road vibration has to be isolated from the passenger compartment, there are rubber bushings. For example, nearly every modern car has upper and lower control arms. These keep the front wheel at the same camber angle as the wheel goes up and down over bumps. Each of these control arms has a bushing or a ball joint at one end. And they all eventually wear out. A German car's unique addictive magic combination of ride and handling is due partially to the bushings. It's not that these things never go bad on a Camry or an Accord. They certainly do. But when you're used to that whole-is-greater-than-the-sum-of-the-parts feeling of driving a German car, and when the front end of your BMW starts to clunk and groan, the degradation in performance and ride quality can be dramatic. If you were driving a claptrap '85 Ford Escort with bad front end bushings, you might not ever notice.

Bushings are one of those Goldilocks things. If they're too soft, they provide great vibration isolation but wear prematurely. If they're too hard, they last a long time but give the car a harsh feel. BMW's version of "just right" seems to hew closer to the former than the latter. Unlike shocks and struts, many bushings require special tools to press them in and out. For a BMW, you can buy control arms with harder, more durable urethane bushings pressed into them, thereby freeing you from the need for the special tool as well as providing the more durable bushing. To determine whether this is the best course for you and your car, you really need to read a variety of opinions on enthusiast forums.

In case you feel you need my permission, it's okay to replace shocks and struts yourself but draw the line at control arms and their pressed-in bushings. When I do so much of my own work, I rarely resent the small handful of repairs that I choose to pay someone else for.

All Eva needed was rear shocks and shock tower bushings, and front struts. I did the front strut bushings while I was in the neighborhood, but stopped there. The control arms all felt fine.

And we lived happily ever after.

CHAPTER 35

THE CAR COUNT HITS DOUBLE DIGITS

With the purchase of the Z3 M Coupe, the car count was at seven; I had fulfilled Siegel's Seven-Car Rule. But rather than bringing some kind of closure, this seemed only to provide momentum in simply blowing the lid off the rule and buying whatever the hell I wanted.

In 2008 I bought a somewhat ratty '73 BMW 2002 with some small dents and surface rust. It had been sitting outside under a tree for several years, and was literally coated in sap impregnated with dead bugs (which Maire Anne examined closely), but it was surprisingly solid for a New England car. Once I washed the crap off (which, after the experience of getting soaked with soap when I took the Saudi 3.0CS through the car wash, I did by hand) and found someone who knew how to polish single-stage paint, some of the shine came back and exposed a lovely patina. However there were numerous spots where rust blisters were forming under the molding. On one hand, this is about as trivial as rust can be, but on the other hand, if I pulled off the molding and took a grinder to the rust … what then? I could touch it up with rust-inhibiting primer, but if I did that, it would take a car that looked great from 10 feet away and make it look like it had the measles from 50 feet away. I took it around to body shops, and no one would spot-paint it. There were too many rust spots, and because of the age of the paint and the patina, there was no way to match the color; everyone said, "Just paint the whole car" and I didn't want to, for all of the reasons above. So, for now, I haven't done anything. I vowed just to use it as a knock-around 2002 and not turn it into something it isn't. I've done a poor job at that; the car now has a 5-speed, Recaro seats, and pretty gold basketweave wheels from an E30 convertible. But I love the fact that it's not a car I worry about getting dinged in parking lots; it's still just a shade away from being a rat rod.

As Maire Anne's bug business started taking off and her travel increased, we needed to get her out of the aging Mazda van and into something neither of us had to worry about, so in 2008 we bought a one year-old Honda Fit. This made nine cars. I had planned to sell the Mazda, but somehow it hung around. Earlier I mentioned that I used it as a winter daily driver when doing the Big Job on my wagon. Plus, it has been useful to have around when Kyle is home from school, and I am mindful of the fact that Aaron is about to get his learner's permit and it is the only automatic we own.

So there we hovered, flirting with the glass ceiling of ten. Then, in the spring of 2008, just as gas prices began rising but before they spiked at nearly five bucks a gallon, I became curious whether you needed to spend 25 grand to purchase a new Prius or whether you could in fact get similar gas mileage out of one of the throwaway econoboxes no one had cared about when gas was cheap. There are several of these—the Ford Festiva, the Dodge Colt, the Subaru Justy, to name a few—but the best known is the Geo Metro.

"Geo" was never an actual manufacturer; it was a nameplate established by General Motors that enabled them to sell a line of cars that had the cachet of being "foreign." While the bigger Geo Prisms were actually rebadged Toyota Corollas, the little Geo Metro (and the Geo Tracker mini-SUV) were built by Suzuki. There were several varieties of the Metro, but the high-mileage king was the somewhat oddly shaped two-door hatchback with the three-cylinder engine (yes, you read that right), and the 5-speed manual transmission. This car had only 55 hp (yes, you read that right too; snow blowers have more horsepower; well, okay, not snow blowers, but motorcycles) and weighed just 1800 pounds. I began reading internet reports of people getting 50 mpg on the highway in their Metros. But you never know what to believe on the web; it may get 50 mpg, and Bigfoot may have sired children with Paris Hilton.

It turned out that I was not the only person looking for a Metro; as fuel prices rose, these formerly disposable cars were rapidly becoming hot commodities, with CNN and the *Wall Street Journal* doing pro-files of people buying, resurrecting, and selling Metros to satisfy hot demand. I called about a Metro that was nearby, but the woman said that someone was already riding the bus up from New York with cash to buy it. However, to my surprise, she called back the next day to say that the gentleman had never showed up, and the car was available. I drove over, checked it out, and I bought it on the spot. So the lowly Geo Metro was the car that rolled the count into double digits.

Now, any ten-year-old car will need work, and the Metro was no exception. I found myself replacing its battery, alternator, oil, spark plugs, brakes, and exhaust. This naturally led to finding Metro-related web sites and user forums. On the internet, of course, you're always one mouse click away from something really strange. In this corner of the world, it's "ultra mileage"—how to squeeze the most miles out of a gallon of gas by, oh, coasting, parking on hills, drafting behind trucks, etc. I realized, with some amusement, that the Metro was, in fact, an enthusiast car.

So how well did the Metro work out? In around-town driving, I was averaging high 30s. Then I took Kyle for a few out-of-town college interviews during which I had the chance to accurately measure highway mileage. On one drive, holding with the traffic speed (65-ish), I averaged about 45 mpg. And when on the drive back, I held it to 55 mph (difficult without cruise control), the car, indeed, averaged 53 mpg. Most impressive.

But all this is to be traded off against the fact that the Metro is, in fact, a tuna can with wheels and a radio. It's tinny and buzzy, with seats about as comfortable and supportive as a beach chair. It does have air-conditioning (nonfunctional), but it has no power steering, no cruise, no intermittent wipers, and manual crank windows. For most people, a nicer, slightly larger car that gets less stratospheric gas mileage would be a better compromise.

Of course, the problem with owning ten cars was that, other than the new Honda, they all needed to be repaired. This proved a bit much, even for me, so I sold the Suburban before it ate its automatic transmission, and I sold the green '73 2002tii right before the economy crashed in 2008. This whacked the counter back down to eight.

It's completely indefensible to say you own eight cars, so I often say, "Well, there's my daily driver, and my wife's, and my son's car, so it's really only five enthusiast cars. And they're not all on the road at the same time." As if this somehow makes it sane. The thing is, the City of Newton sends me the annual excise tax bills at the same time, and when all eight of them arrive in the mail, there's no hiding it. I open up the front door expecting to find that the black helicopters are waiting to take me away.

So, go ahead. Use me as a warning, a cautionary tale, a portent of what can happen due to lack of restraint. But you haven't met Ben. A BMW Club member in Chicago, Ben Thongsai, is a pro (he owns a repair shop), and, as such, a lot of cars pass through his hands. When Ben was at my house last year, I asked, just to see Maire Anne's reaction, "Hey Ben, how many cars do *you* own?"

I had a knowing little moment, like the scene in the movie *My Cousin Vinny* when Joe Pesci puts his girlfriend Marisa Tomei on the stand, knowing that what she's about to say will blow everyone away.

"You know," said Ben, "I'm not exactly sure."

CHAPTER 36

ALPHA MALE BEHAVIOR AMONG CAR GUYS

So. You're a car guy. Now you need to establish your dominance in the pack. How do you do it?

The classic thing to do is to procure some American iron. A muscle car. Something big, nasty, and brutish, with fat tires, a loud exhaust, and lots of swagger. Maybe a '69 Camaro with glass packs. Vin Diesel on wheels. Or you could go expensive and metrosexual, maybe a late-model Porsche. Forget the image of Porsche guys with gold chains and slicked-back hair; it's the money that does the talking, baby, and nothing says money like dropping "the Porsche" into a sentence. Especially when it's mispronounced using the popular but incorrect single-syllabic form, rhyming it with "porch" (it's actually pronounced "Por-sha," and don't get it wrong if you wish to be taken seriously in the car world).

(The alert reader will notice that, before the end of this book, I, in fact, will have dropped the P-bomb multiple times, but the Porsche that I own is an '82 911SC, worth less than ten grand, and I pronounce it correctly, so we're good.)

We've all seen those commercials featuring people and their dogs that look alike, or at least have some superficial personality traits. You know: big strong guys with Dobermans; overly coiffed women with little frou-frou poodles. There often appears to be some similar sort of correspondence between people, particularly men, and their cars. Big, strong, wave-the-flag-beer-drinking guys with classic American muscle cars; gay men with VW Beetles ("Not that there's anything wrong with that," to quote Jerry Seinfeld).

Oddly enough, even the Metro provided me with car guy interactions. I expected it would engender about as much respect from hard-core car guys as one would garner ordering a glass of warm milk in a biker bar. But to my stunned surprise the car actually generated grudging admiration from folks who knew what it was. For example, when I went to a junkyard in Lawrence, Massachusetts to buy a wheel for the snow tires I planned to put on the car, the guy behind the counter—who was sporting slicked-back hair, a backwards ball cap, and gold chains—saw the Metro through the window, and said, "Is that one of them three-cylinda jobs?" "Yup," I said, "all 55 horsepower of it." "Wow," he said, "what kinda mileage ya get?" When I told him, I instantly had street cred. "I never seen one of these. Can I look under the hood? Hey, Jimmie, get out here. Ya gotta check this out! Oh man that engine is so tiny I could pull it outa there with my hands!"

Gas mileage as the new horsepower. You gotta love it.

One way to show where you are in the pecking order is to simply drop the number and kinds of cars you own into every casual conversation, just in case another car guy is within hearing range. I, however, never do that. You'd never know that I own eight cars, including an '82 Porsche, a '73 2002, a '73 3.0CSi, a '99 Z3 M Coupe, and a '99 528iT with a stick and the sport package. You don't own eight cars including an '82 Porsche, a '73 2002, a '73 3.0CSi, a '99 Z3 M Coupe, and a '99 528iT with a stick and the sport package, do you? Just asking.

Or you can talk about your projects with random people you meet at social events—how you disassembled your baby and took three years of nights and weekends to put her back together. Nothing says car guy like a frame-off restoration. I suppose these things are the car guy equivalent of "let me tell you about my grandchildren." Maire Anne will tell you that when I'm deep into the throes of a project, it's all I want to talk about; I might as well be wearing a T-shirt that says "let me tell you about my subframe bushings."

Chest beating can also be part of establishing pack dominance. On the online forums, there's always some asshole who seems intent on wanting you to know that he knows more than you do. Stand up to the prick. Rock his world. *Show him that he's wrong.*

But even with people you know and like, subtle one-upsmanship can creep in during the natural trading of war stories. One night we were having dinner with my wife's business partner, Andrea, and her husband, Mark. I knew Mark was a car guy, but we'd never rolled and gotten the scent on each other before. I was outlining some of the BMWs I'd gone through. Mark said he'd been into TVRs (an obscure but very cool British car) and had owned three of them, but recently had had several Subaru WRXs. I said I'd owned over two dozen BMW 2002s. He mentioned a suspension modification he recently did. I described installing air-conditioning in one of my cars. He countered with the story of putting a 500 hp engine into his Subaru. I let it drop that I had retrofitted fuel injection into my '73 3.0CSi, thereby subtly countering his thrust of raw horsepower with my parry of complexity and ingenuity, performed on a classic car that is actually *worth something*.

And then he lunged in for the kill. The sucker punch started two towns over, approached me in slow motion, then gathered speed as it approached my face, like in a classic Popeye cartoon. I did *not* see it coming. The twin-punch of the air-conditioning and the fuel injection retrofit usually shuts most of 'em down.

"Of course," he said, with a wonderful air of nonchalance, "that probably wasn't as involved as building the plane."

"You … built … *a plane*?"

"Yeah, one of those kit planes, two-cycle snowmobile engine, fully acrobatic. Pretty cool. And not as hard as it sounds. You do have to be kind of careful attaching the wings to make sure that the bolts are torqued right, though; wouldn't want to get that wrong."

Checkmate.

WHAT TO BUY (CLASSIC CARS)

What are you, nuts? I'm not going to tell you what to buy. If you think the Pacer is the most beautifully proportioned automobile since the Porsche 911, live your dream. If you lost your virginity in a Simca and have always had a hard-on to recapture that moment, go for it, big guy.

(Truth be told, the Simca reference dates back 25 years to a BMW CCA Oktoberfest where six guys—including former *Roundel* editor Yale Rachlin—and one woman were sitting at the bar swapping car stories round-robin. The guys' stories were all about speed or massively inconvenient mechanical malfunction and invariably concluded with either "I loved that car" or "I freaking hated that freaking car." The woman slew us all. After a pause in the conversation, she uttered the seven words six men will never forget. Those seven words: *"I lost my virginity in a Simca."* Six guys nearly spat out their beer.)

I've asked for input from BMW CCA *Roundel* Technical Editor Mike Miller on this chapter, as it gives you the benefit of not just one quirky unsubstantiated enthusiast point of view, but two.

FIRST, A CAVEAT

My body of experience is with 1960s and '70s German cars, mostly BMWs. Nice shiny rust-free BMW 2002s can be had for less than half the price of a low-end new BMW. Cool driver-quality cars can still be found for five grand. In the big scheme of things, this is very short money. I'm not talking about six- and seven-figure Ferraris, nor Ralph Lauren showing his Bugatti Type 57SC Atlantic at Pebble Beach (not that there's anything wrong with that). Yes, I have watched the cable show *Chasing Classic Cars*. I do not have the money to throw around that "master Ferrari restorer" Wayne Carini has. I'm not advising people on which Auburn boat-tailed speedster to buy (not that there's anything wrong with that either).

Editor's Note: This memoir is **not** a repair manual. Please read Warnings & Cautions on p. 410.

Jay Leno once said, in an interview with *Popular Mechanics*, "I like to restore a car to 98 or 100 points, then drive it down to 10 or 20 points, and if you really want to, restore it again." That's great. I sleep better at night knowing that Jay has this sort of live-in-the-moment-don't-worry-be-happy-stop-and-smell-the-oil worldview and isn't anal about his collection of over 80 cars. *He'll just restore them again.* Once I begin earning a tenth his salary, I'm so onboard. In the meantime, my not having the money to afford a restoration dovetails nicely with the fact that I don't want to own a car if it's so nice that I'm afraid to put tools down on painted surfaces in the engine compartment.

KNOW WHAT YOU WANT

To the maximum extent possible, you should go into the classic car buying process knowing what you want. Is that a restored show-quality car you can trailer to and from events and win trophies with? A low-mileage time capsule that's original right down to its skinny dry-rotted tires? A tight, rattle-free, sorted-out driver you can enjoy right out of the box? Or something affordable, in need of work, that you can tinker with in the garage? If you're never going to be happy unless you own a '67 Alfa Duetto with original paint, or a BMW 3.0CS with a retrofitted modern drivetrain and air-conditioning, that's what you should look for. You should buy whatever gives you the most pleasure, even if that pleasure comes from just looking at it in the garage (or the living room).

CONDITION, CONDITION, CONDITION

Once you know which of these broad categories you're operating in, the advice is pretty simple: Buy the nicest car, with the best option package, you can afford. In real estate it's "location, location, location." When you're checking out a classic car, it's "condition, condition, condition." What that means is, whether you're in the market for a '72 BMW 2002tii, a '63 Rambler Classic, or anything else, don't try to turn a sow's ear into a silk purse. Money spent up front is rarely regretted and usually recovered if you need to sell the car. A well-optioned car in great condition will always be worth more than a base model in so-so shape. Preserve it long enough and well enough (meaning covered in a dry environment) and you'll probably make a profit. Mike Miller adds, "There's a good argument that collector cars in excellent condition have proven to be safer investments than stocks. At least you'll know some robber baron can't wave his cigar and make your car disappear overnight."

"Condition" refers primarily to the body and interior. Looking first at body condition, the three main elements to check are paint, trim, and amount of rust. Shiny paint and bright chrome immediately catch the eye and cause the heart to race. This, combined with lack of rust, is the central pillar holding up the value of a car. Particularly in an area like New England, it's almost unheard of for an older car to be rust-free by accident. Either it's cared for (garaged and not driven during wet weather) or it isn't. If it isn't, rust gets it. So cars naturally bifurcate into three classes: perfect, nearly perfect, and basket cases. When it comes to the condition of the interior, look for beautiful seats, door panels that aren't sagging or cut up, intact headliner, crack-free dash, decent rug. Finding a car with each of these interior items in good condition is important because, while any one of these components can be replaced at a cost that is perhaps less than a month's mortgage, dealing with *all* of them becomes prohibitively expensive.

Thus, on older cars, condition is everything, and by comparison, the mechanicals are far less important. It's an exaggeration to say that you should buy an old car without driving it or even hearing it run, but you can certainly rule the car in or out based only on condition. If the car is rust-free with shiny paint and an intact original interior, and the price is right, who cares if it needs brakes, shocks, and exhaust? It's one of those times when people who know nothing about cars and go *oooooooh* when they see some cherry old classic on the basis of nothing except its appearance are in fact absolutely right.

BUDGET

So you should buy the best car you can afford. How much *can* you afford? Well, you ask, what do I have to spend in order to get what I want? This is often an iterative process. You may start off wanting a bone-stock mint original low-mileage car, then get sticker shock and retrench to a lightly-restored example. If even that's too dear, you may entertain something in "restore or drive as-is" territory. If you have the fever particularly bad, you may even succumb to driving something that's one rust hole away from being a parts car to satisfy your passion.

Mike warns, "I always tell people to come up with a budget for the car purchase, remedial maintenance, and repairs, then triple it. That should be about right."

This brings to mind two very practical matters. In Massachusetts, the annual vehicle inspection is supposed to verify that the car doesn't have "holes or cracks, due to rust or otherwise, in the floor pans or other body panels which would permit the passage of exhaust gasses into the passenger or trunk compartments" and "rusted structural parts of the undercarriage or unibody so as to cause a hazard or structural weakness." If your rust bucket fails inspection, you can try a lawyer's defense and argue that the rotted fenders on your 2002 are neither structural parts nor in a place which allows the entry of exhaust gasses, but they *can* fail you if they see rust holes *anywhere* in the body. Obviously, vehicle laws vary wildly state-to-state, but my crack about driving a parts car notwithstanding, there are in fact limits to how ratty a rat rod you can drive around.

But the good news is that, if you use a classic car insurer, the insurance for a low- to mid-priced classic can be peanuts. I recently bought a rust-free California 1985 635 CSi with a 5-speed, Recaros, badly faded paint, and 200K on the clock, for chump change. It's a knock-around driver. Once painted and cleaned up, it's worth maybe four grand. When I snagged it, I was very conscious of the fact that the car was 25 years old and thus was eligible to be insured as a classic in the state of Massachusetts. I called Hagerty, with whom I already insure several other cars, and told them I wanted to add the 635 CSi.

"What stated value do you want to put on the policy?" the nice woman asked.

"Four thousand dollars."

"Okay, just a minute … the incremental cost to your policy is $18. When your policy is renewed, the full annual cost of the added car will be $24." I swear I am not making this up.

"I *LOVE* you guys!"

ORIGINAL CARS

As the saying goes, it's only original once. Right now, original cars are hot, with lightly blemished, imperfect examples sometimes besting completely restored ones at auction.

Like "restored," "original" has an imprecise meaning. There's *looks like it just rolled out of the showroom ultra low miles as close to "kept in a hermetically sealed bubble for 50 years" as you'll ever find.* At the ultra-high-end of collecting, I've read about people who search out and buy cars still coated in the factory Cosmoline, never titled, never driven, as close to the fountain of originality as possible. Ultra-low-mileage cars are for investment and artistic appreciation, not driving. Are *you* going to be the one to start racking up the miles on that '63 split-windowed Corvette with 7,500 clicks on the clock and the original redline tires? If you own a car like this, odds are the only driving it sees is on and off the trailer that transports it to and from car shows. The irony is that, if you wanted to begin putting hundreds of miles on a perfect, original, ultra-low-mileage car, it would require preparation. I don't care how "original" it is—I wouldn't want to do much more than move it in the garage if it was running on nearly 50-year-old tires, belts, and hoses.

Then there are "barn find" cars. Popularized by Tom Cotter's *The Cobra in the Barn* series, barn finds are generally non-rust-buckets that are whole and intact, but because the paint has degraded past saving, the interior and wiring have been eaten by mice, and all drivetrain and braking systems have seized themselves solid, they usually need total restoration. Some concours events now even have a Barn Find class, with cars trailered in and shown in the condition they were in when extracted from the barn. In this context, "patina" literally extends to dirt, leaves, and spiders. There's something fascinating to me about bringing part of the environment along when a car is shown at an event. The detritus of the Depression isn't usually displayed around a '37 Cord 812. The smoke of Berlin and Bauhaus buildings don't surround a 1930 Mercedes. Perhaps they should. I guess "barn find patina" is the physical manifestation of the car's most recent context, like seeing a mummy wrapped in its burial gauze.

When I see a "barn find" car, I can't help but think about a rough hierarchy: Sitting in a barn is preferable to sitting outside; covered in a barn is better than uncovered in a barn; stored inside a building beats being abandoned in a barn. In the same way that investment planners tell you that your chosen mix of stocks and bonds affects the growth of your 401k more than any other factor, the choice of one of these three storage options has a more dramatic effect on the condition, and thus the value, of the car 30 years down the road than virtually anything else you do.

I'm sure every car guy who ever found a cool car in a barn would give his eyeteeth to go back in time, find the owner, hand him a car cover, and beat the crap out of him until he agrees to *go out to the barn and put the cover on the damned car.* The fact that you can't also say, "And here's 20 thousand dollars go and rent yourself a storage space for 20 years trust me it'll be worth it" highlights why long-term preservation is difficult and many killer cars were sacrificed to the elements and rodents. We all kick ourselves for selling, or passing on, certain cars that now are worth big bucks, but very few of us have access to cheap long-term indoor storage, much less had that access when we made the decision to pass or sell. We make the tough choices we need to make. You might want to kill the guy who relegated the '63 split-windowed Corvette to his grandparents' barn, but it is understandable that the barn looked better than nothing. But I digress.

The current cache of "barn patina" notwithstanding, most of us are looking for a car we can afford to buy and not be afraid to drive, and the sweet spot of originality is between the extremes of rotting barn finds and ultra-low-mileage hanger queens. In this context, "original" usually means the car is wearing the paint that was sprayed at the factory, hasn't had any body panels or major interior components replaced, has the original (or correct replacement) drivetrain, bumpers, trim, and wheels, and the interior hasn't been cut up for an aftermarket stereo or air-conditioning. Of course, a car can satisfy those requirements and easily be a dead rusty mouse-infested piece of crap.

The term "survivor" is sometimes used to connote a presentable, running, drivable original car whose condition can vary from a pristine 20,000-mile-only-driven-by-a-little-old-lady-to-church-on-Sundays car, to more of a rat rod with faded don't-worry-about-parking-it-where-you-might-get-door-dings paint. Personally, cars whose faded paint, dulled chrome, and lived-in interior are in balance with one another have a lot of appeal to me. These B- and C-grade condition cars are unlikely to appreciate dramatically like pristine examples, but they can provide a fun, cost-effective path to satisfying your lust as long as you don't try to turn them into something they're not. If a car is presentable

and largely original but has some rust, sometimes you see the phrase "an honest car"—a car that's not trying to be something it isn't.

You'll also sometimes see a car described as "a driver." I know this is meant to connote what the car is by not saying what it isn't: a show-quality car. But I find it funny. It's a *car*. Of *course* it's a "driver." What else is it going to be? A guest room? A potting shed?

Looking for cars in the rust belt, there's an important category I claim to have invented: *As rust-free as one can expect for an unrestored New England car*. This seems to accurately capture the reality of what I find, for a reasonable price, within a few hours' drive.

The swings of the pendulum of demand for originality are funny to observe. When a car is five or ten years old, modifications are all the rage, but once a car obtains classic status, the more bone-stock it is, the more desirable it is. The original skinny 13" steel wheels on a BMW 2002 used to be one of the first things an enthusiast would relegate to the who-cares pile, replaced by wider 13" alloys from a 320i, or, later, 14x6" bottlecap rims from a 325e. Now the original steelies with their cereal-bowl hubcaps have all the cachet. You're even starting to see this with E36 BMW M3s from the mid- to late-1990s. The original double-spoke alloys (the DS1 and DS2 styles) were pretty weird looking, and many were replaced with the aftermarket wheel du jour. Now they're the bomb.

The stereo in a classic car undergoes this same dynamic. Even the term "stereo" is often incorrect. Most 2002 owners discarded the original monophonic Blaupunkt radio and its console-mounted single speaker in favor of a stereo cassette player. This required cutting speaker holes in the door panels, under-dash pieces, or the rear deck, but, hey, you didn't care once you had *Fragile* or *Dark Side of the Moon* cranking. Nowadays it's harder and harder to find cars that aren't cut up or modified, and having the original Blaupunkt radio, center speaker, and virgin interior panels is a highly prized indication of an unmolested or correctly restored car.

Likewise with seats. I love the look of original German pleated leather seats with horsehair padding; they're a thing of period-correct beauty. But early 1970s BMWs are now nearly 40 years old, and finding a decent set of seats without worn-out horsehair padding, ripped upholstery, and protruding springs is very difficult. Plus, they're just bloody uncomfortable. These days I'm a 53-year-old man with a bad back. Screw originality. Give me a set of Recaros. If the original seats are intact I'll put them in storage.

It's difficult for the layperson to tell an original car from a restored one. I'm not sure I can, even with older BMWs I know quite well. Knowledgeable folks talk about examining the weld points and the undercoating. I'd like to think I'm that good, but I'm not. I thought my sweet little early '72 tii was a completely original car, but it turned out its rear right quarter panel had been replaced, and it had a "snorkel nose" (a nose panel with a short tubular section for the air intake box of a carbureted 2002—the fuel-injected tii didn't have the snorkel), an indication that the nose had probably been replaced. (Actually there's active debate about this; some folks say they bought their tii new and it came from the factory with a snorkel nose, an indication that the BMW factory had run out of tii-specific nonsnorkel noses.)

If a car is presented as both original and having low mileage, there's no substitute for provenance—the documented history of the car. A stack of receipts dating back to the car's purchase that show the mileage slowly increasing to its current value is powerful evidence. Prove the mileage and you substantially imply the originality. The more provenance a car has, the less risk, but the higher the cost— you're not going to bargain someone down much if they have a perfect, low-mileage, fully documented car.

If you're attracted to a car, no matter how original it seems or how low the mileage is, you need to inspect it thoroughly for rust. Walk around the car and give all external body panels the once-over. Crouch down and look at the rocker panels beneath the doors. Open all doors and examine the lip at the bottom. Take a flashlight and look up inside the fender arches. Open the hood and look at the front shock towers and around the headlights. Open the trunk and examine at the rear shock towers and in the spare tire well. If you're seriously considering this car, there's no way around getting down and dirty and crawling beneath it to look at the bottom inside edge of the rocker panels, the floor pans, and the frame rails. Remember that rust is like an iceberg— what you can see is only a fraction of what's there.

In addition to these nearly universal areas to check, many models have specific places that rust which are difficult to see. The BMW 3.0CS, for example, poses a triple threat. First, there's a cavity that

traps water up under the front fenders, allowing rust to form and bur-
row outward, eventually perforating the firewall and getting into the
passenger compartment. Often, the first indication of trouble is electrical problems caused by water dumping onto the fuse box. Although
you can't see this water trap, you can check for firewall perforation by
lowering the glove box and the hood latch cover and looking above
them with a flashlight.

Second, what looks like a rocker panel on a 3.0CS is actually a very
wide piece of trim extending from the top of the door sill to the floor
pan. There's no way to know the true condition of the rocker without
removing this trim. Unfortunately the trim is held on with several
dozen tiny screws that are likely rusted in place. Asking a seller if you
can remove the rocker trim to check beneath it for rust is outside the
bounds of reasonability. The best you can do is to infer the rocker's
condition by checking for rust at the joint between the floor and the
bottom of the rocker trim.

Last, unlike later BMWs whose rear shock towers are covered
with felt that is easy to pull away for inspection, those on the 3.0 are
obscured by thin plastic coverings. It is not terribly difficult to remove
these for inspection, but they are extremely brittle and can easily shatter if attempts are made to bend them. If you're serious about paying
nontrivial coin for a car in great condition, you need to know about
these model-specific rust areas, or pay to take the car to someone who
does for inspection.

RESTORED CARS

As I discussed extensively in Chapter 15: "Restoration and Why It
Makes No Freaking Sense," you're *always* better off spending the most
you can afford and buying a car someone else has restored rather than
trying to restore a less expensive one. Purchasing a classic car may be
an investment, but, with very few exceptions, restoring one isn't. So
now that I've talked you out of taking on a major restoration project,
I'll share what I've learned about buying an already restored car.

Even if you're not an expert, your eye is a pretty good indicator
of the overall level of restoration. Look for shiny, flat reflective paint
on all surfaces, both horizontal and vertical. Walk around the car and
run your thumb along the gaps between all body panels to check for

evenness. (In addition to the thumb providing more detail than the eye, this is a great way to unnerve a seller. All of a sudden you look like someone who knows what they're doing. I highly recommend it.) Look for brightness and lack of bumpiness on all chrome pieces. Inside the car, check for rips and wear in the seats, and lack of fading and cracking of dashboard and door panels. You can wash and wax a car and wipe the inside down with Armor All, but it's difficult to "fake" a restoration and get the totality of these things right.

Pay careful attention to the paint. Look for overspray—areas that are painted the body color that aren't supposed to be. For a very high-quality paint job, the glass and rubber seals are removed, allowing the car to be painted beneath the seals, so if you see a little paint on the edges of the front and rear windshield seals, you know the car was repainted with the glass left in. That's not the end of the world— it just means the car didn't have a glass-out restoration. But if you see paint on the edges of, for example, the trim in the middle of the door, you'll know the trim wasn't removed; it was just painted around as part of a low- to moderately-priced paint job. If you pull the trim off, you'll see strips that were not repainted. Pretty cheesy. It's not that you shouldn't *ever* buy a car with *any* amount of overspray, or whose trim was painted around; it's that these things are indicative of the quality of the work. In my humble opinion, using the word "restored" to describe a car painted with the trim left on it is misleading to the point of fraud, whereas a glass-out paint job indicates a higher degree of restoration than a car painted with the glass left in, and thus is worth more. Others may disagree and say that for *any* car to call itself "restored" it must have had a glass-out repaint. I think the fundamental issue is that you shouldn't pay Y for a car that's only worth X.

For example, a memorable eBay ad for a BMW 2002 touting its "recent open-checkbook restoration" showed freshly sprayed Inka (orange) paint extending into the trunk. While a resprayed trunk can certainly be part of a high-quality paint job, a trunk's rubber, wood, fabric, and plastic pieces—and preferably the gas tank—should all be removed or masked off and left unpainted, and on this car it was all just blasted orange. Not only did it look silly, it was an instant loss of credibility for the seller.

The interior of any car that calls itself "restored" should be just about perfect. It should have the correct seats, door panels, dashboard, and console. I'd expect a set of recently reupholstered seats with fresh padding and no rips or even visible wear. There should be no cracks in the dash. The headliner should be clean and rip-free. On an older car, an aftermarket stereo may be installed that required cutting speaker holes in the door, under-dash, or rear deck. The tolerance for this is a personal thing, but if the seller is asking top dollar, at a minimum the installation should look professional and the visible components shouldn't look like they time-traveled in from a different era.

HOW CORRECT DO YOU WANT TO BE?

This term "correct" hangs above potential automotive transactions like the sword of Damocles. When enthusiasts talk about a "correct" car, they mean one outfitted with the type of parts originally supplied with it. While this list encompasses thousands of parts, the enthusiast eye is most sensitive to exterior trim and interior pieces. Enthusiasts shy away from something that looks like a Frankencar—a car assembled from parts from disparate sources. Nonetheless, it's easy to understand how a car loses its correctness. The unholy trinity of age, sun, and heat is merciless on cloth and vinyl. If your seats are ripped and the springs are poking through, or your dashboard is cracked from sun exposure, you recoil in horror when you find that many of these parts are no longer available (NLA) new from the manufacturer, and the cost of used examples in mint condition has gone through the roof. You pause. You love your baby, but there are limits. Then, in your search, you find a set of seats or a dashboard from a slightly later or earlier model of the same car. They look decent. They bolt right in. They're reasonably priced. Even if you're aware they're slightly different (and you may not be), what's the harm? Probably none, at the time, to you. But it can affect the value of the car. The closer the car is to mint, the greater the potential affect.

For example, although the most obvious changes on a BMW 2002 took place in 1974 to the exterior when the round taillights and small chrome bumpers were replaced by square taillights and big bumpers, there were numerous interior changes that happened at the same time. These include faux wood grain on the instrument cluster, a one-piece dashboard, a one-piece rug, and different seat pleating. It's common to see those newer interior pieces find their way into pre-1974 cars. And pre- and post-1974 isn't the only schism over which parts are transported; there were even significant variations in grilles, dashboards, consoles, instrument clusters, seats, and seat belts among the small-bumpered '68 through '73 cars. The earlier the car, the greater the odds it's wearing some parts from a later car. For example, pre-'74 small-bumpered cars had the roundel on the vertical part of the rear clip, while big-bumpered cars have it integrated with the trunk lid. It's not uncommon to see a car wearing the wrong trunk lid with the roundel in the wrong place.

On the site www.bmw2002faq.com, trashing cars, particularly those that are presented pretentiously in high-dollar ads and auctions, is something of a blood sport. Heaven help you if you advertise a car as "original," "restored," "correct," or "unmolested" (if any term embodies the whole *cars as women* thing, it's "unmolested") and something is amiss. If the dashboard and the wheels aren't right, or it's wearing the wrong rearview mirrors, these guys smell blood and jump on it like lions on a limping gazelle. It gets ugly. To some, spotting the wrong components on a car takes on the shrill tone of aliens identifying humans in *Invasion of the Body Snatchers*. Personally, I think, if a car is rust-free and nicely painted, and its price puts it within your budget, and you're not dead set on owning a "correct" car and aware of its issues, it's not a big deal. It's more that, as I keep saying, you shouldn't pay Y for a car if it's only worth X.

Trying to get *everything* "correct" on a car is a never-ending series of expenses with diminishing returns. For example, the 3.0CS has a drop-down tool kit mounted in a five-sided plastic tray on the underside of the trunk lid. Because of the weight of the tools, the tray eventually cracks. They are NLA from BMW. The going rate for a reconditioned tool tray is nearly $500. *It's a plastic tray. In the trunk.* Forgive me if I don't dedicate my life to finding and installing the best one on the planet. And the $500 doesn't include the tools. Those *are* available, but the original Heyco tools included red-handled plastic screwdrivers, and the replacements, for reasons unknown, are green-handled. The red-handled Heyco screwdrivers are now highly sought-after items on eBay. My tool tray went AWOL after the coupe's body restoration in 1988. I'd swear it's around here somewhere. I laughed when I stumbled across one of my red-handled Heyco screwdrivers. It was in the basement, thrown in with the house painting supplies. I'd been using it to pry open paint cans.

They're just parts, and it's just a car. It's not as if, when you install that last correct piece, the car shimmers and glows and takes on special powers and you and the car are awarded extra life like in some video game.

But sometimes lack of correctness is a huge tip-off that something is drastically amiss. A recent eBay auction offered a '73 2002tii in what appeared to be beautiful condition, nicely optioned with air-conditioning, sunroof, and a 5-speed. And … the description said the car had just 42,000 miles, adding substantial headroom to its potential value. When a car's odometer indicates low mileage, the seller can take one of three tacks. He can claim "low miles and I have all documentation to back it up." Or he can say, "It says 42K but it probably rolled over" (i.e., it probably has 142,000 miles). Or he can claim ignorance and blithely state "the odometer reads 42,000 miles" and feign that he has no opinion on the matter.

Personally, I hate it when people take this latter tack. Of *course* they have an opinion. It's unusual for a car to have low mileage without supporting documentation. The ad for this '73 tii was closer to the former. It mentioned the car's 42,000 miles five times in the auction, and said, "Speedo reads 42,000 miles. No reason not to think this is not correct. The mileage shown corresponds with all the receipts & the Mass. title, which states it's original." Note how this is faintly weasel-worded. However, the auction description had an overall tone that seemed open, friendly, and unpretentious, and the seller had a high feedback rating, so it did not raise any obvious red flags with me of a blatant scam. Then, someone on www.bmw2002faq.com pointed out that the car's speedometer had crosshairs on it—the style of gauge used in a post-'74 2002 with a faux wood-grained instrument cluster. In other words, the speedometer and odometer had been replaced. *No reason not to think this is not correct* became *you've got some serious 'splainin' to do, pal*. The auction was taken down the next day.

This is a cautionary tale. Even with cars I know well, there's risk in getting it wrong. The risk is compounded when you feel pressured to make a snap decision. Perhaps this is why I tend to err on the side of inexpensive cars, with little claim of correctness or originality, being sold cheaply because they need work. Perhaps someday I'll have the financial muscle to go out and pay top dollar for that correctly restored early '72 tii, but for now, if I only lay out four grand for a car, even if I'm half wrong about it, that's a maximum of only two grand of financial risk.

RESTORED CARS CAN BE RUSTY, TOO

All of the rust issues on original cars apply to restored cars. Just because someone uses the word "restored" doesn't mean you don't need to check thoroughly for rust. On a car like a 3.0CS where rust hides in places which are difficult to inspect, I wouldn't believe a restored car was truly rust-free unless I saw photos taken during the restoration process, and that restoration was recent or there was documented low mileage since it was done. Someone who shelled out the money to restore a 3.0 would have to be pretty careless—or have something to hide—to not have photos of the car stripped to bare metal and of the rocker panels and rear shock towers without their cover pieces.

While the absence of rust, the shine and lack of overspray of the paint, and the state of the interior constitute 90 percent of a car's condition, a detailed engine compartment kicks the car into another restoration class. If you open up the hood and see paint just as shiny as the outer body, an engine clean enough to eat off, and original-looking labels and decals, someone has gone to a lot of work to put it into and keep it at that condition. If you see zinc-plated metal components that literally look new, you've wandered into some pricey real estate. You might not particularly care about the level of restoration of the engine compartment, but it adds substantially to the value of the car. Conversely, if the engine compartment looks like the apartment of your crazy aunt Mildred who keeps twelve cats, all other factors being equal, the car is not worth as much as one whose engine compartment looks like your bachelor uncle Rudy's New York penthouse.

Lastly is the undercarriage. A detailed undercarriage (front and rear suspension, drivetrain under-components, and floor pans) is the corsage of restoration. My drop-dead gorgeous '73 3.0CSi doesn't have one; crawl beneath it and you'll see it proudly wears its nearly 40-year patina of dirt, grease, and old undercoating. For the most part, you don't restore an undercarriage—you get a restored undercarriage as a by-product of completely restoring a car. For this reason, knowledge-able folks will give a detailed undercarriage particular scrutiny. If a few subframe components were repainted and a new layer of under-coating was sprayed, that's fine, but it's not the same as the car having a ground-up restoration.

"RESTOMODS"

Note that a car can be neither original nor 100 percent correct and still bring big bucks if it's tastefully modified or a flat-out fire-breathing track rat. Sometimes you'll see the term "restomod" used to connote this "modified while restored" approach. While I loathe the term, few BMW 2002 aficionados would thumb their nose at a well-painted car outfitted with a 5-speed, front air dam, driving lights, Recaro seats, Bil-stein shocks and struts, a 1" lowered stance, and 15" Panasport wheels. (In fact, I just read you my wish list. Now you all know what to get me for Christmas. Just make it a Turkis or Tiaga or Ceylon roundie tii with a/c, and leave the front bumper on; I don't like that sucking-up-the-track-look.) A so-called "M2" (a 2002 with an S14 engine retrofitted from an E30 M3) can bring a lot of money if the work is done properly. Similarly, the retrofit of a modern Motronic fuel-injected engine into a 3.0CS, when done correctly to a nice driver, doesn't seem to hurt its value. But de-chrome a car, put on big fender flares and some non-original trunk spoiler, do an extreme interior makeover with burled walnut where none originally was and TV monitors in the backs of the headrests, or (gulp!) gull-wing doors, and now you're into matters of taste that can decrease its value unless you find the right buyer with exactly the same desires.

Sometimes you'll see an ad that says "older restoration." That's very honest. And it conjures up the image of a car that is loved and sees actual use. Expect a repainted car that now has a few nicks and flaws, and a no-longer-mint interior showing some signs of use. Personally, I could care less if a dashboard has a few cracks in it, as it affects the functionality of the car not a whit.

"AS BUILT"

There's also the issue of whether a car is true to its original build sheet. That is, all other factors being equal, a car ordered from the factory with, say, a limited slip differential and air-conditioning should be worth more than a car which had those parts retrofitted. You can send a VIN and $5 to BMW and they'll e-mail you the build sheet, allowing you to see whether, for example, your car actually came with an LSD. I'd say that this reaches the point of silliness, but there's a line that's very important. A BMW 2002tii is worth way more than a 2002. You can bolt a fuel-injected engine, bigger brakes, boxed rear trailing arms, and a clock into a 2002, but that doesn't make it a tii. Firstly, the VINs are different. Far more important, though, is the issue of authenticity and scarcity. Tiis are worth more not only because of their higher performance, but also because *there are far fewer of them*. In the world of vintage Porsches, this dynamic is even more dramatic; the value of the fuel-injected 911E and 911S dwarfs that of the base 911. Cars to which every single bit of a higher-performance variant have been bolted are sometimes called "tribute cars," and there's nothing wrong with it as long as the seller is upfront about it with the buyer. Unfortunately, two transactions down the road, a new seller might not be so upstanding. Passing a car off as something it's not is fraud.

The build sheet also lists the original interior and exterior colors of the car so you can see if they've been changed. Speaking of which, a few words on matching numbers and changing colors: Particularly with American muscle cars, you hear a big deal made out of numbers-matching cars (where the stamps on the engine and transmission match those on the body). I haven't heard much importance placed on it in the BMW world, in which my feeling is that matching numbers provide additional provenance as to the car's originality, but in and of itself doesn't cause a quantum leap in a car's value. And a car whose color has been changed … the "correct restoration" crowd regards this as nothing short of an affront to God. If you're the one restoring a car, changing the color certainly shouldn't be done on a whim. While I'm firmly in the camp that if it's your car, and if you want to change the color, you should tell everyone else to pound sand, you *should* understand the implications down the road. One school of thought is that

changing the color from the original hue to another hue in which the car was available is not nearly as detrimental to the value as changing the color to one what was never originally sprayed on the model in question. Then again, BMW CCA member Gary Pyle has one of the most striking 2002s I've ever seen, painted a highly nonoriginal Monte Carlo yellow with a lot of red in it. It's visually arresting and drop-dead gorgeous.

I think that, if you're a buyer operating at the right edge of the curve, have few financial constraints, and are looking for the finest example of an award-winning car that may experience the greatest amount of asset appreciation, you are right to be concerned about these things. The top end of the value of an original or correctly restored car in its original desirable paint color, outfitted with its original numbers-matching drivetrain, is going to be higher than a color-changed or non-numbers-matching car. But if you're not in it specifically for trophies or asset appreciation, and if you find a car repainted a nonoriginal color or without matching numbers, and there's ample other reasons to like the car, quit worrying about it.

And remember: Ralph Lauren, who owns over 70 cars, changed the color of his Bugatti Type 57SC Atlantic—arguably one of the most unique collectible cars in the world—from blue to black.

ONE LAST WORD ABOUT COLOR

You *should* love the color of your car. You *should* be excited to see it every time you open the garage door. There is absolutely nothing wrong with wanting to buy an Inka 2002 or a Guards Red 911 and spending months stalking your prey before pouncing on the right car. Hell, that process alone will keep you occupied (and, thus, probably, faithful) for months. But you may find your requirement for one and only one hue is forcing you to fish in a pretty sparsely populated pond. Keep an open mind. You may stumble across another car, and find that it has been well cared-for, drives well, and is set up just the way you want it. It may just steal your heart, and you may warm to the color, yea, even grow to love it.

HOW MUCH RESTORATION SHOULD YOU BUY?

How much of the above should you obsess over? Well, what's your lust-to-finances ratio? If you want a 100 percent correct car with a detailed engine compartment and undercarriage and you can afford it without damaging your family's finances, buy it. As an investment, there's little doubt the best car will experience the greatest degree of return. But it's simply a choice driven by a budget, not some kind of moral stand. Men with the blessing of age and disposable income often intone, with the kind of solemn pomposity accompanying political grandstanding, that there's only one way to restore a car: The correct way. Fuck them. Don't these "correct restoration" guys remember what it was like to want a car so bad you'd lock yourself in a dark room and wait for the pain to pass?

TIGHTNESS

To me, for a car that's actually driven, the debate between original and restored, or correct versus color-changed, misses the point. What you want is a tight car. It is incredibly time-consuming to turn a rattle-y clunk-y car into a smooth-riding tight one, and believe me, it's more than just installing a $20 set of urethane bushings. You need to drive a car over a variety of roads to verify whether it is a tight car. Much more about this is in Chapter 55: "Shake, Rattle and Roll."

AIR-CONDITIONING

I love having air-conditioning in my classic cars. Yes, a well-optioned car with air will bring more money than a base model, but this isn't the issue. By allowing me to drive the cars in hot weather, a/c dramatically increases my enjoyment of them. Think about this carefully when you're selecting a car. If you want a car with air-conditioning, and if you won't drive it much if it doesn't have it, buy a car with air-conditioning, and don't let anyone else's opinion about whether a/c is "necessary" sway you.

WHERE TO BUY

I am an inveterate bargain-hunter who looks specifically for old cars—mainly BMWs—in need of work and sold at below market value so I can buy them, own them for a while, nurse them back to health, experience them, love them, maybe make a few bucks, and shepherd them on to the next owner. As such, I never decide to buy model X, then go out and find one and pay market value for it (my Porsche 911SC being perhaps the sole exception). But that is in fact what most people do—they decide they want, say, an E30 M3, then set out to find the best one they can for the right price. Sure, price is important, but it's a condition-driven process rather than a price-driven process. If you're doing this, there's a well-known saying you should pay attention to: When you buy a used car, you're buying the previous owner. The more evidence you have the previous owner loved the car, the thicker the stack of receipts, the more you feel like you can come back and ask him questions, the better. Buying from someone known and respected, someone who posts regularly on an enthusiast-related forum, is worth a lot. The BMW CCA website has classified ads, as do model-specific forums such as www.bmw2002faq.com, www.E9coupe.com (the 3.0CS site), and www.BigCoupe.com (the E24 6 Series site).

Unlike searching for best-condition market-value cars, bargain hunting is a crime of opportunity. This is especially true when you live in the rust belt and have a jones for older cars. You can look longingly on eBay at the rust-free examples in the Southwest, but the fact that *everyone* is looking on eBay, coupled with the cost of trucking a car across the country, means that there are rarely deals to be had there. So when promising ads for cars pop up close to home, you have to go and look. I used to read the classifieds in the newspaper and a regional publication called *The WantAd*, but these days for me it's all Craigslist. I check easily ten times a day during the week, and probably 50 times a day on weekends. When something hot pops up, you have to be ready to drop everything and pounce, because if you don't, someone else will beat you to it. It's frustrating when there are no photos, or the only pictures are blurry and don't show the problem areas, but sometimes you have to pack up and run on scant information, because if you insist on waiting for someone to e-mail you photos, the car may be gone. Basically I call about any BMW 2002 or 3.0CS within a 150-mile radius, and if it sounds promising, I check it out in person. Most of the time I take the 30 seconds needed to determine that it's a rusty pile of junk, mutter to myself, "Well *that* was a complete waste of time," and turn right around and head home, but there's really no way to know without going and looking. Remember that rust-free 3.0CS from Saudi Arabia I found advertised for half its value? Hope springs eternal.

WHEN TO BUY

From a cost standpoint, winter is a great time to buy a classic car as long as you have somewhere to put it. Of course, if you *don't* have somewhere to put it, you shouldn't be looking at it. A convertible or sports car practically sells itself in nice weather, so if someone is selling their baby in the howling jaws of February when there's three feet of snow in the East, he's got a reason, usually divorce, job loss, or relocation. You're not a scum-sucking vulture for responding to his ad. Bad weather, though, makes it difficult to thoroughly evaluate a car. This is another one of those classic risk-versus-reward trade-offs.

EBAY

The basic situation with eBay is this: Cars (and everything else for that matter) sold on eBay have to be "as described." So if a car is sold with an auction description that says it's "100% original" and it isn't, or "has absolutely positively zero rust" and it doesn't, then the car is not "as described" and the buyer has grounds to file a dispute. While this offers some protection to the buyer, it also has an unintended consequence: There are many cars on eBay advertised with four crummy photographs and a one-paragraph description because the less a seller says, the smaller the chance someone can legitimately say the car was not "as described." As a buyer, you might think this is the standard risk-versus-reward tradeoff, but think about it. If you're the seller, and you know the car is rust-free, and you're aware communicating this information would increase its value dramatically, wouldn't you scream in a 48-point font "this car is rust-free" and post photographs proving it? I do when I sell cars. I photograph the living daylights out of the underbody.

Okay, perhaps the seller doesn't honestly know. You occasionally see auctions saying "husband died car sitting in the garage." But be steely-eyed about this. There are three possibilities: a) Owner honestly doesn't know. b) Owner has simply left it out of the description. c) Owner is obfuscating. I hate to say it, but which scenario do *you* think is more likely? If you're bidding on a classic car on eBay and it looks shiny and pretty but the seller makes no claim about rust and there are no photos of the undercarriage, there's a good likelihood you're being suckered. If you buy the car and it's rotted underneath, you have no recourse. A guy who looked at my tii told me a heartbreaking story about buying a beautiful late-'60s Porsche 911 on eBay, and seeing, when the shipping company came and the car was still on the upper deck of the trailer, the extensive rot on the underside of the car. Can you imagine knowing that you'd been swindled before the car was even unloaded in your driveway?

Let me give you an example where I was, in fact, wrong. Andrew Wilson, the BMW CCA Maine Chapter president, paid top dollar on eBay for a Verona (red) '73 2002tii. The car had been discussed heavily on www.bmw2002faq.com and was generally blessed as an original, correct car, but I thought the auction description was a little thin in terms of presenting evidence the car was actually rust-free. By chance, I met Andrew and saw his car at a BMW CCA event. The car, christened "Vern" because of its Verona paint, was beautiful. After I introduced myself, Andrew said, "Oh, *you're* the guy who posted on the faq that I overpaid for my car!" I couldn't imagine what I'd said that was interpreted that way. That night, I searched through my old posts. What I'd said was that I was surprised the car sold for the amount it did when the eBay ad did not in fact claim the car was rust-free, and included only one photograph of the undercarriage. I never would've taken the risk merely on the basis of the eBay description and couldn't understand why anyone would. However, talking with Andrew, I learned that he had extensive conversations with both the owner and the mechanic who knew and maintained the car for two years, and the mechanic said there was no rust under the car. Based on those conversations, Andrew felt confident Vern was the right car to buy, and he enjoys her thoroughly and shows her enthusiastically at many BMW CCA events.

GOING OUTSIDE YOUR COMFORT ZONE

We're humans. We tend to go with what we know. When you know a lot about one particular marque, it's difficult to buy something different because it seems like there's an insurmountable knowledge deficit to overcome. If I look at a 2002 or a 3.0CS, I can tell in a heartbeat if it's a car I'm interested in. I know what the common problems are. I know where rust hides. I know the electric dashboard clock in a tii has become a $300 part. I know if you see a puff of blue smoke in the exhaust when you lift your foot off the gas it isn't really a big deal but if you smoke all the time it is. I know carpet kits are relatively inexpensive but original intact seats are getting hard to find however you can throw in Recaro sport seats from a BMW 320i you just bolt them onto the same seat rails but these are getting hard to find in decent shape as well and no you *can't* just bolt in the seats out of an E30 325i. Hell, I know about the "snorkel nose" in a 2002 and to look above the glove box in a 3.0CS for rust. How specific is *that*? How many years of accumulated knowledge and what number of individual cars does this represent? If I'm going to look at another make and model, where do I even start?

Ever since I worked for a guy in junior high school who had one ("A car like that, *you can get sex out of*"), I've had a hard-on for an early '70s Lotus Europa. Wicked low, sensationally angular, and looking like nothing else, I think they're gorgeous. And affordable--nice-driving cars sell in the teens. But I don't know any of these corresponding things about them. I called about a Europa that popped up on Craigslist in Connecticut. First question I asked was the same first question I always ask when I call about a BMW because it is the only question that really matters: "How's the body? Are there any rust holes, anywhere?" The gentleman patiently replied, "Well, as you probably know, Europas have a tubular frame with a fiberglass body, so, no, there aren't any rust holes in the body." Ooops. It stopped me dead in my tracks. I realized that this was the tip of the iceberg; he had all the niche knowledge, I had none. He could tell me—or withhold—anything.

These wonderful web-enabled days, of course, all you need to do is type "Lotus Europa buyer's guide" or "Europa FAQ" into Google and you'll hit on most of what you need to get started. I chickened out on the Europa, but I did buy the Porsche 911SC. Getting up to speed, learning that the '78–'82 SCs are fairly bulletproof 911s with the bugs worked out of them, knowing to look for cars with the Carrera oil-fed timing chain tensioners and the pop valve mod, and finally pulling the trigger and buying one, was one of the most satisfying and exciting experiences of my automotive life.

But what about the story of the '73 2002tii purportedly with 42,000 miles yet wearing a speedometer from a '74? If you're coming in from the outside, how the hell are you supposed to know to look for *that*? It's enough to give anyone cold feet. But don't let this scare you off. All it shows is that there's risk in a sight-unseen purchase of a car of questionable provenance from an unknown seller. You already knew that. If you're looking at the upper end of the scale, the best way to reduce risk is to purchase a car from someone knowledgeable with a good reputation in that car's user community. Absent that, you can contract a knowledgeable third party to evaluate the car for you.

Don't be too afraid to wander outside your comfort zone. Passion involves a certain amount of risk. Take it slow, study the subject, trust your gut. And enjoy the ride.

CHAPTER 38

THE THRILL OF THE CHASE
BUYING A CLASSIC CAR

There's a scene in the dystopian sci-fi movie *Blade Runner* where Harrison Ford and Sean Young exchange the following dialog:

"Do you love me?"

"I love you."

"Do you trust me?"

"I trust you."

These four lines completely encapsulate the portion of my relationship with Maire Anne that intersects with my relationship with cars. Which is to say, most of our combined lives.

It has been noted by my family that I really do chase cars the way other men chase women. When I get the scent on me, my palms sweat. My breathing gets shallow. I become more than a little obsessive. It is difficult for me to think clearly—or indeed to think at all—while I am in the midst of running down some hot prospect. At this point in my life, in terms of job and family, I am totally mister middle class suburban, which may be why there are few things as exciting to me as the thrill of the chase.

There are three parts to the chase: scouring the ads, checking out the car, and the end game (deciding whether to close the deal or walk away).

In 2008 I stumbled downstairs on a Sunday morning in November, poured a cup of coffee, pointed the browser at SearchTempest (a variant of Craigslist that lets you search across multiple cities), and found nothing that would make me drop everything and drive up to Maine or someplace equally distant. I went into the kitchen, got a muffin, came back to the computer, searched again, and saw that in the three minutes I'd been gone, an ad had been posted for a round taillight 2002tii in Portland that, in fact, made me drop everything and drive up to Maine. (Well, wouldn't you? I have a theory about this: The

Automotive Powers That Be dangle these things in front of you, and if you miss responding to even one, they say, "Oh, I was going to materialize that ad for the 1963 Series I Jaguar XKE sitting 30 years zero rust perfect interior just needs tune-up and tires must sell $5,000 *two miles from your house you'll beat everyone* but he missed the tii so screw him.")

The ad said "1974 BMW 2002tii great condition just had major service call for details" but the photo clearly showed a pre-'74 small-bumpered car with round taillights. I spoke with the owner—a car guy who was mainly into American iron. He'd bought the car from a friend and had not had it very long before he happened into a fastback Mustang and needed the cash and the garage space. I asked what rust it had and whether the fuel injection was still intact. He said it did have a golf-ball-sized rust hole just behind the pedal cluster, but that was about it, and yes it still had the injection system on it. Regarding the year, the ad was a misprint; he said the car was a '73. After extracting a gentleman's promise that he wouldn't sell it out from under me during my two-hour drive to Portland, I took the coffee, the muffin, the GPS, a floor jack, a Tyvek suit, and a few tools, and headed north.

The address I'd been given turned out to be a beautiful old townhouse just outside downtown Portland. The car was in the driveway—a pretty Sahara (tan) chrome-bumpered tii, original interior, perfect seats and door panels, a bit of a mildew smell inside, shiny paint with a few small rust bubbles, but essentially an unmolested car right down to the original bus-sized wheel, working door buzzer, and original rug. The rust hole behind the pedal cluster was more tennis ball- than golf ball-sized, and there was rust-through at the corner of the front rocker panel, but all in all, for a New England car, it was very solid

And something else ... the car had a tidy, compact appearance. It took me a moment, but then I recognized it as an early '72 with tight bumpers. These early cars have no gap whatsoever between the rear bumper and the body, and the front bumper is tucked in closer than on the later cars. I opened the hood to find the black plastic intake plenums that indicate an early '72 tii. It had been more than 20 years since I'd owned one of these, and it took a little while for the mental encyclopedia to kick in ... early '72s are the only tiis with the 121 head with 46mm intake valves and 10:1 pistons. In the glove box were the original owner's manual and the tii supplement that verified the high compression ratio. Very cool.

The grail for me really is finding a car with little to no rust, an undented body, shiny paint, and an original intact interior, but in need of enough mechanical attention that it's being sold at a good price. Living in New England, this doesn't happen often. And yet I was looking right at one. Fortune smiles on the prepared.

The tii wore a set of Maine plates with year 2003 tags, so not only was it unregistered, it clearly hadn't been on the road in quite a while. Thus my test drive was limited to two quick sets of four right turns around the block. The car started right up and ran passably, but even at very low speeds it had a driveline vibration and an unforgivable shake in the right front wheel that I assumed was due to a flat spot in the ancient tires. To get it home, I would need to have it towed or trailered. I was there, I was first, I made a quick decision. The owner and I shook hands somewhere slightly south of five grand, and I told him I would pick up the car the following weekend.

I called Maire Anne and explained about the car's being an early '72 tii and what that meant. I told her about the tight bumpers and the high compression pistons. I said that I had bought it, but would probably sort out its drivability issues and pass it on to another buyer, which would probably swell the college coffers by a couple of grand. I paused, exhaled, and said, "I think I know what I'm doing." She said, "I think you do too." No, you can't have this woman; she is *mine*!

There were two big challenges with this car. One was not violating its originality. The other was not falling in love with it—that is, being true to the plan and selling it. I rationalized this very carefully. If the car were truly rust-free (which it wasn't), or a zingy color that I craved (Sahara doesn't light my fire), or had air-conditioning (it didn't), I might have done my impression of Frodo on Mount Doom (Me: "The car is *MINE*!" Maire Anne as Sam: "*NNNNNOOOOOOOOO!*").

But I did what I said I'd do. I sorted out its mechanical problems and sold it. The car was just lovely—near-perfect interior, incredibly strong engine, remarkably solid—but in addition to the hole in the floor, it had one nontrivial rust perforation of the front fender arch, and enough rust bubbles under the trim and window rubber that it couldn't be spot-painted. I got it to the point of being a nice driver, but because of the rust and paint issues and the fact that I do mechanical but not paint and bodywork, I couldn't figure out how to do anything other then spend X and move the price by less than X. And really, the body and paint issues were best left to the next owner. So I put it up for sale and a car guy named Howard quickly snatched it up. In addition to the fact that he'd always wanted a tii, he lived in Philadelphia and was a huge Flyers fan, and the little Sahara tii sported a faded Flyers sticker on the bumper. Little things like this can be intimate vectors that connect people to cars.

Now, if I wanted to dip into the familiar well of cars-as-women analogies, I could say that this was the one I let get away; that I rescued her from an abusive relationship; that I was not entirely rational about her; that we had a brief but intensely passionate fling before I went back to my loving family; that I was thrilled when she found the lasting love of a new man; and that I've second-guessed the decision ever since. Probably a better analogy, however, would be that of foster care. Although I had this car for only a short period, I was honored to be able to play a role in its life, to care for it, to get it cleaned up, give it milk and cookies, put it in its jammies, read it *Where the Wild Things Are*, and ultimately pass it on to someone who would love it for the long term (see, I told you that caring for a car is an intimate thing). Howard *loves* it, which I know because of his continuing e-mails—another example of cars connecting people.

So you have to keep these bargains. You have to go and look. After all, you never know when the Automotive Powers That Be will dangle that '63 Jaguar XKE. With the '72 tii it worked out great, but, in fact, the majority of the time, I drive for several hours, spend ten seconds looking, then walk away and mumble to myself, "Well, that was a complete waste of time." Of course, knowing this has yet to stop me from continuing to look.

WHAT TO BUY (DAILY DRIVERS)

Again, I'm not going to tell you what to buy. If your heart is set on getting a BMW E39 540i Sport so you can experience a $60K German tire-smoking autobahn inhaler that now through the magic of depreciation sells for a tenth of its original price, do it, as long as you go into it with your eyes open and can keep up with the upkeep. In fact, no matter where your passion carries you, "do it with your eyes open" is probably the single best piece of advice I can give.

To be clear, when I say "daily driver," I'm not talking about a new car or a classic. I'm talking about something in between. I've never bought a new car in my life. However, buying a used daily driver is such a time-consuming pain in the ass that it's nearly enough to drive me into the arms of a new car dealer—at least that process is relatively efficient, and there's little question about what it is you're buying.

In the opening of his novel *The Crying of Lot 49,* author Thomas Pynchon describes the pathos of a low-end used car lot, where people exchange their broken dreams for someone else's, with the piteous expectation that this will make a measurable difference in their miserable lives. Many people sell or trade a car in order to avoid the cost of maintenance or repairs. If car a is replaced with comparable new or newer car for this reason alone, the owner has not necessarily saved money—he's just paying in a different way.

DRIVE WHAT YOU SEE YOURSELF IN ... WITH LIMITS

For the past few years I've gravitated toward BMW wagons, as they provide me the combination of stuff-hauling capability, driving enjoyment, and a manual transmission. Recently, I tried to wean myself off the BMW-as-daily-driver habit and get into a less expensive (presumably), more reliable (probably) Japanese 5-speed wagon, but Toyota and Honda haven't imported one since the late '90s. And I am not— *not*—going to drive a fucking Subaru. I eventually decided that, since

---

I'm not going to spend the money to buy something nearly new and low-mileage, any $5,000 car I buy is going to need work, so I might as well drive something I like. I bought a 2001 325Xi wagon with a 5-speed, the sport package, and 145,000 miles on it. This is my current daily driver. If your self-image has you wrapped in a late-model VW Golf with phone dial wheels, do it.

Similar trade-offs of cost versus risk exist for daily drivers and classic cars, but the nature of the risk is different. For a classic car, the risk is that the car isn't what you thought (it has more rust, wasn't restored as thoroughly or correctly, etc.). In contrast, for a daily driver with, say, 85K miles, the risk is the chance of breakdown. For high-mileage DDs, the risk is not only the chance of a breakdown but also the expense of possible failure of a major component. If you want to drive risk through the floor and are not sensitive to cost, buy a new or low-mileage well-reviewed Japanese product. In my humble opinion, there's very little risk in a late-model low-mileage Accord, Camry, or similar darling of *Consumer Reports* (autos.msn.com, by the way, is another very good place to see at-a-glance trouble spots for potential used car purchases). But you'll pay for it. At the other end of the cost scale, if you buy a thousand-dollar car for your kid to get back and forth to that dream job at CVS, you'll only have risked a thousand dollars. But the risk of breakdown is very real.

Everyone wants to know: How much do I need to spend to get a dependable used car? What is the formula for maximizing reliability (minimizing risk) yet paying as little as possible? Where is the knee in the cost curve? What year, make and model should I buy, and with what mileage? I can't tell you those things. As the Bottle Rockets said, "If a thousand dollar car was ever worth a damn, why would anybody ever pay ten grand?"

GO INTO A HIGH-MILEAGE GERMAN CAR WITH YOUR EYES OPEN

I *can* tell you that, my love of German machinery notwithstanding, if you're looking simply to minimize cost and maximize reliability, I don't recommend you buy a German car. Yes, I, the BMW guy, just said that. A consensus of folks whose opinions I respect tell me BMW, Mercedes, and Audi seem to be designing cars for lease—engineered so lessees have a good experience for 60,000 miles, at which point the lease is up and they turn in the car. It's not that the cars are designed specifically to detonate after that; it's just an unintended consequence. Heaven help you if you own a late-model German car as the cooling system and suspension components go bad and the sensors degrade. It's one damned thing after another. High-mileage BMWs can be a handful even for folks like me who love them and fix them themselves. But if you don't love them, they'll make you pull your hair out. And if you have to take them into the dealer whenever they hiccup, they will make you cry.

I have yet to fully understand why German cars have this problem and Japanese cars, by and large, don't. I want to believe, in buying a German car, in purchasing a product designed to be driven on *der Autobahn* as fast as it can possibly go, all day long, that that is more than just fahrvergnügen marketing fluff. Japanese and American manufacturers offer sacrifices at the shrine of this mythology when they do the whole "we took our car to the autobahn" or "we drove our car on the Nürburgring" thing. My E39 528iT wagon had a very sophisticated suspension, with oil-filled bushings on the thrust arms, the tension struts, and the rear subframe. This strikes me as the perfect representative microcosm of the issue, the universe in an oil-filled bushing. These bushings contribute to magical unique combination of ride and handling in a BMW. And in about 60,000 miles, the rubber hardens and cracks and the oil leaks out, adding to E39's reputation as a car which funds mechanics' children's college education. If you don't replace these worn-out bushings, the car clunks over bumps and doesn't track correctly. So the bushings become a required maintenance item. And maybe this is an acceptable cost for driving something rarefied, something that possesses that "this is why people in Germany can drive this thing at 130 mph" pedigree.

But the cooling system? Really? Most modern BMWs have a straight six-cylinder engine with an aluminum head. Older model BMWs like the 2002 and 3.0CS had all-metal radiators, expansion tanks, and thermostats that eventually succumbed to corrosion but almost never failed catastrophically. If the hoses felt pillowy or bulged over the hose clamps, you replaced them. But for nearly 20 years, BMW cooling systems have had a lot of plastic in them. There are plastic tanks on the top and bottom of the radiator. There is a plastic expansion tank. Hoses have plastic ends that slide over plastic fittings and snap in place rather than being held with old-fashioned hose clamps. Some models have thermostats with plastic housings and water pumps with plastic impellors. Coupled with a straight six-cylinder engine, this is a deadly combination. As the plastic ages and is exposed to the heat of the engine, it gets brittle and eventually cracks. The tanks can crack and lose coolant slowly. The hose necks can simply shear off when you hit a bump and lose coolant suddenly. Either way, the engine overheats. Run that temperature gauge into the red once on a BMW with a straight six and you can easily crack the head. Mike Miller recommends a water pump, thermostat, and belts at 60K, radiator and expansion tank at 90K, and every hose at 150K. If you purchase a late-model BMW whose provenance is unknown, Mike's recommendation is that the cooling system should be done as a prophylactic repair. He calls these replacement parts a "plastic kit" and his recommendation is based upon overwhelming anecdotal information from over 100,000 readers who drive BMWs, as well as their technicians. I follow this recommendation to the letter. Understand what this means: the cooling system becomes a routine maintenance item, like spark plugs.

But why design a car in this fashion? With the oil-filled bushings, at least the maintenance is a by-product of a design that is purportedly buying you some additional uniquely German performance. With the cooling system, it's the opposite—it's the absence of performance that requires the additional maintenance and expense. I haven't heard of Japanese cars whose entire cooling system is considered to be a maintenance-replaceable item. Bentley Publishers Senior Technical Editor Charlie Burke hypothesizes that it's a consequence of Germany's stringent recycling laws—that the primary design requirement of the plastic in the cooling system is recyclability, and the effect on longevity is simply an accepted consequence.

Mike Miller, who in addition to his BMW-nut street cred holds a master's degree in environmental law, agrees. He adds,

> Car manufacturers are often pressured into illogical choices due to politics, while genuine environmental analysis is dispassionate. Genuine analysis begins with recognizing that all human activity creates pollution. It then proceeds to examine whether a remedial measure—such as mandating recyclable plastic automotive cooling system parts—is

likely to mitigate more pollution than it creates, create more pollution than it mitigates, or wind up too close to call and therefore probably not worth the effort. Recycling involves significant energy costs in the process of recycling itself, as well as human activity and transportation of recycled material and recycled goods—often in hyper-polluting diesel trucks. There is also the matter of overall vehicle service life—of not having to produce as many cars when those cars last longer, thereby reducing pollution resulting from vehicle production. Finally, in the context of Germany, recycling also involves a physical footprint in a country where space is highly valued. So, we sometimes wind up not really knowing if any environmental benefit was actually achieved by a given remedial measure. Recyclable BMWs are good examples of that." Mike also speculates that the choice of plastic for cooling system parts was probably motivated by weight savings as well as recyclability, at least in BMW's case.

In addition to the above dispassionate analysis, Mike offers the following insight into the German psyche:

Another aspect of this subject is the different vehicle ownership paradigms in Germany vs. the U.S. Here, a driver's license is practically a birthright and everyone has a car. Many BMW owners own their cars for decades. I've had my 1977 320i for 24 years and my 1976 2002 for 21 years, I have an E46, and I'm poorer than snot.

But you have to be fairly well-off to even get a driver's license in Germany much less buy a car and keep it on the road. The TUV inspections are so stringent that one rarely sees a ten-year-old car. The Germans don't need or want a car capable of 200,000 miles because it will be sold out of the country or stolen long before then. Moreover, the Germans absolutely love their gizmotronics and there is a cultural thing of "keeping up with the Schultzes across the street." People don't want their neighbors to think they can't afford a new car.

Quick story on the last point: My friend Helmut, who has lived in Vermont since 1986, tells the story of replacing the front door to his house in Bavaria. The house was a few hundred years old, having survived a few wars. The front door had been broken and repaired multiple times, the wood was deteriorating, and Helmut was sick of fixing it. So he did what people with 300-year-old houses do: He went to the door maker and had a new hardwood door custom made.

Within two years, every house on his block had a new front door, and the door maker had brought him sausage several times in thanks.

Now, in fairness to the Germans, I doubt the overall pain level is much different if you own a Volvo or other European luxury import. And the act of buying Japanese doesn't inoculate you completely against all trouble either; I owned two Japanese minivans—a 1991 Toyota Previa and a 2000 Mazda MPV—both purchased as two-year-old cars, neither of which lived up to the Japanese image of toaster-like reliability. My friend's 1997 Lexus LS450 suffered exactly the same sort of oil separator freeze-up that felled my 528iT (which, I have to admit, made me feel better, perhaps my only episode of automotive *schadenfreude*). Still, I meet people who tell me, "I drove that [insert Japanese car model here] 150,000 miles and did *nothing* to it and *nothing* ever broke." If you know anyone who can say that about a German car, give me their number—I'd love to ask them a few questions. While they're hooked up to a polygraph.

On the one hand, really, it's just not reasonable to think that you'll spend four or five thousand dollars on a car with over 100K and never have to fix anything on it. But there are some reasonable expectations, and BMWs sometimes violate them. The lowest mileage BMW I ever owned was the 318ti I purchased with 42K on the clock so I'd have something reliable I could let Ethan drive after he got his license. The bloody thing cracked the plastic coolant neck off the back of the head and dropped all its antifreeze on the ground (everyone say it together—*they all do that*). It was one of only three BMWs I've ever had die on me that had to be towed home. Mechanics tell me they pull the transmission to replace this broken plastic neck. WTF?

Why the hell would you design a car that way? It's enough to make a diehard BMW enthusiast appreciate his wife's Honda.

All in all, selecting, buying, and maintaining a daily driver is an exercise in driving yourself nuts. The best you can do is roll the dice, buy something you enjoy driving, and stockpile Valium.

BOOK VALUE

Although it is useless for older cars and can be wildly inaccurate for certain newer enthusiast cars, book value is a useful thing to know when shopping for a particular model. Kelley Blue Book (www.kbb.com) will tell you the private-party value (how much you should expect to pay for a private-party sale) for a given model, graded by mileage and condition of the car. It will also tell you the car's retail value if sold at a dealership. The National Automobile Dealers Association website (www.nada.org) will tell you the car's trade-in value—what a dealer will give you for the car if you trade it in, also graded by mileage and condition. I figure if I can buy a car at a price between trade-in and private sale, and closer to trade-in, I'm doing well.

THE SALES TAX WHACK

Realize that, when you buy a new or used car, you're going to have to pay sales tax on it. In Massachusetts, the tax is 6.25 percent, and it's not on what you actually paid for the car, but on the book value of the car, so if you get a particularly good deal, you're still assessed the tax on the higher value (don't get me started on this). The 6.25 percent tax on a car with a $10,000 book value is $625. If you're selling your current car because it needs repairs, $625 would buy a lot of repairs. Also, the cost of insurance is higher on newer cars, especially if the car is driven by a teenager. I mention these things because whenever I upgrade my ride, these tax and insurance numbers are always higher than I thought, and will be very high if you choose the low-risk option of buying a nearly new low-mileage car. My neighbor recently went through the "what do I have to pay for a dependable used car for my kid" process, bought a five-year-old Accord, and nearly passed out when she saw the total of the purchase, the tax, and the insurance.

CARFAX AND AUTOCHECK

CARFAX and AutoCheck (the Coke and Pepsi of vehicle history reports) provide an invaluable service, telling you how many owners a car has had, if it was a fleet or lease car, whether it has been in an accident, and most important, whether it has been declared a total loss by an insurance company for reasons of wreck, flood, or theft. These services are not flawless—they can only tell you information that is in their database. For example, if a car was submerged in a flood and simply left to dry out, or had an accident and was fixed privately without an insurance claim being filed, they have no way to know. But I would never buy a daily driver without running the CARFAX or AutoCheck. The risk of buying a car with a tainted history is simply too great. Note that the Vehicle Identification Number (VIN) system was not standardized until 1981, so older classic cars are not in databases that CARFAX or AutoCheck can access.

Any used car dealer worth their salt should run a CARFAX for you if you're considering their car. For a private sale you need to do it yourself. My BMW 325Xi wagon was being advertised at a very good price and I needed to make a quick decision whether to drive to Rhode Island and see it or risk losing it. I'd been paying someone else five bucks a whack to run AutoCheck reports for me, but they weren't answering their phone. I paid the $45 for an AutoCheck account, ran the VIN, it showed up as a totally clean two-owner car, I drove down to see it, and bought it on the spot. Well worth the $45.

Even if CARFAX shows an accident, or the car having been a fleet or lease vehicle, or even an insurance total, this should not necessarily be a show-stopper; it's more that well-worn issue of knowing what you're buying and not overpaying for it. Years back my mother bought a Honda Civic that was a salvage car for an excellent price. We bought it from the guy who put it back together. He had a very large, complete, professional shop. She had great luck with it. My niece is still driving it.

MAINTENANCE, MAINTENANCE, MAINTENANCE

When looking at a daily driver, the "condition, condition, condition" maxim for original and restored cars flips around to "maintenance, maintenance, maintenance." That is, if you're looking for, say, a five-year-old car, *all* of them are rust-free, have shiny paint, and an intact interior, so what you want is a car that has had the required maintenance. This is especially true on modern BMWs whose cooling systems are ticking time bombs. If that water pump hasn't been changed in 60,000 miles, you want to know that and get it replaced ASAP.

PRIVATE PARTIES VERSUS DEALERS

Ideally you'd buy the car from the original owner who can show you a stack of receipts and assure you (hopefully truthfully) he loves the car and there's nothing wrong with it but he needs something bigger for the family yadda yadda yadda. But many people rely on going to dealers for used cars because the car has presumably been checked out and anything wrong fixed, and a warranty is offered. Personally, I get such a strong unclean feeling every time I walk into a new or used car dealership that I want to run home and take a hot shower. *Do you have a trade-in?* I'm just here to look at the car. *Are you paying cash or financing?* I'm just here to look at the car. *Are you interested in an extended warranty?* I'm just here to look at the car. *We're going to need you to sign this form and Xerox your license.* I'm just here to … actually, never mind; I'm not here any more. Damn that hot water feels good.

If you want to lower cost as much as possible at the expense of increased risk, you can go to a public auction where cars are being wholesaled. These are cars that have been traded in to dealers, but the dealer has decided not to keep them on their lot. Unfortunately, when a car is traded in and wholesaled, any records are lost (a form of automotive amnesia). You don't know who the previous owner was. You don't know what's been done. So much for "maintenance, maintenance, maintenance." The best you can do is try to infer maintenance from the condition of the car. Does it look well cared-for or abused? Have the leaves and acorns ever been cleaned out from under the hood? Make no mistake—you are assuming increased risk. But if it's a car you're familiar with, or if you've prescreened that make and model, identified the trouble areas, and inspected them, the risk may be manageable.

In my case, high-mileage all-wheel-drive BMWs can eat their transfer case and differentials if the fluids were never changed, so what you want to see is a paper trail showing these fluids were serviced within 100K miles. Because my 325Xi wagon had been recently auctioned, I had no idea whether or when these fluids were changed. But because the car was in such great condition, I bought it anyway and immediately changed all the fluids. Then I did "the plastic kit"— the radiator, expansion tank, thermostat, water pump, and every hose. So far, it has worked out fine.

Here's hoping you do as satisfactory a job balancing your passion, your finances, and your repair time in the selection and care and feeding of your daily driver.

CHAPTER 40

THE THRILL OF THE CHASE

WALKING AWAY FROM A DAILY DRIVER

Even through I'm primarily into older cars, I am certainly not immune to the wiles of newer ones. I've long wanted a 1998 BMW M3 four-door sedan in an interesting color as a daily driver. So when a Techno Violet M3 with 99,000 miles popped up on Craigslist for $5,400, those portions of my brain devoted to things like work and family suffered serious oxygen deprivation.

The ad said the car was being sold cheaply because it needed work and because the owner had lost his license. Actually I'll just show you the ad, which I swear is absolutely verbatim:

> THIS A 1998 M3 TECHNO VIOLET 99,XXX MILES 5 SPEED
> NEED IGNITION SWITCH, BRAKE DISC 1GRILL 1CORNER
> LIGHT 02 SENSOR AND WHEEL SENNSOR FOR THE ABS
> LIGHT TURN ON ONLY WHEN DRIVING THE CAR. THE
> CAR IS IN THE ROAD INSURED COME AND TEST DRIVE
> DONT GET IT TWISTED THE CAR RUNS IM ASKING $5400
> B/O. ANY OTHER QUESTION CALL [XXX-XXX-XXXX]
> THANKS THE CROME WHEELS ARE NOT INCLUDED
> (IM NOT LOOKING FOR ANY TRADES BUT IF U GONNA
> OFFER ME SOMETHING TO TRADE PLEASE DONT INSULT
> ME THANK YOU THIS CAR IS WORTH LIKE $12K TO $14K
> AROUND THERE I KNOW WHAT I GOT THE REASON WHY
> IM SELLING IT SO CHEAP IS BECAUSE I UNDERSTAND
> THAT THE CAR NEED A LITTLE BIT OF WORK TO GET IT
> PERFECT BUT I DONT HAVE THE MONEY RIGHT NOW TO
> FIX IT PLUS I DONT HAVE A LISENCE ANYMORE TO DRIVE
> IT THIS IS A GOOD OPPORTUNITY FOR SOMEBODY THAT
> CAN MAKE THIS CAR WORTH AT LEAST $13000 AGAIN
> WITH LIKE $1000 ROUGHLTY TALKING THINK FIRST
> BEFORE JUGING THIS TECHNO E36 4DR M3 :))ATT:EDWIN

Let me say that equality, dignity, and respect are absolute bedrock values for me (thanks Mom), and I would never think less of anyone simply because his ad was written in something that isn't exactly the King's English. That having been said, what unfolded was pretty funny.

I called and got the VIN so I could run CARFAX and AutoCheck reports. One showed up two minor accidents; the other revealed a possible discrepancy of 25,000 miles, which could be a simple recording error. Both were noted; neither was a deal breaker.

I drove out to a somewhat sketchy part of Worcester, Massachusetts on a freezing morning, and there she was. Techno Violet is a love-it-or-hate-it color, but when the sun hits it, I think it's gorgeous. I've long said that I can tell in ten seconds if I'm going to buy a car, and the rest of the check-out is just to seek confirming evidence. I immediately thought *she will be mine. Oh yes, she will be mine.* Fortunately my left brain was active enough to ask, "What's the catch?"

Simply put, "the catch" was that "she" was beat to shit. But that realization would come slowly. I walked around the car. It had recently been repainted. It was pretty and straight, but the sunroof seal and right grille and corner lens were missing. And the fenders had boy-racer side-vent cutouts like a newer BWM M3, but the vent grilles were gone. And the car had mismatched wheels. And the interior was a mess: The ignition had been popped out, the radio was missing, the headrests were gone, the headliner was sagging, one rear door panel was damaged, and the climate control module was hanging by its cables.

As I was peering in, a street person in a trench coat slowly walked up to me and said, "What are you? A repo man?"

The owner appeared in his pajamas and a light winter jacket. As we were talking, a guy pulled up in a pickup truck and yelled to the owner, "Four grand! I'll give you four grand for it!" and then drove off. The owner laughed and said, "He's a friend of mine; he says that to me whenever he sees the car." I thought to myself that, even with the odd fenders and messy interior, four grand would be a great price for this car, and noted sadly that, if he had in fact repeatedly rejected this offer from his friend, he probably wouldn't take it from me.

Suddenly, two other guys rounded the corner. One of them called, in the highly exaggerated tone of a carnie barker, "Get your crack cocaine! Get your crack cocaine right here!" I'm not sure what the context of this was—if they actually were drug dealers, if the owner of the car was a drug dealer, or if the whole thing was just for show because I looked so out of place. "Are *they* friends of yours too?" I asked the owner. He didn't say anything.

Like I said, a sketchy part of town.

My bubble of lust began losing air when I checked the fluids. The engine was so low on oil that it did not register at all on the dipstick. The owner didn't have any oil, and I didn't have the right kind with me. We drove to a parts store and bought three quarts of synthetic. It drank all three. While adding the oil, I noticed that the radiator's plastic upper tank had been repaired with epoxy. Sheesh. Low on oil *and* had leaked coolant. Danger Will Robinson.

Then, when I drove it, it got worse. Much worse. The owner showed me that, in addition to putting in the key, I had to start the car with a screwdriver because the whole ignition module had been ripped out and was hanging beneath the steering column (yes he had the title). It started right up and idled okay with no obvious noises or oil or coolant smoke. But nearly every dashboard warning light was on. The power steering wasn't working; what I could feel of the steering was horribly loose. The front right wheel felt like it was about to fly off due to a cracked brake rotor. The transmission munched second gear. The car banged horribly over bumps. When I looked underneath, I found a go-fast aftermarket coil-over suspension, but also a bent rear trailing arm and a barely attached exhaust.

I started to think about the offer shouted by the guy in the pickup truck … four grand? At first I thought it'd be a steal for that. Now I began to imagine four thousand dollars of buyer's remorse.

I know I keep saying that you should always think these things through so that, when you do make an offer, you are equally okay with whatever the outcome, but I'd never considered a car that was such a pretty, freshly-painted color that tugged at my right brain, but had so much downside and risk, and was so *beat*. I estimated the cost to make it whole, guessing at the price for certain used parts like headrests, stereo, and a matching fourth wheel. It quickly hit two grand. And that was only for the things I *knew* about. It would probably take at least a grand just to get it drivable enough to find out what else it really needed, and the odds were that list would include every tie rod, ball joint, and bushing. I would have been more sanguine if the car had any two fewer demerits (say, intact ignition and original fenders). Because I already owned a 528iT wagon and a Z3 M Coupe, the M3 only made sense if it was something to buy and resell, or, if I was buying it to replace the wagon, if after paying X and fixing it for Y, I'd have a nicer M3 than if I'd bought one costing X+Y. For a keeper, I should find a nicer car. For a flipper, I could lose my shirt. The ineffable calculus was that it made no sense. I left making no offer.

Of course, there's a third category—a dirt-cheap project car to get multiple Hack Mechanic articles out of. With that in mind, "it makes no sense" turns into "wonder what he'll take" (a road I find myself on quite often). We negotiated via e-mail. I offered $3,000. He came down to $4,500. I inched up to $3,750 ("I paid less than four grand for a running, rust-free, freshly-painted M3 sedan" has some nice bragging rights). He squeaked down to $4,300. We were only $550 apart. I thought I could pry it away with cash before an impending snowstorm; I literally e-mailed him a photograph of the money spread out on the table with the caption *"See I really do have the cash."* No, he said. "Someone will pay $4,500 for it." Perhaps. But that someone will not be me.

Two weeks later he called me back and offered me the car for $4,000 (showing that, whatever the story was with the guy who shouted "four grand" from the pickup truck, he understood that my money was, in fact, real). I drove out there with a truck, a trailer, cash, and my son, Ethan, as hired muscle, prepared to cut a deal. Due to a comedy of errors, the owner didn't have the keys. But that enabled me to give the car another long, cold look. I closely examined the nonoriginal front fenders, and found that the metal was paper-thin and that they had been installed without proper undercoating—a recipe for rust. I walked away from it for good, and this time I didn't look back.

It was a good chase; it kept me occupied for several weeks. A bit of a malaise settled in after it was over, but I slept better. My friends and family made Techno Violet jokes until spring. On Valentine's day morning I went out to the garage to find the seats of my daily driver covered with a shimmering violet fabric and a note from Maire Anne saying, "Roses are red / Violets are blue / Here's your BMW / in Techno-Violet hue …"

But the best part of the whole Techno Violet M3 episode was the feedback from BMW Club members. *Roundel* editor Satch Carlson himself said, "Just tell me you did not buy this hideous rat." Technical editor Mike Miller offered, "Thank God you didn't buy this car. It is sojourning on its way to the junkyard. Remember we're shopping for a used car owner as much as we're shopping for a used car. I wouldn't even have replied to this ad." (Damn, Mikey, where's your sense of *adventure*?) My old friend and Club Service Advisor Terry Sayther said, "We see them like that all the time. *DO NOT BUY IT.*" Friend and CCA member Brad Meyer delightfully twisted an old Monty Python line by saying, "This is not a car for buying. This is a car for laying down and avoiding."

But my absolute favorite comment was the following unsolicited e-mail from CCA member Mike Roach. Keep in mind that Mike and I have never met. "I was getting ready to board a plane, send out an e-mail to everyone I know in Boston, call the state mental hospital, basically do anything to keep you from getting it. This is the car that would have been your undoing. It would have crushed your spirit. It's tragic to see a car guy tormented to the point of hobby desertion. You would have shuffled around, staring at the floor for years. The return of Bertha's tender love would have been our only hope, and lord knows where she is. Your family, CCA friends, band, etc. would have still loved you, but missed the Old Rob." Note that, while I've written in detail in these pages that Bertha is the 2002 that I sold to my friend Alex in 1988, I hadn't written about Bertha in the *Roundel* in many, many years when I received Mike's e-mail. I told Mike that anyone who throws around the phrase "the return of Bertha's tender love" knows me better than I feel, uh, comfortable with.

Who would've expected a beat-to-shit M3 to be the mechanism that fostered such delightful human connection, even without my buying the car?

CHAPTER 41

MY INCREASINGLY DECREPIT FLESH

During the winter the garage was being built, I needed to work on the brakes on my daily driver BMW sedan. The old garage was already torn down, and my 3.0CSi was occupying the only other nearby garage space, that of a neighbor who has an unused garage nearly as ancient as the one I tore down (in return, I blow out his driveway every time it snows, an implicit quid pro quo I regard more seriously than he does). So where exactly was I going to do this brake job? Fortunately the building I work in has heated warehouse space, so I ordered the parts, and planned that when they arrived, I'd drive into work and bang out the repair there. I didn't even consider taking the car to a shop and having someone else do it; when you know that a basic rotors-and-pads brake job is a hundred dollars in parts and a couple hours of your time, damn it's hard to pay someone 500 bucks.

Before it was demolished, my old garage housed almost 15 years worth of oil, antifreeze, transmission fluid, and God knows what else. It was disgusting, but I thought of it as my private Hack Mechanic fluid cellar. Why, yes, over there we have a cask of blended 3.0CSi motor oil; note the slightly metallic aftertaste from where the rod bearings have worn right through to the copper. We've let it age for 15 years; it's just starting to get good. And this insouciant little vintage over here, that's original 2002 hypoid differential fluid. You never forget the smell of that. We shall serve no scum before its time.

A quick digression is in order to explain why I still change my own oil. It's not that I like doing it. Actually, I don't. But I do it anyway. One reason is the desire to do it right for a reasonable price (dealers charge a ridiculous amount for an oil change and, at the low end of the spectrum, those $16.99 oil changes at the chains or the corner garage use cheap oil filters). But, more important, when you own high-mileage cars, *someone* has to maintain them, which means jacking them up and crawling under them at regular intervals to look for leaks. If you don't have a regular mechanic, that someone is … you. Changing the oil is the "I'm greasy might as well crawl all the way under and have a good look" event that allows me to see other problems before they become more serious. It's like the car's well-visit to the doctor.

Many years of these good, responsible sentiments had generated numerous containers of disgusting dreck. When the garage was torn down, I'd temporarily stored them under the deck, but obviously they needed to be carted off. So one Saturday morning, while I was waiting for the BMW brake parts to arrive, I loaded the nasty fluids into the van and took them to the recycling depot—you know, the place that they used to call "the dump" until the dump stopped accepting trash. I considered putting a big "Valdez" banner on the side of the van for the duration of the drive to impart the cargo with the appropriate caution and sense of doom. After I unloaded the unspeakably filthy containers into the tank for recycled oil, I checked out the electronics recycling area (part of the ritual—hey, it's Newton; people get rid of a lot of good stuff here), and there was a very nice looking 27" Sony Trinitron television. Remember that this was back in the day when big CRTs were still king; the first 42" flat screen plasma sets had just come out, but they literally cost twelve grand. So I picked up the television, which weighed about as much as a pregnant cow, and put it in the back of the van.

Now, I am not large, or particularly strong or athletic, but having been in and out of rock and roll bands for years, I've developed skill at lifting big heavy objects. When your gig is over at 2 A.M., no one's going to load your stuff into the back of your car except you, so you just man-up and get it done. It didn't seem to me that this object was that different, or that much heavier, than the countless guitar amps or PA cabinets I'd lifted.

So I got home, opened up the van, unlocked the basement, picked up the television (again), and carried it inside. Maire Anne saw this and immediately said, "Rob, don't lift that by yourself." Ah, she's sweet, but such unwarranted wifely concern. Nonsense. I am a man. I will lift what I want, when I want to, and no, I don't need any help, thank you very much.

Once the television set was inside, I plugged it in, turned it on, and was pleased to see that the menus came up, but found that when

I hooked up an antenna, it didn't lock onto any channels. I did ten minutes of web-sleuthing, determined what was probably wrong, and read that it was not an easy fix. I sighed and realized that, of course, this was why the damned thing was at the dump I mean recycle center to begin with. So I picked it up again and put it back in the van. Maire Anne said, again, perhaps with more urgency, *"Rob! Don't lift that by yourself!"* Feh. I am a man. I will lift what I want, when I want to. I then drove back to the dump, where I lifted it *a fourth time* to return it to the scrap section.

So, yes, I lifted a 27″ Sony Trinitron, by myself, not once, not twice, but *four times* (kind of reminds you of that business with the Triumph and the fog, doesn't it?). Since the specifications for even obsolete electronics live forever on the web, I can now confidently report that the Sony KV27HS420 I hoisted weighs 110lbs. (I loved the review I found on epinions.com that says *"but one person can carry it."* Yes! You are a man too! And how is *your* L5 vertebrae and S1 nerve root?)

But I wasn't done.

Saturday night, the water heater suffered a most abrupt and spectacular demise, with water literally streaming out the bottom and flooding the basement. At least there was a clear diagnosis. (I imagined calling a plumber, having him look at the mini-Niagara in my basement, scratch his head, and say, "Well, *there's* your problem. It's fooked.") So I drove to Home Depot, bought a water heater, muscled it into the back of the van, drove home, and muscled it out of the van and into the basement. On Sunday I unhooked the dead one and muscled it out to the curb. And yes I did that all by myself, because I am a man, and I will lift what I want blah blah blah.

Incredibly, my back was fine.

Or so it seemed.

The brake parts for the 318ti arrived that Saturday. So after Saturday's wrestle with the television and Sunday's tussle with the water heater, on Sunday night I drove the car to work and put it inside the warehouse. I jacked it up, set it on jack stands, removed the front wheels, and began replacing the rotors and pads. I was sitting on the floor, facing one of the front hubs, when I reached diagonally in front of me to pick up a wrench that was to the right of my right knee.

Ouch.

That's not right.

And it didn't go away. It wasn't a searing pain, but something was clearly very wrong. It was all I could do to finish the repair, put the car back together, and drive home.

When the pain was still with me two days later, I saw my doctor. He did the full round of reflex testing, and was almost giddy with academic interest when I presented absolutely no patellar reflex in my right knee.

I had bulged a disc and pinched a nerve.

That was 2007. An initial round of physical therapy resurrected the patellar reflex and ameliorated most of the acute discomfort, but even with repeated therapy and cortisone shots, my back has never been right since, and apparently it never will be.

I used to pick up transmissions and bench-press them into place. No more. Now, I have to be very careful even doing something as pedestrian as dismounting and mounting wheels. Even bending at certain angles is hard; it is very uncomfortable for me to work under the hood of a low car like the Z3 M Coupe. And muscling a battery in and out of any car now carries substantial risk.

Now, I know other people who have serious back problems, and in the spectrum of things, mine are trivial: I have never been felled by excruciating pain; I have never been bedridden; I have never missed a day of work. I also know that the key to aging gracefully is to accept these changes and limitations with humor and adroitness, and not constantly look back with longing at what you can no longer do or have.

But it sucks.

However, I simply refuse to stop working on cars. I enjoy it too much. In this new slightly hobbled paradigm, the mid-rise scissors lift has proven to be a godsend. The ability to sit fully upright beneath the lift, once a luxury beyond measure, is now an absolute necessity.

I now understand how my mother feels when we implore her to stop moving rocks around in her garden.

I just try not to do anything stupid. And that is exceedingly difficult. I am, after all, a man.

CHAPTER 42

WHY I DON'T FIX CARS FOR OTHER PEOPLE
(PART III: BAD LUCK WITH FRIENDS' SUBARUS)

In 2010, my old high school friend Mary Jane posted on Facebook that she had just lost her job, and her Subaru really needed brake work, and if anyone knew a cheap mechanic who did good work, she would appreciate the referral. At first I didn't respond because, well, I don't fix cars for other people, and she wasn't specifically asking me. But then the posts turned more urgent. And I remembered some history that MJ and I shared with our friend Dave, a larger-than-life figure who was a great backyard mechanic and enormously helpful in our circle of friends, bailing me and my Triumph out more than once, usually at odd hours of the morning and in odder states of consciousness. Dave passed away in 1991. I thought, "Dave would've fixed her brakes, and he's gone, so I should."

So I relented. I called her up and told her that I was the cheapest mechanic she was going to find (free being pretty damned cheap), and that basically I never did this but I would do it for her. I would channel Dave. I said that brakes are brakes, that I do them all the time. I said that I even had a garage, air tools and a lift, and assured her I would probably have her in and out in a couple of hours, and there was very little that could go wrong.

And for about a week we were welcomed into Iraq as liberators.

MJ had in her possession a diagnosis from a repair shop that included a parts list, so, starting out, I had the benefit of knowing that the car needed not only brake pads and rotors but also a brake caliper. I tried to order the parts at a local store, but there seemed to be some confusion over the size of the brake rotors. MJ came over and we put her car up on the lift. I measured the Subaru's rotors to be certain, and then went to the store and picked up the parts. When I got back, I pulled off the bad caliper on the right, replaced it, bled the brake line (whenever you disconnect a brake line you have to bleed the air out of it), and replaced the brake rotor. But when I tried to fit the new brake pads, something wasn't right. I couldn't make the pads fit. I compared them to the old ones, and they were the wrong size. Somewhere in the confusion over rotor sizes, the guy had sold me the wrong pads. I called the parts place, but they had just closed (it was Sunday). Here we were, faced with the age-old rhythm of repair issue, and it was marching to its own drummer.

I normally don't buy brake parts at chains like AutoZone, but the car was up on the lift, and both of our lives would've gotten complicated if I couldn't complete the job and she couldn't drive home. Fortunately I found a place that was open Sunday evening and had brake pads of the correct size. I got the pads, installed them, and lowered the car off the lift. When I got in it to test it, however, the brake pedal went right to the floor. Not good.

As I said above, whenever you disconnect a brake line, air can get into it, and that air needs to be bled out by running pressurized brake fluid through the system and catching it in a container. Sometimes it takes a number of tries to get this right. Often you can get away with bleeding only the line that you've opened, but sometimes you need to bleed all of them. I bled the entire system three times. Finally the pedal firmed up, but something still didn't feel quite right. But it was now 9 P.M. on Sunday night. I had put the car on the lift at noon. I'd been working on it for nine hours.

In the end, although it was a mitzvah (and, lapsed Jew that I am, I do not use that word lightly) and MJ was extremely grateful, I'm still not entirely sure that I completely fixed the problem. There's no doubt that the car had a seized brake caliper and was in dire need of pads and rotors, and I replaced all that, but I'm not certain there wasn't some other problem, like a bad master cylinder or a leaking power assist valve. I would've preferred to totally nail it. Whenever I asked MJ about it, she'd say, "Oh, yeah, the brakes are great," but I was never sure if she was just telling me what I wanted to hear. On the "cars as a conduit for human interaction" scale, this third repair for someone else was vastly more satisfying than the first two, but, again, I had fixed someone's car, and had this feeling that, despite my best efforts, I'd done something wrong. I could make this a couchable moment and talk about how Jewish guilt apparently still applies even to the non-practicing, but I'm uncertain what the actual causality is.

I know they say that charity is its own reward, but if you know someone who does mechanical work, don't press him (or her) for favors. There's more going on here psychologically than you realize.

CHAPTER 43

THE BEST RHYTHM OF REPAIR EXAMPLE EVER

Earlier I wrote about the rhythm of repair—the process by which, as a do-it-yourselfer, repairs are fit into your life. The major dynamic in the rhythm of repair is the interplay between diagnosis, ordering parts, and actually fixing the car. That is, on a car that's a daily driver, since you don't want to take the car "down" for any longer than necessary, you are tempted to try to diagnose the thing on the fly, order the parts you think you need, and take the car down only over the weekend and only when you already have the parts in hand. Most of the time this works out pretty well, but sometimes you're left scrambling to put the thing back together before Monday morning's unsympathetic thunder.

I recently had a rhythm-of-repair-related experience so profound it practically bitch-slapped my little Zen Hack Mechanic world.

After Ethan and Kyle started college, they stopped coming on vacation with us. (I know … why would anyone pass up an all-expenses paid vacation to Nantucket? You raise your kids to be independent, and what do they do? They go and be independent. Even with bugs, bombs, cars, and guitars, I guess we're not as cool as we think.) Thus we no longer needed a gargantuan vehicle for all of us to get to Nantucket. I sold the Suburban. However, Maire Anne, Aaron, and I still go down there and rendezvous with my brother-in-law Dan and his delightful daughters Aidan and Guthrie, so although I no longer need to transport five of us from Boston, I still need a decent-sized vehicle once there. I bought a 1993 Toyota Land Cruiser.

Like the Suburbans preceding it, the TLC was used only for vacation and pulled off the road for the winter. With the 'Burbs, this was because neither Maire Anne nor I wanted to be driving a vehicle that big the rest of the year. In contrast, I actually enjoy driving the Land Cruiser; it's smaller than the 'Burb, far more maneuverable, and has a lot of mojo. Unfortunately it is a 5,000 pound vehicle with all-time all-wheel drive and a primitive digital engine management system, the three of which conspire to deliver an average fuel economy of eleven miles per gallon. Now, I have no moral issue with this. I think people should drive what they want. But if I'm going to be driving something that gets eleven miles per gallon, it should be impossibly angular, have an Italian name that ends in *i* and about two inches of ground clearance, wear paint whose finish you can fall into, and leave shrieking acrid plumes of tire smoke in its wake. The Land Cruiser is handy, but eleven-worthy? I think not. So it stays parked until vacation calls.

With vacation about three weeks away, I registered and insured the Land Cruiser. I noticed that the two problems it had when I parked it last year—a loud exhaust and a sticky hand brake—had both gotten much worse over the winter. Knowing full well the car would never pass inspection in that condition, I began to deal with these issues.

The exhaust had holes in the two headpipes. Experience has shown it is generally false economy to replace individual exhaust pieces; you should bite the bullet and replace the whole thing. If one part of the exhaust is rusty enough to be perforated, odds are the rest of it is weak. Plus, individual exhaust pieces are bloody unlikely to come out without a fight; it's far easier just to wreck the whole thing with a Sawzall. Nonetheless, economic issues sometimes win out. Modern cars have catalytic converters that can be pretty pricey, so the "just replace everything" mantra can cost you dearly. When I found out certain of the exhaust pieces on the TLC are dealer-only and a whole exhaust would set me back nearly a thousand bucks *for the parts,* I did what I said I wouldn't do and replaced only the headpipes. The result was predictable; the new headpipes didn't seal perfectly against the old catalytic converters. However, it was much quieter than it had been—enough to stand a chance inspection-wise.

The hand brake was a total pain in the ass. There is a lever called the bell crank that goes through the backing plate of the rear brakes, connecting the hand brake cable with the rear brake shoes, and it was totally seized. I soaked the bell crank on both sides in penetrating oil overnight, then spent two hours beating on them with a hammer, back and forth, back and forth, trying to get them to free up. I got the levers moving enough that the brakes did *something* when I pulled the hand

brake lever. Like the exhaust, it was not completely fixed, but functional enough that I was willing to play inspection roulette.

I take all of my cars to the same local service station for inspection.
They know me pretty well and cut me some amount of slack, giving
me the benefit of the doubt wherever possible (think of it as a volume
discount). To my delight, the Land Cruiser emerged from their inspection bay with a shiny new sticker. I expected them to not-so-gently re-
monstrate me on the exhaust and/or the hand brake, but instead, to my
surprise, they said the right front wheel had a lot of play and strongly
recommended I take care of it as soon as possible. I swore I would,
then promptly forgot about it in the prevacation crush.

About a week later, with vacation only four days away, I drove the
Land Cruiser to work and heard a loud metallic scraping sound. And
I mean *loud*—loud enough that pedestrians turned and looked at the
truck as I drove by. It seemed to be coming from the right front wheel,
to vary with speed, and to come and go when I applied the brakes.
This is all consistent with a bad front wheel bearing. I had loaned the
truck to Ethan the day before, but it's doubtful his use could've made
a wheel bearing go bad. I remembered what the inspection station had
said about play in the right front wheel. I assumed they were talking
about a loose tie rod, but I jacked the truck up, grabbed the wheel at
6:00 and 12:00 and then again at 3:00 and 9:00 and moved it, and sure
enough, the wheel bearing was clearly loose.

Now, there are some repairs I look forward to tangling with, but
the idea of jacking up a 5,000 pound vehicle, pulling off that big-ass
wheel and tire, and changing both the inner and outer wheel bearings
was not my idea of fun. And, in addition, it was about 90 degrees in
Boston and we were leaving for vacation in four days.

Directly across the street from where I work (and I mean *directly*—
spitting distance) there is a car and truck repair shop. They do mostly
fleet and commercial vehicles, but the guys I work with will sometimes
bring their cars to them out of convenience. I took the truck to Tony,
described the situation, told him I'd already verified the front wheel
bearing was loose, and asked him for an estimate. Tony called me back
an hour later, confirmed the outer wheel bearing was not only loose
but bad, and quoted me $326 to replace both it and the inner one. This
seemed like money well spent—no worries, no sweating in the heat,

and perhaps only the fourth time in ten years I'd paid *anyone* else to do *anything* on *any* of my cars. My only worry was I might get used to it.

So imagine my surprise when, after picking up the Land Cruiser at the end of the day and beginning to drive it home, it still made exactly the same scraping noise.

Let me be clear about this. The inspection station told me the car had something loose in the right front end. I diagnosed it as a bad wheel bearing. I told Tony the car had a bad wheel bearing and asked him to replace it. Tony verified the car had a bad wheel bearing and replaced it. The car, apparently, *really did* have a bad wheel bearing. However, *this was not the source of the noise.*

So, now, with three days before vacation, what do I do? Do I take the car back to Tony who did exactly what I asked, correctly replaced a bad wheel bearing, yet returned the car to me with the same noise? Do I take it somewhere else? Do I gamble it's something minor and ignore it? Or do I try to fix it myself?

As you know, I have a mid-rise lift, which in theory would've made it very easy to pick the truck off the ground and allow me to spin all four wheels and see which one was making the noise, but the chance that I could misjudge both the capacity of the mid-rise and the weight of the TLC made me circumspect about putting it up on the lift.

At work, however, we have a truck floor jack big enough to lift a tank. The next day I drove the TLC into work. It was still beastly hot outside, but inside the warehouse it was hot but not actively deleterious to human health. I jacked up the Land Cruiser one wheel at a time and isolated the metallic sound to the right rear wheel. I supported that corner of the truck with two jack stands *plus* the floor jack, pulled the wheel off, and saw about what you'd expect of an 18-year-old vehicle with 180K miles. It looked like the rear brakes had never been changed. The brake pad was very thin and the outside circumference of the rotor had large flakes of rust. Geez, I thought, the scraping sound could be coming from anywhere within this mess. Using a chisel, I knocked most of the rust off the outside of the rotor and verified as best as I could nothing was hitting the caliper. I put the wheel back on and spun it, and still heard the scraping sound. Damn.

Maybe, I thought, the sound is coming from the hand brake. After all, the bell crank levers were so seized I was beating on them with a hammer. Even on a car with rear disk brakes, the hand brake is still an old-fashioned drum inside the rotor, with the cable pulling a pair of shoes. I took off the caliper, pulled off the rotor and drum, and saw the hand brake shoes were about the thickness of deli meat before you ask them to slice it as thin as they can get it. I backed off the hand brake adjuster until there was no chance the shoes could be touching the drum, put everything together, spun the wheel, and the noise was still there. Damn again.

At this point I was hot, tired, and unhappy. I thought *this scraping sound is probably nothing, almost certainly something minor like a rust flake wedged between the caliper and the rotor.* But then I'd flip-flop and think *are you SURE? Are you willing to risk a wheel bearing seizing up on you on vacation?* The practical angel on my left shoulder whispered *just take the car in to someone else and pay them to fix it—that's what normal people do.* But the mechanic on my right shoulder said *what are you, nuts? You know a full rear brake job on this truck will probably run you 15 hundred bucks* (nearly half what the truck is worth). And I'd rather spend that money in 15 hundred different ways.

Well, I thought, if I'm going to fix it, I need parts. Brakes are brakes. There's no great mystery in how to replace them, or what to order. I looked at online price and delivery times for rear pads, rotors, and hand brake shoes. Then I realized: What was the purpose of replacing the hand brake shoes if I didn't also deal with the seized bell crank levers? Those *are* very specific to the car. The bell crank levers are dealer-only items. It started to snowball. I didn't have a complete list of every part I'd need. And, even calling the dealer, there was no way to get mail-ordered parts here before vacation. I struggled to focus through the heat. Something inside me said *stop—don't buy anything. You don't even know it needs ANY of these parts. Take a deep breath and DIAGNOSE THE PROBLEM.*

So I looked at it one more time. With my eyes stinging with sweat, up went the truck on the jack and stands. Again. Off came the wheel. Again. I already had backed the hand brake shoes completely off, so they can't be scraping. What else can I take out of the loop? The caliper. I completely removed the caliper from the rotor and zip-tied it to the shock absorber. I spun the hub. Noise gone.

I put the wheel back on and spun it. Noise still gone.

To be certain, I took the car down off the jack and drove it around the parking lot with the caliper still tied up. Noise still gone. I jacked the car back up, put the caliper back on, and spun the hub without the wheel on it. Noise still gone. So it's *not* something wedged between the caliper and the rotor. This is good. This is progress.

Then I put the wheel back on, spun it, and the noise was back. Hmmn.

Even with the sweat running into my eyes, my brain slowly began to engage. *It's almost as if,* my brain said to me, *it's almost as if the noise is only happening when BOTH the caliper and the wheel are on.*

And then it happened. Once in a while, your brain breaks out of the little box you've built for it and follows its own path down the hill in the back of the house through the weeds, and finds a pretty little section in the garden you've never seen before.

The wheel was lying face-up on the floor. I flipped it over and looked on the inside. And then I saw it, plain as day—a bright silver circular scrape mark, like the space between two songs on a vinyl record album. This was the source of the noise. *Something on the caliper was scraping the inside of the wheel.* I looked at the caliper. Sure enough, attached to the caliper, there was a small heat shield, about the size of a book of matches, intended to conduct heat away from the brake pads. One corner was bent up. The bent corner was rounded from where it had been hitting the inside of the wheel. It made perfect sense that, if either the caliper or wheel was removed, the noise was gone, but when both were installed, the noise was back.

What bent the heat shield? Why did it happen all of a sudden? Could a rock have gotten kicked up in there? Did it have anything to do with Ethan's borrowing the car? Don't know, don't care. I bent the offending little sucker down, put the wheel back on *for the fifth time,* drove the car around the parking lot, and was visited by the Zen presence of blissful quiet (what is the sound of one brake shield not scraping, grasshopper?).

So here's the life-changing epiphany. Had I taken the truck in to a repair shop, be it Tony's across the street, a Midas Muffler, an independent mechanic specializing in Land Cruisers, or a Toyota dealer, *any* competent mechanic would've looked at this corroded mess of rear brakes which hadn't seen human hands since it left the factory 180,000 miles ago and said, "It all has to be replaced—rotors, pads, calipers, handbrake shoes, bell crank levers, all of it." And they would've been right. And if they'd changed the rear calipers—and they probably would've because the dust boots were in terrible shape—then the scraping noise would've vanished because the new caliper would not have had a bent heat shield. And it would've cost me 15 hundred bucks. The truck did need rear brakes (and I've since replaced them, by the way). *But that had nothing to do with the noise.*

If this doesn't make you understand why the vibe of John Muir's Volkswagen "Idiot Manual" resonated so deeply in my soul all those years ago when it proposed that not only *can* you fix it yourself, but you can do a better job than anyone else; why anyone who says *do it once do it right* around me risks getting smacked in the face with a sock filled with horse manure soaked in brake fluid; and why car guys the world over so often fall back to their knee-jerk reaction of *damn it I'll just do it myself*—I can't help you.

CHAPTER 44

AN ECONOBOX FOR FIREBIRD BOY

Like me, my ex-boss has three sons. He said he told all of them: "Here's how it is. I buy your first car. It's a shitbox. You pay for everything."

I liked that. Very clear. No room for misunderstandings. I determined that that's what I would do.

But, of course, parenting is more complex than that.

During the summer of 2008, right before the economy crashed, gas peaked in the Northeast at about $4.50/gallon, and I felt like a freaking genius because I was driving the Geo Metro. But as prices eased, and the ribbing I took from my friends did not ("Why are you still driving that piece of shit?"), I was content to give up my little experiment and go back to driving a car that was more interesting and substantial. Eventually I gave the Metro to Ethan while he was at college. *Yes! Firebird Boy Is Forced to Publicly Drive the Tuna Can! This is like wearing the Scarlet M! THE UNIVERSE IS JUST!*

At first he was chagrined by the fact that, of all the cool cars in the garage, *this* was the one I said he could have. But once he warmed to it, he began to like the car. There is quite possibly no cheaper vehicle to drive. "Dad," he called me one weekend, "I drove from Amherst to New York and back. I think I spent 15 dollars in gas!"

Last fall, Ethan told me that, two months prior, the car had failed inspection because the check engine light was on. I told him that if he kept driving it, he was risking a ticket that would increase our insurance rates, so the options were: he could pay someone to fix it, he could fix it himself, or he could ask for my help. Now, as much as I like the clarity of my ex-boss's approach, I don't have the heart to enforce the "you pay for everything" part because I know he can't. So, in truth, he pays for gas, and we pay for insurance, registration, parts, inspection, the electronic toll pass bill … in short, everything. And I'm the one who maintains it and keeps it running. (This all shows that the "family" exception to "I don't work on cars for other people" is big enough to, well, drive a Geo Metro through, as well it should be.) So I fully expected that this check engine light issue would fall to me, and it did.

Two days before Thanksgiving, I drove out to Amherst and swapped cars with Ethan, driving the Metro home under cover of darkness and leaving him with my BMW station wagon so he could get home for Thanksgiving. I fixed the check engine light (a rather ingenious workaround, if I say so myself, involving replacing a no-longer-available emissions-related component with a light bulb of the same resistance) and gave it back to him.

When Ethan came home for the summer, the Metro, like the prodigal son himself, returned. And it was beat to shit. The check engine light was back on. He'd never changed the oil. The muffler was cracked off and hanging. It had a good-sized dent in the left rear quarter panel. It needed shocks and struts. It had a bad ball joint. The windshield washer pump wasn't working. The rear hatch lock was broken. The interior just stank. His basic strategy seemed to be to run it into the ground.

So I did what fathers do. I chewed him out. Sometimes we can't help ourselves. If many women are wired to nurture, many men are wired to "teach lessons," no matter how annoying or destructive that may be.

But on Ethan's end, it's not personal. He's just one of those kids who is hard on physical objects like cars. And the house. And computers. And cell phones. And iPods. Part of this is certainly just generational *zeitgeist*, where everything is disposable and there is the ridiculous expectation of every twelve-year-old that they will have an iPhone, and if it breaks, mom and dad will just get them another one. But part of it is Ethan's personality. It's not that he intentionally trashes things; it's just that he's so often focused on some other goal. To paraphrase Stephen Covey's very useful book *The 7 Habits of Highly Effective People*, there is a balance to be maintained between Production versus Production Capability, which means if you have an asset (for example, a lawn mower) and you use it but don't maintain it (for example, never changing the oil or sharpening the blades), one day you'll find it doesn't work—it's broken, you've used it up, it's done—and you can't cut the grass. When you realize that the "lawn mower" can be a car, or your body, or the environment, or a relationship, his point—that when we focus too much on the short term we often use up valuable assets—is enormously powerful.

Many chapters ago I quoted John Muir's brilliant insight from his "Idiot Manual" that working on a car changes your relationship not only with the car, but also with yourself. He and Mr. Covey are really talking about the same thing: that the act of caring for something brings you into the process by which that thing continues to produce something you find to be of value. This is a deep and important observation.

But it's nearly impossible to teach someone to care. This was more than I could reasonably expect Ethan to absorb. So, instead, I explained that physical objects are just that, and fundamentally Maire Anne and I don't care about them, but being careful with physical objects that belong to other people (us) is a sign of respect for other people (us).

It made me think back to when I was in my late teens or early twenties. My mother, at her most breathtakingly levelheaded, once explained to me that it was great that I had all these friends about whom I obviously cared deeply, but I shouldn't treat my family any *worse* than those friends. It was an astonishing observation for her to make; it was astonishing that she found it necessary to share the observation with me; and it was astonishing that it was so rational that it actually made sense to me and caused me to modify my behavior.

Parenthood is a mystery. You never know what will sink in, or when your kids will mentally hit the mute button on you. When most of the women I know thought about having children, they imagined themselves nurturing babies. In contrast, an informal poll of my male friends confirms that when most men anticipate fatherhood, they skip right over infanthood and childhood and fast-forward straight to adolescence, imagining facing slightly smaller less rational versions of themselves. Do you know what men fear most? Well, sure, raising daughters, but after that, what men fear most is facing "the drug conversation." What am I going to say, men wonder, when Johnny asks me, "Well, Dad, what did *you* do?" We imagine those big eyes staring up at us, hungry for truth and guidance. Are we going to be truthful, or another lying hypocritical scum-sucking adult? "I'll just lie," said one friend. "I'll take the Fifth," said another.

Women are, of course, correct, as they are about most things. When the kids are born, they're not adolescents—they're babies. The immediate need is to nurture. You have a good 13 years before you have to face up to "the drug conversation." But what no man sees coming is what, in fact, actually happens—*it never comes up*. Your kids never ask. You know why? *They could care less about what you did 30 years ago.* It has as much relevance to them as Vietnam. Every generation thinks they invented sex and drugs. What possible bearing could your experience have to them? If you even try to broach the subject, the response is *ick*; they're about as receptive as if you tried to friend them on Facebook.

Oh, hell, I must've fallen asleep on the couch. I'm sorry, our time is up.

I gave Ethan the shitbox I mean Metro not only because it's incredibly easy on gas, but also because, as part of his general education on responsibility, I wanted to teach him a lesson about the cost of car ownership. If the lesson failed, it is probably because because I kept doing all the maintenance and absorbing all of the costs. I'd like it if he showed initiative and maintained it. I'd like it if he came into the garage and helped me out while I maintained it for him. But I guess it's simply his job to be a young man, and my job to keep his car running. That's what I do, right?

I suppose I should just find him a nicer car, something with a lower shitbox quotient that I don't have to keep working on.

Oh my God. Maybe he's just smarter than I am. He's ... he's waiting me out. This was his plan all along. The ungrateful little shit. I'll kill him.

CHAPTER 45

VINTAGE AT THE VINEYARDS: HOME AMONG THE CAR GUYS

When I put my arrest-me-red 1973 BMW 3.0CSi on the Hagerty collector car insurance policy, and according to the terms of the policy could no longer use it as a daily driver, my use of the car naturally plummeted. The policy gives me 3,000 miles a year, but I doubt I was averaging *300* miles a year. Some years, probably not even 30 miles. On one hand, with a classic car, infrequent use is not a bad thing. Limited exposure means limited stone chips, paint fading, and rust, and fewer miles mean fewer repairs. Plus, absence does, in fact, make the heart grow fonder. Drive an old car every day and the rattles can start to drive you nuts. But drive it every few months and you experience it fresh. Man, this thing is *great*; why don't I drive it more? But even by these standards, I was barely using the car.

And then something unexpected happened. I stumbled into a BMW 635CSi Alpina B7 parts car with a set of rare, killer, period-correct 16" open-lug Alpina wheels that I knew would look great on my 3.0CSi. I bought the parts car, pulled off the wheels, and sold the rest of the car to Mario Langston up at Vintage Sports and Racing in New Hampshire. The wheels were the spark that lit the fire: I began to consider driving the 3.0CSi down to the Vintage at the Vineyards classic BMW festival held annually in on Memorial Day weekend in North Carolina so I could show off the old girl and her new shoes.

Once I got the scent on me, I was possessed. I feverishly prepared the car. Work ranged from basic maintenance to long-desired modifications. I flushed fluids that hadn't been changed in 15 years. I replaced the brakes. I lowered the suspension an inch and installed the correct Bilstein HD shocks. I found an inexpensive set of Recaro seats on Craigslist and installed them. I addressed a whole bunch of minor appearance issues. Those long trim pieces that cover the rocker panels that I took off ten years ago to check for rust? I finally put them back on. Other small pieces that had never been reintegrated after the outer body restoration, such as the windshield washer system and the chrome trim on the door sills, were located and installed. It was sort of like watching the Iron Giant reassembling himself.

I planned to drive the 800 miles from Boston to North Carolina in a single day, but Maire Anne convinced me that there was no reason to kill myself. Instead I stopped at the north end of the Blue Ridge Parkway and stayed at a hole-in-the-wall Motel 6 in Harrisonburg, Virginia. When I came back from dinner, a young couple in their mid-30s were ogling my coupe. "Zees," the man said, "ees mei dream kar!" They were German. I said, "Mine too!" He explained enthusiastically that, because of the German TUV (effectively, their Department of Transportation), any car with a rust hole is crushed, so these old BMWs are exceedingly rare in Germany. When I said that I was going to an event featuring *three hundred* vintage BMWs, he and his wife both gasped; they had no idea vintage BMWs had such a following in this country. As the sun was going down, I took photos of them with their camera in front of his "dream car." Such a nice moment, the car providing a most unexpected connection.

The following morning, I woke up at 5:30 and drove down a deserted section of the Blue Ridge Parkway. I was on one of the most spectacular sections that literally runs along the ridge, with views down both sides. Me, the car, the scenery, the twisties … at one point I literally had tears of joy.

When I pulled into the hotel parking lot, filled to bursting with vintage BMWs and their owners, I felt like the Bee Girl in the Blind Lemon video finding her own people. I was, instantly and joyfully, reunited with folks I knew and folks I'd never met but who knew me because of my 25 years of monthly "Hack Mechanic" columns for BMW CCA *Roundel* magazine. During the weekend, dozens of car guys came up to me. "Hey Rob—How's *Firebird Boy*? Diggin' the Metro, is he?" "Do you still have that 528iT wagon? I can't believe it broke a spring! Did you ever get it all sorted out?" "Can my wife meet your wife and absorb whatever it is she's got?" "Still having trouble with your neighbor?" Perhaps the most frequent comment was "Thank *God* you didn't buy that piece of crap Techno Violet M3!" (nice to know the faithful are watching my back). In addition to this ribbing, a number of folks told me, "Your column is the first thing I read every month." As Yale used to tell me, anyone who says this does not flatter them is simply lying.

The event featured over 300 vintage BMWs, including *a hundred and ten 2002s*. In every possible configuration. There were tourings. There were rare turbos. There were rarer convertibles. There was one 2002 onto which some wacko had grafted the body of an early '60s British panel van. There were impossibly bright colors, some of which were stock colors I hadn't ever known existed, and some of which were *damn it it's my car I'll paint it whatever color I like* (men after my own heart). Now, there are two shades of original BMW orange—Inka, which is deep, and Colorado, which is paler. Seeing so many well-maintained/restored cars, I finally learned how to tell Inka from Colorado. Or so I thought. At the hotel, two orange cars of different hues were adjacent to one another when a passer-by asked his friend, "Are these supposed to be the same color?" I thought I'd show off my newly won observational skills. "The one on the left," I offered, "is deeper, so it's Inka, whereas the one on the right is Colorado." *Yes!* I thought to myself, *30 years of 2002 ownership and I can still learn something new.* But then the owner of one of the cars corrected me. "Actually," he smiled, "they're both Colorado, but mine has the original Glasurit paint so it's paler." I was reminded of the cat show Maire Anne and I went to nearly 30 years earlier, where I had misidentified a lilac point Siamese as a blue point. (The BMW people were nicer; I was one of them.)

I was struck by what a glorious expression of individuality it all was. There were perfect cars whose owners had maintained as original right down to the big European front license plate. There were highly modified 2002s with M3 engines whose price tag exceeded the down payment on my house. Many had driving lights mounted on the front bumper. Some had a front bumper and an air dam. Some had no front bumper, an air dam, and a lowered suspension, giving them that vacuum-cleaner-sucking-up-the-race-track look. There were bone-stock interiors, custom interiors, hand-built wood consoles, and every kind of wheel you could possibly imagine. There were cars whose every bit of rubber and trim looked factory-fresh, and cars whose owner had said, "Screw it, I'm not paying a thousand bucks for new chrome trim" and painted it all black. And the owners were all different, too. Some were young, practically kids. A handful looked like aging hippies. But most were just a cross-section of 30- to 60-year-old men. Each one of them beamed with pride when talking about his car and explaining why the choices he'd made were right for him.

Now, I don't think of my arrest-me-red 3.0CSi as a show car, but it more than held its own in this illustrious company; in fact, it was incredibly well received. Even though the outer body restoration was done in 1988, I've been careful with the car, keeping it garaged and under a cover (this simple act does wonders). The red paint and chrome absolutely popped in the North Carolina sun. Indeed, of the ten coupes parked together at this event, five were Polaris (silver), one was black, one green, one tan, and one white, so my red car positively screamed *look at me*. Most people mistook the color for Verona (the BMW shade of red originally used on these cars). Verona coupes are fairly rare. When I explained that my car was originally Polaris but I'd had it repainted Mercedes Signal Red, no one tried to lecture me on the importance of maintaining originality; to a person, the response was, "Well I love it; it's just gorgeous." Over the years, whenever I saw a coupe in an understated color such as Agave (deep green), I would think how elegant it looked. I mean, who changes the color of a car from silver to Signal Red? A kid! I *was* a kid when I did it! But the choice of color I made in 1988 was at last vindicated.

Strolling among the cars on the lawn of the North Carolina vineyard was like being in a waking dream. It was like coming home. I compared notes on daily drivers with the other men. We discussed repair as therapy. I told my stories and they told theirs. And I realized—they do what I do. *These guys are just like me*. The only difference is that I pound out 1,100 words a month about it.

While I felt very much at home among the car guys, I did have an interesting epiphany. Although there were a handful of guys who were "worse than I am" (meaning they owned more cars, or a set of cars that was more valuable or interesting), they were pros; that is, they all owned or worked in car-related businesses. Of the amateurs, in terms of the number of cars owned, I appeared to be "the worst."

However, I discovered that when measured by another metric—car cleanliness—I was substantially left of center. This event is designed by its organizers to be an organic informal get-together, not a "concours" where cars are officially judged, but still, owners want to present their babies at their best. For me, this means spit on the birdshit, wipe it off with a paper towel, and throw out the espresso cups littering the floor. But other folks really get into preparing and cleaning a car to show it. When I arrived at the event, I noticed that there was a wash station (hoses and buckets) set up. My pretty red coupe did have a couple of bird bulls-eyes and speed-spattered bugs from the 800-mile drive, so I queued up to use the wash station. A fellow came up to me. "I'm surprised you're washing it," he said. I thought my Hack Mechanic habits had preceded me, but that's not what he meant. "Water," he said, with an ominous tone designed to connote seriousness, *"is not your friend."* He showed me a spray bottle with some magic potion he mists-on and towels-off, saving the car from the indignity of public bathing. Then I noticed that probably 20 cars were lined up in the shade, their open trunks having disgorged boxes holding a bewildering variety of cleaning products. I didn't even have a sponge. Of course, that night it rained torrentially, showing that water is going to get to know you whether you want to be its friend or not.

Before the festival was over, a bunch of us went for a drive along some impossibly corkscrew-twisty roads through the North Carolina hills. I'll be damned if these 2002 guys are going to lose me, I thought. I nailed and wailed. My big red coupe, with its fat rubber, lowered stance, and new brakes, behaved magnificently. One 2002 guy said it was downright intimidating as it came roaring up in his rearview mirror. As we arrived at our destination (a vintage gas station), and I parked and looked back up the road and saw wave after wave of 2002s approaching through the twisties, I thought ... my God. What a symphony of sound and shape and color. What a glorious parade of passion. These cars are nearly 40 years old, and all these guys just love them.

Why do men love cars? I mean, for heaven's sake, just *look* at them.

GETTING A COOL CAR COOL

While part of the charm of an older car is its simplicity, I never have been an adherent to the tenet that that simplicity necessarily precludes air-conditioning. When nearly everyone's daily driver these days has a/c, not having air in an enthusiast car can reduce the amount of time it is driven. After all, if it's 90 degrees out and you're going to dinner with your wife and need to buy some milk on the way home, are you really going to take the classic car when it doesn't have a/c but her Accord does? Here in New England, where we keep our beloved classics off the road during the salty months, the driving season becomes awfully short if you also shy away from using the car during the heat of summer.

Classics notwithstanding, if you're buying a daily driver and you need working air-conditioning, I can't stress enough that *you should buy a car with working air-conditioning*, or factor into the purchase price that it could cost you thousands of dollars to get it fixed. If someone tells you, "It just needs a recharge," that's simply *never* true. Cars don't consume refrigerant in the same way that they use oil and brake pads. Air-conditioners are sealed systems. You don't need to top them off. If a car needs a recharge, it's because the refrigerant leaked out, therefore something is broken, therefore it doesn't "just" need a recharge. It would be more correct to say, "It worked last fall. Now it doesn't. This happens every spring. It must have a slow leak somewhere." At least that would be honest. But realize that those "$79 A/C Service" shingles hung out at repair shops are optimism bordering on fraud. Best case: There's one leaking O-ring, they find it quickly, replace it, and charge you $200. More likely the a/c system needs a major component replaced and the bill is two grand.

You can see, whether your car is a daily driver or a pampered classic, there's the potential to save a boatload of money working on your a/c yourself. A lot of DIY mechanics shy away from air-conditioning

---

Editor's Note: This memoir is **not** a repair manual. Please read Warnings & Cautions on p. 410.

work and I've never understood why. There's even some degree of chest-beating in classic car circles that "I don't need a/c in this car—in fact I took it out to save weight—I just roll down the windows." Some folks refer to using R75/2 refrigerant—75 mph, 2 windows down.

If that's your thing, fine, but I am not at all in this camp. I like having air-conditioning in my old cars. It dramatically increases my enjoyment and therefore my use of them. And few repairs are more satisfying to me than starting with a nonfunctional a/c system and finishing with a cold car.

Let's talk a bit about how air-conditioning works. The image most people have of an air-conditioner is a box sticking out the window of a house. You plug it in, turn it on, and cold air blows out the front with the same magic as a picture appearing on a television screen. But it's not terribly complicated. Like refrigeration, an air-conditioner works on the principle that a gas cools as it expands. Most people have experienced this when cooking with a propane-powered barbeque grill, feeling the propane tank, and noticing that it's cold. Air-conditioning uses energy to compress a gas so the gas can expand—and thus get one of the components cold. Then it blows air across that cold component and sends it "inside" where you want it. Then it dumps the heat created by the act of compression "outside."

The beating heart is the compressor. In a home a/c unit the compressor is powered by an electric motor, but in a car the compressor is run off a belt from the engine. The part that gets cold is called the evaporator core. It lives under the dash, along with the expansion valve that the gas actually expands through, and the fan that blows the cold air at you, in an evaporator assembly. The part that dumps the heat—essentially an air-conditioning radiator—is called the condenser and lives in the nose of the car, in front of the radiator, often with an auxiliary electric fan in front of it to help cool it off. So the components are distributed throughout the car. Contrast this with a home window air-conditioning unit where everything is packed into one neat box. A combination of aesthetic and aerodynamic requirements makes this impossible on a car, but if you look at a refrigerated tractor/trailer (a/c mounted on the front) or an RV (a/c mounted on the roof), you'll see exactly these sorts of stand-alone units. If they break, you can just unbolt them and install another one. Wouldn't that be sweet to do in a car?

Whether repairing an a/c system that recently died or resurrecting a long-dead system, there is a basic sequence of steps. If you've replaced a single obviously failed component in a system that recently worked, you may need only to evacuate and recharge, but if you're dealing with a 40-year-old car whose a/c hasn't worked in an unknown amount of time, you should understand that the odds are you'll need to replace the compressor, dryer, and every hose.

How do I know all this? There's a great site called www.aircondition.com. Through there, I learned enough to begin repairing the a/c on all my cars. You can too. Read. Learn. Do.

The basic steps for a/c rejuvenation are:

- Decide if you're changing refrigerant from R12 to R134a
- Decide if you're replacing the compressor
- Perform a visual inspection
- Decide if you're replacing all the hoses
- Check that the compressor clutch works and the compressor is not seized
- Perform a gross leak test
- Check that the compressor does its compression thing
- Perform a pressure holding test and look for smaller leaks
- Flush the system
- Fill the system with the proper type and amount of oil
- Replace the receiver / dryer
- Evacuate the system
- Recharge
- If necessary, perform small leak detection

DECIDE IF YOU'RE CHANGING REFRIGERANT FROM R12 (FREON) TO R134A

Because of the evidence of Freon's role in harming the ozone layer, it was phased out in the early 1990s in favor of R134a. For this reason, the little 12- and 16-ounce cans of R12 stopped being sold commercially in this country in 1993. There was, and is, a widely held belief that R12 is illegal. This is untrue. Both the big propane-sized canisters and a nearly endless old stock of small cans are commercially and legally available to those with an EPA Section 608 certification which you can easily obtain via an online exam. What *is* illegal is venting R12 (or R134a) into

the atmosphere (though, at the price that R12 costs, I don't know why anyone would intentionally vent it). But misinformation, the initially skyrocketing price of R12, and the low initial price of R134a (it used to be about two bucks a can) caused a rush to convert old cars that originally had R12 to R134a. These two refrigerants use different and incompatible types of oil (mineral oil for R12, PAG oil for R134a), and a correct conversion was thought to require not only completely flushing all the old oil out, but also changing the compressor, hoses, and O-rings. Ester oil, however, is compatible with *both* R12 and R134a, and over time, an accepted retrofit technique has been to flush the system, drain but not replace the compressor, refill with ester oil, and leave the hoses alone. Regardless, since a conversion involves completely flushing all the old oil out, a rejuvenation or major a/c repair on an old car presents an opportunity to convert to R134a. Whether this is wise or desirable is a matter of endless debate.

These days, the cost difference between R12 and R134a is less dramatic—the going price for cans of R12 on eBay is about $25, whereas walking into AutoZone for a can of R134a will set you back about $15. More germane is the fact that older German cars like BMWs and Porsches didn't have great a/c systems to begin with, and many folks who converted these cars to R134a were less than happy with the results. Carl Nelson, owner of La Jolla Independent BMW and one of the premier 2002 and 3.0CS experts, says his customers want a cold car, and reports that keeping their '02s and coupes pumping R12 gives him happy customers. However, I can tell you that Boston ain't SoCal—there are very few shops left in the Boston area that work with R12. Note that there are other choices than R12 and R134a, but you have to be knowledgeable and committed—they're the refrigeration equivalent of voting for Lyndon LaRouche.

You need to be aware that R12 and R134a use different hose and charging fittings. On most older cars, the R12 a/c components are connected by hoses with flare fittings, and use small screw-on charging fittings like a tire valve. When new cars incorporated R134a, everything changed over to O-ring hose fittings, and larger snap-on charging fittings were employed to avoid any chance of accidentally crossconnecting R12 and R134a recovery tanks. Aftermarket a/c components for your car may be available in both R12 (flare) and R134a (O-ring) versions, and you need to know which version to purchase. For these reasons, if you're resurrecting a dead a/c system, you really need to decide on which refrigerant you're using at the start of the project.

DECIDE IF YOU'RE REPLACING THE COMPRESSOR

If you're rejuvenating the a/c on an older car with an original big bulky noisy piston compressor, you may well want to skip testing the compressor and simply replace it with a smaller, quieter, more efficient rotary-style unit. These generally require a new bracket to bolt them to the block, or an adapter to bolt them to the original bracket. If you are buying a rotary-style compressor like a Sanden, the hose and charging fittings are on a plate called the "head" on the back of the compressor. Be certain you're buying a compressor with the correct head—that is, if your car has R12 and your hoses have the original flare fittings, be certain the compressor head has flare connections and R12 charging ports. Even this diligence isn't always enough to avoid surprises—on compressor replacements on both my Porsche 911SC and my BMW 2002, I stuck with Freon and sourced a Sanden replacement compressor with flare fittings, only to find that the car's original hoses had two #10 flares, whereas the compressor head had a #10 and a #8.

Even if you know that the old compressor is going to the scrap heap, don't yank it out just yet; it's useful to leave it in for the gross leak detection step below.

VISUAL INSPECTION

This is particularly important when rejuvenating a long-dormant system. Are all of the components even still there? If it's an old car, the large bulky piston compressor may have died at some point and been pitched into the scrap heap when the engine was rebuilt. Does the crankshaft have the pulley needed to run the belt to the compressor? Is the condenser present in front of the radiator? If the car has had a front-end accident and the a/c wasn't working, sometimes the condenser doesn't make it back in. Are all of the hoses present and attached? Have any of them burned up against a hot exhaust manifold? You can't begin to assess leaks if the system isn't closed, and it can't be closed if it isn't even complete. Turn on the a/c switch. Do both fans (the one in front of the condenser and the one inside the evaporator assembly) blow air without squealing and howling? In addition to visually accounting for the major components and evaluating the state they're in, this is a chance to truly look at the project with eyes wide open, because you may wind up having to replace every single component you see. Grok it. Be at peace with it.

REFRIGERANT PRESENT TEST

It's possible to do this test, and other a/c work, without a set of gauges, but you shouldn't. As part of your embracing a/c work, you should just buy the gauges. That way you can hang them on your garage wall and act nonchalant when someone sees them and comments, "Wow! Gauges! Do you do your own a/c repair? That's so cool!" The use of gauges to fine-diagnose a/c issues and troubleshoot down to the component level is a topic too lengthy for this chapter, but for the refrigerant present test, we're basically just using the gauge set to see if there's *any* gas in the system. Gauges can be purchased in any automotive shop. The fittings are specific to R12 or R134a. If you have different cars with each, you need a set of adapters or two sets of gauges. The blue gauge is for the low pressure (suction) side, and the red gauge for the high pressure (discharge) side. In the middle of the two gauges is a service port with a hose that allows the gauge set to be connected to a can of refrigerant, vacuum pump, nitrogen bottle, or other service device.

There are blue and red knobs on the gauge set. Understand that the knobs have no effect on what the gauges read—they affect whether the low (blue) and/or high (red) sides are connected to the service port. *Make sure both knobs on the gauges are closed (rotated clockwise).* Using the blue and red hoses, connect the gauges to the car's service fittings. These may be on the compressor, or the low side fitting may be on the line from the receiver to the compressor and the high side fitting may be on the line from the compressor to the condenser. Once the gauges are connected, they will register the pressure of the refrigerant in the system.

If the gauges read zero, then there's no refrigerant, and you can proceed with the leak test. But if the gauges read non-zero (a good rule of thumb is that, with the car off, the gauges should read approximately the ambient temperature—that is, 60 degrees Fahrenheit, 60 psi on the gauges), your system is full of refrigerant, and lack of cooling is likely due to something else, in which case, you can proceed directly to the compressor test.

You may ask, "Do I really need to use gauges? Can't I just depress the compressor fitting with the tip of a screwdriver and see if anything hisses out?" The answer is: It's illegal to vent refrigerant. You're a car guy. You *like* tools. Just buy the gauges. You're going to need them anyway.

DECIDE IF YOU'RE REPLACING ALL THE HOSES

Similar to the "just pitch the compressor" approach, if you're resurrecting a long-dead system and you already know that the hoses are junk because they've been sitting unattached or have melted against the manifold, you should plan on replacing them all. On a 1970s BMW, the original hoses are no longer available, so "replace" means "have new hoses made." I cannot state strongly enough that if there is no refrigerant in the system, it's because it leaked out from somewhere, and in addition to finding *the* leak(s), hose replacement is a great prophylactic measure so you don't have to go through the leak detection process again in a few months. If you have the original hoses, don't throw them out even if they're junk. They may be of value in case you need to take them or send them to a custom hose shop and have them duplicated. I say "may be of value" because the degree to which a duplicate of an old hose will help you depends on what else you're replacing. If every a/c component is original, sure, duplicate the hoses, but if any have been updated, it gets complicated. For example, the dryer in a Behr a/c system in a BMW 2002 has a #6 flare input facing down and a #8 flare output facing sideways—very specific and highly unusual. The hoses connecting to the dryer are equally specific. If need be, you can replace the dryer with the original part and have the hoses duplicated. But if you're doing a whole-hog a/c upgrade and replacing the compressor and condenser as well, you'd be wise to select components with modern O-ring fittings, so why not just use O-rings on everything and use a conventional dryer with two side-facing fittings? Once you cross this Rubicon, your old hoses no longer matter—the components may be mounted in different locations than original, the fittings are different, the angles at which the hoses connect to the fittings probably changes, etc. It's custom hoses for you, Jack.

But make no mistake—there's time, expense, and risk in replacing every hose. The ones that are especially challenging are the two running inside the passenger compartment, attaching to the evaporator assembly up under the dash. On a newer car, O-ring connections are employed, but on older cars like a BMW 2002, they're flare fittings that were tightened with a dying strain in 1972 and haven't been touched since. Although the fittings are generally accessible at the side of the console, the tubing connecting them to the evaporator core is fragile and easy to damage when trying to unscrew fittings wedded with 40 years of corrosion. Pursuing the goal of a tight a/c system, I've tried to undo these connections to replace the hoses, and snapped one of the fittings off, which, I can assure you, pegs the ruins-your-day-meter.

There's not one all-sizes-fits-all answer to this. If the car has been sitting with the a/c system intact (i.e., closed up with all hoses attached), I will sometimes give the system a gross leak test (below), and if it passes, flush it, replace the dryer, and hope I get lucky, but if it fails the leak test and any leaks are traceable to a hose, I'll usually just replace them all. Another way to look at it is, if you have other reasons to disassemble the console, such as a dead evaporator blower motor, a leaky heater core, or heater flaps whose foam has deteriorated so they're letting in ambient air, then the evaporator assembly has to come out anyway, and it's wise to replace the evaporator hoses and possibly even the expansion valve at the same time.

COMPRESSOR CLUTCH AND SEIZE TEST

If you know you're replacing the compressor, obviously you can skip this and the compressor functionality test. The first test in the compressor's bill of health is whether its electric clutch engages and, if so, whether the compressor turns freely. On anything but the most primitive a/c system, a low-pressure cutoff switch will prevent the compressor from engaging if the system is out of refrigerant, and if the a/c isn't working, the odds are overwhelming that it *is* out of refrigerant, so to test the compressor you may need to hot-wire it directly to the battery. Find the wire powering the compressor. Generally there's a single positive wire because the body of the compressor is grounded to the engine, eliminating the need for a ground wire. Trace the power wire back from the compressor until you find a connector, then disconnect it. If I can't quickly find the connector, I simply cut the wire and splice it later, but that's why I'm the Hack Mechanic. Attach a length of wire to the compressor that's long enough to reach the battery. Touch the wire to the positive terminal of the car's battery, then release. Do this two or three times. You should hear a clicking sound from the compressor as electrical contact is made and broken. That's the electric clutch. If you don't hear the click, the clutch is probably bad. The clutch may be separately available, but don't bother; if the compressor is old, just change the whole unit. It would need to come out to do the clutch anyway.

If the clutch is working, make sure the compressor belt is installed, then start the car and again touch the compressor wire to the positive battery terminal. If, when you touch the wire to the battery, you hear a spectacular squealing sound and smell burning rubber, then you are the proud owner of a seized compressor—when the clutch is engaged, the belt can't spin the compressor. It sucks when you find this, but at least it's a clear unambiguous diagnosis. If it's a newer car, there may be good cost-effective options for a used compressor. As with buying any used part, this is a judgment call that's a function of cost, risk, and how long you plan to keep the car.

GROSS LEAK TEST

Before going further, you need to have some idea if the system has obvious leaks. Many years ago I learned the trick of using a tank of nitrogen to pressure-test an air-conditioning system. It's a two-stage process. In the first, you literally listen for hissing from massive leaks; in the second, you pressurize it and leave it overnight and see if it maintains pressure. For the gross leak test, we're using the gauge set primarily as an adapter for the nitrogen bottle, secondarily to check if the pressure drops overnight.

Buy or rent a small nitrogen bottle at a welding supply shop. Use an ¼" NPT to ¼" flare adapter to connect the regulator on the nitrogen tank to the center hose of the gauge set. Close the knobs on the gauge set (screw them in clockwise). Close the regulator on the nitrogen bottle by unscrewing it all the way. Open the valve on the top of the nitrogen bottle. Then screw in the regulator until the gauge on the regulator reads 100 psi. Now slowly open both knobs on the

gauge set to allow the nitrogen to flow into the low and high pressure sides of the system.

With the valve on the nitrogen bottle and the knobs on the gauges open, the bottle is going to try to maintain 100 psi into the system. The system is either going to hold it, or it's going to leak out. You're going to need to *listen*. Turn off the radio and any other devices making noise. If there's a massive leak, you'll hear it. Follow your ears. Put your hands around hoses and connections. Eventually you'll need to use a bottle of soapy water, spray it on all components (particularly around connections—don't forget the pressure cut-off switches) and look for air bubbles. If you find a leaky component, shut off the nitrogen bottle and repair or replace the part. If it's leaking at a threaded connection, try tightening the nut. On newer cars with O-rings, the rubber ring is responsible for the seal so the nuts don't need to be tightened down with a dying strain, but on older cars like the BMW 2002 and 3.0CS that originally used Freon and still have flare fittings, these connections need to be tight.

Pressure-testing is an iterative process. Let's say you pressure-test the system and discover a leak in the condenser—fairly common due to its front-mounted location and exposure to weather and stones. You'll need to procure another condenser, install it, and pressure-test again.

If there's no obvious audible leak, close the valve on the nitrogen tank and the knobs on the gauges, and watch the gauges for 30 seconds. If they don't move, the system may still have small leaks but at least it is tight enough to see if the compressor functions.

COMPRESSOR FUNCTIONALITY TEST

If there are no massive leaks, and the compressor clutch is engaging, and the engaged compressor is not seized, the next step is to see if the compressor is actually compressing anything. If the gauges showed no gas in the system, shut off the nitrogen bottle and unscrew the hose to the gauges. Open the knobs at the top of the gauges to vent any nitrogen, then close them. The gauges will read zero. Start the car. Hold the compressor wire on the positive battery terminal and look at the gauges. The high side gauge won't deflect because there's nothing to compress, but if there's deflection of the low (suction) side gauge, then the compressor is at least doing something, and it's worth a try pressure-testing, evacuating, and recharging the system. If the gauges remain at zero, then the compressor is not compressing anything and probably needs to be replaced.

PRESSURE-HOLDING TEST

Once any obvious leaks have been addressed, the next step is seeing if there are small leaks. The easiest way to do this is by verifying that the system will hold pressure for several hours. This time, you'll want the flow from the nitrogen bottle closed, as you don't want a constant source of pressure—that is, you'll want to pressurize the system, leave it, and see if the system holds the pressure you put into it. Hook the nitrogen bottle back up to the center hose of the gauge set. I usually crank up the pressure to 150 psi for this pressure-holding test, but one has to be very careful, as nitrogen bottles are pressurized to thousands of pounds, which can rip apart an air-conditioning system in a New York second. Close both knobs on the gauge set. Open the knob on the nitrogen bottle. Adjust the regulator to 150 psi. Slowly open both knobs on the gauges. Then close the knob on the nitrogen bottle. The gauges should now read about 150 psi. There may be some slight difference in calibration of the gauges, but that's not important. What you're looking for is change over time. Write down the reading or mark it with erasable marker or tape. Then, walk away for several hours, ideally until morning. Pressure varies with temperature, so the readings will naturally fall if you pressurized in the heat of the day and it cools off overnight, but if the car is sitting in the garage at a relatively constant temperature, in the morning the pressure should be the same. If it is, you have a tight, leak-free system.

If, however, it has lost a substantial portion of its pressure, don't kid yourself—you have a leak. And the fact that it took overnight to lose pressure means that it is a small leak. You can try spraying soapy water again, but you may need to resort to dye and chemical sniffing leak detection methods that require the system to have oil and refrigerant in it (see below).

FLUSH AND FILL WITH OIL

Air-conditioning systems use several ounces of oil to lubricate the compressor. When working on a system, ideally you should completely flush it and refill it with the right amount and type of oil. This is for a

number of reasons. Firstly, as a system is run, the oil gets distributed through the components of the system, and because there is no way to directly measure how much oil is in there (it's a sealed system—there's no equivalent of a dipstick), in order to be absolutely certain of the amount of oil, you need to flush it all out, drain the compressor, and start from scratch. Because this is a pain, people sometimes use a rule of thumb to add two ounces of oil whenever a major component is replaced. Secondly, R12 and R134a systems use different types of oil, so if you're considering converting an R12 system to R134a (or vice versa), the old oil *must* be flushed out. Thirdly, having nothing to do with oil, if you're rejuvenating a system that was left open (e.g., compressor removed 20 years ago, hoses left dangling), it *must* be thoroughly flushed to remove contaminants. Lastly, if the compressor seized, metal shavings may have been thrown into the system. If they were, they must be flushed out.

Thus, for all of these reasons, the "do it once, do it right" approach to a/c repair is to completely flush the system of any old oil and contaminants, then refill it with the correct amount of the correct type of oil. If the system is completely apart, you add one-third of the oil to the compressor, condenser, and evaporator respectively. If the vendor from whom you purchased the compressor is adamant that the compressor comes filled with the correct amount of oil for the entire system, and you've verified it's the correct oil for your configuration, you can take them at their word, but you must make sure other oil has been flushed out of the system. If your system had been working and recently died, and if you identified the failed component as, for example, the condenser, you can probably get away with replacing just that one component, not flushing, adding two ounces of oil to it, and evacuating and recharging. This usually works fine, but over time, with multiple repairs, it can result in a car with too little or too much oil in the a/c system. You have to trade off the risk of taking things apart so you can flush (see Chapter 28: "Of Klingons and Kluges") against the risk that the system is so full of crap that it will fail if you don't flush.

Flushing is performed either by using pressurized cans of a/c flush, or by filling a container with a/c flush or a volatile compound such as mineral spirits, putting it in line with an air compressor, and blasting it through sections of the system. For example, you can undo the hoses coming from the condenser to the dryer and from the condenser to the compressor, put the flush nozzle in the end of one hose, and flush through the condenser and out the other hose. But there are complications. You shouldn't flush through the dryer; you should just replace it. You can't flush through an evaporator because the expansion valve stops the flow, but you can "pop flush" where you let the pressure build up and pop the flush nozzle off (wear goggles!!!). And you should never try to flush a compressor; you just turn it upside down and drain it as thoroughly as possible into a coffee filter. If nasty stuff comes out of it, you'd be wise to replace it.

REPLACE RECEIVER/DRYER

Air-conditioning systems have a dryer (also called a receiver), basically a beer-can-sized bottle of desiccant that removes moisture. If the system is opened to replace any component, unless the dryer is very recent, it should be replaced.

If you've gone through the above steps, you've identified any grossly leaking components and replaced them. You now presumably have a system that stands a good chance of being capable of cooling the car. You've already saved a big chunk of change. What's next? You could simply take the car in to be recharged (more accurately, evacuated, leak-tested, and recharged), and that's fine. I worked that way for years. Or you can go for the gold.

EVACUATE THE SYSTEM

If you have a tight system that has survived an overnight pressure test, you need to evacuate it—pump it down to a deep vacuum—before you recharge it. The purpose of this is to remove any moisture that might've crept in (moisture, when combined with the lubricant, can create acids). Your high school chemistry tells you that lowering the pressure lowers the boiling point of a liquid. By pulling a deep vacuum, you literally cause any moisture to boil off. To pull a vacuum, you buy or rent a specialized vacuum pump, hook it to the center hose of the gauge set, open up the low and high pressure knobs, then run the pump for at least an hour. For extra credit on the leak-test exam, after the vacuum has been pulled, you can shut all the knobs and let the system sit overnight and verify that it holds the vacuum.

AND FINALLY ... RECHARGE THE SYSTEM

It's a simplification to say that you procure the correct number of cans of the correct kind of refrigerant, connect a can tap to the center hose of the gauge set, tap one can at a time (always keeping the can upright), open the knob *for the low side only*, and let the evaporated gas get sucked in while watching to make sure that the pressure doesn't climb too high, but that's basically what you do. While it's possible to do this "blind" with only an inexpensive low-side gauge that's part of a can tap, it is strongly advised to look at both the low and high side pressures to have an idea of what's going on. There are good descriptions of the details of reading the gauges on www.aircondition.com. I have to tell you—recharging the car is the dessert at the end of the meal, the sex at the end of the date. When you feel that air start to blow cold, it's a rush.

SMALL LEAK DETECTION

If you pressure-tested the system overnight and verified it held pressure, and if you let it sit for several hours after evacuation and verified it held vacuum, it should be pretty tight, but there can still be small leaks. The two weapons deployed against leaks in a charged system are chemical sniffers and dye. Sniffers directly detect the presence of refrigerants and alert you with an audible tone, a flashing light, or both. They're not cheap, but I have a Yokogawa leak detector and it works great. Ultraviolet dye is inexpensive and can either be purchased in liquid form and mixed with the oil prior to system assembly, or bought in a pressurized can and injected like refrigerant into a closed system. Then the system is run and an ultraviolet light and a pair of special glasses are used to hunt for the dye. I'm not a big fan of dye—it's messy, and it's difficult to distinguish old dye from that which is from a fresh leak.

If the system is leaking from inside the evaporator assembly, you're probably not going to hear it hissing, and you can't spray soapy water in places you can't reach or look for dye in places you can't see. Sometimes the only way to diagnose an evaporator leak it is to use a chemical sniffer in the general vicinity of the under dash. In a newer car, replacing the evaporator may not be too bad. On my E36 BMW, the evaporator core and expansion valve slid out from behind a panel, and on my Toyota Land Cruiser the entire evaporator assembly was trivial

to unbolt from under the glove box. But if you have an older car like a
2002 or a 3.0CS with a leaky evaporator, just drink yourself into a stu-
por for a few days because it's simply going to suck. The delicate dance
necessary to remove and reinstall the console and evaporator assembly
in my 3.0CS has to be one of my least favorite automotive repairs.

Understand that it is illegal to vent either R12 or R134a. This means
that if you identify the source of a leak in a charged system, and if this
requires you to open the system back up to repair the leak, you need
to take the car somewhere to have the refrigerant recovered. I thought
about buying recovery equipment, but it's expensive, and by pressure-
testing with nitrogen and letting it sit overnight, I've almost always
been able to verify that a system is tight before I charge it up. Only once
have I had to pay someone to recover refrigerant. When the compressor seized on my Suburban with rear air, the system was full-up with
a massive 84 ounces of Freon. I'd hoped to be able to find a repair shop
who would, essentially, hold the Freon for me, or buy it from me and
sell it back, but the paucity of shops in Boston who work with Freon did
not leave me with any leverage. In the end I paid half an hour of shop
time for someone to recover nearly $200 worth of Freon and got nothing
for it, but I left with my environmental conscience absolutely clear.

That Suburban was also the car where, earlier in the book, I
enumerated the horrible cascading failure that ensued when I tried
undoing the lines to the rear evaporator to flush them. This was fresh
in my mind when I began to rejuvenate the a/c in the Porsche. After
diagnosing and replacing a bad compressor, I thought I'd flush the
system. I looked at the connections between the hoses and the evaporator and condensers, saw 25 years of corrosion, recalled how I'd twisted
the lines off the rear evaporator in the 'Burb, realized the odds of these
connections coming off without damage were slim, and did the "back
slowly out of the cave" thing. The 911's compressor was bad but it
had not seized, and I wasn't converting from R12 to R134a, so flushing
was not absolutely necessary. I backed off. After compressor replacement and evacuation and recharge, the Porsche's a/c worked great, so I
made the right call.

When I bought my '93 Toyota Land Cruiser, it was cheap, partially
due to my driving a hard bargain because the air-conditioning was not
working. The compressor checked out okay (that is, the clutch worked

and it wasn't seized). I pressure-tested the system with nitrogen and found a major leak in the condenser. I replaced it with a used one, but when I pressure-tested the system again overnight, it was still leaking. I isolated the leak to the evaporator assembly. When I pulled the assembly out, the backside of the evaporator core was oily and filthy — clear indication of it leaking. The evaporator core wasn't available as an a la carte part, only the entire assembly, and that listed at nearly $1,500 from Toyota. Fortunately I was able to locate a used evaporator assembly. Since I now was replacing two of the three major system components, I elected to "do it right." I flushed the system and replaced every O-ring. I wanted to add the correct amount of oil, but the only way to know how much oil is in the compressor is to take it out, turn it upside down, and drain it. I did, and found that the compressor was completely dry — the system had blown all its oil out the evaporator leak. If I hadn't "done it right," I probably would have burned out the compressor in short order.

NOTES ON CONDITIONING THE COUPE

Many years go I did a from-scratch a/c installation into my '73 3.0CSi. It was a lot of work, but highly do-able and tremendously satisfying. The experience gave me a roadmap that can be used to approach a/c retrofit into any car. In addition to the basic sequence for a/c rejuvenation described above, breaking the retrofit into the following pieces made it tractable:

Decide on your overall approach — how much are you improving while you're retrofitting? There are three primary approaches to retrofit. You can install an original system (factory or dealer-available) with no modifications, you can install a largely original system with some reasonable improvements, or you can roll your own. Most folks opt for the middle option, since if you're going to go to all that work, you want to come out of it with a cold car, and replacing the compressor with a smaller lighter quieter rotary-style one and updating the condenser to a newer more efficient parallel-flow unit are cost-effective, proven, and low-risk. The big questions revolve around the evaporator assembly and the console it sits in.

First, understand that old German cars like '70s-era BMWs do not have climate control systems. This means there is no mixing (well, no *intentional* mixing) between the a/c and the heat. Each has its own fan. Each has its own temperature control. The a/c blows cold air out the evaporator assembly, and the cold air emerges from the center vent of the console. That's it. It doesn't let you direct the cold dehumidified air at the windshield to defog it, and it doesn't mix the cold air with heated air to allow you to set a less-than-freezing temperature. That temperature knob on the evaporator assembly governs only how frequently the compressor cycles (turns on and off), which makes the air alternately warm and cold, but this is *not* the same as a modern car where adjusting a single temperature knob will mix cold air with heated air and produce a single stream of air at a relatively constant temperature. If you're freezing in an old car because the a/c is too cold, first you count yourself lucky, then you don't complain about it too loudly for fear your friends with non-air-conditioned cars will beat the crap out of you, and finally you lower the fan speed and aim the blowers away from you.

Now that you understand this, you can appreciate the different options for the evaporator console and how they affect the look and feel of the interior. There *are* aftermarket a/c systems that offer climate control—an evaporator and heater core in the same box—giving you a modern single-knob single-fan single-air-stream solution, but when it comes to interfacing one of these units with the existing dash sliders and ductwork on your car, you're on your own. In addition, because these units contain a heater core, the car's existing heater box needs to come out so the new heater core can be connected. Since a stock heater box and fan usually sits against the firewall in a very specifically sized cut-out, adapting a climate control unit is a pretty tall order. And, since none of this is even remotely stock, wrapping it all in an original console, or at least one that looks remotely period-correct, is unlikely. Of course, you might not care how it looks, and if that's the case, more power to you.

The second option is abandoning the pipe dream of climate control but opting for a modern aftermarket evaporator assembly. This gives the benefit of an evaporator core and expansion valve optimized for R134a, and a modern fan that moves more air than the original antiquated unit (Mike Miller's memorable assessment of the combination of the fan and core in a stock 2002 evaporator is that it is "like a hamster blowing over a snow cone"). You won't have to remove the heater box like with the climate control option, but you're on your own regarding getting the new evaporator assembly to fit under the dashboard and on the transmission hump. And there's no guarantee you can sandwich one of these units inside an original console. The fallback position is ditching the original console and installing the universal under-dash vent kit that is available with the unit. You may start off thinking that a universal evaporator assembly from a company such as Vintage Air will fit the bill perfectly fine, but then decide that it's out of sync with the look and feel of your car (trust me, there's no value judgment here).

The last option is the one many people select—finding an original, used evaporator assembly, replacing and/or upgrading its internal components, and surrounding it with a stock console. Particularly when combined with a new rotary compressor and a larger parallel-flow condenser, many folks find this is an acceptable compromise of look, feel, and performance.

R12 or R134a? As described above, many other decisions bifurcate from this choice.

Verify that there aren't showstoppers. For example, the stock crankshaft pulley on a 2002tii doesn't have a groove for the compressor belt. You need the special air-conditioned version of the pulley. You don't want to find that out halfway into the job. Read up on your car and plan your assault carefully.

If possible, buy a complete a/c system out of a junked car. Photograph the living snot out of it as you remove it—every nut, bolt, and wire. You'll throw away the compressor, hoses, and dryer, but it will provide you with a template, and with that all-important air-conditioned console.

Compressor. Source a new rotary-style compressor and the correct bracket. Remember that the compressor model is specific to whether the car will be using R12 or R134a. I vividly remember, when doing the 3.0CS, bolting that shiny new compressor and bracket up to the engine and thinking "first step is the hardest—now I'm on my way."

Condenser. Either find an original one or simply source the biggest aftermarket condenser you can physically stuff into the nose (which is what I did—strongly recommended if converting to R134a).

Unless there's a body of knowledge in an online forum that tells you what will fit and what won't, this is an iterative process involving measuring, ordering, test-fitting, and, unless you damage the condenser, returning. Whenever I've done this, the final size was smaller than I'd estimated because unless your brain automatically performs AutoCAD clearance calculations, you can't really know where the clearance problems will be until you actually try to install a candidate unit. In other words, the limiting factor in selecting "the biggest aftermarket condenser you can physically stuff into the nose" isn't mounting it there, it's getting it into position. Install the electric fan as well.

Evaporator assembly. For me, this was by far the most time-consuming part of the process. Because I decided on an R134a installation and wanted to do whatever I could to maximize cooling while not doing anything to preclude an original-looking interior, I bought an original evaporator assembly, took out the old two-row evaporator core, and paid someone to fabricate a custom three-row core that was exactly the same dimensions. That way I got the benefit of improved evaporator efficiency while retaining the original evaporator case, which allowed me to use an original console.

If you're using an original evaporator assembly out of a junked car, you'll kick yourself if you install it, install the console trim pieces around it, recharge the system, and then have trouble with the evaporator and have to take it back out. Prophylactic maintenance is the name of the game. I would recommend you take the assembly apart, flush through the evaporator core, and replace the expansion valve. If you can rig something up to pressure-test the core and the attached valve, do it. Feed the fan motor 12v and test it. It has to move enough air over that evaporator core to make this whole exercise worthwhile. If the motor seems anemic, you might want to have it and the squirrel cages rebuilt. At a minimum you can oil the bearings and wash the fan motor brushes down with contact cleaner. Remember that the evaporator has to allow water to drain; typically there's a small rubber hose that needs to protrude through the transmission tunnel. If your tunnel doesn't have a hole, you need to drill one. A particularly harrowing part of my 3.0CS retrofit was getting the evaporator assembly in place without shattering the ancient brittle plastic interface piece between it and the ductwork above it.

If, on the other hand, you're installing an aftermarket evaporator assembly, or going for the gold with a climate control unit that replaces both the evaporator and the heater core, you're a braver man than I, and have many fun-filled evenings of engineering and adaptation ahead.

Punch holes in firewall for hoses. This was a particularly stressful part of the installation in my 3.0CS. Looking at another a/c equipped car, careful measurement, drilling pilot holes, and using a high-quality Greenlee two-sided chassis punch produced flawless holes. Remember to coat the newly-cut edges of the holes with zinc primer so they don't rust.

Hoses. For a from-scratch a/c retrofit, you're going to need to have hoses custom-fabricated. If at all possible, install the compressor, condenser, evaporator assembly, and dryer, then take the car to a custom hose shop. That way they can crimp one fitting onto a length of hose, take the hose out to the car, cut it to the correct length, and crimp on the other fitting. As said above, be aware that the a/c components on old cars used flare fittings, whereas most new components use O-rings, so if you're installing a new R134a compressor and receiver but using an original evaporator and condenser, your new hoses will need to have flare fittings on one end and O-ring fittings on the other. And be certain that your system has charging fittings. On my from-scratch installation, the guy doing the hoses noticed that there were no charging fittings anywhere (oops!) so he spliced them into the hoses he was making (whew!).

Wiring. The wiring isn't rocket science (fan speed switch turns on compressor, condenser fan, and evaporator fan), but you might want to make it as clean and stock-looking as possible so other more anal-retentive car guys don't give you a hard time about it. Or not.

Console trim. Depending on the car, this can cause financial ruin. Original air-conditioned console pieces for the 3.0CS are unique to that car and hellishly expensive. For many years I just let the evaporator assembly sit bare on the transmission tunnel. Then I adapted a non-a/c console, cut holes for the squirrel cages, screwed on some slotted side covers from a 530i, and left the front open. Finally I found original a/c side console pieces that were in horrible shape and paid an upholstery shop to have them re-covered.

Don't let anyone tell you not to bother with a cold car. Whenever I see someone driving a classic car in sweltering heat with the windows rolled down, I think *how's that R75/2 workin' for you NOW, buddy?* Conditioning my coupe was one of the smartest projects I ever undertook. During the summer, it makes the difference between my driving the car and leaving it parked. And when someone yells, "Hey! Cool car!" I think, *buddy, you don't know the half of it.*

CHAPTER 47

I DON'T GET TO DATE 18-YEAR-OLDS

My son Ethan is a strikingly handsome, cocksure young man, with a manner that makes him stand a good chance of talking just about anyone into just about anything. For a time, he was bringing home one young woman after another. And not just any young women—the most attractive young women you've ever seen.

One summer, when he vacationed with us at the beach, he brought along a girl who was so gorgeous that it pushed me over the line. (As Bill Cosby used to say about looking at his teenage daughter's teenage friends, "A man gets to thinking thoughts that *just aren't right*.") In a quiet moment, I told him, "Okay. It's official. I admit it. I am sexually jealous of my son."

He laughed. His response: "Now you know how I feel, looking at that garage full of cars, and the only thing you let me drive is the Geo Metro."

I thought about this. "Well," I said, "that's just the way it is, kid. I don't get to fuck 18-year-olds, and you don't get to drive the Porsche."

My response was cute, and flip, but it is actually a deep observation.

I've always been amazed by people who make big hard life decisions like leaving jobs and going back to college. The cost of these changes, both financially and emotionally, can be pretty high. I've observed that they're often driven by the fact that the person making the change is very unhappy in his or her current path. It's not that you can't change professions late in life. You can, but it's out of sync with a natural rhythm, and you have to expend a lot of energy to overcome that.

Similarly, it's not that you can't chase younger women when you're older. You can. People certainly do. But if you're married, the damage and the cost will be enormously high.

Most of life is about choices. Oh, sure, things happen, feather-in-the-wind stuff—car accidents, cancer—but for the most part, events are the results of choices. When I was younger I didn't view sexual desire in this way. Meeting someone new was not a "choice," it was a ships-in-the-night-love-the-one-you're-with-we-might-not-pass-this-way-again thing (damn you, 1970s radio). When you're young, it doesn't feel like infidelity is an issue of self-control; it feels like following through on attraction and indulging passion are the most natural things in the world, and fidelity is an unnatural straightjacket. But there are emotions other than passion, and there are things to value other than simple physical sensation.

I can proudly say that age and wisdom have kicked youth's ass. I've survived the potential wreckage of my own libido. And I really do believe that the cars—being tempted by them, lusting after them, chasing them, fixing them, caring for them, and occasionally nailing them until we both scream—has provided me with a channel for these energies and helped to keep my baser physical impulses in check. To quote Beldar Conehead, "Stability and contentment have been achieved."

So, no, I don't get to date 18-year-olds. But I do get to drive the '99 M Coupe. And the '73 2002. And the '73 3.0CSi. Oh, and the Por-sha.

It's just the way it is.

Besides, if I strayed, Maire Anne would set fire to the garage.

CHAPTER 48

SOME PEOPLE ARE MUCH MORE OF A WHACK JOB THAN YOU

After Vintage at the Vineyards, I truly thought that, in terms of number of cars owned by a nonrich amateur, I was the furthest out on the right edge of the bell curve. And then I met "The Collector."

As with many things, it started with answering an ad on Craigslist: "Barn Find! 1972 BMW 2002tii, California car, sunroof, a/c, Recaros, 50K miles, no rust. I have owned this car for over 20 years. It has been sitting in my barn for 15. This is the nicest unrestored 2002tii you will ever find." A rust-free tii with air. You really couldn't have composed an ad that would ring my bell harder had you tried. I called the owner. He was very curt on the phone, but I did manage to schedule an appointment. The car was in New Hampshire. I drove up the next day.

When I arrived at the address, I drove through an opening in a stone wall into a very large, long circular driveway. There were cars, trucks, and boats parked everywhere. About a hundred yards back there was a very large Victorian main residence, plus a carriage house easily twice the size of my home, plus a gigantic rambling structure the owner referred to as "the barn." I'm not good at judging sizes, but I work in a 12,000-square-foot facility, and this place looked comparable to that in footprint, and it had four floors, the lower two of which had drive-in access.

I introduced myself to the owner ("Tommy"). He opened up "the barn" to reveal cars crammed everywhere. He appeared to have a particular passion for old Minis and diesel Mercedes, but there were also Alfas and Peugeots, three Nissan Skylines, a 60-year-old hand-built race car with a drivetrain from a BMW 328, a Land Rover, a Vanagon camper, a few old Chevy Blazers, VW turbodiesel wagons, a Citroën DS, a 1962 Ford Falcon two-door station wagon … on and on they went. There were 20 Mazda 323s, likely constituting a sizable percentage of the remaining U.S. population. And, in addition to the cars, there were rows of vintage motorcycles, stacks of stained glass windows, the fuselage of a plane, and the airframe of a helicopter. My jaw was hanging. I couldn't resist asking, "How many cars do you own?" He said he hadn't actually itemized what was on the property at this moment, but counting what were inside and outside the barn, probably about 70.

Okay, Rob, eyes on the prize. Tommy showed me the BMW. The lighting in the barn was terrible. I pored over the car slowly with a flashlight. It was, as he said, a '72 2002tii, with air-conditioning, factory sunroof, and some desirable aftermarket options such as Recaro seats, exhaust headers, and an air dam. It was impossible to accurately assess the condition of the Malaga (maroon) paint through the dirt and poor lighting.

If you've learned anything from me, it's that the go-or-no-go condition for buying any old car is the condition of the body. I looked at it very closely. There was one nontrivial rust blister on the left rear quarter panel. When examining someone else's car, you can't just go digging at rust spots with a scratch awl to see whether the rust can be sanded or ground off or whether it's a rust-through hole that actually needs to be patched, but it seemed likely that this spot was more of the latter (rust-through) rather than the former (sand it off) variety.

There was also a fair amount of surface rust forming beneath some flaking paint along the bottom of the car. And the front fenders concerned me. They were missing the lower trim pieces (the molding stopped abruptly at the front doors) as well as the front side reflectors. The holes for the trim and reflectors weren't even present. People do sometimes de-trim a car to give it that "California look" where large sections of paint are unbroken by chrome trim, but here the de-trimming was *only* on the front fenders. It was obviously wrong; any enthusiast would notice it immediately. And, when I looked underneath the fenders, I saw non-original tar-like black undercoating. Clearly the fenders had been replaced. Now, that's far from the end of the world—any 2002 that has spent its life in New England is probably on its second or third set of front fenders—but this car was supposed to be from California. And it was odd that the owner of such a nicely optioned vehicle would have chosen to do such a slap-dash fender job. I wondered what rust monsters lurked beneath.

Since I was dying to know more about the barn full of cars, I momentarily sidestepped the question of my interest in the 2002 and gently probed. Once Tommy opened up, he let loose a number of amazing stories. He said he was a doctor—the last independent family physician in the state of New Hampshire to see poor and moderate-income patients. He told me that, many years ago, he was the physician to the Saudi royal family. He said he treated some of them for heroin addiction, a major no-no under Islamic law, and that, in gratitude for his discretion, he had sometimes been paid in cars; Ferraris and Lamborghinis would show up in the driveway of his rented villa. This, he said, was the start of his wheeling and dealing in cars, and it continued when he returned to the states. Since my visit was occurring during the 2009 debate over heath care, we chatted at some length about the political fracas.

It was fascinating. I asked Tommy how he reconciled his altruistic professional life with his quirky but obviously passionate collecting impulses. He stopped and thought. "This is untidy entropic behavior," he said, "but I've got a good eye, and I've made a hell of a lot of money."

I turned *my* good eye back to his car. He said he had gone through a number of BMWs in the 1980s, and this tii was the nicest, most options-laden 2002 that he'd ever gotten his hands on, so it was the one he kept. It was highly desirable on paper, but the fact that it wasn't completely rust-free and had been sitting for 15 years tempered my desire considerably. Any car that's been parked that long will need all the hydraulics, the clutch, the rubber lines, and the shocks replaced, at a bare minimum. Tommy was candid enough to say that it did not run. I didn't attempt to prove him wrong. However, that's where the candor ended. Anyone who understands old cars knows that an odometer reading of 50,000 miles means 150,000 miles. People do this all the time; they say, "Odometer reads 50,000 miles," as if not saying "the car has 50,000 miles" is ethically defensible. Unless there's paperwork to prove it's a low-mileage car, to pretend otherwise is, in my humble opinion, perilously close to fraud.

Plus, he was asking $8,500—a sum which, in 2009, was clearly in excess of the current value of the car. I offered him six grand, which is what I thought it was worth—at least what it was worth to me—and he quickly dismissed it.

So that was that.

Then, about three months later, the car showed up on an eBay auction with a Texas address. Clearly it was the same car; the auction photos were even taken inside the barn. I e-mailed the seller, curious to know what was up. Had he bought it but not even moved it, and was trying to flip it in place? He explained that, in fact, he was a broker working for Tommy, trying to help him unload some of his cars. He said that Tommy had him put a reserve price on the auction for $8,500. "Well, good luck with that," I said. I watched as the auction closed with a top bid of $5,600.

But I continued speaking with and e-mailing the broker over the span of several weeks. "Tommy is a wheeler-dealer," he said. "What he wants is for someone to show up there with cash and *haggle* with him." This was intriguing. I'm so used to thinking things through and deciding what something is worth to *me* that I never considered that the other party might enjoy the blood sport of negotiation. In the meantime, the car was relisted, and the second eBay auction closed with a final bid of $5,400, then a third time at $5,700. All of this re-inforced my belief the amount I'd offered several months prior—six grand—was probably about right. The broker said that if I showed up with cash, I could probably pry both the tii and a 2002 parts car from Tommy for $6,500.

So I did what I do—I thought about it very carefully. I decided that I needed to look at the car again. If my initial assessment of the body proved correct and I found no additional rust of any consequence, and if the engine did not obviously need a rebuild, I'd probably make something happen. So I drove back up to New Hampshire, this time with cash and a truck and a trailer, prepared to do the deed. This time Tommy had rolled the car out of the barn, but had done nothing else to it; he still hadn't even washed it.

First I looked at the parts car. It was a big-bumpered '74 that had suffered an engine fire. The interior parts and much of the outer body trim were different from those of the '72 tii. Taking the parts car would've meant a lot of work with no clear reward. Not interested.

Then I looked, again, very carefully, at the '72 tii. Fundamentally, nothing had changed from my initial assessment of the body. However, I did notice some pinholes in the rocker panels, and more paint flaking and surface rust forming under the hood and trunk lids. The moment this car got wet, rust would explode everywhere. If I were writing an ad for it, I'd classify it using my neo-realist category *as rust-free as one can reasonably expect for an unrestored New England car.*

To assess the engine, I needed to do a compression test. To do this, you have to spin over the engine, and that requires a fresh battery. I'd brought along a battery, but on a tii, the brake master cylinder impinges into the battery compartment, requiring you to use a special smaller battery, and the battery I'd brought didn't fit. With some wiring adaptation, I managed to connect the one I'd brought. I pulled the fuel pump fuse out to make sure that, when I turned the key, there was no risk of fire. I did the compression test and found 110 to 120 psi in all four cylinders—not great, but not bad for a car that's been sitting.

Since I had a battery hooked up, I was perhaps minutes away from potentially being able to hear the car run. I put the fuel pump fuse back in, had my fire extinguisher at the ready, turned the key to the ignition setting, and was not at all surprised to see gasoline spurting everywhere; the rubber fuel lines on a car that has been sitting for 15 years will almost certainly be dry-rotted. When this happens, you stop. I thought about changing the fuel lines, but a) I didn't have any with me, and b) if the seller wants to sell a car as a running car and thereby increase its value, it's really incumbent upon him to put in the time and effort to do this.

Tommy was on me for a decision. Malaga is not a crave-it color for me, and with the car not washed, I couldn't even tell if the paint was shiny or cracked with age. The body was very solid, but its condition didn't jibe with the supposed California pedigree, and this, coupled with the front fender situation, added a fair amount of risk. Thus, even though on paper this was the air-conditioned tii I'd always wanted, it was probably a flipper rather than a keeper. I did some quick mental calculus and figured that the value of the car—if I did the "rolling resurrection" thing—simply got it running, sorted out its mechanical issues but did no paint or bodywork—probably topped out around nine grand. I thought, yeah I want it, but I should pay no more than six. I'd gotten the price about right the first time.

So, as the broker had recommended, there I was, with cash, and a truck and trailer to take it away. I reminded Tommy that the broker had essentially offered me the tii *and* the parts car for $6,500. I said that I didn't want the parts car. I said that while it wasn't my intention to come back up there and make him the same offer I'd made three months prior, in fact, my initial offer of six grand was about right. I produced a wad of cash from my pocket. Obviously he saw the truck and the trailer. I waited for the negotiating part.

There was none. Tommy said the broker took a $500 fee, and that, subtracted from my offer of six grand, was a deal breaker. He said that I should've contacted him directly. I was stunned. I wanted to say, "You should've taken my offer three months ago and then you would've saved your 500 bucks," but I held my tongue. "So," he said, "you can come up with another 500 bucks, or we can agree to part as friends." I extended my hand. "Friends it is, then." I hopped into the truck and drove off with my trailer and six grand.

When you decide to end a negotiation by leaving, you can't do it as a negotiating ploy, hoping the seller will run after you or call you on your cell. You have to mean it. I meant it. I've gotten very good at this part. Actually, this is a major life lesson. I find that, in many areas of my life, whether it's buying a car or bidding on a job for work, if I think things through, I can craft a situation in which I'm happy with either of two outcomes. What you don't want is the ending of that episode of *The Simpsons* where someone offers to trade Homer an expensive Italian sports car for the last Krusty burger, a "ribwich" that turns out to have been made from an animal that is now extinct, so "when they're gone, they're *gone*." Homer accepts the trade and drives off in the sports car. The other guy bites into the ribwich, then says, "I am having ze buyer's remorse."

Now, it is a seller's right to try to get as much for a car as he can. I'd walked away from cars countless times before, but there was something about this particular interaction that bothered me. It took me a while to put my finger on it, but eventually I realized what it was: laziness. Had Tommy simply washed and cleaned the car, replaced the fuel lines, and gotten it running, it would've been well worth what he was asking for it. But he didn't. And there was sufficient risk that it wasn't worth a premium to me.

When I got home, I was more than a little miffed to find that Tommy had just re-listed the car on Craigslist, and had included the compression test numbers that I'd just taken the time to generate. With the drive up to New Hampshire and back, I'd basically just wasted the better part of a day.

Coincidentally, the broker then called me. "How'd it go with Tommy?" he asked. I kept my cool, but chewed him out a little bit for supplying me with erroneous information. "You said he wanted to haggle," I said. "There was no haggling. I made him an offer. There was no counteroffer. There was simply 'no.'"

Then the broker said something that stopped me in my tracks. "Well," he said, "you have to remember that Tommy's a pack rat and sometimes has trouble letting things go."

I get it. *He's not a collector; he's a hoarder.* I'll recognize this time-wasting behavior the next time I see it.

You see, I work very hard to avoid "ze buyer's remorse." This is why Maire Anne trusts me.

(Over time, with the appreciating value of 2002s—especially tiis—I have had to admit that passing on this car was a mistake. The wily old collector/hoarder got the better of me. Damn!)

CHAPTER 49

THE WHAC-A-MOLE MAINTENANCE MODEL

It's Saturday morning. The family is asleep. You grab a cup of coffee, wander out to the garage, look at your baby, and think: What shall I fix?

In a busy life where automotive repair competes with other important activities, how do you actually apportion your car-related time?

Whac-a-Mole. You know — the kids' arcade game where a mole comes out of one of a bunch of holes, and as quickly as you can, you beat it to death with a hammer. This is the perfect metaphor for how most automotive work gets done.

Okay. Maybe that's not how it works with you. Maybe you're up to your hips in the Big Job like a 5-speed retrofit and you go to bed thinking about reaching that bitch of a nut at the top of the transmission, rehearsing in your sleep the necessary sequence of universal joints, long extensions, and wobble adapters, and in the morning hit the ground running like a Navy Seal taking out Bin Laden.

But, much of the time, the Whac-a-Mole analogy is useful. You do the repair that has most recently broken the otherwise smooth surface of functionality.

Let me explain. I recently bought a rust-free 1985 BMW 635CSi, with a 5-speed, leather Recaro interior, badly faded paint, and 200,000 miles on the clock, for short money. The car had repeatedly died on its owner, who had a young family, and he promised his wife he'd get rid of it. So when I got it home, there was one big hairy ugly mole staring me right in the face. Task one was to duplicate and solve the dying problem. It took about 20 miles of driving it in ever-widening circles around the block, but when it got dark and foggy and I turned on the lights and the defroster, it died. The voltage regulator turned out to be bad. I replaced it and verified the problem was solved. *Whack!*

But in the process of driving circles around the neighborhood, I observed and recorded a litany of issues the car had. The most serious was low oil pressure—the car behaved fine when cold, but when it was hot, the oil pressure light came on as soon as I took my foot off the gas. I replaced the sensor and tightened the banjo bolts in the head, but neither made a difference. I was nearly resigned to the car's needing an oil pump—an expensive and time-consuming repair. But there was one more easy thing to try—changing the oil and filter. Sure enough, it turned out the car had the incorrect filter in it. Once it was replaced, the problem was solved. *Whack!*

I then began clocking through the punch list. Clunk in the steering? Tightened up a loose tie rod. *Whack!* Clunk going over bumps? Replaced a bad sway bar link. *Whack!* Squeal while accelerating? Replaced a bad center support bearing. While I was in there, I replaced the shifter bushings to get rid of the slop in the gearshift. *Whack! Whack!*

After a couple of weeks of this, I realized that I was driving a 1985 BMW 635CSi with nothing obviously wrong with it. Now, this doesn't mean that the car was perfect, or even that it needed no work—far from it. The front end was still a bit loose; there were small drips of oil and power steering fluid; the dashboard and seats were cracked, and the paint was badly faded. But all of these are what one would expect of an unrestored 27-year-old 200K German car. It was balanced. No moles were sticking up their heads. Nothing to whack.

In contrast, one morning, when playing the Whac-a-Mole game on my 1999 Z3 M Coupe, you know what I did? I pulled out a pair of scissors and snipped a thread that was hanging from the stitching of the steering wheel. I had to laugh that this was the most pressing thing on the car, but it was. Now, it's not that the M Coupe lives in a bubble; in the past year I've done the clutch and the entire cooling system. But it's a much newer car than the 635CSi, in much better shape.

Instead of Whac-a-Mole, another way to think of the car's condition is as a surface, a topographic relief map of needs, where the highest elevation peaks are what get attention first. The question is whether, as the car ages, you can put up with the basic roughness of the underlying surface.

Most people put their $2,300 down, pay their $199 a month, and buy or lease something new, figuring that that buys them four years of a smooth surface, four years of driving with nary a mole on the horizon. The first mole is usually squealing brakes caused by worn pads, or the car needing tires. Once that is repaired, the car probably needs very little—there are probably no other glaring and obvious peaks to lop off, no other moles to whack. Perfection returns. Then the car may need an exhaust. Or shocks and struts. Or steering components like tie rods and ball joints. Or (and BMWs are highly prone to this) work on the cooling system. Now you're really into it. *Whack! Whack! Whack! Whack!*

And though you're trying to keep up, the car won't let you. It's aging. The paint is getting all scratched. The interior is wearing. The air dam is cracked. And there are creaks and rattles whose source you can only guess at. Are you going to whack these moles too, or let them become part of a new, rougher landscape, and only whack the big ones?

The important thing is to understand how rough a surface—how relentless a game of Whac-a-Mole—you can tolerate. The older the car, the more difficult it is to achieve and retain perfection. You can change the rubber engine mounts and suspension bushings. You can rebuild the drivetrain and brakes. You can put in new carpeting. You can install fresh door seals to cut down on wind noise. You can replace the sound insulation on the firewall. You can paint the car. You can put it on a rotisserie and detail the undercarriage. But in doing these things in a Whac-a-Mole fashion, you're trying to approach restoration incrementally. I've always been happy with that. But for some people, the perpetually rough surface becomes intolerable, the goal is owning a vehicle whose condition asymptotically approaches that of a new car, and nothing will do short of full restoration. This is akin to Bill Murray no longer being content to shoot the gopher when it comes out of the hole in *Caddyshack* and deciding to go in after it.

Either way, what's really taking a whack is your wallet.

CHAPTER 50

THE BLUEFISH RACES (OR, "WANNA DRIVE?")

When I was 13, my mother and I were driving down Middle Street, the unpaved road we lived on in Amherst Massachusetts, in our 1969 Plymouth Satellite, when she stopped the car, shifted the automatic transmission to park, turned sideways, looked at me, and said, "Wanna drive?"

The offer was wholly unexpected, and one of the kindest and most surprising things she could've done. But my mother has always been like that. "Practice random acts of kindness" is a bumper sticker. My mother practices remarkably well-targeted acts of kindness.

Amherst was pretty rural then. We were on a long straight section of road with fields on both sides. Nothing really could go wrong. And nothing did. I drove perhaps half a mile to our house. I even piloted it into the driveway without hitting anything.

I've always remembered that moment, the simple grace of an unexpected gift.

On Nantucket, you can drive on certain sections of the beach if you have a four-wheel-drive vehicle and an over-sand permit. I like to fish when I'm on vacation, and this is the only practical way to reach some very nice fishing spots. When Ethan was 13, one night I surreptitiously pried him away from the family with an invitation to "help me fish." We drove onto the road heading out to the beach. I stopped the car, shifted the automatic transmission to park, turned sideways, looked at him, and said, "Wanna drive?" He went wide-eyed and wordlessly but vigorously nodded. It was a big, wide section of beach, nothing but dunes on the left and the Atlantic on the right. I even let him drive the truck all the way back up to the house. Nothing really could go wrong, and nothing did.

We repeated this in the years until he got his license, at which point the novelty had worn off. When he started bringing girls on vacation, he still wanted to drive my truck on the beach; he just didn't want me in it.

When my middle boy, Kyle, was 13, I did the same thing. But my youngest son, Aaron, felt like he was being excluded from something. "Where are you guys *going*?" he peeped. I didn't have the fishing rods strapped to the truck, so excuse-wise, that was out. I thought fast. "To the Bluefish Races," I said. He looked suspicious. "Seriously," I offered, "it's a Nantucket tradition. They have the bluefish in these tanks on the shore. They're tagged with radio transmitters. You choose a fish and bet on it. Then they release them into Surfside rip. The first one to reach the Sankaty Head lighthouse wins." He looked highly skeptical. "But because of the betting thing, you have to be 13. I took Ethan to the Bluefish Races when he turned 13. This year Kyle is old enough. Your turn will come." I doubt that Aaron really bought into the concept of the Bluefish Races; more likely Maire Anne applied some well-timed misdirection involving ice cream. (A parenting genius, my wife. I'll want to patiently, or not so patiently, argue and correct; she'll say, "Who wants pie?")

Kyle, oddly enough, didn't ask me anything. He just came with me. Kyle is very Zen like that. We drove onto the road heading out to the beach. I stopped the car, shifted the automatic transmission to park, turned sideways, looked at him, and said, "Wanna drive?" "Sure," he deadpanned, but his eyes said so much more.

So Kyle and I went driving on the beach, just as Ethan and I had. It was a big, wide section of beach, nothing but dunes on the left and the Atlantic on the right. Nothing really could go wrong, and nothing did. He enjoyed it so much and was so grateful that we did it again the next year.

Only next year Aaron was not to be bamboozled.

"Where are you guys going?" he asked.

Again, no rods in the truck. Damn, this kid doesn't miss anything. I'm just not that good at planned subterfuge. "Oh, honey, to the Bluefish Races."

"I don't believe you. I don't think there are any Bluefish Races. It doesn't make any sense. You can't see them when they're in the water. Who pays for those radio transmitters? How do they know to swim around to Sankaty Head lighthouse instead of straight out to sea? Something's fishy, and it isn't bluefish."

Freaking ten-year-old Adrian Monk.

"Sweetheart, you have to trust me on this one. When you turn 13, I promise I'll take you to the Bluefish Races."

And so, three years later, it was my distinct pleasure, one night while on vacation, to say to Aaron, "Come on—let's go to the Bluefish Races." He hadn't forgotten about it, but clearly neither was it something that had been troubling his waking mind for the intervening three years. "Ooooh-kay, Dad" he said.

We drove down to the beach. I stopped the car, put it into park, turned sideways, and looked at him. "Wanna drive?" Oh, the shock and awe. Oh, the wide-eyed affirmative head nod. Due to beach erosion over the years, the beach was not nearly as wide as it used to be, but still, with just dunes on the left and the Atlantic on the right, nothing could go wrong.

And nothing did.

Bet you thought something was going to go wrong, didn't you? Like a kid driving a truck into the ocean?

Nah. Sometimes life really *is* just that easy.

(I have since taken my nieces Aidan and Guthrie to the Bluefish Races as well. When I did my time-tested "wanna drive?" with Guthrie, it took a full three seconds for the reality to break over her consciousness, at which point her face lit up and she said, "For *real*?" If anyone needs a reason to have kids, or to borrow them from a relative, this is a good one. I could heat my house for a year with that smile.)

CHAPTER 51

THE TORCH IS PASSED

Life is rarely what you expect. Earlier I expressed a certain degree of measured disappointment tempered by a New Englander's realism (nothing like being both a lapsed Jew and a geographic Calvinist) at the fact that none of my kids ever wandered into the garage to absorb my maleness, to learn something about fixing cars, or even simply to hang out and learn something about *me*.

So imagine my delight when one of them did, and turned the tables on me.

I had removed the exhaust from the Z3 M Coupe to replace the clutch. In the process, I'd snapped off four of the six pressed-in studs that hold the exhaust to the manifold. When this happens, you're in a world of hurt, and none of the options are good. I tried beating the studs out with a hammer and they wouldn't budge. I tried drilling through them and the drill bit broke. People talk about using heat to remove stuck nuts and bolts. I never had great luck with heat, but I was told that's because I wasn't using enough of it. Propane is good for cooking steaks, I learned, but useless for mechanics' applications. To get things hot enough to make a difference, you need an oxyacetylene torch, commonly referred to as a blowtorch. I found a lightly used oxy setup on Craigslist but had trouble correctly adjusting the flame. I tried reading online, even viewing how-to videos on YouTube, but I couldn't get it. I needed a Zen torch master.

Enter Kyle.

Kyle is in a conservatory program studying technical direction, the backstage part of theater. He's not a scenic designer; he's the person who figures out how to build someone else's design, make it sustain the required physical loads, have it split in two to come offstage or fly upward between acts, and break down for transport into a trailer. This is equal parts art, applied engineering, and construction. As part of his training, he has become fluent in both torch and weld.

Kyle and I spent a delightful few hours in the garage, with the oxy-acetylene torch putting out an ungodly large flame, trying not to light the bottom of my M Coupe on fire. He taught me the trick to dialing in the gas mixture (making the inner tip of the oxygen flame coincident with that of the acetylene). Once he showed it to me, and I did it my-self, I got it in a way that you can't just by watching a video.

So, the exchange of maleness and the transfer of knowledge happened after all. It just flowed in the other direction. The simply-hanging out part was, I hope, mutually satisfying.

Now, talking about stuck bolts, folks may remember that Robert Pirsig devoted a chapter in *Zen and the Art of Motorcycle Maintenance* to "stuckness." I had read it 30 years earlier and remembered that the dis-cussion on stuckness was, like much of the book, rooted in a somewhat esoteric dissertation on the metaphysics of Quality, but I couldn't recall the specifics. Here is Mr. Pirsig's advice:

> Stuckness shouldn't be avoided. It's the psychic prede-cessor of all real understanding. An egoless acceptance of stuckness is a key to an understanding of all Quality, in mechanical work as in other endeavors. It's this un-derstanding of Quality as revealed by stuckness which so often makes self-taught mechanics so superior to institute-trained men who have learned how to handle everything except a new situation.

Yeah yeah ... so tell me how to get the broken stud out.

> What your actual solution is is unimportant as long as it has Quality. Thoughts about the screw as combined rigidness and adhesiveness and about its special helical interlock might lead naturally to solutions of impac-tion and use of solvents. That is one kind of Quality track. Another track may be to go to the library and look through a catalog of mechanic's tools, in which you might come across a screw extractor that would do the job. Or to call a friend who knows something about me-chanical work. Or just to drill the screw out, or just burn it out with a torch. Or you might just, as a result of your meditative attention to the screw, come up with some new way of extracting it that has never been thought of

before and that beats all the rest and is patentable and makes you a millionaire five years from now. There's no predicting what's on that Quality track. The solutions all are simple ... after you have arrived at them. But they're simple only when you know already what they are.

Yup. Fucking useless.

STUCKNESS, FOR REAL

All good-natured jabs at Robert Pirsig's implication that a stuck bolt merely requires high-quality creative thought aside, there *are* tried-and-true procedures you can rely on when nuts and bolts are stuck. These are perhaps the most useful items in a mechanic's bag of tricks. Without them, we wouldn't be able to work on any car that's had exposure to the vicissitudes of time (which is to say, anything worthy of our love).

Let's start with the *oh crap* moment. When I was pulling the exhaust out of the Z3 M Coupe, I hadn't yet bought the oxyacetylene torch. I got impatient, used a breaker bar with a cheater pipe, and snapped four of the six exhaust studs. Ouch. By the way, what normally happens when using a breaker bar is, when the nut gives way, you literally hear a loud *crack* and then the nut becomes easy to turn. That's why this is sometimes called "breaking the nut" or "cracking the nut." In contrast, when you snap a stud or bolt, you can feel the breaker bar and pipe starting to turn with no accompanying *crack*. When this happens, I react immediately and viscerally with a sick feeling at the base of my rib cage because I know the next four hours of my life are going to be occupied by this one freaking bolt. This episode explains why it really is best to have a systematic approach to dealing with stuckness.

First, if you have a set of "Easy Outs"—those counterclockwise-spiraled bits you're supposed to insert into a hole you've drilled into a snapped-off bolt—go to your toolbox, right now, find every one of them, and throw them in the garbage. Trust me: If a bolt is so frozen that, with a clear access and ample amounts of torque, you snapped the head clean off it, the Easy Out is not going to loosen it. *Ever.* It is, however, almost certain to break in half and leave part of itself inside the bolt. And then you're even more boned than you were before.

Let's use several specific exhaust removal examples to highlight solutions to "stuckness." Due to the combination of heat, exposure, and (in rust belt states) salt, stuck nuts and bolts are routinely encountered during exhaust work, probably more than in any other class of repair. The smart approach used to be to simply wreck the old exhaust (rip it apart with a Sawzall), get it out of the car, and install all new components. This is, however, not true on cars outfitted with a catalytic converter. That baby is expensive. Unless the cat is toast, you want to reuse it. This means having to separate it from the other exhaust components. Typically the pipes heading into and out of the cat have a flared tube with a captured two- or three-bolt flange which mates with its counterpart on the muffler or resonator. The bolts holding the flanges together are usually small, with 12 or 13mm heads. And if they've been on there 20 years, I can guarantee you they're not going to come off without spitting in your eye.

GO FOR A SOAK

When you see rusty nuts, the first thing to do is soak the threads in penetrating oil. WD-40 is not penetrating oil. It is not going to soak into and free anything. Many DIY-ers swear by PB B'laster. I prefer SiliKroil. You have to order it online, but it's worth it. Penetrating oil needs time to work. Repeated soakings are often necessary. How many times you soak stuck nuts depends on your patience and whether there are other acceptable alternatives for getting them off. For mated flange bolts, as you'll see, there are in fact several other methods. I soak 'em once, and if that doesn't work, I snap 'em or cut 'em.

THE BROOKE SHIELDS APPROACH

Once you've soaked the threads in penetrating oil, you can try to get a socket and a wrench on the nut and bolt. Some manuals make a big deal of putting the socket on the nut and the box-end wrench on the bolt head, the idea being you want to spin the nut and hold the bolt head still, but I don't think it matters much. In fact, as you'll see below, sometimes you'll actually *want* to snap the bolt. If the nuts and bolts have been on there for many years, you'll have to deal with the fact that corrosion actually makes the nut and bolt heads smaller. It's not uncommon to use a 13mm socket on a 13mm nut or bolt, only to find the outer surface has rusted and crumbled away and the thing is now closer to 12mm. When this happens, take two of your good 12mm six-point impact sockets and bang them on (one onto the nut, the other onto the bolt) with a hammer. Whenever I do this, I think about Brooke Shields slipping into those Calvin Klein jeans which were clearly two sizes too small in that 1981 ad. Hey, it works for me.

OH, SNAP!

With sockets (or a socket and a box-end wrench) securely on the nut and bolt, you now can try to loosen them. Put a ratchet or a breaker bar on the socket and crank away. Maybe the nut will come off. Maybe it won't. If it doesn't, break out the air impact wrench. These are great for these little 13mm flange bolts. With all that torque, it'll either spin the nut off (yay!) or snap the bolt (yay!). Either way, you simply withdraw the bolt from the hole (unless it's rusted in the hole; see below) and move on to the next bolt.

CUT THE SUCKER IN HALF

Sometimes the nut or bolt head is so rusted and munged up you can't get a socket to stay on it. In this case, if there's a gap between the two flanges (and there usually is), you can take advantage of it and cut the bolt where it comes through the gap. Use a Sawzall, a Dremel tool with a cutting wheel, or perhaps even a conventional hacksaw. When lying beneath a car, clearance is frequently an issue; it may be necessary to jack the car up high (Jackstands! Double-jack the car!! Safety!!!) to allow sufficient access.

Let's talk for a moment about these tools. Many years ago, when Maire Anne and I used to do a lot of hiking and backpacking, we noticed we no longer remembered what we paid for well-performing equipment once we were in the wilderness, but boy we resented stuff that didn't work well. That is, if your stove wouldn't boil water, or your tent leaked, you didn't think *I'm glad I saved the 20 bucks and didn't buy the good equipment.* It's like that with the Sawzall and the Dremel tool. You need them. You can't deal with stuck exhaust nuts without them. Go out and buy yourself a Sawzall (or other brand of reciprocating saw) and two packs of metal-cutting blades of various lengths. Before starting to cut through exhaust bolts, take the blade that's on the saw, throw it away (or put it in your old blade coffee can), and put on a fresh one. Trust me, when lying beneath a car with crap falling in your face, this is not the time to save the two bucks on the blade.

The same holds with the Dremel tool. Buy one. Then spend the 20 extra bucks and buy the EZ Lock quick-disconnect mandrel and a stack of metal cutting wheels that fit the EZ Lock. You need these things. Don't use the ceramic wheels which have the screw hole in the middle; they shatter very easily, and when they do, the pieces fly everywhere. When starting on an exhaust removal job, put in a fresh cutting wheel. These things are not like expensive wine to be saved for a special occasion. Use 'em up.

BE SAFE!! You are using power tools that can easily sever a brake line, the floor of the car, and your finger. If you're using the Sawzall, be very aware of the reach of the reciprocating blade before you pull the trigger and start cutting. For our flange example, get the blade out as far as it'll go, then lay it in the gap against the bolt, and orient the saw in the position you're going to use, and make sure it's not going to rip a hole in the floor of the car. If you're using the Dremel tool, be aware the cutting wheel can grab, causing the tool to careen off in the direction the wheel is spinning. You see how shallow those tendons are on the back of your hand? Imagine that cutting wheel skitting across them before you know what has happened. Even where clearances are tight, it is always advised to hold the Dremel tool with both hands to prevent this sudden unanticipated movement.

Whether the Sawzall or the Dremel tool is better for cutting the flange bolts is a function of positioning and clearance. I'll often start with one tool, then switch to the other, then switch back. I also have a small air hacksaw that I sometimes can position into places I can't reach with the Sawzall.

When dealing with triangular exhaust flanges with three bolts, you'll usually be able to get at the bolt closest to the bottom. Once that bolt is cut, the flange is usually loose enough that you can rotate it around to position the other bolts at the bottom one at a time.

OFF WITH ITS HEAD

Sometimes you can't cut the bolt because there's not a gap between the flanges or because you can't position the Sawzall or Dremel. In this instance, you can try to chop its head off. The Dremel is usually the better tool for this. Cut the bolt head (or nut) flush with the flange, even digging slightly into the surface of the flange as necessary. Note that this is more time-consuming than cutting the body of the bolt, since the head (or nut) is bigger than the shank. If the bolt turns freely, you can sometimes trim the head off perpendicular to the axis of the bolt (i.e., cut a corner at a right angle to the flange, rotate the bolt, cut another corner, etc.), then withdraw the bolt through the hole.

PUNCH IT IN THE FACE. DRILL, BABY, DRILL.

Sometimes, even after you've snapped or twisted or sawed the head off, the shank of the bolt is still rusted frozen solid in the hole in the flange. Because the ends of most exhaust pipes are flared, the flange is almost always captured on the exhaust, so there's no easy way to replace just the flange. In this case, you have to drill the bolt out. This is tedious and tiring work. It's far easier if you can remove the piece from the car and set it on a drill press, but if the flange is on an exhaust component that's still attached to the car, you're in for a long session on the garage floor.

First, make sure you have a good center punch. You need to mark the starting point for the drill. You have one shot at this. Position the punch as close to the center of the bolt as possible and smack it with a hammer.

Next, make sure you have the best set of drill bits you can find. Those old rusty ones you have? Relegate them to the old drill bits box. Maybe they're useful for wood and plastic, but you don't want them here. You're going to be spending as much as an hour drilling out one bolt. Like with the Sawzall blades and Dremel cutting wheels, this isn't the time or place to be saving money. Unless you have a drill bit sharpener, run down to your favorite hardware store and buy the best set of cobalt or titanium-coated bits they sell. Believe me, when you're lying beneath your car and you're using old bits and it's taking forever and the stores have closed, you're going to wish you'd simply spent the 40 bucks on the new drill bits.

The key to drilling out a bolt is starting with a small bit, drilling it through the bolt, then going to the next larger sized bit, enlarging the hole, and repeating. Don't use a bit so small it flexes (meaning you might not want to start with the ⅟₁₆" bit). If you can bend it in your hand, you'll probably break if you press on the drill too hard. And once you've snapped off a bit and left part of it in the bolt you're drilling, you're boned; it's nearly impossible to drill out a bolt once there's a bit (or an Easy Out) embedded in it.

A word on drilling itself. I'm not a machinist, but the mantra is "speed kills and dulls tools." So in addition to the fact you don't want to snap the bit, you want to go slow to keep the bit sharp. Don't run the drill at its maximum rpm, don't lean too hard on the drill, and use some kind of cutting oil (3-in-1 oil is better than nothing).

Be careful! As you increase the size of the drill bit, the amount of new metal being cut increases, making it more likely that the bit will grab. When the drill bit is small, grabbing will probably snap it, which sucks, but if a larger-sized bit like a ⅜" grabs, what happens is that the bit stops *but the body of the drill tries to keep rotating.* You'd think the spinning drill would simply rotate out of your hand. Perhaps that's true if you're a leftie, but for right-handed people, in fact, it catches your hand in a way that makes it difficult even to release your fingers from the power button, and can snap your wrist. You can deal with this in a few ways. You can hold the drill with your left hand; you can use a drill chuck with clutch with a torque setting that'll trip if it binds up; you can intentionally leave the bit slightly loose (i.e., don't tighten the bit down with a dying strain) so if it binds, the bit will spin in the chuck, or you can try to be very careful and not push the drill hard.

As you've moved to bigger drill bits that are nearly the size of the bolt you're drilling, sometimes you can remove pieces of the shell of the bolt. If you're drilling an exhaust flange, the exact hole size doesn't matter, but if you're drilling out a bolt which has snapped off in a threaded hole, you don't want to drill the hole any larger than the original threads. It's rare you get that first center punch exactly in the middle, or hold the drill exactly parallel with the axis of the bolt, so it's common for the hole you've made to come closer to one side of the original threaded hole than the other. Once I've run a good-sized bit through and made a hole that's close to the diameter of the original bolt, I've sometimes been able to take a metal pick and needle-nosed pliers and work the pieces of the shell free of the original threads. If you're very careful, sometimes you can expose the original threads and just run a tap through them to clean them up.

SOME LIKE IT HOT

Last chapter I talked about using a torch. For many years, I heard people say "if it's stuck, heat it up," and tried attacking a variety of stuck nuts with heat, never to any success. Only after I bought an oxyacetylene setup did heat actually make a difference. Having had the chance to use the torch a number of times, I can offer the following insights.

There is some debate as to what the mechanism is by which heat actually helps. A commonly repeated school of thought holds that heat is effective because of differential expansion—that is, if you heat a stuck nut, you cause its metal to expand, loosening it from the bolt it is threaded onto. In fact if you look on the Pelican Parts website on which owner Wayne Dempsey has a particularly good section on stuckness and the use of heat, Wayne recommends, when trying to remove a stuck exhaust stud, you shouldn't heat the stud—you should heat the *aluminum around the stud*, letting it expand and loosen the stud. While this makes sense, there are websites that debunk it, doing the calculation of the actual amount of expansion and showing it is negligible.

The second school of thought is that differential expansion has little to do with it, and the salient mechanism is that instead the heat is helping to break the bond of corrosion between the parts.

The third theory is that, by getting the offending part cherry-red-hot, you are making the metal malleable. Imagine your frozen nut is not steel but Play-Doh; it is probably more likely to release its death-grip and spin off the bolt. However, imagine you've heated an exhaust stud to taffy-like consistency. It may well just twist off flush with the head—exactly what you don't want.

In looking at the application of heat, let's switch from our flared exhaust flange example to the common problem of headpipe nuts. Typically the output end of an exhaust manifold has a flat surface which mates with the top of an exhaust headpipe. The manifold has two or three studs protruding from the flat surface; they're either threaded into the surface or press-fit in from the back. The headpipe slides over the studs, and is held in place by large nuts (usually 17mm) threaded onto them. With the previous flared flange example, snapping the bolts isn't a big deal because they're not captured—the two bolt halves should fall out of the hole if you cut or snap the bolt. But here, manifold studs *are* captured. If you snap one, you have to get the snapped piece out of the manifold, which is bolted directly to the engine and not nearly as accessible as an exhaust flange hanging beneath the center of the car. Because of these factors, you really, *really* don't want to snap these studs off.

Remember what I said in the tool chapter about how an air impact wrench isn't for taking off incredibly tightly stuck nuts—it's for taking off normally tight nuts incredibly quickly? One nice thing about an impact wrench is, when used on a decent-sized nut and bolt like a 17mm, it is highly unlikely to snap it. It may well snap an old rusted 13mm exhaust flange bolt, but a 17mm headpipe nut and the stud it's threaded onto are quite a bit beefier. So it's pretty safe to soak the headpipe nuts in penetrating oil, and then let the impact wrench do its *whacketa-whacketa* thing. If the wrench goes *whacketa-whacketa-WHEEEEE*, it's spun the nut off and you're good. If it keeps chugging *whacketa-whacketa-whacketa-whacketa*, the nut isn't budging and you must resort to other measures.

So you have three choices. You can soak the nut in more penetrating oil and try again in the morning with the impact wrench. You can heat the nut with a torch and try again with the impact wrench. Or you can try torque—using a breaker bar with a pipe on the end. Using this setup, you can easily apply *waaaaay* more torque than your impact wrench.

The problem with applying massive amounts of torque is something *will* give, and it might not be what you want. If you have a ¾" breaker bar, you're not going to snap the bar or twist off its square chuck. If you have thick-walled impact sockets, you're unlikely to crack the wall of the socket. So either the nut is going to come off, or you're going to snap the stud.

ASSIST AND TWIST? HEAT-YOU AND UNSCREW? BORK AND TORQUE? (SORRY)

Now that I own the oxyacetylene torch, my default approach is to try penetrating oil and the impact wrench, and if that doesn't work, go right for the torch—get those headpipe nuts cherry red (if I can reach them), *then* put the impact wrench on them. I recently did this on my '93 Land Cruiser, and it successfully got off five of the six stuck nuts. I couldn't reach the sixth one with the torch (the headpipe itself was in the way), and that's the one stud that broke.

Interestingly, with the headpipe off, I *could* reach the broken stud. These Land Cruiser studs are threaded into the manifold. I heated the stud with the torch and tried to unscrew the short snapped-off section with a Vise-Grip. The Vise-Grip got very hot very quickly. I put on a welder's glove but still got nowhere trying to unscrew the snapped-off stud. I spent real money and bought a professional-grade stud remover meant to work with an impact wrench by gripping the stud tighter and tighter, but it just snapped off the stud flush with the manifold. I wound up having to drill it out and re-tap the hole.

HEAT AND BEAT

On the Z3 M, the exhaust studs aren't threaded; they're pressed-fit in from the back. The studs have ridges along the sides and a flat cap on the top. Tightening the nuts seats the studs in their holes. This is good because, unlike threaded studs, in theory, you should be able to bang them out from the front. All the web forums I read said to "heat and beat"—heat up the studs and smack them with a hammer. I used my MAPP gas torch, got them red, and banged on them with a small sledgehammer so hard I was concerned about damaging the manifold or the head. They would not budge.

I bought the oxyacetylene setup specifically to deal with these studs. Let me say the torch, like the impact wrench, is *not* a panacea for stuckness. As I said last chapter, you have to learn how to dial in the flame. And that flame is long and hot and will melt a brake line or a CV boot in a second. I was so concerned about burning something important in the engine compartment of the Z3 M Coupe that I took two disposable aluminum roasting pans, cut them up, folded the pieces over four times, and packed them around and behind the exhaust manifold studs to act as heat shields.

SMELT AND PELT

Once I convinced myself I could in fact maneuver the torch safely beneath the Z3 M and around the engine, I took the Dremel tool and cut the broken studs off flush with the manifold, thus leaving the smallest amount of metal to heat. I then put the torch directly on these short sections of snapped stud. When the heat was just short of melting the stud, I took a punch and a small sledge, smacked the bottom of the stud, and out it popped. In this case, the operative mechanism clearly was that the metal was made malleable; because the stud was no longer rigid, the ridges on the sides of the stud no longer had a deathgrip on the inside of the hole. I explained this to Maire Anne, drawing the distinction between it and "heat and beat." She came up with "smelt and pelt." I like it. Accurate. Punchy. Has a good beat. Easy to dance to. I give it a 73.

BURN, BABY, BURN

In addition to the snapped exhaust studs on the Z3 M, several of the flange bolts were inextricably embedded in the flange holes. I pulled the exhaust completely out from beneath the car, enabling me to beat on the bolts with all my might using a sledge, and they weren't going anywhere. I tried to drill one of them out and broke the drill bit. There seemed little choice but to try using the cutting head of the oxy-acetylene torch with its lever that injects extra oxygen into the stream. This is the configuration commonly called a "blowtorch." It is far from dentist drill precision, at least for this novice user with the torch tips that came with the package. It's a big flame that cuts a big hole.

The exhaust flange—and the bolt stuck inside it—was nearly an inch thick. By the time the flame had burned through to the far side of the bolt, the near side of the flange had a big ugly hole like an impact crater, and the force of gravity had tugged at the flange's molten metal and distorted it, making the flange resemble one of those dripping clocks in a Dali painting. In this case, I didn't care. This was just an exhaust flange; it wasn't a mating surface. All it had to do was have a hole through which a bolt could pass. But it made me very circumspect about using the cutting head (the "blowtorch") on something that *is* a mating surface, like burning out a stud on an exhaust manifold. Here's hoping that, now I know to rely on "heat-you and unscrew," I never need to.

REMOVE THE NEXT LARGER ASSEMBLY

There is another dynamic which is sometimes employed—that of removing the next larger assembly. For example, if a manifold-to-headpipe stud is snapped off in the manifold and you don't have a drill or a torch, you could remove the manifold from the head and take it to a machine shop. It's useful to realize that this is an option, but in practice, on old high-mileage cars, it is rarely productive. It was a possible solution on my Z3 M Coupe since it is a relatively recent car and the manifold-to-head studs look intact. But when I looked at the rusty nuts holding the exhaust manifold to the head of the '93 Land Cruiser with its 180K miles, with the studs corroded to the diameter of toothpicks, the idea that these studs would come out easily when I'd just snapped off a bigger more robust one was ludicrous.

A Dremel tool with a cutting wheel. A Sawzall. A decent drill with brand-new high-quality bits. An oxyacetylene torch with a cutting head. Soak. Snap. Cut. Decapitate. Punch and drill. Heat-you and unscrew. Heat and beat. Smelt and pelt. Burn baby burn. Remove the next larger assembly. This is a pretty good bag of tricks. And now you know them too.

Someone should buy me a hat that says, "Women love me. Exhausts fear me."

CHAPTER 53

THE MAD DASH

Ethan, who is pursuing a career in film, recently entered the 48 Hour Film Project—a crazy-ass endeavor in which teams of amateur film makers head to a central location (in this case, a bar in downtown Boston) and are handed film topics drawn at random. They have 48 hours to script, shoot, score, edit, and credit a short film, which must then be submitted as a Quick-Time file, on a thumb drive, at the location where the original drawing was done (the bar), no later than 48 hours after the drawing. If you're late, you're disqualified. Cat ate my thumb drive, my grandmother died, I had a flat tire, alien abduction—doesn't matter. No excuses, no retries, no mulligans.

Ethan adroitly assembled and prepositioned his team, stationing them at our house so that as soon as he received his assignment at the bar ("heist film"), he could phone it in and have them immediately begin work, thus efficiently making use of the 20-minute drive back from downtown Boston. One group started roughing out a plot centered on the botched robbery of a coke dealer. Another contingent ran to Walmart to buy a safe. A third took some of the cardboard building blocks the boys used to play with, painted them white, coated them with baby powder, and wrapped them in plastic bags to make them look like bricks of cocaine. Using the safe and a scale, they set up a fairly convincing coke lab in our basement. There were actors, hair and makeup people, lights, computers on every horizontal surface … it was the wonderful controlled anarchy that is the currency in which youth traffics.

Given the drug-themed plot, Ethan asked if he could use one of "the cool cars" as a prop. We settled on the Z3 M Coupe. (Maire Anne lobbied to have her bugs make an appearance. It was interesting hearing Ethan explaining that the link between coke dealers and exotic insects was perhaps not as compelling as that with fast cars.) I was hesitant to simply hand over the keys to Eva so I elected to go with them to the filming location. The shot called for an actor to exit a building, walk down a flight of stairs to the street, get into the car, and drive off. Ethan explained that, once the actor got in the car, they'd cut, the actor would get out, I'd hop in, and they'd film the car driving away. I was a bit puzzled. "Are you doing that because you think I don't want anyone else to drive the car, even for a moment?" Ethan nodded. I explained that I had no objection to someone else's pulling the car away from the curb. He was grateful for the simplification.

You can probably tell where this is heading.

So there I was, off to one side, out of the camera shot, when they yelled "action." As the actor began descending the stairs, I noticed another car coming down the one-way street. I thought, no problem, I can't be the only one who sees this; they'll have to stop filming. But they didn't. The car came closer. The actor climbed into my M Coupe. Be calm, Rob, don't be a nervous Nelly, there are at least four sets of eyeballs on the scene other than yours. Then the actor started the engine, put the car in gear, and began to pull away from the curb. The other car continued to come down the street. No one intervened. Did they not see? My limbic system apparently overruled my desire to not seem like a hovering overprotective car guy; at the last moment, when it was clear that no one else would, I heard myself shriek *STOP!* The approaching car's front bumper came to rest approximately six inches from the M Coupe's beautifully sculpted right front fender.

The actor was mortified. He rolled down the window.

"Do you just want to drive it yourself?" he asked somewhat sheepishly.

"I have no objection to your pulling the car away from the curb," I said, mustering all of my rationality, *"but you have to look, just like with any other car."*

When they brought back the film to be edited, the editing crew, who were not present when the scene was shot, literally gasped in horror at how close the car came to actually being hit. Even Ethan, who was right there during filming, was visibly shaken when we saw the replay. I elected not to watch.

For two nights, the crew slept very little. The film had to be submitted at the bar in downtown Boston by 7:30 P.M. Ethan benchmarked the distance from our house to the bar at, according to Google maps, a

highly optimistic twelve minutes. Yeah, I said, maybe with zero traffic
and driving 90. I advised him that it was more like 20 minutes. Work
always expands to fill the amount of time allotted for it, but the reverse
is never true. The editing portion of the project proved quite time-consuming. Ethan planned that, at 6:45 P.M., they'd export whatever they
had from the computer onto the thumb drive, get in the car, and go.
At 6 P.M. they did their first test export and found that their 4-gigabyte
thumb drive wasn't large enough to hold the exported movie. I volun-
teered to find a bigger thumb drive, an endeavor made more difficult
than expected by the 6 P.M. Sunday closing time of the nearby Staples.
I sped from store to store in the silver M Coupe in search of the elusive
thumb drive. Mercifully a nearby Walgreens had a single 8gb drive on
the rack. I got back home with my prize at 6:45 P.M. and they began the
final export of the movie.

Now, it is well known in quantum mechanics that observation of
a system interferes with the system. Although this is a microscopic
phenomenon, it has long been noted that the macroscopic world is
rife with what appear to be analogous examples. A watched pot never
boils; anthropologists observing primitive cultures wind up responsible for their reverence of the Budweiser logo and their addiction to
iPhones; etc. In this spirit, it is well documented that a watched progress bar moves slower than an unwatched one. But suffice it to say that
in the entire recorded history of humans observing computers, no one
has ever observed a progress bar moving slower than the one on the
computer performing the final export of this particular movie onto this
particular thumb drive. It was agonizing.

The clocked marked the minutes mercilessly. 7:00. 7:05. 7:10. 7:15.
Ethan and his crew were looking at what had been unthinkable—not
getting the movie in on time. Finally, at a dream-crushing 7:20 P.M., the
export was done. They double-clicked on the movie file on the thumb-
drive just to make sure it was playable (it was—not that it would've
made any difference if it wasn't; there was no time to recover), and
Ethan and I grabbed the thumb drive, ran out the door, jumped in the
silver M Coupe, and burned rubber toward downtown Boston.

These days, I'm usually pretty sedate behind the wheel, but if ever
there was a time to stand on it, this was it. At a red traffic light I went
around a guy on the left, then hung a right directly in front of him. I

cornered onto the West Newton entrance ramp to the Mass Pike with enough lateral force to mash Ethan against the door, and then redlined it through second and third, coming just short of triple-digit speeds. It was my Dustin Hoffman moment, with the timely submission of Ethan's film playing the part of Katharine Ross. I flew past cars, even passing people on the right where necessary (and I *never* do this).

In short, I drove like some asshole in a BMW.

As the clock ticked 7:25 and we were passing the Watertown exit, I turned to Ethan and said, "I think you need to prepare yourself that we're not going to make it."

"I know, Dad," he said.

Perhaps I was driving sufficiently fast that relativistic time dilation effects were becoming significant, but whatever the reason, as we approached the Copley Square exit, the clock on the dashboard read, incredibly, 7:29. Holy nick of time, Batman, we thought—with Ethan's legendary charm and some Irish luck from Maire Anne's side of the family we might actually make this. We got off the Pike, made three quick rights, endured a maddening 15 seconds behind one car that did not share our urgency, then Ethan said, *"That's the bar—STOP!"* and jumped out and dashed across the street. The clock on my cell phone read 7:33. I prepared myself to console a dejected child. At least I knew that I couldn't have gotten there any faster without risking both public safety and possible jail time for reckless vehicular endangerment.

Then, Ethan strutted out of the bar with a Cheshire cat-sized grin. "I ran in," he said, "to *HUGE* applause, as they were counting down to the deadline. People hugged me and took my picture."

"So you made it?"

"With ten seconds to spare."

Ethan and I hugged and high-fived, then sat in the car and just laughed. *Any* alteration—a single red light—would've rocked the outcome. He called his crew back at the house and told them they'd just made it. As we were driving back, Ethan said that the mad dash might have been his favorite part of the weekend.

That night, on Facebook, Ethan posted the following:

"NO ONE drives like my dad."

Taking the risk for my son, giving it my best shot, and not only having it pay off, but sharing it with him and having him viscerally appreciate it—it may have been my single most enjoyable moment as a parent.

The next day, Ethan called me up and told me that they'd been disqualified. The submission had been rejected because the movie file on the thumb drive was unplayable. Apparently when they exported the movie, they hadn't checked the box to embed all video sources. Some of the video was still on the hard drive. The movie had only been playable on the thumb drive because they tested it on the computer whose hard drive still held the video. Ethan used all of his considerable persuasive skills to try to get them to accept a re-exported version, but the answer was a carefully scripted, "It's a 48 hour contest, and I'm sure that you can appreciate that someone less scrupulous than you could have constructed this situation to gain an extra day to continue editing the movie." No excuses, no retries, no mulligans.

Ethan, obviously, was crushed. The hardest part was telling the other crew members that their work had been for naught. Since it was his project and he was the one who actually performed the export, he felt responsible. I reminded him that the reason he was the person at the controls of an unfamiliar piece of film editing software was that the film editor was literally passed out at the kitchen table, having had virtually no sleep in the preceding 48 hours.

In the end, it wasn't so bad. The film was still shown as part of the festival, but with the asterisk that it was a late submission. And Ethan probably learned an incredibly valuable lesson about not pushing things so close to the line.

But, for 13 amazing minutes, in a silver M Coupe, father and son had shared an adrenaline rush, slowed time, risked arrest, beat the odds, and nearly slipped the surly bonds of Earth. It was glorious. I thought about the impossibly fast hour-and-15-minute run in my Triumph from Cambridge to Amherst 34 years before. This was better.

Next year, though, I will have a stock of gargantuan thumb drives and will stubbornly insist that they begin the export at 5 P.M. and test the file on a different computer. I mean *someone* has to be the responsible adult.

CHAPTER 54

THOUGHTS ON REFRIGERATORS, RELIABILITY, AND WHY YOU CAN'T GO BACK

I want to discuss the failure of the "smart" cooling fan in my daily-driver 325Xi wagon, but I need to begin by talking about my mother-in-law's refrigerator.

Rita has a spare refrigerator in her basement. It must be at least 50 years old. She and Tom used it to store, mostly, soda, which it chilled to a temperature that could shatter the enamel on your teeth if you hiccupped too hard. It ran and ran and ran, through 12 presidential administrations, four wars, and oscillations in hemlines and monetary policy. At one point the handle broke off, and Tom deftly grafted on a pull-tight latch like the kind used on a guitar case. Everyone commented, "Boy, they don't make 'em like that anymore." Of course, energy efficient it wasn't; it probably cost them $300 a year in electricity. But still, it was a marvel. I asked Maire Anne, and she thinks the damned thing is, in fact, still running.

Well, they *don't* make 'em like that anymore, true, but much of this is an illusion. Here's why.

When we marvel at Tom and Rita's wunder-fridge, we leave out the fact that the freezer frosts up so badly that if it isn't shut off and defrosted every few months, it freezes itself solid. That is, it's not a "frost-free" freezer. Those small dorm-room refrigerators aren't frost-free either, and thus also experience the shrinking freezer phenomenon, but for full-sized refrigerators, manual defrosting is an anachronism. Even to those of us old enough to remember, it's a Kodak Brownie memory, as distant as moonshots and American servicemen in Indochina. And no one is nostalgic for it either; it was a pain having to take out all the food, put it in a cooler, and wait for the sheets of ice to crack and the water to run out onto the floor. I once ruined the refrigerator in a rented apartment when I got impatient, began chipping ice off the coils with a screwdriver, and punctured one. With Tom and Rita's fridge, since all they had in it was soda, they didn't even need to empty it out to defrost it; they could simply unplug it for a day and then plug it back in. In fact, since they never used the freezer, they probably didn't need to defrost it at all. I doubt memory would be so kind to the wunder-fridge if its behavior caused people to perform actual work.

So frost-free is better, right? Well, it depends what you mean by "better." Every refrigerator has the cold-generating coils located in the freezer. Some amount of cold air is then channeled down from the freezer into the refrigerator section to cool it, but this also allows moisture to get into the freezer and ice up the coils. So how do frost-free freezers work? Was there a refrigerator engineer's equivalent of Robert Johnson at the crossroads, selling his soul to the devil so he could design a supernatural method of producing cold air without generating frost? The answer is far more mundane, but still quite surprising.

Heaters.

Yes, every refrigerator with a frost-free freezer has heating elements. *Inside the freezer.*

In your refrigerator you have a timer, and in the freezer you have heating elements and temperature sensors. About every six hours, the timer interrupts the refrigerator's normal cooling cycle and tells the heaters to run for 15 minutes (or until the temperature is above freezing) and melt the ice that's forming on the freezer coils. Think about this. If you're curious, empty out your freezer sometime, remove the inner cover to expose the coils, and watch the heaters glow red and reduce the ice to rainwater. It looks like a fire in winter. It's beautiful, haunting, counterintuitive, and a little creepy to think of it happening inches from the ice cream and the frozen shrimp.

The problem comes, of course, when something fails. And something *will fail.* The timer can put the system into a defrost cycle, then die and never get back to a refrigeration cycle, in which case both freezer and fridge get warm. Or the heaters or the temperature sensors can fail, causing the freezer to ice up, which, ironically, often blocks the flow of cold air into the fridge, causing it to get warm.

So the freezer in the 50-year-old fridge can freeze itself solid and still let the refrigerator chill the beer, but if the defroster in the fridge with the frost-free freezer fails, the milk spoils.

It's estimated that most refrigerator repairs are due to failures of some portion of the defroster circuit. When a freezer is cold but a refrigerator is warm, the advice is—and I love this—unplug it for 24 hours, then plug it in. In other words, *manually defrost it*. If both the freezer and the fridge come back up cold, you know the problem is in the defroster circuit and you can then begin the process of diagnosing which element is bad. Or you can just run it like this, indefinitely, and manually defrost it.

Of course, I'm the kind of guy who *likes* pulling the cover off the back of the freezer compartment, exposing the heater elements, and troubleshooting them. The feeling of accomplishment gained by successfully doing this and getting the fridge back up and running for 40 bucks instead of feeling like you have no choice but to drop $800 and kick the old friend summarily out on the curb is huge. When I see a refrigerator on the curb, discarded, probably prematurely spent, I can't help but think *I could save you; it's probably just those damned defroster heaters.* If the design aesthetics of refrigerators approached that of cars, I might have a garage full of them, waiting for me to nurse them back to health.

But here's the point. Even knowing how failure-prone the defroster circuit is, that it is largely responsible for decreasing refrigerator lifetime from 50 years to perhaps 10, there's no market for old-fashioned "dumb but reliable" refrigerators you need to defrost manually. We're happy to use them until they die, pitch the old box when it's out of style anyway, and go to Sears and buy a new one. Likewise, there's virtually no market for "vintage" refrigerators. Even manual defrosting notwithstanding, they're too small and suck too much power. This same dynamic exists with many new technologies, or improvements to old ones. We know there's no free lunch, but we want the pie, too, and we don't want it to be too fattening.

And with that foray into "better" refrigeration, we come to the cooling fan in my daily-driver 325Xi wagon. The trend over the last 40 years has been to make nearly everything in a car "smart," and the cooling system has not escaped the wave. Cars originally had a mechanical fan mounted directly to the water pump and driven by the aptly named fan belt. As long as the water pump was turning, you could be certain the fan would be pushing air at the radiator. I can guarantee you that no BMW 2002 or other old car with an intact fan belt ever overheated because the fan simply stopped spinning.

However, the spinning fan generated a fair amount of noise. Somewhere, someone decided that, if the engine wasn't hot or the car was barreling down the highway with lots of air passing through the radiator, this noise was "unnecessary," and a fan clutch was introduced that disconnected the fan from the spinning water pump. This always struck me as an inherently bad idea. The first fan clutches were centrifugal, failure-prone, and easily bypassed. Later, many cars incorporated a viscous fan clutch. The consequence was that fans were quieter, but if the fan clutch failed, the car would overheat in traffic because of lack of air flow. Personally, I've never understood the engineering trade-off inherent in the fan clutch. "May well cause the engine to overheat if it fails" versus "some buyers might think it's too loud," in fact, *isn't* an engineering tradeoff; it's a *marketing* trade-off.

Then came front-wheel-drive cars. Because these generally have transverse-mounted engines, the water pump faces the side of the car, not the front, making a mechanically driven front-facing cooling fan aimed at the radiator a contraption that would make Rube Goldberg jealous. So manufacturers began incorporating electric cooling fans. In addition to solving the orientation problem, the electric fans were thermostatically controlled, turning on only when needed. This made the car nice and quiet if the engine wasn't hot, but also created the odd circumstance where the fan might continue to run even after you shut the car off and walked away from it. No one bats an eyelash at this anymore.

Though BMWs remain steadfastly rear-wheel drive (except for you MINI renegades), the long engines, particularly the six-cylinder motors, create an engine compartment that's starved for space, so at some point BMW started using electric cooling fans. Such is the case with my E46 325Xi wagon. It relies on a single electric fan for both the radiator and the a/c condenser. The fan is more than just thermostatically controlled—it is "smart." The ECU combines many inputs, including vehicle speed, coolant temperature and a/c system pressure, and sends a speed signal, in the form of a frequency-varying strobe, to the fan. Well, not directly to the fan—to a fan controller and relay that are integral parts of the fan and not orderable a la carte. The fan controller reads the strobe signal and commands the fan to produce a wide range of airflow across the radiator and a/c condenser.

I will admit that, in traffic, when the air temperature is hot, an electric fan can move more air than a mechanical fan if the engine is idling slowly, and that is an advantage. Of course, like the frost-free refrigerator, this advantage comes at a price, and the price is the potential of failure. The fan motor can out-and-out die, or the controller/relay can flake out, or one of the sensors the ECU monitors in order to create the strobe signal can flatline.

Earlier I described how BMW went over to the Dark Side many years ago by incorporating plastic into the cooling system, and how owning a high-mileage BMW requires prophylactic replacement of the water pump, thermostat, expansion tank, radiator, and hoses. When I bought the 325XiT in the summer of 2011 I dutifully did all that. Turns out, it wasn't enough. I should've replaced the electric cooling fan. I didn't, because there was nothing obviously wrong with it, and because, like most German electric motors, it was not cheap. This was a mistake.

First I began noticing the a/c in the wagon would sometimes get warm, particularly in traffic. Since the car's temperature gauge still read in the middle, I didn't suspect the cooling fan. Then, one evening, the fan kept running after I parked the car. This in itself wasn't unusual, but the fact that, 30 minutes later it was still whirring, indicated something was wrong. I unplugged it and left myself a note to plug it back in in the morning. Things again seemed fine but a few mornings later I went to drive to work and found the battery had been drained to the point where it couldn't start the car, presumably because the fan had been running all night.

Then, one day, sitting at a red light with the air-conditioning on, I realized I was getting hot. I looked at the temperature gauge and found it uncomfortably close to the red. I pulled into a nearby parking lot and checked the electric fan. It wasn't turning. This is incredibly dangerous turf. The car is running hot but has not yet overheated. You *know* it's running hot because the cooling fan isn't turning. I had not taken my own advice and prepositioned a set of heavy-gauge wires in the car to allow me to hot-wire the fan directly to the battery. As long as the car keeps moving, there's sufficient air flow through the radiator, and you'll be fine. But you don't have control over traffic and red lights. Do you go for it, or do you call for a tow? I rolled the dice, figuring I could beat rush hour home. I won, but get this wrong and this is *exactly* how you crack a head.

So, here, in the span of a few days, the "smart" cooling fan malfunctioned one way, running all night when it wasn't supposed to and draining the battery so that in the morning the car was dead, then malfunctioned the other far more dangerous way, not running when it was sorely needed.

Now, one reaction to this is "The cooling fan lasted 150,000 miles. That's not bad. If you want to be able to trust that the car won't overheat, add replacement of that electric fan into the rest of the prophylactic cooling system maintenance." I have. I did. I will. It's a mistake I will not make a second time.

But that misses the point. Here's what frosts my noodle. The combination of a long straight aluminum head and a marginal cooling system creates a situation where you overheat the thing once and you've bought yourself an engine. That's important. That's a situation to be avoided at all costs. As an engineer, wouldn't you want to design the system to include a fan that is highly unlikely to fail? That would be a mechanical fan. Perhaps, on this car, due to space constraints, you can't. But *design the system to warn the driver if the fan isn't working*. This ain't your freezer frosting up. You crack the head and it could cost you ten grand.

And *the technology exists* to warn the driver if the fan isn't working. It is already in the car. That annoying *check engine* light is a federally mandated self-monitoring system for emissions-related activities. If it senses anything that *might* result in increased emissions—incorrect current load, wrong resistance, open circuit—it trips the light. Excuse me, but in my book, a cracked head is more important. Why not use the same technology the check engine light circuitry uses? There could easily be something that senses if the electric fan isn't turning while the engine is at operating temperature (i.e., *before it swings into the red*). It could detect if the fan is drawing not enough or too much current, and light a big red flashing *DANGER FAN NOT WORKING GET SERVICE IMMEDIATELY* message—something absolutely clear, keyed to the importance of the problem, and not lost in the sea of comparatively unimportant "check engine" information. But it'll never happen. BMWs are designed for how they behave in the first 60K miles, not for fail-safe operation past that.

I looked on www.e46fanatics.com, found my flaky set of symptoms were all well inside the envelope of fan/controller failure, and ordered a Behr replacement fan. While waiting for it to arrive, I wired the fan directly to the battery with 10-gauge wire and an in-line 30 amp fuse so I could continue to use the car, but I noticed that, sometimes when I plugged the fuse in, there would be no spark and the fan would not turn on at all, indicating problems with the fan motor itself. At that point, I quit driving the car until the new fan arrived, as the risk of overheating the engine was simply too great.

I also read posts from owners who either bypassed their fan controller or installed a less "smart" aftermarket fan, in both cases wiring the fan with a relay and a switch on the dashboard so *they* had control over when to turn it on. If you *want* to do this, that's fine, and very creative, but it struck me as out of step with the feel of the car (it's a fairly nice, intact 2001 BMW, not something older that's already been kluged seven ways from Sunday). Me, if a new OEM $200 fan solves the problem once and for all, I can live with it. It arrived, I installed it in ten minutes, and have had no cooling problems on the car since, though I still watch the temperature of this car closely when it's hot and I'm in traffic.

If I may continue this antimodernist rant for a moment, a similar situation exists with the crankcase ventilation valve (CVV) or oil separator that froze in my 528iT wagon. The CVV, sort of a souped-up PCV, is a fact of life in many modern cars. It separates moisture from the oil and allows it to boil off. But if you drive a car a short distance in very cold weather and then shut it off, moisture that has accumulated but not yet boiled away can freeze in the valve. When you start the car again, the frozen valve can send oil directly into the intake manifold, hydro-lock the engine, and bend the connecting rods. And when you replace the CVV, you see that the parts are cheap plastic. Of *course* they fail over time. The perception is that this part, that isn't present on older cars, has no real benefit. It doesn't buy extra performance or reliability; its only reason for existence appears to be enabling a very large repair bill. This is *exactly* the sort of thing that makes you want to run back into the arms of a '65 Falcon.

But why live with this at all? Why *not* roll the clock back and drive something older, with a mechanical fan, without all that plastic in the cooling system, without all those relays and computers, without a CVV? You can, and some do, but you'd be hard-pressed to convince most people to give up the power, gas mileage, comfort, quiet, safety, winter weather performance, etc., that accompany newer cars. In fact, as with the refrigerator, most folks go the other way—when it breaks, they simply buy something brand-new.

There are, however, exceptions. I recently met a young man at a dinner party who is totally into his 1972 Type II VW bus. He lives John Muir's philosophy about the relationship with your vehicle changing your relationship with yourself. He travels everywhere with his tools and crucial spare parts. When I observed, "Even with tools and parts, it still sucks if you break down on the Tappan Zee Bridge," he was unfazed and replied that he plans his routes carefully and takes smaller roads so he can pull over and perform an extended repair if necessary. "You have *no other daily driver*? The bus is your only car?" I asked. He nodded proudly.

I thought, wow, this is one committed guy. I mean I love my old BMWs, but that love is enabled by also owning a modern daily driver. The idea of him keeping his bus off the interstate, slowing down, selecting routes in harmony with his larger journey, and enjoying that journey is poetic, but it also struck me as similar to the last few years of the Space Shuttle program, where whatever the stated mission was in terms of satellite launching and experimentation, the practical goal was getting the thing up and back without killing everybody. "Do you have the bus here?" I asked. He hesitated. "The inspection sticker's expired," he said. Then his girlfriend leaned forward and gently interjected a crucial piece of enabling context: "We took my Subaru."

It's enough to make me want to go over to my in-laws' house and grab a cracklingly cold soda out of the wunder-fridge. It's a good thing it'll be so cold it doesn't need ice cubes. I'd need to chisel those out of the freezer. They've probably been in there since the Eisenhower administration. I don't think they're coming out without a fight.

SHAKE, RATTLE AND ROLL

I've referred several times to a "tight car"—one that doesn't constantly distract you with annoying rattles, or make you swear oaths whenever you hit a pothole or run over a set of railroad tracks. This is not easy to achieve. Rattles and clunks are the broth in which old cars marinate. The old joke is "If the car is loud, turn up the radio," but most of us want our ride to ride as nicely as it looks without resorting to electronic countermeasures. The usual suspects hauled in for the police lineup may be bad shocks and worn-out suspension bushings, but noise can come from *anywhere,* and often seems to be coming from *everywhere.* Most often it's multiple things. A mis-fitted hood, maladjusted door latches, a loose power window motor, a passenger-side window whose rubber seal has worn out, or trim that's detached at one end and *thwaaaang*-ing like a yardstick pulled backwards on a desktop … I've hunted down, found, and fixed all these, and more. It is difficult, time-consuming, and expensive to de-rattle a car to the level it was when new. And, even if you did, the good old days weren't all that good; compared to the fit, finish, and quiet of the modern car you likely drive every day, your beloved classic was probably redolent with rattles and a cacophony of clunks when it rolled new off the assembly line anyway.

Even if you drop big coin on restoration work, tightness has surprisingly less to do with restoration than you might think. After my 3.0CSi was repainted, at which point anyone who saw it would've called it "restored," it rattled horribly *because* so much of had been taken apart. The guy who painted it did a great job wet-sanding and polishing it to a deep, mirror finish, but he rushed through the reassembly. In fairness, it was loud before the outer body restoration, but it came back with more, not fewer, noises; I found loose molding and unsecured power window motors. Sorting out the clunks and rattles and getting the car to the quiet solid place where it is now has been a 25-year-long process.

Editor's Note: This memoir is **not** a repair manual. Please read Warnings & Cautions on p. 410.

Those caveats aside, I am, I believe, like the majority of classic car owners who think, "I'm a reasonable guy. I don't expect my baby to ride like a new car. Really. I don't. But I'd give my left nut to get rid of *THAT noise because THAT noise is DRIVING ME FREAKING NUTS! Can you hear THAT? You can't? REALLY? I can't BELIEVE you can't hear THAT!*"

CLUNKS VERSUS RATTLES

If a particular noise is driving you crazy, the distinction between clunks and rattles may be academic, but I hold that they are different. *Clunks* are caused by something hitting something it's not supposed to when the car is jerked up and down over bumpier-than-normal pavement. *Rattles*, on the other hand, can occur on pavement of only nominal roughness, and are caused by two things rubbing or gently knocking together with some sort of characteristic frequency.

Although rattles and clunks *can* come from anywhere, I do have something of a procedure I go through when trying to quiet down a car. It helps to think of it as peeling layers off an onion, with the clunks on the outside and the rattles on the inside. You can only track down and fix one noise at a time. Once you've nailed it, the next layer will make itself known.

DE-CLUNK THE TRUNK

First, you want to completely—and I mean *completely*—empty out the trunk. Don't laugh. People talk about getting the biggest "bang for the buck." Well, this can be the biggest no-bang for no bucks. In addition to unsecured spare tires, jacks, and lug nut wrenches, I've found loose fire extinguishers, cans of Fix-A-Flat, and entire ratchet wrench and socket sets banging around in the spare tire well. Seriously. Do this first.

SEAT THE SEATS

A next quick and easy thing to check is the state of the seats. The odds of an original set of seats and slider brackets in a classic car *not* being a source of noise are slim. Grab both front seats by the headrests and rock them back and forth. I can almost guarantee you'll see an inch of play from the worn-out sliders. The act of sitting in the driver's seat usually keeps the noise to a minimum, but without weight in the pas-senger seat, it may be contributing to the noise chorus. If it is, I some-times simply remove the passenger seat while I'm doing further noise testing so as not to be distracted by it.

EXHAUST CLUNKS

The next layer is the exhaust. It's usually pretty obvious that the exhaust is the source when you hear a resonant ringing sound of metal clanging against metal while going over bumps. You can verify this easily by going to the back of the car and, with the engine cold, grabbing the tailpipe and shaking it side-to-side and up and down. Perhaps all that's wrong is that a rubber hanger has worn out—easy and inexpensive to replace. Other sources of exhaust banging, though, can be more subtle. When exhaust pipes are designed to take a bend as they head up and over the rear suspension components, there may not be enough clearance if they weren't installed with the correct orientation, causing them to hit the subframe or floor. If you find this is the source of banging, correcting it may be as easy as loosening the U-bolts and/or flange nuts and rotating the exhaust sections to where they should be. Unfortunately you may find that the section where the muffler slides over the back of the resonator has welded itself in place with heat, exposure, and rust, and can't be budged. Sometimes you can get around this problem by looking at the exhaust and finding the attachment point for the next section, like where the front of the center resonator bolts to the end of the headpipes, and rotating it there.

While you're checking the exhaust, if your car has a bracket se-curing the exhaust to the transmission, be sure to inspect it. If pieces are missing, it can clunk, rattle, or both. This is a common failure point on old BMWs. There should be a two-piece bracket. One piece should be clamped to the exhaust with a U-bolt. The other piece is supposed to be secured to the transmission via rubber bushings, but it's common to see the bushings degraded from the oil and transmis-sion leaks common in these cars, leaving the bracket free to sound like a chainsaw.

SUSPENSION CLUNKS

If the exhaust isn't hitting anything but there is obvious loud clunk-ing over bumps, you need to thoroughly examine the suspension. This begins with the shocks and struts and their mounts. Go to all four corners of the car and do the bounce test, pushing down, letting it come up, and pushing down again to set up an oscillation. Really work it—you're trying to get it to make noise. On a newer car with bridge-abutment bumpers, I'll sometimes stand on the bumper and work it up and down that way. On an older car you can't do this, as those skinny chrome bumpers weren't really meant to absorb much of anything. In fact, when a classic car is in cherry condition, you have to be careful even pushing down hard on the body panels. On a 2002, I sometimes open up the hood and push down on the tops of the fenders or the shock towers, or open the trunk lid and push down at the corner of the rear fender and the back panel. Of course, now you have to be careful not to have the hood or trunk lid slam shut on your hand.

But in doing this, you may unearth a *clunk*. If you do, you now need to isolate it. Having a friend assist you is invaluable in this pro-cess. Someone has to physically lay his or her hands on the moving parts to isolate the offending one.

Even if the shocks and struts themselves are fine, it's not uncom-mon to discover something related is wrong. In my Z3 M Coupe, the rear shock tower bushings had worn out, leaving the top of the shocks to bang around. In my 3.0CSi, I once found that the collar nut holding one of the front strut cartridges in its tube had loosened up, enabling the whole cartridge to move up and down inside the tube. This was one of those golden *eureka!* moments, after which I drove the car, veri-fied the noise was gone, and felt my entire automotive soul exhale.

If you can reproduce the clunk when bouncing the car but the noise isn't coming from the shocks or struts, another common source is the sway bar bushings or end links. The sway bars themselves are held to the subframe by U-shaped clamps in the middle, with rubber bushings between the clamps and the sway bar. If these rubber bush-ing have completely deteriorated, it is possible for the metal sway bar to hit the metal clamp. However, the sway bar is merely twisting at this central attachment point, whereas it is moving up and down at the ends. Thus it is more likely that a clunking or banging noise is coming from the ends rather than the middle. However, these central sway bar bushings can emit an incredibly annoying *screeeee* similar to a squeaky hinge in a slowly-opening door. My 3.0CSi has urethane sway bar bushings, and if I don't grease them every few years, they start to sound like monkeys doing the nasty.

The simple sway bar design on older cars employs a long threaded bolt connecting each end with the control arms (in the front of the car) or the trailing arms (in the rear). There are round rubber bushings above and below where the bolt comes out of the end of the sway bar, and above and below where it goes through the control or trailing arm. Any of these can be worn to the point where metal is hitting metal. If this is the case, it is visible upon inspection.

Many newer cars use a different sway bar attachment mechanism called an end link that has a small ball joint at both the top and bottom. When these fail, they can raise quite a racket. Because the little ball joints have rubber boots around them, the failure point is often not visible, but if you have someone bounce the car while you wrap your hand around each end of the link, you can easily tell if it is the source of the clunking. If your car is banging over bumps and you isolate it to a sway bar link, count yourself lucky. They're cheap and easy to replace.

If the components above have passed muster, you need to look at the suspension bushings. Part of the pleasure of older BMWs like the 2002 and 3.0CS is that they have very simple suspensions whose bushings are generally quite robust but are easy to change when they go to that big bushing graveyard in the sky. There are two cylindrical rear bushings, slightly smaller than a beer can, located at both ends of the rear subframe. As with any rubber part, with age these get brittle and can crack. It is possible for the rear subframe bushings to fail to the point that the subframe actually moves around. Fortunately these bushings are plainly visible, easy to inspect, and can be replaced with the subframe in the car. Such is not the case, however, with the rear trailing arm bushings. I have never replaced these, and would require ironclad evidence that they are a source of noise before considering doing so.

Generally speaking, the newer the car, the more complex the suspension is, and the greater the bewildering assortment of bushings.

If that's not bad enough, on many newer cars some of the bushings are press-fit into other components. These require special tools to remove and install, leaving you to either try to fabricate a tool using threaded rods, nuts and washers, or buy the next larger assembly with the bushings already pressed in—or pay someone else to do it. If some clunk is driving you nuts and you've read on message boards that the sound is probably due to a pressed-in steering or suspension bushing—and you've checked everything else you can think of—you may just need to bite the bullet, pay someone to change it, and see if the clunk goes away. Remember that it is, of course, quite possible for a bushing to be bad or worn-out and *not* be the cause of a particular sound you're hearing.

In addition to de-noising, there's a secondary benefit to doing all this. While you're checking for suspension clunks, you're laying your eyes and hands on most of the suspension and steering components. This is a good thing. I'm a believer in *if it ain't broke don't fix it*. But if you see, for example, rear shocks that carry the car's 38 years on them, it's probably time to replace them anyway, and doing so removes them as a question mark in the sentence of noise. You also may see a torn boot on a tie rod or ball joint that may not be the source of any noise, but is probably an indication that the aged component should be replaced.

DRIVETRAIN CLUNKS

Another likely set of culprits is the drivetrain mounts. The engine and transmission sit on top of rubber mounts, and the differential is suspended from above by a bracket with mounts inset into it. These are all necessary to prevent drivetrain noise from coupling into the body of the car. The differential mounts often last the life of the car, but engine and transmission mounts are done in by exposure to oil and heat. If the engine mounts are spongy to the touch and the engine visibly rocks back and forth a good bit when started or rev'd, they should be replaced. On a BMW, the transmission mount is a single vibration isolator the size of a large spool of thread and is often replaced in conjunction with the guibo (the flex disk at the front of the driveshaft). When the guibo and driveshaft are removed, the transmission shift platform is exposed, allowing access to the shift bushings and shifter

knuckle. These items may or may not be rattling or clunking, but replacing them to tighten up the shifter feel is one of the nicest, most cost-effective, and satisfying things you can do to an old BMW.

HOOD CLUNKS

Having peeled several layers of clunks off the onion, the next layer consists of the body panels. Hoods, trunk lids, and doors are common sources of clunks and thunks. I have, at times, removed each of these panels and driven cars without them in order to ascertain whether they were the source of an offending noise. Nothing says hard-core do-it-yourself mechanic like driving a car without a hood. (Or—shades of the first time I met Alex—a door.)

Let's look at the hood first. The hood on most cars uses a spring-loaded latch located in the nose panel, near the radiator. There is a small metal bar called the striker on a bracket bolted to the front underside of the hood. When the hood is closed, the striker pushes the latch out of the way, then the latch slides into place behind it, clicking once. Then, when the hood is pushed all the way down, the striker slides deeper into a groove in the latch, and the latch clicks a second time, firmly holding the hood down. The latch is released by pulling the release lever, which yanks a cable, which frees the latch. On most cars, when you pull the hood release lever, it pops the latch from the second to the first position, but then you need to walk around to the hood, raise it slightly, find the safety lever, and move it to free the latch completely before opening up the hood.

While newer BMWs have conventional front-opening hoods and momentary-release latches, the hood latch on an older BMW is a little different. The hood opens from the rear, not the front. When you pull the cable, it isn't releasing a spring-loaded latch; instead, it's actually pulling down on (and releasing) the latch itself. And there's no safety catch.

Some degree of adjustability is almost always built into the latch system. Either the bracket for the striker has elongated holes, or the latch does. Sometimes both do. Either way, this enables you to loosen the bolts holding one of them, and slide the latch or the striker to change the point at which the latch locks the hood. (I say "almost always" because I recently found, in trying to squelch an annoying clunk in a 2005 Ford Focus, that *neither* the striker nor the latch was adjust-able, clearly demonstrating the use-it-and-throw-it-away intent of the design of the car.)

From a noise standpoint, the other relevant components of the hood are the standoffs. Even if the latch is completely removed, most cars have a pair of rubber or plastic standoffs that the underside of the hood rests against when it is closed. The standoffs usually thread into holes, allowing their height to be adjusted. The latch and the standoffs work together as a system, allowing the hood to be latched tight in a position where it is aligned with the rest of the front body panels. The latch isn't supposed to be adjusted to pull the hood down as far as it'll go; it's supposed to be adjusted to pull the hood against the standoffs.

With that context, let's look at your hood. Walk to the front of your hood (or the rear if it opens from the rear) and grab it and try to move it up and down. Do this in the center and at both corners of the hood. If the hood is well-aligned with the nose of the car and it doesn't move, you're done. If it moves up an inch or more, it's likely the latch is only holding the hood in the first safety position, not in the second latched position, which in addition to allowing the incredibly unsafe possibili-ty of the hood flying up in your face while you're driving, will result in one hell of a lot of banging. In this case you can try adjusting the latch position to try to get the striker to go further into the latch groove. You may need to thread the standoffs in deeper to allow the hood to move further. If you can't get the hood to latch in the locked position, the latch may be broken and should be replaced immediately.

However, if the hood is clearly locked but still moves up and down and clunks when it does, you've found a source of noise. First thing to do is inspect the standoffs. I've often found one of them damaged or missing, in which case this may be the whole problem. If the standoffs are intact, you can either try adjusting them further up or the latch further down. If the gap between the hood and the nose is about right, leave the standoffs alone and adjust the latch. If the gap is wrong, ad-just the standoffs until it looks right, then adjust the latch.

Noise from the trunk lid is very similar to hood noise. The latch design is similar except that passenger cars generally don't have a le-ver to release the trunk lid from a safety position; there's only the fully latched position that is popped open with the key or a button release.

And most trunks don't have standoffs; instead they pull the trunk lid tight against the weather stripping. Wagons and hatchbacks, however, may have standoffs and a "soft closing" feature with an actuator that pulls the hatch door tight against them; this mechanism is pretty notorious for electrically malfunctioning or breaking in BMW wagons. But the method of checking for play and adjusting the latch and/or standoffs is the same as for a hood. Sometimes you need to adjust the latch so tight that you have to practically slam the trunk lid in order to make it snug enough against the seal that you can't make it clunk with your hand. I like to do this, then drive the car, then back it off a bit and drive it again and see if I can tell the difference. But it's important in pursuit of the goal; I've quieted down cars substantially by simply adjusting the hood and trunk latches.

DOOR CLUNKS

Next are the doors. Like the hood, the doors have a latch and striker mechanism; generally it is the striker (the side on the body, not on the door) that is adjustable. Unlike the hood, though, there is no adjustable standoff. The door has to be held tight against the rubber door seal, and on an older car, this seal often has deteriorated. Grab the door handle and pull it up and down, then in and out. If the door moves, there is play that must be adjusted out. I've found this to be a major source of clunks on old BMWs. There are usually bolts or Phillips screws holding the striker plate to the body. Loosen these and move the plate in (toward the center of the car), then tighten and retry. You may also try moving it slightly up or down. In order to hold the doors tight and rattle-free on the Porsche, I had to adjust these so the latch would actually hit the striker as it went past it. There's an additional trick on older BMWs. A corn-kernel-shaped piece of rubber is supposed to go on the latch (door) side. After being opened and closed thousands of times, this part is often worn out or missing, and without it, the doors are almost certain to bang. Sometimes replacing this small inexpensive piece of rubber is all that is needed.

If the door doesn't budge when latched but there's clearly noise emanating from it when you drive, you need to see what's going on inside. Pull off the door panel, which generally means unscrewing the armrest and release lever, gently prying the panel from the door by popping the plastic clips out of their holes, and gently pulling the panel upward. Pull back the plastic vapor barrier (if it has one) and look inside the bottom of the door. Every door has a door brake of some sort that prevents the door from swinging too far open. On older BMWs the door brake has a springy piece of metal that looks like someone wrapped a long stick of gum around the front, tip, and back of your index finger. If the brake has failed, it is usually because this piece of metal has snapped in the middle, and odds are half of it is banging around the bottom of the door. There could be other stuff too. I've found speakers, wrenches, and shattered glass from busted windows that were replaced without cleaning out the shards (I'm the Hack Mechanic but even I would never do *that*).

If there's nothing visible banging around at the bottom of the door, grab the top of the window and move it in and out, and see if the track at the bottom of the door moves. Sometimes the bolts holding the window track have loosened up. In fact, since you have the door panel off, take a ratchet wrench and check every bolt you can see. Inspect where the window itself attaches to the window regulator. Window regulators on modern BMWs are pretty poor, and are considered normal-wear-and-tear parts you're almost certain to replace with a 150K-mile ownership life. These can fail in a number of ways that are likely to make the window unable to go up and down, but can cause rattles and clunks as well.

DE-RATTLING

Having addressed the exhaust, shocks and struts, major suspension bushings, and hood, trunk, and doors, hopefully you've peeled off the outer clunky layers of the onion of noise. And now you're left with the rattles. And boy, there are a lot of places for rattles to hide. One could do a dissertation on the physics of rattles, the resonant frequencies at which they occur, the correspondence of vehicle speed and surface roughness to those resonant frequencies, but in the end, at the practical level, the only useful functional correspondence I've found is that rattles that vary with engine speed tend to be associated with the drivetrain. That is, if your car sounds like a chainsaw when the engine hits 3,000 rpm, the odds are good that you have a loose exhaust shield, muffler clamp, or other unsecured drivetrain component. Of course the source still could be something deep up under your dashboard that just happens to vibrate at that resonant frequency.

One thing I do is walk around to every body panel, window, bumper segment, license plate, headlight, taillight, parking light, and piece of molding, and bang on it gently with a closed fist, and see if it buzzes or rattles. It's amazing how many of them do. Then I open up the hood and do the same thing to every engine compartment component I can reach. This includes the valve cover, radiator fill tank, windshield washer reservoir ... everything. Then, if something buzzes or rattles, I jam pieces of foam or sections of cut-up rubber coolant hoses behind it to immobilize it. Then I drive the car to see if it makes any difference. Usually it doesn't (the frustrating "that wasn't it" scenario), in which case I then remove these foreign shims from their unwelcoming crevices.

Don't discount the value of looking on message boards to find what a body of like-minded souls have to say about characteristic rattles for your chosen ride. My Z3 M Coupe had an incredibly annoying tinny rattle coming from the back of the car. I was unable to reproduce it when the car was still, and could not isolate it when it was moving. I looked on the M roadster and coupe section of Bimmerforums and learned that, if the hand-brake cables aren't tight enough, the clip holding the ear of the hand-brake shoes has no tension on it and can rattle. That was it. I fixed it in minutes. The noise was gone forever. Bliss.

Sometimes even the simplest, loudest rattles are maddeningly difficult to locate. My 2001 325XiT—a fairly quiet, tight car—suddenly developed a really snotty rattle that seemed to be coming from the vicinity of the dashboard. I drove while my son Aaron laid his hands on everything he could think of and couldn't find it. It was really starting to piss me off when I discovered that it was coming from my sun visor. I'd unclipped it and swung it to the left to block some lateral glare, then swung it back in front but hadn't clipped it in. I laughed when I figured it out, but it showed how, even for something as obvious as this, the ear did not immediately lead to the location.

Despite the above example, driving in the car (or riding as a passenger with someone else driving) and simply listening, moving your head around, and laying your hands on everything within reach *can* be very effective. While attempting to localize some offensive clunking in my 528iT wagon, I rode around in the back while Maire Anne drove down a variety of roads. I ultimately diagnosed a combination of bad rear subframe bushings and a battery tray weld that had broken loose. I even rode around in the trunk of the 3.0CSi for a few laps around the block in a desperate attempt to locate a noise that had plagued me for years. Hell, how else are you going to lay your hands directly on the tops of the rear shock towers to feel them clunking under actual load?

For these reasons, you can see that it would be incredibly helpful to have a set of remote ears. A few years back, when I was trying to diagnose the source of chainsaw-like engine noise in my 2002, I discovered the mechanic's stethoscope. This is exactly what it sounds like — a device that looks like a doctor's stethoscope but has a pencil-thin probe at the end instead of a round disk. I found use of this instrument absolutely hypnotic. I spent an hour lying beneath my running 2002, poking here, listening there, absolutely transfixed at the way certain sounds coupled through certain parts of the car (though after putting several of my cars on the lift and listening to their rear ends, I was convinced they were all going to self-destruct at any moment). The stethoscope was invaluable for correctly diagnosing a slack oil pump chain in the 2002 before going to the effort of dropping the oil pan. I later used it in the 635CSi to diagnose a rumble and squeak on acceleration as a bad center support bearing. I had Maire Anne drive the car while I sat in the passenger seat and poked the probe down through the hole in the hand-brake lever.

However, a rumble is a somewhat constant, systemic sound, whereas clunks and rattles are by their nature episodic and elusive. The mechanic's stethoscope has not proven terribly helpful in isolating or diagnosing the clunks and rattles that plague older cars and drive their owners up a wall.

But then there was a flash of hope. A colleague of mine told me that, during the 1990s, he saw a product that interfaced six acoustic transducers to a box that connected to a PC. You could attach the transducers anywhere you wanted with tape, then record the data and look at the result. I thought … I'd give my eyeteeth for one of these. Spread the six transducers across the car. Drive the car. Listen to the results. Find which one recorded the noise. Move all six transducers near that one. Lather, rinse, repeat. I mean, how valuable would *that* be in

368 CHAPTER 55 MEMOIRS OF A HACK MECHANIC

isolating rattles? When I asked him, however, if he could find product info, unfortunately the device slipped, Brigadoon-like, back into the Scottish mists, to vanish for another hundred years. I guess I still need to use my actual physical ears.

When I drive my beautiful red 3.0CSi over moderately smooth roads, I think, "Man, this thing is *tight*. All the work I've done on it over the last 25 years has paid off in spades." When I drive it over uneven pavement and hear something in the doors lightly clunk, I rationalize, "This is a true coupe. It has no B-pillar holding up the roof or stiffening the chassis. There's a certain amount of twist inherent in these Karmann-built bodies. I've been over this a dozen times. I can't get the door latches adjusted any better than they are. It was probably like this when it was new. Get over it." And these days, when I hit railroad tracks or a bad pothole, and something deep in the bowels of the car emits a dull *clunk*, instead of obsessing about the source (or turning up the radio), my attention is diverted by something else—the fear I feel for the health of the car's beautiful but soft Alpina open-lug wheels which seem to dent if you look at them too hard. So that's my advice. Don't obsess. Don't turn up the radio. Buy really expensive wheels instead.

And then I hop in either of our modern daily drivers and am instantly reminded what *tight* really is, and of the chasm between here and there. This is a reality check, but in no way a depressing one. More like having a nice dream about an old lover, then waking up in the arms of your spouse.

CHAPTER 56

THE PORSCHE PASSES

As the calendar turned to the spring of 2011, my employment at the job I'd held for 27 years became unstable. It's not that all the unexploded ordnance in the world had suddenly been cleaned up—far from it. Rather, shrinking government budgets were testing my luck at writing winning proposals, and my luck was failing the test. In order to stretch out the available funding and preserve my job, I reduced my hours to one day a week for months at a stretch, with a corresponding precipitous drop in my income. Some tough decisions needed to be made.

Men sell enthusiast cars for two main reasons—money and space. If we had infinite amounts of both, we'd never sell anything. On the money side, like Charlie Chaplin playing the starving Tramp who looks at rich tycoons and imagines them trussed up like roast turkey dinners, I began looking at my cars and seeing thought balloons hovering above them depicting how many mortgage payments they'd bring. The Porsche, once the paradigm for *frivolous but not irresponsible,* now shrieked at me *I am frivolous and indefensible and represent four mortgage payments.* On the space side of the curve, despite my opening this book by asking, "Who the hell do *you* know with a warehouse," I have, in fact, made tantalizing references to "the warehouse at work." Among the many ways I've been blessed has been the ability to stash cars in this warehouse so I have room in my garage to actually *fix* something (the garage can hold four cars—five if you include the space under the porch—but with that many in there, they're jammed in so tight you can only drive the one immediately behind the roll-up door). Losing the warehouse space at work due to closure or job change effectively required shedding at least one car, or parking one outside over the winter, and I'd been down that road before (remember the Porsche's ECU encased in a block of ice?).

So it's gone. The Porsche. The '82 911SC. The frog-faced interloper with the fat sculpted haunches, the audacious whale tail, and the Targa top that cost me less than ten grand, looked like a million bucks, and never failed to get stares from grown men and whooping thumbs up from zit-faced teenaged boys.

Although I'd originally wanted a classic small-bumpered pre-'74 911, I grew to love this car. I owned it for eight years—a lengthy sojourn in my stable. I loved coming in cold to Porsche-land and walking up the learning curve. I loved finding the right one and pulling the trigger on it. I loved how the seating position and the gearing were absolutely flawless. I loved how, with the Targa top off, it felt nearly as open as a full convertible. I loved driving it in the spring and fall with the top off and the heat cranked. I loved dropping the engine to fix the oil leaks. I loved the "packed" sound of its air-cooled engine. I loved the faint but persistent smell of oil and exhaust. I loved how it smelled and sounded like an old Beetle if an old Beetle was really angry and fast and stuck to the ground like a cat on Velcro. I loved how my knuckles literally got white when I drove it hard. I loved how, with all that oil flowing through all that plumbing, I could hear it gurgle. I loved the fat ass and the halfway-to-turbo fender flares. I loved turning around and looking at it after I parked it and thinking, yeah, I'm going to come back and drive you home and experience all those sensations again. And again. And again.

I watched the closing prices of 1981 through 1983 911SCs on eBay for several weeks, determined what I thought the car might be worth, constructed an incredibly thorough and well-photographed auction, and got within $200 of my target price. I sold the car for within $600 of what I paid for it. To say I got $600 worth of enjoyment over the eight years is an understatement at the level of "I somewhat enjoy sex."

In addition to gaining money and space, there was another reason to sell it—risk. Although it was running great, it had 138,000 miles on it, and no provenance; there were no records with the car when I bought it. One of the wonderful things about BMW 2002s is that their engines are simple and relatively inexpensive; good used 2002 engines can be found for 800 bucks. In contrast, the eBay price for a used 3.0-liter engine for a 911SC is about $3,500. Even if the engine continued to hum along, there were other concerns. In Chapter 28: "Of Klingons and Kluges," I described squelching an oil leak by replacing the one leaky oil return tube that was easily within reach. The other return tubes were obscured by the heater boxes, and there was little doubt that over time they would begin leaking as well. It was likely the exhaust and heater boxes would need to be removed to service the tubes, and the spindly corroded studs holding the exhaust to the head gave me the willies. Snapping one of these would bring a world of pain down onto my shoulders.

When I was about to put the auction up on eBay, I decided I should augment the photos with a short video demonstrating how well the car winds out, so Ethan and I went for a hot lap in the car on the Mass Pike, one exit up and back, with me redlining it through three gears and him videoing the action. Then we came to exit 16—a right-hand sweeper with an odd moment of reverse-banking. I was enjoying what was probably my last good adrenaline blast in the car. And maybe I was showing off for Ethan. But I flew past a Jeep on the two-lane ramp and went into the curve pretty hot. And then I made the classic mistake—I lifted off the gas in the middle of the curve.

The combination of the car's tires, which were at least seven years old, my lack of hot asphalt time in the car, and, yes, my lifting off the gas resulted in the Porsche's rear end breaking loose. In that half a second where my consciousness was bitch-slapped with the big stinking dead fish of unintended oversteer, I thought, *oh SHIT I'm about to stuff this thing right into the guardrail! Crap! CRAP!!* The ass-end came around left. I corrected it. It snapped right. I corrected again. Then it stabilized. I slowed way down. Ethan and I caught our breath, then laughed as we rolled up to the stoplight.

Then the guy in the Jeep caught up to us, rolled down his window, fist-pumped us, and went "Woo-*WHOOOO! YEAH!!*" I gave him my best coolest *yeah THAT's how you drive a Porsche I meant to do that* look. In truth, I was so spooked by the near-guardrail-stuff that I regarded it as an omen—selling it was not only appropriate, but was necessary to avoid angering automotive powers beyond my influence.

So, it's gone. My bank account acquired a cushion against adversity. Facing an uncertain job future, it was the appropriate thing to do. I'm not resentful. I'm not car-poor. I still own the 3.0CSi, the Z3 M Coupe, the ratty '73 2002, the cheap 635CSi, and a daily-driver 325XiT wagon. That's five BMWs. I've got nothing to complain about.

But none of them have quite the same audaciousness as the whale-tailed Targa-topped 911.

When I go into my garage, I can still see the Porsche-shaped hole in the air.

CHAPTER 57

WHY I DON'T FIX CARS FOR OTHER PEOPLE
(PART IV: THIS TIME, IT'S PERSONAL)

I got a garbled cell phone message from Maire Anne while I was driving. I heard, *something something Alex something something car died something something engine something our driveway.* I called Alex and learned that his 1999 VW Passat wagon had just suffered catastrophic engine failure on the Mass Pike with Alex's two kids and two dogs in the car, and he wanted to know if he could have it towed to our house and put it in our driveway while he figured out what to do with it.

Now, you have to understand that, 90 percent of the time, Alex is one of these big-thinking impossibly cheerful souls with a thousand kilowatt smile to whom all things are possible. He built both the kitchen addition on the back of my house, and then, later, my garage. Earlier I told the story of Alex ripping down half his house because he felt its addition was built incorrectly. His reconstructed house is gorgeous, with a unique rock-surrounded swimming pool built into the sloping yard that backs onto a 35-acre pond. Being around visionaries is as energizing as it is maddening. I am *so* not a visionary. I can be such a practical person that I just want to punch myself. Some people see the glass as half-full. Some see it as half-empty. Me, I see the glass as a source of thirst-quenching capability and want to verify that it can be refilled on demand via some controllable external source when the need arises.

But despite Alex's inestimable talents, he was going through a rough patch. Divorce and consequent financial issues rendered him low on money, which is why he'd bought the Passat wagon for twelve hundred bucks not a month earlier. After fixing a few things like electric windows that would not roll down, it seemed a good fit for him, the dogs, and the kids. Unfortunately, the car had the 1.8-liter turbo—an engine best known for a sludge problem so severe it keeps lawyers employed.

So when, after the flatbed dumped the Passat in my driveway and we pushed it all the way to the end, Alex said, "I'll find an engine and swap it in the driveway," my knee-jerk reaction was "Are you freaking NUTS? What planet do you live on? This thing is a rolling sludge factory. There are recalls and lawsuits over this engine. The car was worth the $1,200 you paid, but now it's dead. I know it's nearly rust-free, but is it really worth the effort? Even if it is, you and I both know what it takes to do an engine swap. It'll be six weeks of nights and weekends. I live here and can run into the garage every night, but you don't. And you have young children to watch. How the hell do you think we're going to get this done? And what you mean we, paleface?"

But I said none of that.

Many years ago, there was an article in the *Harvard Business Review* entitled something like "Good Managers Don't Manage: Rather, they subtly bias the process." The article's basic tenet was that rather than running around like Arnold Schwarzenegger in *Conan the Barbarian* shouting things at people and telling them what to do ("You! Into the boat!"), you should instead give broad goals, shine on actions you like, and treat those you don't like with benign neglect. Over the years I found this approach absolutely invaluable. I don't think of myself as a controlling person, but there's no question that I have an engineer's mind and tend to analyze a situation, break it down in a way that makes sense (to me), and move forward in a manner that is logical (to me) and seems constructive (to me). One year, on vacation, I saw a family where the father was wearing a T-shirt that said, "I am the dad. No questions. No arguments. We'll just do things my way." While a big part of me really liked that shirt, and still wants to psychically wear it, the "shine on what you like and benignly neglect what you don't" approach really is best.

So when Alex talked about swapping engines in my driveway, instead of telling him why I thought it was foolish, I said, "Here are the limits. You *can't* pull an engine in my driveway. I've spent years trying to convince the elderly gentleman on my right that I am not running a repair shop. I'm not going to throw that out the window. However," I said, "you *can* pull the engine in my garage. Tell me when you want to start and I'll move some of the cars out. Then we can roll the Passat in there, put it on the lift, and have room for the engine hoist."

Over the next few weeks, Alex said things like, "I did some reading and the whole engine doesn't have to come out it may just need an oil pump and a head," and I'd say, "Okay, but you realize that that's a lot of work too." Or he'd say, "I'm not sure the car is worth it," and I'd say, "You're probably right," thus trying to ever-so-slightly bias the process by smiling on the idea of donating the poor dead sludged-up beast to charity, and benignly neglecting paths that would necessitate attempted repair in my garage.

It sat in my driveway for two months.

Then, one day, action. Alex told me he'd bought an engine. He came over and we dug the engine hoist I hadn't used in 20 years out of my basement. He said his plan was to set the replacement engine up on an engine stand at his house, drop the oil pan, make sure it was free of sludge, replace the timing belt and water pump, then haul it over to my place. He talked about bringing his boys over to help him do the work. Considering that they're both budding motorheads who, if left unchecked, will watch reruns of *Top Gear* for 18 hours a day, this did not seem outside the bounds of possibility.

So much for benign neglect.

The most questionable engine swap in history was on.

I began to wonder if Alex hadn't, in fact, built my garage for me in preparation for this moment.

I guess there was an odd bit of symmetry between this engine swap and my buying, resurrecting, and installing the engine from Alex's 533i flood car into my 3.0CSi over 20 years ago. As the sorceress Mirri Maz Duur says in George R. R. Martin's *Game of Thrones*, "Only death pays for life." Perhaps the death bill had come due 20 years late.

Now that the project had gone from "maybe" to "this is actually happening," I did what I could to grease the skids. Make no mistake, an engine swap is a Big Job, and you need to think things through. The Passat had to be on the lift—which is in the back of the garage—to access the myriad of things that would need to be unbolted, but because the engine hoist has to be in front of the car and needs clearance to roll the engine forward and away, that meant occupying two spaces in the garage. Add to that room to set up the engine stand, and you've taken up most of another space. So all the cars except one needed to be moved out. I used the Land Cruiser to tow the Passat to the top of the driveway, then rolled it backwards into the garage and onto the lift. Then I waited for the onslaught to begin.

But nothing happened. All was quiet on the suburban front. It was early September. I could easily envision the calendar rapidly rounding third to October with no progress. This piece of crap Passat had usurped precious garage space. I had cars sitting outside. I began to be concerned that I wouldn't get my garage back before the snow flew.

So I started whittling away around the edges of the Passat myself.

This period of acquaintance with the Passat, the intruder in my garage—the automotive equivalent of the party guest who passes out on your sofa and with whom you have an awkward conversation in the morning while they mooch a bowl of cereal and a cup of coffee and you wait for them to get the hell out of your house—did not start off well. I needed to pull off the front wheels, but was immediately stymied by the presence of antitheft lug nuts. I pulled the interior of the car apart before finding the small splined adapter needed to take the lug nuts off. After using it, one of the wheels stuck on the hub, and when I pulled against it, it gave way when I didn't expect and crashed into my thumb, spraining it for several weeks.

This, I grumbled to my old friend the 3.0CSi (the only car left in my garage, since I'd moved everything else out to make room for the big swap), *is why I don't fix cars for other people.*

I expected Alex to take over, but the demands of his myriad of construction projects, coupled with being in the middle of a divorce while being the primary caregiver to his kids, were substantial. He did manage to get over, use the engine hoist to lift the replacement engine out of his truck, and set it up on the stand. Although he'd planned to drop the oil pan and do the timing belt at his place, this was better done in my garage, as there were a multitude of parts that needed to be swapped over from the old engine.

To keep the project moving along, I continued whacking away at the Passat. Yanking out an engine is actually pretty easy. The hard part is detaching everything (I'm sure doctors say the same thing about heart transplants—*once you get all the plumbing disconnected, you just reach in there and yank that baby out*). Every mechanical and electrical connection has to come off the engine and transmission. One of the few pleasant surprises was that I discovered I could leave hoses attached on the a/c condenser and compressor and just swing them away, eliminating the necessity of recharging the a/c afterward.

I e-mailed Alex with long and detailed nightly updates. I talked about the challenges in job-sharing this repair. There's nothing like ripping something apart to clue you in on how to put it back together. How would Alex manage now that I was doing the dismantling? I did my best to photograph things, label every plumbing and electrical connection with paper tags, and organize removed pieces into large labeled envelopes and cardboard boxes.

Surprisingly, there was rarely any answer from Alex to my e-mails. After two more weeks, it was still all me.

So, to ensure I'd get my garage back before the arrival of winter, I switched from *how can I help* mode into *damn it I'll just do it myself* mode. I've been down this road before. Tackle tractable tasks. Detach the shift cable from the transmission. Undo the turbo from the exhaust. Pull the hoses off the power steering pump. Undo all those bloody coolant hoses and electrical connections. Label each one. Unbolt the whole fuel rail with the lines attached, pull it to one side, and stuff it in a baggie. Sometimes I think I could build a rocket and go to Mars in bite-sized chunks.

I was at it every night. I was making great progress. Maire Anne said, "But what about Alex wanting to involve his boys? Maybe he's looking forward to having a bonding experience with them." I said, "*I don't care.*" In truth, it's not that I didn't care; I simply wanted the job to get done so I could have the garage back before winter. Let Alex be the visionary. I just want to be the guy whose cars aren't sitting out in the snow. Sometimes very practical matters require no vision at all to see and execute the solution.

I'm not a total tool junkie, but I do appreciate it when you scope out a repair, think "that gonkulator I've been looking at not only would make this repair go faster, it's almost actually necessary," make the decision to purchase said gonkulator, and are rewarded by speedier work. Because the Passat's engine has to be pulled and installed with the transmission attached, the angle of the engine-transmission pair has to be smoothly varied, shifting the weight between the front and the back. So I bought a load balancer, a device that sits between the hoist and the engine and adjusts the center of gravity. With the turn of a crank, you can change the engine-tranny from hanging flat, to the 45-degree angle needed to clear the obstructions in the engine compartment and transmission tunnel. I didn't buy the cheapest Chinese-made $25 version like I usually do, since web reviews said that, with the engine's weight hanging on it, you can't easily turn the crank, rendering it not terribly useful. Instead, I opted for the $50 American-made OTC Tools version where the crank threads run inside bearings, allowing smooth operation with a load on it. It worked perfectly. I wished I'd bought a load balancer 25 years ago when I used to pull and install engines more regularly.

Whacking away at it every night and weekend for about a month, I got the Passat's engine and transmission out. I stood there in my garage, tools and greasy parts literally everywhere, the engine and tranny dangling from the hoist, the replacement engine on the stand, and the front of the car looking like it had hit a land mine, feeling a tremendous sense of accomplishment, yet also thinking *what have I gotten myself into?* I thought of a younger, less battered Alex all those years ago, standing in the ruins of his half-torn-down house. The fact that I was doing all this work to help out my overwhelmed friend struck me like the empath in the *Star Trek* episode who absorbed other people's diseases. Now I was the one who was sick.

I planned to manage the historic problem of things going wrong (i.e., shearing off the brake lines on Paul's Bug, snapping the stud on the head of Blair's VW Bus) by insisting that Alex handle certain problem areas himself. For example, to change the timing belt requires unbolting the crankshaft pulley, and when I put my impact wrench and 6mm Allen on the first of the four pulley bolts, it did not just *whacketa-WHEEEE* right off, so I stopped and e-mailed Alex a detailed explanation of the problem, saying, "I'm stopping—you need to take these pulley bolts off yourself."

No reply.

When the car continued to sit, I found myself ineluctably pulled out to the garage and confronting the stripped pulley bolts. First I cleaned out the Allen holes with a pick. Then I thought *no, I am NOT going to do this* and went back inside. Then I came back out and lightly tapped the Allen socket into the hole. Just seeing how it fit. Finally

I couldn't stand it anymore. In a rash passionate moment I grabbed the impact wrench, plunged it onto the socket, and pulled the trigger, ready to deal with the consequences, but praying silently to the God of Adhesion to go lightly on my Hack Mechanic soul.

Perhaps the God of Adhesion half heard me, because half the crankshaft pulley bolts stripped.

Okay, I thought, with the sort of Calvinist fatalism we New Englanders revel in, *THIS* was my *THIS is why I don't fix cars for other people* moment. Why oh why didn't I stop? Why didn't I leave it for Alex like I said I would? Stupid! Stupid! Stupid! Oh, this is going to suck, and I am going to revel in its deep suckage.

After trying several of my "stuckness" techniques, the one that worked was the Brooke Shields Approach—hammering a 12mm twelve-point socket onto the outside of the bolt head. I pulled the trigger on the impact wrench, and was greeted by the glorious combination of both *whacketa-whacketa-WHEEEEE* AND the bolt dropping on the floor.

If anything is an example of the Hack Mechanic ethos, it is this. Don't stop. Don't give up. Try another way. Do it again. Soup to nuts, despair to joy, the stripped pulley nut incident probably lasted less than an hour.

Not surprisingly, on a job of this size, nearly every rhythm of repair mechanism was at play. Alex needed to decide what parts to order, and from where. Unfortunately, he was largely AWOL. Again, to keep the project moving, I eventually made the parts decisions and placed the order myself. I ordered the timing belt, water pump, and oil pan gasket from one vendor and paid for two-day air so we could begin the engine reassembly as soon as possible. I scouted out best price with free shipping from another vendor for everything else, having verified that their web site showed all items in stock. I placed both orders on the Monday before the long Columbus Day weekend so we could plan to spend the entire three day weekend jamming on the repair.

I sent Alex detailed e-mails on all this, and rarely received more than a passing reply. I tried not to let it bug me as I kept moving forward.

Finally, Alex was able to break away and planned to spend an afternoon and evening in the garage. To try to assist him when I couldn't be there, I typed up six pages of notes:

The turbo and its hoses need to be cleaned. Have you thought about the order with which the good and the bad engines will need to occupy the hoist? The fitting on the input line to the transmission cooler is frozen. The PCV valve is missing on the replacement engine but the one on the original engine is all clogged up. The seized pulley bolts are off but I haven't removed the pulley because you have to set the engine to top dead center first to do the timing belt. I ordered a timing kit with belt, pulley, and tensioner; it should be here before the weekend. Here's a printed copy of a step-by-step online procedure to do the timing belt. The timing covers on the replacement engine are cracked; you should pull them off the old engine…

On and on it went in my best, thorough, itemized, 14-point Times Roman left-brained glory. I left the printed copy on top of the replacement engine where he couldn't possibly miss it.

That evening, when I came home, Alex was in my garage. He had dropped the oil pan and pulled the valve cover off the replacement engine and showed me that it appeared, mercifully, to be free of the sludge, coke, and turbo turds that felled the original motor. For about an hour we naturally tag-teamed like we used to when we were young men. It was delightful.

Then Alex had to leave. My printed notes were on the floor. It was obvious they hadn't been looked at. I picked them up and handed them to him, joking, "Here's some required reading for you."

"Oh, I can't read that," he said.

"What … what do you mean?"

"My ADHD," Alex said. "I can't digest pages of text unless I've taken my Adderall, and I try to do that only when it's absolutely necessary. I'll do the timing belt, but I need to look at the procedure in the manual that has pictures, not the one you downloaded that's just bulletized text."

Nearly 30 years I've known Alex. I never knew that he had ADHD. Suddenly it made sense. He wasn't ignoring my e-mails. *He literally could not absorb and respond to them.* I wondered if my tendency toward yammering incessant volumes of detail fell on the ears of other friends and colleagues the same way.

The timing belt, water pump, and pan gasket arrived. I carefully installed them myself, then began transferring the other ancillary components (power steering pump, alternator, etc.) from the bad engine. But I grew increasingly nervous when, by Friday, the second order hadn't arrived. In a perfect example of how the parts procurement process can completely bollix up your plans, I called to find the vendor had held up the entire order because they only had two of the replacement bolts for the crankshaft pulley and I'd ordered four. Nothing had been shipped. Nothing would arrive by the weekend. Furious, I cancelled the order and began scrambling. It was the classic rhythm of repair turnaround. As has happened to me many times, *best price free shipping* suddenly became *what do I need to do to lay my hands on these parts RIGHT NOW?*

I called Alex and essentially insisted that he needed to drop whatever he was doing and go to the dealer *immediately*, regardless of the high cost. I tried reading him the parts list, but his phone was cutting in and out. "Are you home or are you driving?" I asked. "I'm in the car, on my way to divorce mediation," he offered. Man, I thought, that's just not *fair*. How am I supposed to be annoyed at the guy when happily married me is yammering in his ear about parts while he's driving to divorce mediation?

Alex paid dealer price (nearly three times what it would've been via the web) and dropped off the parts. I finished assembling the engine, mated it to the transmission, and dropped it in, grateful for my new load balancer (which was helpful on the removal, but absolutely essential for the installation).

On Columbus Day, both Alex and I *finally* got back into the garage at the same time. On went the radiator clip. The myriad of carefully labeled hoses and cables were routed and attached. Despite my having put the dozens of disparate fasteners holding on the car's nose into labeled envelopes, it required both of us doing our best "if this one goes there, these must go there" logic.

The sludge rocket was reassembled.

We filled it with oil and coolant, bled the cooling system, looked at each other, smiled, shrugged, and turned the key. The Passat started immediately (fuel injection will do that), but we were robbed of our *woot woot* moment by alarmingly loud valve clatter followed by the engine running very rough, then dying.

We scratched our heads and did a compression test. Compression was fine. The repeated cranking of the starter during the compression test gave the oil pump a chance to send oil up into the head, which quieted down the valve-train. We swapped the coil packs from the original engine and it seemed to run better.

Alex tried driving the Passat around the block, but smoke started pouring out from beneath the hood, the check engine light came on, and the engine began running very rough, sounding like it was firing on less than four cylinders. He shut it off (right in front of my nosy neighbor's house) and we pushed it back into the garage. So this baby is not going to be born without a fight, eh?

The smoke was coming, alarmingly, from the turbo, but upon examination it was merely burning off grease that got on it during reassembly. I plugged in my OBD-II code reader to find out the source of the check engine light, and saw that three of the four cylinders had posted misfires. I cleared the codes and started it, and it idled smoothly. We let it run for 20 minutes and it threw no codes. But then, as soon as we revved it to 3,000 rpm, it stumbled badly and lit the CEL again.

I could've said *A-Ha! THIS is why I don't fix cars for other people*, but in truth, I saw the big picture. The engine was installed. And it was running. The car moved under its own power. Nothing was leaking beneath it. The patient could go home and recuperate there, even if it was trailing an IV.

The most questionable engine swap in history was a success.

This did raise an interesting distinction between working on newer cars versus diagnosing them. Swapping the engine in Alex's Passat wasn't that different from doing my sister-in-law Tricia's Tercel all those years ago; there were just more things to unhook. In contrast, diagnosing a misfire could be an bottomless well of work.

However, in the end, Alex didn't need to replace anything. The new engine and old electronics seemed to just need time to get acclimated to one another. Despite the transplant, no antirejection drugs were required.

Finally, anticlimactically, about three months after it was dropped off in my driveway, about five weeks after I brought it in under my roof, the problem child Passat lumbered out of the garage and was gone, leaving nothing in its wake but an engine hoist, a load balancer, a transmission jack, a lift table, a giant overflowing trash can, empty containers of antifreeze and oil, a case of empty cans of brake cleaner, Tyvek suits, rubber gloves looking like spent condoms, Band-Aids, paper towels, rags, dozens of hastily-labeled cardboard boxes, envelopes, and tags, an utterly disgusting 12-quart pan of oil just waiting for me to trip over it, a 12-quart pan of antifreeze possibly even more disgusting than the oil because of its pink color and the objects floating in it which included a dead mouse, pages of downloaded procedures (yes I just should've bought the Bentley manual), cheater pipes of varying lengths, 2x4s, milk crates, plastic tins of adhesives, bungee cords, zip ties, nuts and bolts, single-edged razor blades, duct tape, the drill, drill bits, the Sawzall, the Dremel tool and its attachments, nearly every ratchet handle, socket, extension, screwdriver, and Vise-Grip I own, and a good deal more, all unceremoniously shoved to one side of the garage.

So, why did I do it? Why did I spend weeks swapping an engine in a car that wasn't mine, that wasn't lust-producing or even interesting, that I felt no ownership or responsibility for, that I'd prefer to never see again, for free? Am I incapable of ignoring the feeble cries for help of mechanical creatures parked in my driveway? Am I in danger of developing a reputation as a good Samaritan running a rescue shelter for abused automobiles?

Nonsense.

Every time I've gone against my judgment and worked on a car for someone, it was to help out a friend, pure and simple. This was no different. Alex has helped *me,* many times. He needed me to do this, just like my sister-in-law Tricia needed me to rescue her Tercel with an engine swap.

A month later, when Alex was in California helping a mutual friend do some work on his house (talk about paying it forward), he stumbled into the unrestored rust-free 1967 Datsun 1600 roadster he'd always craved, for $3400. He bought it on the spot. The car guy part of me totally understood the "this was the last of my money, I deserve this, I'm 50 years old, and if not now, when?" spirit of the purchase, but the part of me that had just spent weeks replacing the damned engine in the damned Passat because he said he was broke wanted to kill him.

And then it occurred to me: All the times Alex was working on my house and something went wrong and he didn't charge me extra, and he saw me buy another car, did he swear *this is the last time I do a job for a friend?* If so, he never said it out loud.

It's not about keeping score. It's about helping friends, with what they need, when they need it.

Why do men love cars? Because they can provide an opportunity to help out a dear friend. Because that "you can't work on newer cars" thing is such a crock of shit. Because I might not want to do this when I'm 70, but I wanted to do it now. Because I could prove to myself that sometimes I actually am the Hack Mechanic—and human being—I often pretend to be.

CHAPTER 58

WHY I DON'T FIX CARS FOR OTHER PEOPLE. REALLY. NO, REALLY.

I'm not a man who lives with many regrets. Recently I left a bag of Trader Joe's chocolate-covered toffee popcorn in the refrigerator of a hotel, and regretted I didn't have it for the drive home. That's about it.

And yet, with time, I came to regret having sold that sweet little early '72 Sahara tii to Howard. This was curious, because I went back and re-read my reasoning, and it was sound. I'd bought it with college money to flip it and turn it into more college money, and you have to be true to those sort of things. Check. I sorted it out mechanically but there were no easy solutions to the body and paint issues, and those were best left to the next buyer. Check. I decided that, had it been rust-free (it wasn't), been a color I liked (it wasn't), or had air-conditioning (it didn't), I would've kept it, but it failed on all three counts. Check, check, and check. And Howard loved it. My head and heart were clearly separate on this one. My head's checkboxes were satisfied, but the heart is a lonely hunter.

As it happened, shortly after selling it, the value of tiis whunged upward like, well, like a tii hitting the sweet spot of its advance and fuel injection curves. The car I sold to Howard is now probably worth twice what he paid me for it. I thought, I blew it. I had a nice, early, fairly clean tii, I had buy-in, and I bailed out. With escalating prices, it looked like I was never going to be able to buy back into a tii. The window had closed.

On one hand, it was funny that I felt a stronger ache of absence with the tii than the Porsche, but it made sense. 911SCs are great cars, but they're commodities—ubiquitous and, as of this writing, not appreciating dramatically. My right brain goes *oooooh* when I see a whale-tailed Targa, but then my left brain takes over. *You had one*, it says, *and it was fun, but next time, do it differently. Don't be so timid. Jump all the way in. Sell some cars, save up 30 grand, and buy a 993.* Firstly, I've never spent even half that on a car. And second, in truth, I didn't crave another Porsche at the bone level like another small-bumpered round-taillight tii.

As my work situation stabilized somewhat, I entertained buying another car. Unlike 911SCs, Porsche 914s *are* appreciating, and they're simple and straightforward and zippy and Targa-topped so they satisfy a good portion of the convertible urge to boot. I walked up the learning curve, learned the two-liter cars with the newer transmission are the ones to buy, and read up on the "hell hole" where they all rust, but never pulled the trigger. I checked out Vanagons, as I still have an adolescent gonzo desire to do the 240 hp Subaru SVX engine conversion in a late Vanagon Wolfsburg Weekender with the fold-out bed, the picnic table, the side cladding, and the little air dam in the front.

And I pursued my lifelong desire to absolve myself of my Rambler-related sins, looking at several '63 Rambler Classics, including one with a factory V-8 and air. The air-conditioning in a '63 Rambler Classic is a thing of beauty. There are three big round chrome louvered vents in the dash, each about the size of a pool ball. Very American. But the kicker is that the a/c switch on the left side of the steering column has three settings. They read "cold," "colder," and (wait for it) "desert only." I kid you not. I imagine a cartoon with police officers called to an *X-Files*-like scene of a man encased in ice inside his Rambler, where one stoic officer turns to the other and deadpans, "Joe, looks like another 524. *He used the desert only setting in Hackensack.*" (It turns out that the "desert only" setting is, in fact, a bit more than just marketing Pablum; it disables the compressor cycling. The compressor comes on and stays on. So if you're driving in a humid environment it may ice up. I used to wire up my 2002 compressors this way. I was "desert only" before "desert only" was cool.) Had the Rambler been rust-free I may not have been able to resist the wiles of its "desert only" setting.

But, even with the blessing of being able to store cars in the warehouse where I work, and even with the through-the-floor cost of insurance for my non-daily drivers through Hagerty, the cars still occupy space, take up time, and have to be kept running. In a rare moment of clarity, I asked myself … what would I actually *do* with one of these

WHY I DON'T FIX CARS FOR OTHER PEOPLE. REALLY.   387

other cars? True, the 914 would be fun with the top off on a Sunday morning. And I'd love winding the living snot out of an SVX-equipped Vanagon and chirping second gear, but how often would I drive it? Would it be worth all the time? And Maire Anne and I don't "camp" or "sleep" in cars anymore; we like hotels, thank you very much. Similarly, I'd love to sit in the Kennedy-era American industrial design of the Rambler's interior and laugh at the "desert only" setting, but would I go to Rambler-related club events? Would I actually *drive* the car? Would I enjoy owning it? Would I park it, walk away, and turn around and look at it like the BMWs I love?

In business they talk about opportunity costs—what you're ne-glecting while you're spending time on something not particularly well thought-out. Incredibly, surprisingly, instinctively, I felt I should wait for what I wanted. Which was a nice, tight, roundie tii.

With air-conditioning.

And very little rust.

That I could afford.

Yeah, right.

And then, on a Monday morning in late May, I saw the following ad on Craigslist for a car on the Downeast Maine coast:

> 1972 BMW 2002tii. White, 92K miles, 4 speed, excellent survivor, great shape, not a rust bucket, floor, trunk great, runs great, could use paint job, small rust bub-ble on LF fender and bottom of door. Interior is excel-lent, has factory AC, everything is there.

The asking price was within $500 of what I'd sold the tii to Howard for. I potentially had the chance to buy back in.

I called and spoke with the owner, an affable German gentleman named Josef who was a BMW CCA member and had read my column for years. I asked him as directly as possible about the rust, since mid-coast Maine is about 200 miles from me and the thought of driving four hours each way only to experience the usual "well *that* was a complete waste of time" scenario was unsettling. Josef repeated the Craigslist description, with the gentle warning that the car was not per-fect. Then he added that the car had a small line of rust forming on one rear shock tower. This certainly raised alarm bells, but he assured me that, even so, the car was extremely solid. I asked if he could send me some photos. They arrived several minutes later but, as is frequently the case, they were cell phone pics and I couldn't tell much from them other than that there did not appear to be rust holes large enough to host nesting birds.

I then called Andrew Wilson, president of the BMW CCA Maine chapter and an acquaintance turned friend, and asked him if he knew the car. Not only did Andrew know it, he produced a photo of the car next to his tii at a Club event at the Owl's Head Transportation Museum. "It's a nice car," Andrew said. When I told him what Josef wanted for it, Andrew advised that he didn't think I'd be disappointed.

Okay. Drop everything.

Now, I used to joke with Maire Anne that anyone familiar with my automotive tastes who ever wanted to kill me could just run a Craigslist ad saying "rust-free roundie tii $4,000," wait for me to show up, then drop an anvil on my head. But what is my Craigslist obsessive-compulsive disorder good for if I don't act on it and beat everyone else to the punch? One of my favorite movies is *The Big Sleep,* with that wonderful scene at the end where Bogart arranges to meet the heavy (Eddie Mars) at a house, only Bogie is already there and sets things up to his advantage. "Everything's changed now, Eddie," he says, "*because I got here first.*" If you're going to snatch up cars, you have to be Bogie. You have to get there first. The car showed up on my radar at a less-than-convenient time—a day after I'd gotten back from a thousand-mile drive for work, and four days before I was going to drive my 3.0CSi 800 miles again to Vintage at the Vineyards—but is anyone likely to beat me out chasing a tii in Downeast Maine on a Monday morning? I think not.

I went into the office to clear a few must-do things off the desk, then set out to figure what the best approach was to scale this mountain. There are two basic ways to deal with a car a day's drive away— swoop in for a quick look-see, or mobilize for the full assault and be prepared to haul it home on the spot. Each has its advantages. For a quick look-see, I could hop in my nice quiet smooth fast BMW wagon and take advantage of the radar detector and the great stereo and be up and back in perhaps seven hours of driving, but if I liked the tii, there would be no way to come home with it; I might need to do the drive all over again.

To get a car home, you need to either fly in alone (in which case you don't leave yourself much of an out, and isn't even possible when a car is in a rural setting), or head up with two people prepared for one of you drive the car home, or contract a flatbed tow, or hire someone with a trailer, or drag the car back yourself with a truck and a transporter. Which one of these you choose is a function of many things, including cost, but nothing says *I am ready to buy* like showing up in the driveway with the means to haul it away. If you're shopping for a nicely restored car at the upper end of the price range, it's not unreasonable to expect to be able to drive it home, but I tend to be a bottom-feeder; I'm trading off price against risk. You compound that risk dramatically by hopping into an ill-maintained car and driving it hundreds of miles before you've sorted it out and fully familiarized yourself with its foibles.

People think that if they have AAA they can call them and have a just-purchased car towed home, but be careful—tow truck operators responding to calls from AAA are not supposed to tow unregistered uninsured cars. Sometimes, as long as the car has a plate on it, you're good, but I've had operators check the plates against the registration and the registration against the VIN, say "sorry Charlie," and leave me high and dry. If the seller has the car registered, ask him if you can leave his plates on it for the tow, then mail them back. If you've bought a car with no plates but only need it towed it a short distance, the cost for directly contracting a flatbed (not involving AAA) may not be too bad, and the "it has to be insured" requirement is between you and the operator.

I have yet to buy a car far enough away that I've contracted for commercial shipping, but people do it all the time for eBay sales. I've *sold* cars, though, and had the gargantuan multi-level shippers come to my door, and seen a great range of care in the placement of the car on those long ramps, from *this guy is a freakin' artist* to *oh god I can't watch*.

I am fortunate in that I have access at work to a truck and a 32' trailer. That's a good-sized trailer, and getting to mid-coast Maine from Boston is 150 miles on interstate, then 50 miles each way along Route 1; the thought of towing a big trailer 100 miles round-trip on windy roads wasn't my idea of fun. So I called U-Haul to try to source an auto transporter. That's the kind that has all four wheels off the ground, necessary for towing an unregistered car (in contrast, a tow dolly picks up the only the front wheels, but because the car is still technically on the road, it must be registered and insured). By luck, I was able to arrange to pick up a U-Haul transporter a mile from Josef's house. This made it so I didn't even need to commit the hundred bucks for the transporter until I decided to buy the car, though I would've gladly done so if this was an enabling requirement. Lastly, I found the nearest Bank of America, called them, and verified they were open till 4:00 if I needed to pull out cash.

With the logistics in place for both the purchase and transport of the car I had not yet even seen, off I went to Downeast Maine.

Now, if there's any doubt I am married to The Most Wonderful Woman a Car Guy Could Ask For, I give you this. I'd just returned the day before from one of several multiweek trips on the road for my real-world job, and in three days was leaving again for The Vintage. While en route northward, I played phone tag with Maire Anne. I left a message telling her what I was doing—driving the truck to Maine to, hopefully, buy a '72 tii. I heard her reply. It did not say *you've been away a lot I'd really like to have you around before you leave again*. It did not say *I need you to come to Costco and carry cat litter*. It said, "Do you have any idea how animated and passionate you sounded in your message?" Yeah, baby. *This* is the glue that holds a successful marriage together, right here.

I arrived about 2:30 in the afternoon and found a house with a mechanic's sign hung out and a medium-sized garage in the back. I walked up the driveway and heard, to my delight, the strains of someone banging on a guitar and playing Neil Young songs. The seller, Josef, was wearing a mechanic's suit. We shook hands, and he graciously said how nice it was to meet the person behind my *Roundel* articles. Looking at the shingle, his coveralls, and the layout of the garage, I said, "I didn't realize you were a pro." He explained that he worked mostly on late-model German cars for longtime customers.

The tii was right there in his garage bay. It looked neat, tidy, and intact. The Chaminox (white) paint was pretty and shiny, but as described in the CL ad, there were rust bubbles on one fender, door, and quarter panel, and some surface rust where the roof gutter trim is attached was streaking down into the paint. Like the tii I sold to Howard, it was an early-'72 car, with the bumpers tight in against the body. There was a cool looking set of period-correct Carello driving lamps on the front bumper. Josef reiterated what he said on the phone about the car not being perfect, and pointed out the slightly skewed front bumper, the corrosion on the inside of one of the Carellos, the light layer of oxidation forming on the rear bumper, and some other imperfections I regarded as minor.

I opened up the trunk to check out the ominous-sounding shock tower rust. As Josef had said on the phone, there was a line of rust bubbling on the right shock tower, but it was not, however, nearly as bad as I'd expected; the rust line was short and had not yet burst through. The spare tire well was rust-free.

The interior of the car had a very cool, eye-popping set of black Konig Recaro-style sport seats with blue and red stripes. The rug was original and intact. The headliner was flawless. The dash had an air-conditioned console with the original Blaupunkt radio in it. The 14" MSW basketweave wheels might not have been my personal choice, but they were in nice shape and looked at home on the car.

Then I crawled beneath the car to check the floors, frame rails, and rockers, and could scarcely believe my eyes. The floorboards had no undercoating. I'd never seen bare metal floorboards on a 2002. There was a small amount of surface oxidation, and one rust hole smaller than a pencil eraser, and that was it. Rust, it's often said, is like an iceberg, where what you see is the tip. On this car, what you saw was what there was. *Plus,* while underneath, I saw a set of Bilstein shocks and big Suspension Techniques sway bars.

I asked Josef for "the story." He said the car originally came from New Mexico but at some point was sold to the family of one of his customers and had been in storage for about ten years. The owner was going to auction it, but Josef wound up buying it from her. He said he put a battery in it, replaced a caliper, didn't do much else, and put about a hundred miles on it in the two years. As I walked around the car, I noticed the rear window had no defroster grid. Like the bare floorboards, I'd never seen this. In the absence of true provenance like a folder of receipts dating back to the original owner, it's helpful to see if the facts jibe, and the lack of a defroster, combined with the absence of undercoating, fit with the story of the car being sold into the Southwest. I later found the original service pamphlet in the glovebox that confirmed the car was delivered and serviced at a dealership in Santa Fe.

I opened the hood and immediately saw the original black plastic intake plenums that mark an early '72 tii. I also saw, however, a snorkel nose associated with a carbureted 2002. I looked more closely and found obvious differences in the shades of white paint on the nose versus the rest of the engine compartment. Clearly the car had been "nosed" at some point in its past. Finding a discrepancy makes you look more deeply. Once I looked more closely at the body, I found the fenders had been replaced as well, and *were* undercoated. This isn't the end of the world so long as the car isn't being represented as wearing all its original panels and paint. It's a rare 2002 that *hasn't* had its fenders replaced.

I started the tii and took it for a short drive. After letting it warm up, I did the hard-off hard-on the accelerator test to check for worn valve guides and seals (rev it up to 4,000, let the revs fall to about 2,000, then boot it and check for smoke on both deceleration and acceleration). I looked in the mirror and saw … nothing. No smoke. This indicated it was likely the head had seen some work—a good thing. Acceleration-wise it felt like the ignition and fuel injection could use a bit of adjustment, but ride-wise it was surprisingly tight and fairly rattle-free for a car that sat for ten years. A nice, tight tii. I was instantly in love. With the seats, Bilsteins, sway bars, close bumpers, driving lights, and a/c, other than installing a 5-speed I couldn't have found a car better set up to my liking if I had custom-ordered it.

I verified that the car possessed its air-conditioning components (compressor, pulley, condenser, evaporator console, hoses), but did not bother to turn the a/c on. Why? Because it didn't matter to me if it worked. It mattered that it was *present*. I'll make it work. A car with dead a/c might need *anything,* but a car with no a/c into which you want to retrofit a/c needs *everything,* and that is a big difference, my friend. On an air-conditioned tii, you have to be certain the crankshaft pulley is present, as an air-conditioned tii pulley—with both the toothed gear for the fuel injection belt and the V-slot for the compressor belt—is unique to the car, rarer than hen's teeth (after 30 years, saying this has started to sound natural), and worth more than any other single air-conditioned component, the rest of which swap with standard 2002s.

I put the tii back in the driveway and jumped into the truck to run to the bank and get the cash. Then I stopped. I'd skipped the part about negotiating the price. Hell, it was a formality. The guy knew what the car was worth and it was priced fairly. But I have a routine I use with both cars and guitars. I ask the seller, "What do you need to get for it?" If I want it and the named price is fair, I pay it; I don't haggle just for the sport of it. Savvy sellers may say, "No fair—I posted an asking price and you came because you're interested—it's *your* turn to name a number." If they do, that's reasonable, but you'd be surprised what price people sometimes come back with when you've taken the trouble to show up, you're standing right there, you're clearly interested, you can produce cash, and you simply ask them, "What do you need to get for it?"

But Josef didn't name a price. He said, again, "Well … it's not perfect … but I also have about a thousand dollars worth of parts." "May I see them?" I asked. He went to the back of the shop and produced a box full of window and door moldings, window felt, under-hood foam, little chrome pieces, and more. This was an expensive box. "I suppose if you don't want them," he said, "I could sell the parts separately."

"What do you need to get for all of it—the car plus the parts?" I asked.

He paused a few seconds, then named a number *well below* the price that made me drop everything and drive up there. "I'll do that … right now." I tried not to burn rubber as I drove the truck to the bank, pulled out the cash, drove to the U-Haul place, hitched up the auto transporter, returned to the shop, and loaded up the car, scarcely believing my luck (which does, by the way, favor the well-prepared).

When the car was loaded up, I remembered to ask Josef my number two question. (Number one is, of course, "How much rust does it have, really?") "By the way, how come you're selling it?"

"Well …" he said, "I wanted an old BMW 2002 … now I've had one. I don't want to be working on an old car all weekend."

I was, for a moment, stunned. He's a professional mechanic. I'm not. He said, "I don't want to be working on an old car all weekend."

I thought … *I do.*

Then, of course, like finding the right knob on the binoculars, it all came into focus and made sense. After working all week on other people's cars, he didn't want to spend the weekends working on his own.

That's why I don't work on cars for other people.

Joseph had mentioned the word "perfect" several times, and it kept ringing in my ears. So much of the classic car world seems to be about chasing perfection. Stamping out all rust. Attaching new body panels with welds that are indistinguishable from what was done at the factory. Leveling the body panels with a hammer and dolly because "Bondo is bad." Painting a deep mirror finish with zero overspray in places you can't see. Installing factory-fresh chrome, rubber and felt. Finding and installing that elusive crack-free dashboard. Ordering the under-hood fasteners with the correct zinc plating. On and on and on. For many guys, it never ends.

There's a phenomenon in physics where the act of decreasing entropy (randomness) in a small space actually increases it everywhere else. This is known as—and I love this—*disturbing the universe*. I get that, for many men, they can't make everything in their life perfect, so they may try to do so with this one thing—their car. The quest for perfection becomes an expression of the love they have for the car. The love of perfection and the perfection of love chase each other's tail like a yin-yang symbol. But I can't help but wonder if, in doing so, they're blowing the budget, stressing their familial relationships— in short, disturbing their universe. Maybe not. Maybe their spouses are as wonderful as mine. But I'm keenly aware that Maire Anne's consummate reasonability is intertwined in a golden braid with both my own rationality and my demonstrated ability to live in the real financial world. I don't chase perfection; I pursue functionality. I don't want or need a perfect car. I don't measure a car against what it would take to make it perfect; I measure it against what it would take to bring it in line with what it seems to want to be. This tii wants to be used. And loved. I shall do both. That will be perfect for the both of us.

Josef stretched out his hand to shake goodbye, but I stopped him. "Now," I smiled, "we must go into your garage and play some Neil

Young songs together." He beamed. We spent 20 minutes passing the guitar and swapping songs. Every transaction should end this way.

But as I headed down the road for the four-hour drive home, towing my nice, tight, imperfect tii, I realized we'd forgotten to play the most appropriate, most obvious Neil Young song of all:

"Long May You Run."

(On the drive home, I called Hagerty, read them the VIN of the tii, and added it to my policy with a stated value of ten grand. The woman said, "Okay, your policy renews in March. The pro-rated addition to your policy is … $48." Everybody say it together: *I LOVE you guys!*)

CHAPTER 59

WHEN CARS DIE

Cars are steel, not sinew. They are responsive, but they are not people. They have curves, but they are not women. We may love them, but they do not love us back. I know these things.

And yet, cars run down, like us. We trust them to be faithful, and they sometimes disappoint, like us. They return to dust, like us. And though their life can be extended almost indefinitely—quite unlike us—there comes a point when even *they* run out of road. My cracks about wanting to donate Alex's Passat to charity notwithstanding, I find it sad when a car dies—when the quartet of exposure, neglect, obsolescence, and lack of money causes the wonderful mechanical contrivance to lurch forward under its own power no more.

Truth be told, I plead guilty to having parted out several cars (that is, taken them off the road, stripped them, sold the parts, and junked the body), so I suppose I was the reaper snatching the breath from their jaws. Then again one could argue that parts cars are the equivalent of organ donors. In general I'm one who extends the lives of cars, preferring to purchase them precisely at the point when they are suffering the sort of organ failure that would make a nonenthusiast pitch them onto the scrap heap.

Let's look at what typically happens. Cars have improved enormously in the past 30 years. Sure, there are normal-wear-and-tear repairs like brakes, shocks, and exhausts, but your average owner probably gets 200,000 miles out of a car without experiencing major engine failure. At some point, however, something big and bad happens. Maybe the car starts running hot and it's diagnosed with a bad head gasket or a cracked head. Maybe the automatic transmission needs to be rebuilt (they all do eventually). Maybe it's not even one big thing; maybe—and this happens frequently with BMWs—you take it in for some minor malady and are told that the car needs a full $2,000 upgrade of the cooling system, oh and by the way it really could use another $1,500 worth of work to squelch the oil leaks and another $2,000 to replace the shocks and struts and freshen up the myriad of magic rubber bushings (some of them oil-filled) that contribute to a BMW's unique ride and road feel.

Or maybe it's the death by a thousand cuts. Last month the alternator died. That was 500 bucks. The month before it was a thousand for an exhaust. The month before that it was something the mechanic tried to describe but you couldn't understand. Now the damned thing needs tires. You've already mentally signed the DNR. No heroic measures. You look at the overall condition of the car, estimate its value, balance that against the cost of another repair, and weigh that against the $3,500 down and $250/month to buy or lease something new. Lust—how badly you simply want a new car—is certainly factored in as well, even if subconsciously. Also factored in is the fact that, once a car starts experiencing problems, its veil of reliability is pierced and you may not feel safe or secure continuing to rely on it—particularly if long trips and/or late night driving are part of the routine. Finally, a life change—a family, for example, and their requisite need for more space—may be the event that tips the scales.

Of course, living here in New England or in other locations where they salt the daylights out of the roads in the winter, cars rust. So if they're daily drivers, most cars eventually, at some point, simply become pieces of crap. If it's a common car, and it has blown a motor or eaten a transmission, and the air-conditioning no longer works, *and* there's rust … really, it's done. Stick a fork in it. Say some Christian words and call the junkyard or donate it to your local public television station. There's no incentive to bring it back. Even if you like this particular make and model, go find a clean one.

Now, there's a whole spectrum of possibilities for how you may feel about a car. You may have a deep emotional attachment to it, or you may regard the car no differently than a washing machine or a toaster. Regardless, everything has its time and place, and thus there comes a point when you let the car go. If it literally died and is truly immobile, sitting in an impound lot somewhere, you may feel you have little choice but to junk it—essentially giving it to the towing company for the cost of the tow. What the hell else are you supposed to do? It takes initiative to find out where the car is stored and pay to have it towed to your house so you can ... do what with it? Pay again to have it towed around to different repair shops looking for a second opinion on the repair or a better price? Put it on Craigslist or eBay to try to get more money for it? If you do that, you'll have to deal with questions about what is wrong with it, and you may not know the answers. These are all problems that make it difficult to deal with a dead car.

This is also why dead cars represent opportunity to those who buy and fix them. If you can put your time into a car and pull it back from the brink, it's a great chance to get into something that perhaps you couldn't otherwise afford, like an old house needing sweat equity. And the seller will certainly be putting more cash into his pocket than if the car were abandoned for the tow charge.

The process by which a daily driver transmogrifies into an enthusiast car happens over a period of years, perhaps decades, and thus, like evolution, is difficult to catch in real time. The BMW 2002 is a perfect example. They were common cars. People drove them and loved them. And then, in New England, they started rusting. Perhaps the owner ponied up for one set of fenders, or one repair to the shock towers. But the number of people who, at that point, said, "I love this car so much that I am going to keep it forever so, to avoid killing it, I shall spend the equivalent of a year's college bill to construct a garage to protect the car and after that I shall drive it only when it is not wet out," is minuscule. Most folks sold or junked their 2002 and moved on to something else. Then, 25 years later, maybe the imprinting thing caught up with them (and everyone else), the cars appreciated, they went looking for another one, and found out how much they had to pay for something presentable. Granted, there are some people who still own the 2002 they bought new and babied, but most of us with an enthusiast car are driving a fifth- or sixth-hand dream on its second or third restoration.

Maire Anne and I have a first-generation (2008) Honda Fit, and we love it. Its perky, looks-right, sized-right design, pep, and handling are reminiscent of the original Civic and the CRX Si, both of which are now collectible. I thought ... am I witnessing the process of the Fit becoming an enthusiast car? Let's play a game. Let's assume I know that a low-mileage rust-free Fit will be collectible in 20 years. Ours has 45K miles and is showing its first door dings and stone chips. Should we pull it off the road *now* to preserve it? That means taking up one of the spaces in the garage *and* having to go out and buy another dependable low-mileage car to use as a daily driver. What should we buy? Should we buy something we like *less*? That seems silly. Should we buy another Fit so we have two, a keeper and a driver? If I'm so sure it'll appreciate, why not keep *both* of them? This is why, short of the hedge fund managers who have BMW Z8s stashed away, no one ever does it.

Now, there's an active debate in the old-car community: Having spent big coin to buy or restore a car, how much should you drive it? After all, you could argue that if you die with the car unblemished, you didn't get your money's worth. Do *you* want to die a virgin? Why should your car? Live a little. The outer body restoration on my '73 3.0CSi was done in 1988, and I've been very careful with it; there's barely a scratch on it. Should I drive it more? I don't think there's any right answer to this, other than *move to San Diego* or some other dry climate where you can drive these cars year-round. Most owners natu-rally find a balance that feels right. If you get pleasure out of owning and showing a near-perfect car, you're unlikely to regularly take long drives at times when it might rain, and that's fine. Few classic car own-ers, having restored a car or shelled out for one, jump into it and go *yee-HA! I am going to beat this thing TO DEATH!*

Even hypothetically, the idea of running a beloved classic into the ground is just heartbreaking, and car guys often have a visceral reac-tion when confronted with the possibility. A few chapters back I told the story of Yale's 2002tii being murdered by the guy he sold it to and resurrected by a BMW CCA member. I was instrumental in helping my '73 2002tii avoid a similar fate. When I was ready to sell it, I advertised it locally. A doctor from Boston came to see it, explained that he'd always wanted a 2002, drove it and immediately fell in love with it. He was literally pulling out his checkbook when I started asking him some reasonable questions.

"Wait a minute," I said. "Have you ever owned one of these?"

"No."

"Where do you live?"

"Beacon Hill."

"This would be a weekend car, right?"

"No, it would be my only car."

"Do you have a place to garage it?"

"No."

"We need to talk."

I recounted to him the cautionary tale of Yale's tii, and explained that, whether the object of desire is a 2002 or an MG or a Beetle or a Mustang, if you use an old ungalvanized car as a daily driver and expose it to a lot of moisture (and obviously driving it in snow or salt is *completely* out of the question), in six months you'll think that someone set off a rust bomb under the car. I refused to sell him the car until he thought about it. He went away dejected and confused but called me that evening and profusely thanked me for talking sense into him. In the end, I sold it to a young man who lived in rural North Carolina, had a garage, and pledged the car his love and respect.

On the flip side, I've bought needy cars from guys who clearly love them but have to give them up because they lose their storage space, or have too many projects, or realize that, for a totality of life-intervening reasons, the car's needs simply outstrip their ability to satisfy them. If you have the car of your dreams languishing and crying for restoration in a garage or even under a tarp in the backyard, that collection of dull metal, ripped leather, and cracked vinyl is the physical manifestation of possibility. It's your buy-in. It's your passion simmering on low. You might not be able to get the car pretty and shiny and running today, but perhaps you will tomorrow. When you reach the end of the line and put it on the block, it is admission of the end of possibility. I find this incredibly poignant. When I buy one of these cars, at least the seller knows I'll care for his baby, nurse it back to health, and shepherd it on to a new parent/owner.

I travel a fair amount for the portion of my life upon which I rely for income. I'll sometimes drive past a property with some large but finite number of cars on it, say between four and twenty – too few to be a commercial junkyard. The cars will be in various states. Sometimes it's hard to tell if they're trending up (resurrection) or down (decay). It always makes me wonder—who owns them? Are they loved? Does someone scrimp and scheme and save to see them run again? Are they just sojourning in automotive limbo, their fate unresolved? Or was their fate sealed long ago but someone just can't say goodbye? Is the guy's wife on him to get rid of the junk, or is he blessed, like me, with a spouse who understands the importance of the peculiar rooms in one's head? When was the last time they moved? Was it an event that was commemorated? Did someone have a tear in his eye knowing that, once he turned the key and shut the engine off, that was it?

I still have dreams about the '63 Rambler Classic my friend John gave me before his wedding, the '69 Plymouth Satellite in which I learned to drive, the '73 Triumph GT6 (miserable piece of British garbage that it was) that took Maire Anne and me on our first date, and Sheriff Johnson, Maire Anne's 1972 VW bus that dutifully transported us to Texas. We sold the rusty Sheriff — without an engine — to a VW guy for parts, so that sealed its fate, but really the odds of any of these cars having survived are vanishingly small. I had significant personal experiences in and with all of these cars; why *wouldn't* I feel some sense of loss and longing?

Earlier I referred to the Neil Young song "Long May You Run." Car guys and Neil fans know that the song is in fact not about a woman, it's about a car — his Pontiac hearse, which ate its transmission on the long downhill heading into Blind River, Ontario. The song ends with the dreamy wistful possibility that the car isn't dead but is instead in the hands of The Beach Boys, being driven down some deserted beach road to catch the surf while it's up. I've always felt that knowing it's about a car doesn't diminish the sense of longing; it adds to it. Some fans have tried to piece together the history — it was probably 1965, not 1962 as the song says — and locate the actual car. Unique cars associated with celebrity owners can bring big bucks. John Lennon's psychedelic 1964 Rolls-Royce Phantom V sold at auction for $2.3 million. Imagine if you could produce Neil's hearse along with documented evidence that this was the actual car. Or the vehicles that inspired the Beach Boys' "409" or "Little Deuce Coupe." If you found the Chevy that Don McLean drove to the levee in "American Pie," you could retire.

And then there are the death cars. On a business trip to Alexandria, Louisiana, I unexpectedly came face-to-face with the hearse that carried the Reverend Dr. Martin Luther King Jr.'s body from the hospital to the funeral home that horrible day in Memphis in 1968. It is part of a private exhibit at, of all things, a pawn shop, along with a large collection of civil-rights-era memorabilia. As a car guy, I have mixed feelings about these macabre vehicles. On the one hand, people should follow their passions and collect whatever blows their skirt up, but on the other, I thought, *this is just weird. People don't collect things like this. If they did, the JFK hearse would be out there attracting attention, and it's not.* Then I did a quick web search and found I was wrong: In early 2012, the JFK hearse sold for $160K to a collector. Further, the ambulance that took JFK to Parkview Hospital sold the year before for $132K.

I thought, what kind of collector buys these things? What is the mechanism for enjoyment of this sort of vehicle? How much does the excuse "it's a piece of history" let you get away with? What is the end-point of this sort of collection? A museum of hearses used to carry the bodies of famous people, displayed along with strands of hair found during restoration? ("Imagine, Marilyn Monroe's lifeless body was *right here.*" Next hearse. "Imagine, Kurt Cobain's lifeless body was *right here.*" Next hearse.) I don't think so. Would I pay money to see the hearse that carried John Lennon's body? Hell, I'd pay money *not* to see the hearse that carried John Lennon's body, and it's difficult to imagine *any* context where the display of such a thing is historical as opposed to exploitative. Is the MLK hearse the exception because it's part of the '60s political assassination holy trinity? I don't know.

The guns that shot JFK, RFK, and MLK are evidence in crimes; they *should* be preserved, in the custody of appropriate agencies. Whether the vehicles that carried their bodies have true historical significance is questionable. A part of me would feel better had these vehicles been allowed to pursue their normal life cycle, which is for Neil Young to party in them, then for them to return to dust. Instead they're being kept alive, as if on life support, as mute reminders, like stroke victims who have seen horror but cannot speak.

And you can't speak of death cars without mentioning James Dean's Porsche 550 Spyder—the one in which he was killed in 1955. The wreck was sold by the insurance company and parted out. What remained—and you can Google it and then choose your favorite cliché (horrific, twisted, mangled, etc.)—was lent to the California Highway Patrol and used as part of a traveling safety exhibit. While being trailered around in 1960, the shell mysteriously vanished and has not been seen since. The only documented piece known to exist is the transaxle (number 10046), and in Porsche circles this part receives the kind of reverence normally reserved for the Shroud of Turin. There were only 90 550 Spyders built, and in the rarefied world of high-end collecting, the surviving examples are now million-dollar cars.

In this environment, a bizarre sort of economics takes root; what was previously unrestorable becomes financially viable. Almost any bent sheet metal can be rebuilt. Frame and body pieces can be fabricated from scratch. Imagine what "the James Dean death car" would be worth. So what becomes important—what separates an original car from a replica—is a VIN plate and a title. I've always thought this reminiscent of the Woody Allen film *Sleeper*, like cloning The Leader from his nose.

And when cars are worth a million bucks, why not clone *two* of them? There are documented cases with Shelby Cobras (another high-dollar car) where the original car was wrecked and rebuilt, and now two cars claim the same VIN. How does this happen? Well, it's like the joke about the guy who claims he has the hatchet George Washington used to chop down the cherry tree. It's very old, he says, so over time, the handle was replaced, and then the blade, but it still occupies the same space. Now imagine that someone finds the original handle and blade, reunites them, and restores them. Which hatchet is the original? Well, both. Sort of.

This excess of attention, of course, is far from what awaits most daily drivers. Our friends Marcia and Fred had a Volvo wagon for 19 years. They loved the car. Marcia in particular was very attached to it, as it ferried her children across the waters of their babyhood, childhood, adolescence, and young adulthood. Finally, the car overheated and cracked its head. It was repairable but the repair didn't make economic sense. With great reluctance, they let it go. In a last act of respect, Fred pulled the grilles off the front. They're now hanging on their wall. I *love* that. My long-abandoned Rambler deserved at least that. And a '63 Rambler Classic has great grilles.

I had the opposite experience recently when Ethan totaled the Mazda MPV. I gasped when I saw the wreck in the impound lot where I went to gather possessions and pull the plates. Anyone who saw the car would have immediately wondered who died in it. Ethan was lucky to be alive. The front end crumpled, the airbags deployed, the steering column collapsed, all as designed. Though I was grateful to the Mazda for saving my child's life, I did not want any piece of the car in my house. I even turned in the license plates rather than transfer them to the car's replacement; I never wanted to see that plate number again.

But in a world where it's sometimes remarkable what survives, I recently discovered Sheriff Johnson's middle seat in the basement of my mother's house. I must've taken it out in preparation for the Great Southern Migration when I installed the killer stereo and the bed. I suppose I could go into my mother's basement, sit in the Sheriff's seat and, in a nod to John Muir, imagine happy people back there, balling and talking and laughing and living and listening to a killer stereo (*Hey! They look like us!*) … but it isn't quite the same.

Why do men love cars? Faces fade. People die. Things that die don't come back. But cars do. At the risk of being crass, obviously you can't crack open grandma's chest and stuff a new heart in there. But that's exactly what you can do with a car. You can cheat death. You can spit in its eye. Listen to that baby run. Oh yeah. Suck on *that*, death. You can do anything from making a car move under its own power one last time to performing full honest-to-goodness resurrection. Together, you and the car can warp time and defy decay. You will still age, the kids will grow up and leave, relatives will die, presidents will come and go, there will be some next big thing in music or technology that you don't really understand, but the car can be forever young. You are the car's picture of Dorian Gray. Only, when you are gone, when the big analyst in the sky says your time is up, the car that you poured your passion into will live on.

And what if the car isn't a pampered '63 split-windowed Corvette or a '72 tii but is instead an old friend maintained on a shoestring budget or even a lowly daily driver? With a car guy's laying on of hands, some sweat, and, yes, a little love, it might run a few more years, roll down that empty ocean road, and get to the surf … maybe a little late, but better late than never.

EPILOGUE

As we go to press, Alex is redoing the second-floor bathroom in my house. I could ask him, "How are you making a dime on this job?" but considering I put the engine in his Passat, I suspect I know the answer. His project responsibilities have included, literally, taking Maire Anne shopping at Ikea for a vanity, lighting, and towel bars. Personally, I think this is perfect—he takes her shopping at Ikea, I get to sleep with her. It's every husband's fantasy. Hey, while it's *not* about keeping score, I think I'm coming out ahead.

Maire Anne and I recently became empty nesters. Aaron, our youngest, just finished his first semester at the Massachusetts College of Art. Ethan and Kyle both graduated college, in film and theater, respectively. Maire Anne's bugs are hale and hearty. None of the large ones have escaped recently (though the time the baby red-kneed tarantula went AWOL, then appeared six months later, adult-sized, in the basement, is legend in the Siegel household). The current brace of cars is the 1972 2002tii, 1973 2002, 1973 3.0CSi, 1999 Z3 M Coupe, my daily driver 2001 325XiT, Maire Anne's daily driver 2008 Honda Fit, and a very high-mileage 2000 Suburban.

Though I've been doing this for 35 years, I continue to discover new things. One revelation has been that, Siegel's Seven-Car Rule notwithstanding, I have limits, even if access to the warehouse at work has allowed me to exceed them. It's actually somewhat challenging to keep seven cars running. If you don't drive an old carbureted car for several months, the fuel evaporates from the float bowl, and the car won't start until the engine is cranked over enough for the mechanical fuel pump to fill the bowl back up. Even if it's just a dead battery in one car, or a bad ground on another, simply ensuring that all of them can be started and moved, much less safely and reliably driven any distance, is time-consuming. I recently started up the Suburban, which had been off the road for several months, and the pedal went right to the floor due to a brake line that apparently rotted while the car was just sitting.

This issue of knowing your limits is absolutely crucial to long-term enjoyment. I said earlier that I know a full-on restoration project is beyond me, so I would never buy a car and begin immediately taking it apart. I am proud that, after going through 50 BMWs, I have never gotten in over my head to the point where I had to sell a non-running project.

Except for the hovercraft. But that's another story.

Another discovery has been that my enjoyment of an enthusiast car increases dramatically if the car is actually used for something. I never fell out of love with my 3.0CSi, but as I've begun driving it over hell and creation to attend events, we're into a whole new phase of our relationship. If you don't look forward to driving the car you own, or take it to the track, or go to club or concours events with it, or simply love to look at it—why in fact do you own it?

I haven't lost my job, but it got rocky enough that, for a brief window, I hung out an electronic repair shingle; I sent an e-mail to the Nor'East BMW 2002 Group saying, "I don't *really* work on other people's cars for money, but I do favors for friends. I'm friends with many of you. Let's see if we can work something out." I had the advantage of being able to select customers who were easy to deal with, and cars I wasn't afraid of scratching. In the end, I took on a single customer, an exceedingly easy-going fellow named Charlie with a '73 2002. It turned out Charlie didn't want to simply pay me to fix his car—he wanted to hang out and learn stuff. It was great for both of us. A wonderful way to both begin and end my commercial automotive repair career.

The warehouse I used to work at is gone, and with it, my limitless storage space for every "only three grand and twenty-four bucks a year for insurance? I'm in" car I've ever wanted to own. Boy, though, it was fun while it lasted. I now have to live within the confines of my own garage, meaning three somewhat easily accessible cars, or four if I put one on roller dollies and slide it sideways but then have little room to work, or five if I utilize the sliding door that accesses the under-deck carport space (or, as someone recently noted, "Dude, *your garage has a garage*"), but that space is still stuffed with the engine hoist and other detritus from doing Alex's sludge rocket I mean Passat. Obviously I need to keep the cool cars safely garaged. To make it all work, I sold my '85 635CSi, and have had to put atonement for my Rambler-related sins on hold. If I die in this state, I risk spending eternal damnation in a 1975 Matador.

Along with loss of the warehouse has come a move of my place of employment. The five-mile-each-way commute I've had for nearly 30 years is now 20 miles. It's too early to tell how this impacts my "since I can commute to work in anything, I can own several very high-mileage fun cars instead of one low-mileage reliable car" strategy.

But none of this is hardship.

Of course, the absence of unbounded space doesn't stop me from fantasizing—not even a little. Websites like BringATrailer.com allow one to entertain audacious dreams. I continue to exercise my Craigslist obsessive-compulsive disorder. I have a strong desire to own a BMW E3 (2800, 3.0S, or Bavaria sedan). Added to the 2002s and the 3.0CSi, it would complete my set of BMWs that have basic body styles from the early 1970s (watch, someone will write in to tell me I've left out the Neue Klasse 2000 4-door sedan). I've even been guilty of typing "Triumph GT6" into search engines. This car guy thing is truly a sickness.

However, I'm always amazed that, no matter how bad you are, there's someone worse than you. I heard about a guy who has a warehouse with 40 BMW 2002s *his wife doesn't know about*. This guy is my new hero. And not because his wife doesn't know. That just makes it funny.

On a similar note, I met someone recently who spent 20 grand restoring a 2002. These days, that's very easy to do. I mentioned this to Maire Anne as part of my consistent attempts to establish that I'm not as far out on the right edge of the bell curve as it might appear. "I'd *never* spend 20 grand rejuvenating a car," I said, confident that this would help place matters in their proper context.

"No," she said, "you'd spend two grand on each of ten cars."

Ouch.

But she's right.

Why do I do that? Is it Siegel's Seven-Car Rule run amok? Is it my peculiar attempt to reduce risk by spreading around my bets? Or is it a simple inability to commit to any one car?

I don't know.

I think I need to lie back down on the couch one last time and work this out.

There's no doubt that, in fact, I spent well over $20K rejuvenating the 3.0CSi, in chunks of several thousand dollars at a time, over a period of 25 years. But I fit it into my temporal and financial schedule, doing things when I had the money, performing all of the work except paint and bodywork myself, in a way that rendered the car undrivable only for short amounts of time. This is who I am. I'm an implementation guy. I'm a guy who gets things done. I'm a guy who's gotten very good at seeing a path to the possible. When I die, just chisel on my tombstone: "He was a very practical guy with a really good track record of achieving short-term goals. He thought he could build a rocket and go to Mars in bite-sized chunks, but, sadly, he lacked the garage space." It's not Rimbaud, but neither am I.

I'm sorry, our time *REALLY IS* up.

As I write this, the '72 2002tii is partially apart in the garage. Its fuel injection is being thoroughly sorted out to fix a vexing lean-running condition once and for all, and its air-conditioning is being refurbished, all to support a planned drive to Vintage at the Vineyards in the spring. It will be the first time in 25 years I've driven a 2002 more than a hundred miles. I am deciding whether or not to prophylactically replace the head gasket. My tendency has been to not worry unduly about once-in-a-lifetime-of-ownership repairs, but a recent spate of blown head-gasket-related posts on www.bmw2002faq.com have given me pause.

So, yes, I still very much enjoy working on cars. And I will drive great distances to hang out with other people who feel the same way.

Here's to the lusts and obsessions that keep us moving forward through the miasma of daily life. Here's to the quirks that make us all so interesting, the flaws that make us sparkle like diamonds, the fragility that can make us shatter like beer bottles on a Saturday night. Here's to our spouses who love us, both in spite of and because of our masochistic motorhead tendencies, and who help us manage that line between wide-eyed passion and unbridled madness.

Life is short. Cars are cool. But they are not, in fact, my greatest joy. That would be going to bed with, waking up with, and spending my life with Maire Anne. Now *that's* love. *That's* passion. But you probably figured that out already.

Rob Siegel
Newton, Massachusetts
January 1, 2013

WARNINGS AND CAUTIONS

This book is not a repair manual, nor is it intended to be used as a step-by-step instruction guide to any specific automotive repair. Some chapters have been designated "Actual Useful Stuff" as a way to differentiate the more practical information from the personal content. However, even the more technical content in the book is included purely for philosophical perspective and is not intended to be interpreted as a repair procedure or step-by-step guide.

Your common sense and good judgment are crucial to safe and successful automotive work. There is no substitute for the appropriate repair manual. Read procedures through before starting them. Think about how alert you are feeling, and whether the condition of your vehicle, your level of mechanical skill or your level of reading comprehension might result in or contribute in some way to an occurrence which might cause you injury, damage your vehicle, or result in an unsafe repair or modification. If you have doubts for these or other reasons about your ability to perform safe work on your vehicle, have the work done at an authorized dealer or other qualified shop.

Working on a vehicle can create danger for you, the technician and others in your workshop. Problem repairs may also endanger the driver and other traffic once a vehicle is back on the road. The attempt to perform technical service can easily cause damage to the vehicle, damage to tools and equipment, and may void or change manufacturer's warranties, which are often extensive. Therefore, check warranties before beginning repair work, read the special warnings and cautions that accompany many workshop procedures and the instructions and warnings that accompany tools, equipment, and some replacement parts.

Be mindful of the environment and ecology. Before you drain the crankcase, find out the proper way to dispose of the oil. Do not pour oil or any automotive fluid onto the ground, down a drain, or into a stream, pond or lake. Dispose of used parts, fluids, and other materials in accordance with federal, state and local laws and regulations.

SAFETY AND TECHNICAL DISCLAIMER

Neither the publisher nor the author makes any warranties, express or implied, that the examples, instructions or other information in this book are free of errors or omissions, are consistent with industry standards, or that they will meet the requirements for a particular application, and we expressly disclaim the implied warranties of merchantability and of fitness for a particular purpose, even if the publisher or author have been advised of a particular purpose, and even if a particular purpose is indicated in the book. The publisher and author also disclaim all liability for direct, indirect, incidental or consequential damages that result from any use of the examples, instructions or other information in this book. In no event shall our liability, whether in tort, contract or otherwise, exceed the cost of this book.

INDEX

ACKNOWLEDGMENTS

This book would not exist without my column "The Hack Mechanic" in *Roundel* magazine (the magazine of the BMW Car Club of America). Huge thanks to the BMW CCA, to *Roundel*'s editor, Satch Carlson, and to all my readers who tell me "you do what I do" and "whatever your wife's got, could she rub some of it off on mine?"

My friend Sharon, unbeknownst to me, sent one of my columns to her literary agent Liv. Even though things with Liv did not result in a book deal, I never would've started writing the book without her interest, and there's no doubt the book benefited from her guidance. Sharon and Liv, thank you.

But most of all, I wish to thank the team at Bentley Publishers. In 1992, I signed a contract with Bentley for a book that I never completed. The fact that, 20 years later, I could swing back with Bentley and have that book turn into this one is one of those circle-of-life things you just can't plan on. Special thanks to Michael Bentley, who believed in my writing from the beginning, and has guided and supported this book throughout its development.

When Liv and I parted company, her final advice was "I think you need a boy," by which she meant "a male editor who, like you, understands the car guy thing." I take great pleasure in the fact that that "boy" was Bentley's Janet Barnes. Janet, I never would've gotten through this without your enthusiasm, thoroughness, level-headed-ness, attention to detail, and respect for my voice. Thank you.

ART CREDITS

Rob Siegel: all artwork except as noted below

Aaron Siegel: 416

Dee Dee Diamond: 199 (top)

Doug Weston: 193 (top)

Kimberly Cox: 206

Maire Anne Diamond: 194 (bottom left, bottom right), 195 (top left, top right), 196 (bottom), 200 (top, middle), 205 (bottom)

Yale Rachlin: 197 (bottom), 198, 204 (top)

ABOUT THE AUTHOR

Rob Siegel is a writer, engineer, and performing songwriter. He lives in Newton, Massachusetts with his scrumptious wife Maire Anne, her IOUS (insects of unusual size), whichever of his wonderful interesting children happen to be sojourning at the house, three black cats, and as many cars and guitars as he can get away with. Rob's column, "The Hack Mechanic," appears in *Roundel*, the magazine of the BMW Car Club of America (www.bmwcca.org). Rob's website is www.robsiegel.com, and his blog can be followed at thehackmechanic.blogspot.com.

Photo by Aaron Siegel

Selected Books and Repair Information from Bentley Publishers

BMW

BMW 3 Series (E90, E91, E92, E93) Service Manual: 2006-2010 *Bentley Publishers* ISBN 978-0-8376-1685-8

BMW 3 Series (E46) Service Manual: 1999-2005 *Bentley Publishers* ISBN 978-0-8376-1657-5

BMW 5 Series (E60, E61) Service Manual: 2004-2010 *Bentley Publishers* ISBN 978-0-8376-1621-6

BMW 7 Series (E38) Service Manual: 1995-2001 *Bentley Publishers* ISBN 978-0-8376-1618-6

BMW Z3 (E36/7 E36/8) Service Manual: 1996-2002 *Bentley Publishers* ISBN 978-0-8376-1618-9

More BMW manuals listed online

MINI Cooper

MINI Cooper Service Manual: 2002-2006 *Bentley Publishers* ISBN 978-0-8376-1639-1

MINI Cooper Service Manual: 2007-2011 *Bentley Publishers* ISBN 978-0-8376-1671-1

Porsche

Porsche Boxster Service Manual: 1997-2004 *Bentley Publishers* ISBN 978-0-8376-1645-2

Porsche 911 (996) Service Manual: 1999-2005 *Bentley Publishers* ISBN 978-0-8376-1710-7

Porsche 911 Carrera Service Manual: 1984-1989 *Bentley Publishers* ISBN 978-0-8376-1696-4

Porsche 911 SC Service Manual: 1978-1983 *Bentley Publishers* ISBN 978-0-8376-1705-3

Porsche: Excellence Was Expected *Karl Ludvigsen* ISBN 978-0-8376-0235-6

Porsche—Origin of the Species *Karl Ludvigsen* ISBN 978-0-8376-1331-4

Volkswagen

Volkswagen Rabbit, GTI Service Manual: 2006-2009 *Bentley Publishers* ISBN 978-0-8376-1664-3

Volkswagen Jetta, Golf, GTI Service Manual: 1999-2005 *Bentley Publishers* ISBN 978-0-8376-1678-0

Volkswagen Passat Service Manual: 1998-2005 *Bentley Publishers* ISBN 978-0-8376-1669-8

More VW manuals listed online

Audi

Audi TT Service Manual: 2000-2006, 1.8L turbo, 3.2 L, including Roadster and quattro *Bentley Publishers* ISBN 978-0-8376-1625-4

Audi A6 (C5 platform) Service Manual: 1998-2004, includes A6, all-road quattro, S6, RS6 *Bentley Publishers* ISBN 978-0-8376-1670-4

More Audi manuals listed online

Mercedes

Mercedes-Benz C-Class Service Manual: 1994-2000 *Bentley Publishers* ISBN 978-0-8376-1692-6

Mercedes-Benz Technical Companion *Staff of The Star and members of Mercedes-Benz Club of America* ISBN 978-0-8376-1033-7

Driving

The Unfair Advantage *Mark Donohue* ISBN 978-0-8376-0069-7

A French Kiss With Death: Steve McQueen and the Making of Le Mans *Michael Keyser* ISBN 978-0-8376-1552-3

Alex Zanardi - My Sweetest Victory *Alex Zanardi with Gianluca Gasparini* ISBN 978-0-8376-1249-2

Engineering/Reference

Supercharged! Design, Testing, and Installation of Supercharger Systems *Corky Bell* ISBN 978-0-8376-0168-7

Maximum Boost: Designing, Testing, and Installing Turbocharger Systems *Corky Bell* ISBN 978-0-8376-0160-1

Automotive Reference

Bentley Publishers has published service manuals and automobile books since 1950. Please write to us at 1734 Massachusetts Ave., Cambridge, MA 02138, or visit our web site at **www.BentleyPublishers.com**

ONLINE APPENDIX

BentleyPublishers.com/hack-mechanic

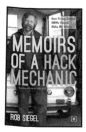

Curious why a BMW 3 Series is sometimes called an E46? Visit the book's Online Appendix where you can find additional information about car models mentioned in the book, decode some automotive jargon, find photo-essays of interesting hacks by Rob Siegel, and post a comment or question for Rob.

TECH VIDEOS

Check out our YouTube channel to find step-by-step videos featuring our own editors and colleagues solving real-world car problems.

Bentley tech videos cover a variety of automotive issues, ranging from cabin microfilter replacement on a BMW 5 Series (E60, E61) to IMS bearing replacement on a Porsche 911 (996).

Featured playlists include dozens of DIY technical videos for:

- BMW
- MINI Cooper
- Audi
- Volkswagen
- Porsche

YouTube.com/BentleyPublishers